ADVENTURES IN CHAOS

American Intervention for Reform in the Third World

Douglas J. Macdonald

Harvard University Press
Cambridge, Massachusetts
London, England
1992

This book is printed on acid-free paper, and its binding
materials have been chosen for strength and durability.

Library of Congress Cataloging-in-Publication Data

Macdonald, Douglas J., 1947–
Adventures in chaos : American intervention for reform in the Third World /
Douglas J. Macdonald.
p. cm.
Includes bibliographical references and index.
ISBN 0-674-00577-5
1. United States—Foreign relations—China.
2. China—Foreign relations—United States.
3. Cold War.   4. United States—Foreign relations—1945–1989.
5. China—Foreign relations—1945–1948.
I. Title.
E183.8.C5M275   1992
327.73051—dc20   91-40615
CIP

*To Mary P. (MacFarlane) Macdonald
and the memory of the late Roderick J. Macdonald,
my parents*

You helped me more than you will ever know

Contents

Acknowledgments

Many people deserve my gratitude—personal, professional, and intellectual. In the early stages of the work, Robert Jervis, James Morley, Thomas Bernstein, and David Baldwin, all affiliated with Columbia University, achieved the difficult task of being both supportive and critical, and helped shape many of my views on the subject of intervention. Bob Jervis in particular was helpful in a manner that was crucial and significant, always exhorting me to keep my attention focused on the critical questions involved. Although there is much contained here with which they would disagree, without their support this book would have been far less thorough and discerning.

Two other Columbia scholars and teachers, Dorothy Borg and the late William T. R. Fox, were kind enough to give me a remarkable amount of their valuable time to discuss the issues involved. Dr. Borg plays the role of skeptic and critic in such an engaging and provocative way that I could not help being deeply influenced by her ideas and insights, especially those dealing with American policy toward Asia. Professor Fox was my academic adviser at Columbia for three years and granted me a significant amount of freedom in my course of studies that perfectly fit my needs—the mark of a great teacher—as well as influencing deeply my views on world politics. Without the sage advice of these two scholars, this book would not have been conceivable. Because of all these individuals, and others too numerous to name, my years as a graduate student at Columbia were among the most intellectually stimulating of my life.

The final stages of the book were completed and the manuscript extensively revised while I was a John M. Olin Postdoctoral Fellow in National Security Studies at the Center for International Affairs at Harvard University. The director of the Center at that time, Samuel

Huntington, deserves my deepest gratitude not only for the financial support extended by the Center, but also for creating an intellectual atmosphere that was genuinely exhilarating. The criticisms of my colleagues at the Center allowed me to view the various policy dilemmas in ways that served to make this a far better work.

While the book was in preparation for publication, Richard Betts, Samuel Huntington, Anthony Joes, and James Wirtz read the entire manuscript with great care and insight, and offered significant advice as well as valuable suggestions. In addition, Robert Kaufman, Timothy Lomperis, Robert Ross, and Robert Rothstein read particular chapters and were most helpful with their constructive comments, which both greatly improved and strengthened the study. Even beyond this invaluable support, Jim Wirtz and Bob Kaufman never tired of my endless questions over several years as I worked out in my own mind the pragmatic, normative, theoretical, and historical issues involved. Their personal and intellectual friendship was, and remains, indispensable to me.

The staffs of the Harry S. Truman Library, the John F. Kennedy Library, Butler Library at Columbia University, Widener Library at Harvard University, and the National Archives of the United States were generous with their time and energy, and thoroughly professional at every level. Financial support for the study was extended by the Graduate School of Arts and Sciences of Columbia University, the V. K. Wellington Koo Fellowship administered by the East Asian Institute of Columbia University, the Harry S. Truman Library, and the John M. Olin Postdoctoral Fellowship in National Security Studies at the Center for International Affairs at Harvard University. The Political Science Department of Colgate University offered agreeable teaching schedules that facilitated the final revisions, and Martha Olcott and Michael Johnston deserve my thanks for such support. The Research Council at Colgate provided necessary financial support in the final stages.

The editorial staff of Harvard University Press exhibited a high degree of professionalism throughout the publication process. In particular, Aida Donald was both a patient editor and a gentle critic. Elizabeth Suttell and Mary Ellen Geer were helpful and cheerful in fielding my many questions, both important and trivial ones.

My good friend Theresa Bowers again demonstrated her extraordinary professional and interpersonal skills as an editor while proofreading the manuscript, and peppered me with intelligent questions that forced me to see the issues from a broader perspective. Cynthia Terrier shared her administrative expertise in preparing the manuscript, while simultaneously carrying out her duties as secretary of the political science department at Colgate, a juggling feat that was, as usual, truly impressive.

For the final responsibility for any errors in judgment or fact, of course, I alone am accountable.

Hamilton, New York
March 1992

Adventures in Chaos

Senator Tom Connally (D–Texas):

"It is all very confusing to me—
perplexing, pusillanimous."

Senator Walter George (D–Georgia):

"It is an adventure in chaos."

—Discussing the formulation and
implementation of a China policy
in executive session in
February 1948

Introduction

Senator Walter George's comment on the difficulties in developing a policy response to the Chinese Civil War was a double entendre. It referred to two "adventures in chaos": the first within the polity of China, the second within the polity of the United States itself. Decision-makers were faced with a set of agonizing dilemmas in China in the late 1940s that have often been repeated in dealings with other nations over the years. These recurring dilemmas have led to a continuing debate over the American role in the developing world, and the role of the developing world in U.S. policy. They have also produced an intellectual and policy incoherence that is unusual even by American standards. This book focuses on these "adventures in chaos," both in the polities of highly unstable client nations (that is, nations that are highly dependent on U.S. support and whose governments are in danger of falling to groups hostile to American interests) and within the American government and society as decision-makers debate what to do about such instability.

The Problem: Reformist Intervention as National Security Policy

When the global containment of Communism became the basis of many American national security goals in the post–World War II era, the United States often found itself embroiled in crises over intervention in the internal politics of clients considered strategically important. With the acceptance of this global role, which was similar to its hemispheric role in the prewar period, American security goals shifted to include most of the non-Communist world. It was then that the United States became more concerned with the internal stability of allies and clients. With several exceptions, this has been primarily true in the non-European world. It is in the Third World that domestic politics in clients have been, and will remain, the greatest potential threat to alliance stability and American national security.[1]

In contrast to containment policies in Europe such as the Marshall Plan and the creation of NATO, which did not lead to a great deal of controversy in the United States, American policies in the Third World have been the subject of continuous debate. Public and congressional support for these policies has oscillated in ways that are largely dependent on the perception of the legitimacy of client governments. Consequently, American policy in these nations has sometimes centered on intervention for the purposes of reform in order to increase the political legitimacy of client governments—locally, internationally, and in the United States. It is therefore not surprising that the legitimacy of client governments also constitutes a main area of attention from anti-interventionist critics.[2] Thus, any theory of alliances in the American context, especially alliances with nations in the Third World, should include the crucial variables of the domestic politics of the United States and of the client.[3]

The recurring problem of legitimacy in Third World clients leads to a particularly acute dilemma of extended deterrence. A successful national security policy requires allies that are politically stable if they are to provide the required reciprocity of strategic interdependence. Protecting a politically stable ally from external attack is a difficult enough problem for defense planners. If the allied government is in danger of collapsing internally, the dilemmas are greatly magnified, and decision-makers have at times felt it necessary to promote reform to prevent the client from being lost to hostile radical groups, usually Communists, that would threaten the American global network of alliances.[4]

This policy dilemma has presented the United States with a role in the world for which it remains largely unprepared and ideologically ill-equipped. Since it is a democratic republic with strong sentiments in favor of self-determination and the theoretical equality of all nations, and with little history of managing a sphere of influence outside its own hemisphere, the United States has had little experience in or knowledge of the military, economic, political, or diplomatic complexities of promoting political stability in client nations.

In attempting to grapple with these complicated policy dilemmas, decision-makers have been constrained by the changing perceptions of the systemic threat, the complexities and limitations of alliance relationships, domestic political considerations, deeply ingrained ideological preferences, and internal governmental incoherence. This has produced an extreme ambivalence over the degree and scope of intervention perceived as possible or desirable in relations with clients. Over time, this ambivalence has resulted in an oscillation in policy toward or away from the promotion of reform.

Thus, it is in the periphery of the containment effort that the greatest problems have arisen in the creation of a stable international system in congruence with U.S. interests. The endemic instability in the client nations has been more likely to produce ruling governments that challenge both American ideological preferences and security needs. This has led to a series of reformist interventions for national security purposes.

The study of reformist intervention is important for several reasons. First, the study of political relations with clients, especially in terms of reform, during periods of intense political instability has been neglected. Much of the literature dealing with counterinsurgency concentrates on the military aspects of the problem and downplays the importance of nonmilitary reforms for the cause of stability.[5] Even those who recognize their importance have often overlooked what Douglas Blaufarb called the "hidden mine" of relations with the client government: convincing or coercing it to put through reforms.[6] It is important to view past policy failures and successes in historical perspective to aid in determining future policies. In addition, following the failure of military intervention in Vietnam, and the apparent end of the Cold War, it is unlikely that the United States will become heavily involved militarily in developing nations for the foreseeable future, at least as a response to internal political instability. If military intervention is largely precluded as a policy option, the role of political and economic intervention will be even more important in securing policy goals in the periphery. The end of the Cold War will reduce, but not eliminate, the need to intervene.

Second, the policy dilemmas and the historical record of these interventions have not been examined in comparative perspective or with a proper understanding of the limits and the possibilities of American power. Most treatments of attempts to reform clients are single case studies of policy failures that often ignore the strenuous efforts of the United States to bargain for reform, and can display a poorly concealed desire to discredit U.S. policy in the periphery altogether.[7] American decision-makers are alternatively, and many times simultaneously, portrayed as greedy, ethnocentric, hopelessly parochial and ignorant about the client society, incompetent, "naive and moralistic," or so fanatically anti-Communist that they will support any behavior of the client government, no matter how brutal.[8] On selected occasions these charges may be deserved. They have not been generally so.

Third, attempts to generalize from single case studies have fallen short of the theoretical mark.[9] In this book I utilize a comparative perspective that aids in the analysis of similar policy dilemmas facing decision-makers across several cases, and across time. This perspective examines social and political processes that generate similar logical policy options available to decision-makers across widely varying cross-cultural circumstances. It therefore identifies and analyzes *types* of behavior that are indicative of recurring situational variables in the clients, are a function of the unequal relations between the superpower and the weaker allies, and were produced in part by the exigencies of the international system. Thus, this method lends itself to greater theoretical generalization than does the single case study approach; it contributes to the generation of theories of international relations dealing with the strategic interdependence of unequal partners, patterns of alliance behavior, and the instruments and uses of leverage more generally.

Fourth, this study of the American foreign policy process synthesizes several levels of analysis. The decisions to intervene for reformist purposes analyzed in the case studies were not made quickly, as is suggested by some cognitive theories of decision-making. Rather, those decisions were made incrementally, and in large part as a response to the consequences of having implemented earlier decisions (the process that is labeled "bargaining behavior" in the case studies). I therefore regard cognitive theories, domestic politics, systemic influences, and the bureaucratic politics model, especially civil-military relations, as equally important components in the understanding of reformist interventions. It is a mistake to think of the United States as a coherent, consistent decision-making unit. There has been an oscillating variation in approaches to instability in clients, generally caused by ideological cognitive dissonance along partisan political lines, and sometimes extreme disagreements within the government over how to approach the problem. This has often led to a great deal of ambivalence at the top levels of the decision-making process. The fact is that sometimes the United States promotes reform, and sometimes it does not. A major purpose of this book is to identify at what times and under what conditions the United States is most likely to promote reform. I will also demonstrate that reformist interventions have been more common and more successful than their descriptions in the historical and social science literature would suggest.[10]

Methodology and Research Design

My goal in this book is to analyze the relative effectiveness of a quid pro quo use of patron commitments (the promise and actual implementation of political, military, and/or economic support) by the United States as a bargaining tool in eliciting reform commitments (the promise and actual implementation of political, military, and/or economic/social reforms) from the client government. I will do this by concentrating on two classes of behavior in the negotiations over the use of commitments: (1) *decision-making* processes, that is, the policy decisions of key individuals and the preferred choices of various bureaucratic components within the U.S. government; and (2) *bargaining behavior,* that is, sequences of interactions between the United States and a client government during a crisis period.[11] Both classes of behavior will be viewed as sequential processes because each is closely interrelated with the other.[12]

These classes of behavior will be analyzed in order to identify the logical alternatives presented to decision-makers within the structure of a particular set of political circumstances, as well as the tendency of these policy alternatives to recur in comparable circumstances in similar situations. I will accomplish this through a relatively detailed historical analysis in the case studies. An examination of policy outcomes alone is insufficient, especially in analyzing a policy process; a detailed description of the diplomatic episodes is necessary to examine how and why the variables interact within a particular bargaining context.[13]

The book proceeds both deductively and inductively. The primary deductive theory to be tested is the inverse relationship between commitments made by a patron state and their negative effects on its resulting leverage with the recipient client state, a relationship that is posited in much of the literature on international relations, as well as sociological and economic theory. I have tested this hypothesis by analyzing its explanatory value in the historical analysis in the cases. In the process of doing so, I reached some complementary theoretical conclusions inductively. I have attempted to maintain a balance between theoretical generalizations and the historical detail in order to concentrate on the generalizable variables, while including the most important idiosyncratic ones. Undoubtedly, this method will not satisfy everyone. Some political scientists will find the historical detail excessive; some historians will question the attempts to theorize. Social science and historical analyses are utilized in roughly equal measure.

Patron-client crisis bargaining is here defined as both implicit and explicit uses of political, economic, military, or technical commitments in give-and-take negotiations, including tacit bargaining through threatening actions, in an attempt to induce (patron) or avoid (client) certain reformist behavior. Since the reformist interventions are typically resisted by the client, negotiations are characterized by coercive bargaining, that is, entailing the use of power to force, persuade, or influence a client government to do something that it ordinarily would not do.

Though both negative and positive sanctions are used or threatened, the former tend to dominate in crises.[14] The book examines how the coercive diplomacy actually works in the cases studied and under what conditions alternative strategies have succeeded or failed.[15]

I also examine the relative utility of two general approaches to bargaining with a client: the unrestricted use of commitments (bolstering/positive sanctions), and a quid pro quo exchange process (reform/positive and negative sanctions) that makes commitments for support contingent upon specific reforms by the client. In all three case studies, the period under consideration was one in which the United States bargained for reforms. Although the quid pro quo bargaining approach was utilized with all three clients, only in the Philippines was it used consistently. I analyze the relative utility of the two approaches by identifying the approach taken by the United States in the particular cases, correlating it with the outcome of the leverage attempt—that is, whether the reforms are agreed to and implemented—and then comparing the cases to identify the efficacy of the respective policy choices. Since the client resists putting through the reforms in the initial bargaining, usually vehemently, one can infer that if implementation occurs it is in large part in reaction to the pressure exerted by the United States. I also analyze the conditions under which such pressure is more likely to be effective. The major point in judging a successful policy is a *resistance overcome* as defined by the client government's compliance with a reform request that had been previously resisted; non-compliance represents a policy failure.[16]

These complementary levels of analysis—decision-making and bargaining behavior—are employed as two separate, yet ultimately interrelated, dependent variables in order to analyze policy outcomes. Thus, the dependent variables are (1) the behavior of the decision-making apparatus (the executive branch and selected key personnel) and the policymaking apparatus (the bureaus and field personnel; for example, the ambassador or chief of the military delegation) of the U.S. government during the crises, that is, those developments that deal with policy *formulation;* and (2) the crisis bargaining behavior of the United States and client governments as they negotiate over the issues involved in intervention for reform, specifically the quid pro quo or relatively unconditional use of commitments in the bargaining approach with the client government and the correlative client actions, that is, those developments that deal with policy *implementation.*

The independent variables for decision-making are related to American policy formulation. They are four: (1) systemic views, that is, perceptions by key decision-makers of international Cold War developments external to the patron-client negotiations which reflect on the necessity for reforms; (2) American decision-makers' views of internal (intra-governmental) and domestic (extra-governmental) political opposition in the clients, and the perception of the chances for client regime collapse if reforms are not initiated; (3) U.S. domestic political pressures, both congressional and public, either in favor of or against the intervention for reform, that affect decision-making processes; and (4) bureaucratic splits over policy direction between civilian and military analysts in the U.S. government.

The independent variables for bargaining behavior relate to American interactions with the client and policy implementation. They are three: (1) the levels of compliance with American entreaties for reforms and the degree of resistant behavior by the client government (including cosmetic reforms to fend off further pressure from the United States; de facto demonstrations that the client has rejected the reforms, for example, attacks on the intra- or extra-governmental opposition; threats to collapse; threats to realign with another patron);[17] (2) the systemic views of the client government and its perception of the likelihood of continued, lessened, or increased American commitments; and (3) attempts by the client to garner commitments from the United States without reforms.

The emphasis throughout the book is on explaining changes in the dependent variables, that is, the decision-making and bargaining behavior of the U.S. government. Ultimately, however, alterations in decision-making will affect changes in bargaining behavior, and vice versa. Thus, the interrelationship between the two dependent variables is examined simultaneously with the interrelationship between the dependent and independent variables in a detailed historical analysis. Though there is an inevitable analytical overlap in the comparison of the dependent variables, I have attempted to keep them as distinct as possible by identifying them in the subheadings of the case studies.

The Cases: China, the Philippines, and Vietnam

The three case studies chosen for this book (Nationalist China, 1945–1948; the Republic of the Philippines, 1949–1953; the Republic of Vietnam, 1960–1963) were all Asian clients of the United States that were undergoing intense political instability, indeed the challenge of a Communist insurgency. It is during such periods of instability that client governments are the most dependent on the patron, yet least receptive to entreaties for reform because of a fear of collapsing. Thus, periods in which the client regime's very existence is called into question present an analyst with a situation that brings into sharp relief issues that may be present but lie dormant in less perilous times. An analysis of these issues can therefore illuminate patron-client power relationships in new ways, offer insights into formulating and implementing policies in other societies where crisis conditions are less evident, and generate more general hypotheses about leverage.

The cases also offer varying outcomes that can be used for a comparative analysis. China and Vietnam, which unlike the Philippines were clear overall policy failures, are intrinsically important lessons of history, or analogues, used by many to discredit U.S. policy in the developing world: China by the political right, Vietnam by the political left. Policy in the Philippines, however, was a quietly successful reformist intervention that has sometimes been overlooked in the policy debates over reform versus bolstering, and inadequately understood until recent declassification of pertinent documents. A comparison of successful and failed policies will identify the salient issue areas in bargaining for reform, will correct the mistaken impression commonly found in the literature that policy failure is inevitable, and will help in choosing optimal strategies for the future. Indeed, even in the failed interventions in China and Vietnam there was some successful, albeit ultimately ephemeral, coercive bargaining.

Other reasons for choosing these three cases include the following: all were instances of reformist intervention; all constituted instances of coercive bargaining with clients; all were influential in determining the approach to other clients; all were considered strategically important by American leaders; and all involved client governments that were highly dependent on American support for their continued existence in power. Though the particular conditions of each client society were unique, the decision-making and bargaining dilemmas facing the United States and the client governments were sufficiently similar to justify a comparison. The fact that they were all examples of Asian policy, and therefore characterized by similar attitudes within the U.S. government on a regional basis that might be quite different in, say, Europe or Latin America, is an added element in their comparability.[18]

Ultimately, however, no cases are comparable at every level of analysis; each represents a unique moment in history. It will be left to the reader to determine whether the comparisons are credible, fair, and judicious, and to ascertain their ultimate worth in determining policies in other societies, in other regions, at other times.

AMERICA AND THE
THIRD WORLD

I

American Policy toward the Third World

1

As the United States emerged from World War II, it gradually became apparent that it was facing a new era in its dealings with the rest of the world. The relative protection and serenity of "splendid isolation," in which basic American goals and values had been nurtured, were finally shattered by the technological, military, and political developments of the war. Though the United States had had bursts of involvement in world affairs outside its own hemisphere at the turn of the century and during and immediately after World War I, and on a few rare occasions before that, many Americans became disillusioned with these experiences.[1] The Japanese attack on Pearl Harbor, the first large-scale, direct attack on American territory since the War of 1812, had a galvanizing effect on the attitudes of most Americans. As the postwar period progressed, and especially with the onset of the Cold War, the earlier faith in the United Nations as the main means of implementation of a peaceful postwar order gradually lessened. Various world developments in the late 1940s, most notably the retreat of the British Empire and Soviet strategic probes in the Middle East and Europe, led to a consensus that the United States must make a greater effort to contain perceived Soviet expansion. A consensus on ends, however, did not translate into a consensus on implementation. Much of the postwar debate on foreign policy in the United States has centered not on the ends of containment, but on the best *means* to achieve those ends.[2] This is as true in relations with allies as it has been with adversaries.

Within the context of the creation and sustainment of its bilateral and multilateral alliance systems in the postwar period, the United States has been presented with immense difficulties. Political instability, economic chaos, internal and external subversion, nascent nationalistic demands in colonial areas, and sagging morale afflicted many actual and potential allies in the early postwar period and threatened to bring to power anti-Western elements viewed as inimical to American interests. The basic problem, as viewed by decision-makers, was this: how was the United States to use its wealth and power to aid in the creation of relatively stable, representative, and independent regimes in order to prevent the spread of Soviet influence, preserve core values, and ensure the military, economic, and political security of the United States itself? This was a tall order by any standard.

The decisions made in the late 1940s led to the acceptance of two major policy decisions by the Truman administration: a containment of Soviet expansion and a Europe-first strategy, that is, a concentration on preventing Soviet dominance of Western Europe and, if possible, a lessening of Soviet dominance in Eastern Europe.[3] This was originally seen as a means of altering Soviet behavior within the context of the United Nations system. As the decade went on, however, it became apparent that a greater effort had to be made on a unilateral basis if the first goal was not to be abandoned.

In late 1949 two major events, among others, brought forth a perception among decision-makers that an even greater effort would be required, and brought to the forefront the American reformist impulse: the Soviet detonation of an atomic weapon in August and the establishment of the People's Republic of China in October. For a variety of internal and external reasons, these events led to a third major policy decision for the United States: the prevention of Communist influence in what came to be called the Third World.[4] What had been a desire now became an imperative. Following the relative success of containment policy in Western Europe and the Middle East, the focus of policy shifted to Asia.[5] The periphery was no longer peripheral.[6]

The Political Debate: Domestic Politics and Reformist Intervention

With the expansion of the area of containment beyond Europe as a new policy goal, the United States increasingly found itself in a position of being allied with regimes that were considered repugnant according to its basic ideals and with newly liberated nations that hardly had regimes of which to speak. These problems were to become more acute during the 1950s and 1960s as colonial empires disintegrated and dozens of new nations were created. The debate over the means of containment policy in the Third World centered around two relevant policy options flowing from the debate over the loss of China and the similarities of the policy dilemma in other client nations:[7] (1) should the United States use its military, economic, and political support of allies for the purpose of inducing needed reforms in "attempts to redress popular grievances before they become fuel for Communist revolutions"? (reformist intervention); or (2) should it "back all existing governments, even those that seem to have lost popular support, against all opposition forces, even those that were not Communist-dominated"? (bolstering).[8] In terms of general policy choices, Democratic administrations have a greater tendency to adopt the former, reformist option, whereas Republican administrations have a tendency to adopt the latter, bolstering option.

This reformist-bolstering dichotomy parallels the foreign policy debate over President Truman's China policy, and it is for this reason that China became such an important "lesson of history" for policy toward the Third World. The Republicans vilified Truman, together with Secretaries of State George Marshall and Dean Acheson, for not sufficiently aiding such a valiant ally as Chiang Kai-shek, whatever his shortcomings. Acheson, however, had apparently learned a different lesson, which he related to Truman in 1950: "If there is one lesson to be learned from the China debacle, it is that if we are confronted with an inadequate vehicle it should be discarded or immobilized in favor of a more propitious one."[9] This attitude reflected a much more intimate involvement in the internal politics of Third World allies that has often characterized American policy since then.

The failure of American policy in China heightened the perception of the potentially disastrous regional and systemic effects of the spread of Communism in the Third World, what came to be called the "falling domino" principle. This was not as implausible at the time as it seemed to many in retrospect. Intermittent Communist insurgencies, of varying intensity, were already under way in 1949 in Indonesia, Malaya, Burma, Indochina, Thailand, and the Philippines. There had been a Communist-led provincial revolt in India in 1948. At Asian conferences in Calcutta in February 1948 and Peking in November 1949, Cominform members, and those from the Chinese Communist Party, were calling for a militant line against both Western colonialism *and* non-Communist nationalists like Nehru and Sukarno. As early as July 1949, Acheson had written Ambassador-at-Large Philip Jessup that the United States could not allow another Asian nation to come under Communist control. Containment had arrived in the Third World.[10]

The vilification of the Truman administration for the loss of China offered another, domestic lesson of history for future decision-makers of both parties. The gradual universalization of containment set a new standard for judging the success or failure of foreign policy. Since the competition with the Soviet Union was now global, it became nearly a zero-sum game. Any advance by the U.S.S.R. or its satellites—that is, if any nation, anywhere, "turned" Communist—was now seen as a loss for the United States and the West. Thus, an extreme fear was created of a policy failure that the opposition party would use politically. This sort of behavior is not confined to the United States. In general, opposition politicians in democratic political systems articulate policy alternatives in simplistic, Manichean terms in order to undermine the political support of incumbents. Those in power are forced to explain the complexities of reality, and their explanations often do not satisfy public expectations.[11]

Examples of this phenomenon during the Cold War are not difficult to find. The Eisenhower administration could not adhere to the Geneva Agreement on Indochina in 1954 in part because, as Press Secretary James Hagerty noted in his diary, the Democrats would charge the Republicans with losing Indochina.[12] In the 1960 presidential campaign, Senator John Kennedy charged the Republicans with losing Cuba. Arthur Schlesinger, Jr., offered an interesting glimpse into how the charge of losing a nation to Communism had become a partisan political weapon, somewhat divorced from the realities of the situation, when he described a Kennedy campaign staff meeting in 1960: "Once, discussing Cuba with his staff, he [Kennedy] asked them, 'All right, but how would we have saved Cuba if we had the power?' Then he paused, looked out the window and said, 'What the hell, they never told us how they would have saved China.'"[13] Lyndon Johnson was beholden in many ways to the conservative Southern wing of the Democratic Party, shared their strong anti-Communist views, and was a congressional leader during the McCarthy period. In his memoirs he made it clear that the fear of an internal debate over "Who lost Vietnam?" was a major determinant of his Southeast Asian policy, and he referred to the Republican right wing as the "Great Beast to be feared."[14] Nor was the Republican right exempt from this kind of political pressure. As President, Richard Nixon once reportedly exclaimed, "The liberals are waiting to see [me] let Cambodia go down the drain the way Eisenhower let Cuba go down the drain."[15] Jimmy Carter attacked Nixon's policy of blindly backing rightist regimes and vowed to restore morality to American foreign policy. Four years later, however, he found himself under attack from Jeane Kirkpatrick and Ronald Reagan for losing Iran and Nicaragua.[16]

Not only have various administrations been attacked politically for losing nations during the Cold War, but their approach to the problem has also come under fire. The Republicans attacked Truman for not backing Chiang Kai-shek; the Democrats attacked Eisenhower for backing status-quo-oriented rightist regimes; the Republicans attacked Kennedy for his ambitious reformist policies; the Democrats attacked Nixon for his backing of rightists; and the Republicans attacked Carter for his reformist human rights campaign. In the 1984 presidential campaign, Democratic contender Walter Mondale attacked Ronald Reagan for backing rightist regimes and an insensitivity to human rights.[17]

In both theory and practice, then, the question of whether to bolster or reform allies has been an important component in the postwar foreign policy debate. This has led to an oscillation between relative activism and relative passivity in American policy toward reform as decision-makers grope for a viable plan of action within the context of international, domestic, and ideological constraints. Much of the debate has centered not on internationalism versus isolationism, as in the past, but on how best to influence the rest of the world in a manner consistent with American security, economic, and ideological interests.

The Scholarly Debate: The Sterile Search for Consistency

The debate over the American approach to reform in client nations has been no less spirited among political analysts than between the political parties. In this section I will summarize the major aspects of that debate as manifested in the scholarly literature and will show that the three main schools of thought, which focus on the particular goals that decision-makers pursue, if used in isolation are inadequate for explaining the phenomenon of reformist intervention.

United States foreign policy is formulated around three sets of inter-related, yet often competing, values and issue areas: security goals, economic goals, and ideological goals.[18] The scholarly literature that explicitly or implicitly deals with reform can be categorized according to these areas of emphasis on the basis of the analyst's view of their interrelationship, and which value he sees as most salient to decision-makers.

Security Goals

There are two groups of scholars that concentrate on security goals in dealing with the reform question, though from widely divergent perspectives. In order to avoid confusion, these groups shall be labeled here "conservative" and "liberal" critics of the American role in the Third World. The analysts referred to are not necessarily conservative or liberal, however, in their views on other issue areas. In general, conservatives believe that the United States has been excessively reformist, to the point of naiveté; liberals believe it has been excessively security-conscious, to the point of cynically backing all anti-Communists, regardless of the cost to the populace of the client nation. In other words, conservatives have argued that the United States does attempt to reform clients but should not; liberals have argued that the United States does not attempt to reform clients but should.

The Conservative Critique. The conservative group is most eloquently represented by Hans Morgenthau, George F. Kennan, Henry Kissinger, and Jeane Kirkpatrick.[19] These analysts have a strong prescriptive bent and often criticize American policy as moralistic because of an alleged mission by the United States to remake the world in its own image. This causes, in their view, an excessive concern with the internal politics of client nations. Conservatives argue that this approach leads decision-makers sometimes to ignore the realities of the national interest and other important issues, and that it actually might undermine America's position in the world by demanding standards of conduct that are impossible for many clients in the Third World to attain. In their view, policy should be based on the hard questions of the global balance of power and should ignore, or at least downplay, the soft questions of ideology and the spread of democratic values in the world. It is not that these analysts like dictators; rather, they feel there is little the United States can do to change them in the short term.

There are major differences among these analysts in their views of a sensible policy. In general, Morgenthau and Kennan argue that the United States should have been much more selective in its use of power in the Third World; Kissinger and Kirkpatrick believed in being involved everywhere. They all agreed, however, that the United States should be less involved in the internal affairs of clients.

Since they emphasized East-West competition with the U.S.S.R. and its clients as the only really important focal point in international politics during the Cold War, conservatives saw the potentially destabilizing effects of a United States promotion of political and social change as not worth the risks involved. A sensible policy, to these analysts, is one that bolsters and stabilizes existing regimes through political, economic, and military aid, with limited concern for the potential excesses of the internal policies of the client government.

The main value of the conservative position is its concentration on the means-ends relationship and its warning against naive crusades that in the long run may lessen, rather than strengthen, America's position in the world.[20] It is not, however, without its problems, especially that strain of conservative thought represented by Kissinger and Kirkpatrick. It is not at all clear that this approach accomplished what was intended. The major emphasis was placed on military and economic aid in order to achieve, in effect, a more efficient, prosperous dictatorship in the client nation to aid in political stabilization in the short run. In the long run, these conservatives argued, a more just and democratic system would evolve.

If there is a naive strain in the American approach to the Third World that states that all the world can be shaped according to democratic ideals, the conservative view represents the opposite side of the ideological coin. According to the Kissinger-Kirkpatrick view, it all boils down to technical and psychological problems that can be solved by greater American commitment and improved efficiency, including more efficient repressive governmental structures to suppress opposition elements. If only the United States would stand by its friends to boost morale in the client government, all would be well. Thus, policy failures in the Third World are viewed primarily, if not exclusively, as the result of a failure of the American political will to aid its clients.

The conservative view can be criticized on three main grounds: (1) it overestimates the capacity of the United States to stay out of the internal politics of the client nation even when taking a bolstering approach, and underestimates the effects of such bolstering on the non-Communist opposition; (2) it unwittingly narrows future policy options; (3) support for a bolstering policy has not been sustained domestically over time.

Because of their excessive concentration on the global balance of power, the conservatives overestimate the importance of the external threat (that is, aid to insurgents from Communist or other hostile nations) and underestimate the importance of potential support emanating from non-Communist groups in contention with the client government. They therefore advise the granting of a relatively unrestricted commitment to the client government to deter the external enemy, and aiding the repressive apparatuses within the client nation to defeat militarily the "externally controlled" insurgents.[21] The problem is that often the client government uses this aid to attack all opponents, including non-Communist ones. This not only pits the government against virtually its entire society, but undermines potential support for a pro-Western majority in the future by radicalizing relatively moderate elements. As a result, it has often been the non-Communist, moderate opposition that is the catalyst in American reformist interventions,[22] in order to prevent these elements from going over to the Communists or becoming otherwise radicalized to an extent where American policy goals are threatened.

These political dynamics appear in all three of the case studies, as they have so often elsewhere. In China in the 1940s, students, intellectuals, journalists, and non-Communist political groups such as the Democratic League, not to mention many peasants, went over to the Communists in droves as the repressive and dictatorial nature of the Nationalist Government manifested itself in attacking anyone advocating even mild reformist policies. The attempt to reform that regime was not so much a simplistic effort to replicate the American political system as it was an attempt, as Secretary of State Marshall later testified, to separate those who were Communists through "indoctrination" from those who were Communists through "disgust."[23] In the Philippines in April 1950, the situation had reached a state where a loyal, non-Communist member of the Filipino Senate threatened to join the Huks himself if abuses by the Filipino Army and Provincial Constabulary were not stopped in his province.[24] In late 1961, a non-Communist leader in Vietnam told a journalist: "If I have to choose between dictatorships, I will choose the Communist one, because it is more efficient. I stay here only because I still feel there is hope for democracy here. If I lose that hope I would not hesitate to go to the Communists."[25] In short, staying out of a client's internal politics does not ensure stability.

Nor is bolstering the client government necessarily staying out of internal politics. As Marshall and Acheson realized, any aid given to particular governments *is* construed as taking sides in deeply polarized societies. Often the United States is blamed for the excesses of the client government,[26] which may further preclude possible options with the moderate opposition in the future.

A second problem with the bolstering approach is that it often prevents a reformist approach in the future. It is a relatively simple task to switch from the latter to the former—the client is always glad to rid itself of this unwanted pressure. It is extremely difficult, and often impossible, to switch from a bolstering to a reformist approach. Chiang Kai-shek successfully fended off American attempts to force him to reform his Kuomintang government and army during World War II, and succeeded in obtaining generous verbal commitments from Franklin Roosevelt.[27] This led to an attitude among the Kuomintang leadership that any reformist approach in the postwar period could be similarly ignored. A similar situation developed in Vietnam. The Eisenhower-Dulles policy of aiding Diem's consolidation of power and strengthening his government by the creation of the semi-secret, repressive Can Lao Party actually fueled the insurgency by pitting the government against all opposition elements.[28] When that policy changed following Dulles's death and the growth of anti-government activity in 1959, Eisenhower and Kennedy found it impossible to convince Diem to cease attacking the non-Communist nationalist elements and include them in his government. The "inadequate vehicles" that Acheson complained of are often created, in part, by previous bolstering.

Finally, the conservative approach has not been sustained within the American political system. The two presidents who most consistently applied this approach, Eisenhower and Nixon, found that domestic political support was disappearing as they reached the end of their tenures because of a generally perceived failure of the policy. The Republicans came under political attack for ceding the political initiative to the Communists in Eisenhower's case, and ceding the moral initiative in Nixon's case. With Dulles's death in 1959, the Eisenhower administration shifted to a more reformist approach, in part because of a shift in congressional and informed public opinion. In Nixon's case, it was not only Watergate that led to a longing for a more "moral" posture in the world, but also a widely held perception that the United States should stand for something more than anti-Communism alone. After Nixon was replaced by Gerald Ford, the United States began to put more emphasis, at least rhetorically, on human rights. In 1976 Secretary of State Kissinger, in a de facto reversal of his policy statements of the past, stated that human rights were "centrally important . . . one of the most compelling issues of our time."[29]

Though many who espouse the conservative view would like to divorce foreign policy from congressional and public pressures to a high degree, this simply is not realistic within the context of the American political system.[30] When the executive branch has given insufficient attention, in the view of Congress, to political and social development, the congressional branch has attempted to force it to do so through legislation linking reform and foreign aid, as in 1966, 1974, and 1976.[31] As a policy prescription, the conservative approach is of limited use because it suggests a model of action that, in the long term, runs counter to some of the basic elements of the American political ideology.

The Liberal Critique. Liberal critics of American policy in the Third World also concentrate on security goals, but usually argue that excessive concern has been given to the security area.[32] This was especially true during the era of disillusionment over the American role in Vietnam. Often projecting the Vietnam experience onto the entire Third World, many liberals charge that the United States has consistently put aside its ideals in order to prop up reactionary regimes because of an excessive fear of Communism and other forms of left-wing radicalism. The United States, the liberals charge, has used the rhetoric of democracy but has followed a "reactionary" policy of backing any government that is anti-Communist, regardless of how despicable its actions may be toward its own people. This view promotes what Samuel Huntington has correctly termed the "myth of U.S. repression."[33] Even Hans Morgenthau, though his earlier condemnation of "moralism" could be con-

strued as an advocacy of a bolstering approach, criticized the United States in the mid-1970s as "repression's friend" and charged that it had backed reactionary regimes with "unfailing consistency."[34]

This group of analysts serves a useful purpose in reminding Americans of their own political traditions and of the fact that if the United States is going to portray itself as the defender of democracy and freedom in the world, it cannot compromise its values as facilely as it has during bolstering periods in the past.

Most Americans, for better or worse, see their nation as a force for good in the world. Though this self-image was badly bruised during the Vietnam era, it was not destroyed because it is based on widely held principles that are the very essence of the American political ideology. Americans have often identified with other democratic societies, and an important aspect of the American belief system is grounded in the assumption that a world of democratic nations would be a much more just and peaceful one. To ask Americans to stop believing this is to ask them to stop thinking like Americans. It is no coincidence, for example, that support for Israel is often justified by the fact that it is the "only democracy in its region." The critics who point to the discrepancies between America's ideology and many of its actions of the past during bolstering periods (though they fail to make the reformist-bolstering distinction) provide an important reminder that if the United States is to avoid fostering cynicism over its values, at home and abroad, it must either alter its view of itself (something that would be traumatic, if not impossible, to do) or follow a more consistently reformist policy in the promotion of democratic values. The oscillation between relatively active and passive postures in the world is based, in large part, on various attempts to close the gap between aspects of the American ideology and actions of the United States abroad.[35]

The liberal analysts can be criticized in four main areas: (1) they ignore the attempts and the real, albeit partial, successes in reformist interventions and call for a consistency in implementation that is unrealistic; (2) they underestimate the ambivalence that decision-makers have experienced in backing dictators; (3) they underestimate the limitations on the American capacity to foster change; and (4) they underestimate the progressive nature of the reforms the United States has attempted to induce.

Liberal critics often overestimate the emphasis the United States has placed on narrowly conceived security goals, at least during reformist periods, and therefore the continuity of decision-makers across party lines. If the United States had simply backed any government that was anti-Communist, it is difficult to explain those real attempts to reform allies that have occurred, especially though not exclusively, during Dem-

ocratic eras. Why did General Marshall attempt to set up a democratic political apparatus in China and use aid to get the Kuomintang to accept it? Why did the Americans insist that Syngman Rhee of the Republic of Korea not cancel elections in the spring of 1950 and implicitly threaten to cut off economic and military aid if this were done?[36] Why did the United States use a similar tactic, with similarly successful short-term results, with the military regime of Park Chung-hee in 1961 and 1963?[37] Why the pressure for democratization in South Korea in the late 1980s? Why did the United States make its aid to the Philippines in the early 1950s contingent upon a program that included land reform, fair elections, and the institution of a minimum wage in order to devolve economic and political power within that society? Why did the Americans constantly badger President Diem of the Republic of Vietnam after 1959 to "broaden the base" of his government by including opposition members in decision-making? Why did Jimmy Carter threaten to reduce aid to the Dominican Republic in 1978 if a rumored military coup were carried out, thereby successfully preventing it?[38]

The list could be considerably lengthened, with the inclusion of major programs in Latin America such as the Alliance for Progress, and land reform programs in a number of nations. The fact is that American reform attempts in developing clients have been more evident than liberal critics would have us believe.[39] Thus, this group not only overestimates the attention given to narrowly conceived security goals, but underestimates the attention given to ideological goals, especially during reformist periods.

Second, the liberal critique underestimates the ambivalence that American decision-makers have experienced when they have had to deal with dictators, even in cases where many argued that clear security goals were manifest. For example, Truman was particularly upset over Spanish dictator Francisco Franco's treatment of Protestants in that country, which the President found "exceedingly obnoxious." In an August 1951 memorandum to Secretary Acheson, the President made it clear that his patience was not unlimited: "I've never been happy about sending an Ambassador to Spain and I'm not happy about it now, and unless Franco changes in his treatment of citizens who do not agree with him religiously I'll be sorely tempted to break off communication with him *in spite of the defense of Europe*."[40] In the same memo, Truman also told Acheson that it was his view that the United States was promoting freedom of religion in the world, and if it could not get its allies to respect this position, these attempts would be undermined. Acheson did not need to be told. He advised giving Franco a loan in 1949 because he was under right-wing pressure, but testified in executive session: "The nature of the regime . . . is not one which you would like to see reproduced in other areas. Intimacy with Spain does not help you in the cold war . . . In fact it causes you great difficulty."[41] Acheson further changed policy toward Spain in January 1950 in an illusory attempt to get right-wing support in Congress, but he was never comfortable with that situation.[42] This is in stark contrast with the ease with which some analysts have portrayed this shift in policy.[43] The United States has made compromises with its basic ideals for security reasons—as indeed it must—but this has often been a difficult and wrenching process.

Third, these analysts underestimate the difficulties in attempting to induce an ally to reform and fail to understand the limitations on American power in this respect. As the cases in this book demonstrate, there is perhaps no more difficult diplomatic task than simultaneously sustaining and pressuring an ally.[44] There is a tendency in the liberal critique to confuse intentions and capabilities, which leads to the conclusion that the United States could have its allies reform if only its leaders wanted this badly enough, if only they had the political will.[45] The tremendous domestic and international constraints under which decision-makers act are largely disregarded or discredited. This often leads liberals to question American intentions in the first place.

Finally, the liberal view often denigrates the reforms the United States seeks as too modest to do any good. This can lead to a curious double standard. American suggestions for rent reductions and land redistribution in China did not "go far enough" even if they had been implemented (which they were not); yet the Chinese Communists had to fall back on similar reforms during the Civil War when their more radical reforms began costing them support among middle-income peasants.[46] American educational campaigns in the Philippines, which gave that nation one of the highest literacy and technical training rates in Southeast Asia at the time of independence in 1946, are judged "irrelevant"; yet when similar programs are put into effect by a Communist regime they are considered "revolutionary."[47] The United States not only has attempted to reform allies, but, at times, has brought real and constructive progress to peoples who have had far too little in their histories.

Economic Goals

There is another, more radical, group that argues that the United States is the foremost capitalist and, therefore, "reactionary" power in the world.[48] Since the United States needs overseas markets and raw materials for its immense productive capabilities, according to this view, it has reached out to the world in order to tie the developing nations to the capitalist "metropolis" on the basis of military, economic, and political relations of permanent dependency. United States foreign policy is but a reflection of its domestic policy, which is based on capitalism, and capitalism, by definition, is based on exploitation. United States foreign policy, by definition, is therefore exploitive. America's interest in security and political freedom has been a chimera, an "ideological gloss" meant to fool the American people and cover the "real" reason for American policy, which is economic greed.[49]

This has been primarily true, it is argued, in the Third World, but characterizes American foreign policy in all its aspects. Therefore, as Gabriel Kolko has posited, the Marshall Plan was meant to ensure not the political independence of Western Europe, but greater profits for American capitalism. The implementation of this policy has also meant "specific opposition to every measure likely to alleviate Third World misery" if such measures do not fit into the overall goals of U.S. economic policy.[50]

This view attained a certain respectability during the Vietnam era, but has since come under increasing scholarly scrutiny.[51] In fact, James Kurth has noted that the theory of the economic basis of American foreign policy could be called the "Vietnam paradigm," given the close association between its popularity and opposition to the war.[52]

The economic explanation correctly calls attention to the connections among political, economic, and national security policies, as seen for example, in the general desire to maintain an "Open Door" to markets. But this view can be criticized on two main grounds: it overestimates the importance and cohesiveness of business interests and their influence on decisions, and it grossly overestimates the coherence of American policy.

The alleged influence of the business community is typically not that important to the crucial question of intervention. Ironically, American policy in Vietnam poses a particular problem for this kind of analysis. In the publicly available materials on Vietnam, including classified memoranda not meant for public consumption, there is little discussion of economic goals. Even in those documents that discuss the economic importance of Southeast Asia, it is the importance of that region to the future of democracy in Japan and India that receives the most attention.[53] As the war continued, it became obvious that the United States could expect no economic gain from that war that could conceivably justify the costs involved.[54] The same could be said for the U.S. intervention in Greece in the 1940s and the Korean War, among others. Yet the interventions went ahead, primarily because of the perceived effects they had on security questions, not economic ones. In fact, the U.S. government experienced difficulty in convincing business interests to invest in those unstable societies, as it has in other unstable regions.

Nor is the business community as cohesive as these analysts portray it. Often any policy the United States follows will help some business interests and hurt others. There are always competing interests that will temper any influence the business community attempts to exert. Those who point to close relationships between some businessmen and some decision-makers make the mistake of confusing access with influence.[55]

Nor is it true that the business community is always in favor of aiding a conservative regime, even in the face of an overwhelming Communist threat. In May 1949, with the Chinese Nationalist regime on the verge of total collapse, Acheson reported to Truman that the American Chambers of Commerce in Tientsin and Shanghai were opposed to the attempts by the China Bloc in Congress to increase aid to the Chinese government.[56] Recent research has suggested that the influence of the China Lobby on governmental policy has been greatly exaggerated, at least in the Truman administration.[57]

The claim that business interests in the United States influence policy-making also fails to represent the reality in the Filipino case. Many American businessmen in the Philippines in the early 1950s were often in favor of the reforms their government was attempting to induce and actually funneled funds surreptitiously through the CIA—though under their own volition—to the presidential campaign of Ramon Magsaysay, a decidedly reformist candidate.[58] Some American businessmen were also influential in the effort to implement the minimum wage laws in the Philippines during the same period, though this was often done at the behest of the U.S. government. This is not to argue that American business interests are reformist in their attitudes; they clearly often are not, and can act as a constraint on decision-makers seeking reforms. But they are only one constraint, and, at times at least, can play a constructive role in implementing a reformist policy.

Second, the view of decision-makers doing the bidding of particular business interests is inaccurate. Political leaders normally see investment in Third World nations as a means to an end (economic development and stability), rather than an end in itself.[59] Self-interested economic gain has played a relatively small role in American policies, and decision-making is a much more complex process than that represented by this view. As Kenneth Waltz has pointed out, foreign aid policy has aimed to create self-sustaining, independent regimes, not dependent ones.[60]

Economic goals at times may be important, but if they challenge other values they may be ignored. In the China case, for instance, the perfect example of this sort of influence would seem to be one Alfred Kohlberg and his association with the infamous China Lobby. Kohlberg was a textile importer who had extensive business interests in China and consistently lobbied, alone and with others, for a more pro-Chiang policy on the part of the United States.[61] Yet not only did the Truman administration not follow this "advice," but the President actually had the entire China Lobby investigated by the Internal Revenue Service, the Treasury Department, and the Justice Department for any irregularities in their financial dealings.[62] As one study found, the economic explanation for American policies "is afflicted with serious flaws. And at best it is only equal to several, alternative non-economic explanations for U.S. interventions."[63]

Ideological Goals

A third group of analysts of intervention concentrate on the ideological goals of decision-makers and trends in the national mood.[64] Many offer broad overviews of American history and point to a pattern of oscillation between an essentially inward-looking, anti-interventionist policy orientation and an outward-looking, interventionist posture toward the rest of the world. The majority of these analysts deal with two contradictory beliefs of national political culture that strongly affect foreign policy, and especially the concept of intervention.

* The first belief is that people, to the greatest possible extent, should be left alone. Government should not get involved in society unless there is an overriding, compelling crisis, and then only on an ad hoc, temporary basis. The proper role for the United States in the international arena is to act as an example to the rest of the world and to protect its interests, but not to attempt actively to change it.

A contrasting belief in the American political culture is based on an evangelical, missionary impulse that promotes the idea of reform on a mass scale in order to bring reality into congruence with the broad generalities of American ideals and values. This "progressive" view has a very different position on the proper role of government. Government should not only take vigorous action to correct present wrongs in society, but should act to avoid future problems as well through a moderate devolution of economic, social, and/or political power.[65]

This reformist view of the proper role of government has deep roots in America. In his examination of the concept of "Mission" in American history, Frederick Merk describes this idea of the devolution of power inherent in the impulse: "From the beginning programs of public welfare were identified with Mission. Programs of political, social, and economic change for the benefit of the underprivileged were fought for throughout the nineteenth century as phases of Mission."[66] He then draws an analogy with the Marshall Plan and the reform-aid programs of the 1960s. Thus, in foreign policy this view leads to demands for a more activist policy in promoting democratic values in the world.

These two views comprise the historical debate between the right and

left of the American political spectrum respectively, but the basic ideological positions both have a great deal of appeal to many Americans.
Americans earnestly want to help other people, but they also want to
leave them alone. The contradictory nature of these desires is apparently not easily grasped by the American mind.[67]

The value of this type of analysis lies in its description of the underlying contradictions, incoherence, and oscillating patterns of the American political system and that system's interaction with the rest of the
world. The bipartisanship of American foreign policy in the postwar
era has been based on an end, that is, the containment of Communism.
An emphasis on ideological goals allows an analyst to identify the variety
of means that various postwar administrations have used to achieve that
end. Those who concentrate on security goals have much to tell us about
why the United States becomes involved in certain nations, but they are
deficient in explaining how that involvement manifests itself and why
policy changes over time. If the ends of policy have remained relatively
constant, why has there not been a consistent bolstering or reformist
approach toward Third World clients? An emphasis on ideological
goals, used in conjunction with security goals, fills that void by better
explaining the processes of decision-making.

Despite these positive aspects, this type of analysis can be criticized
on two major grounds: it relies on vague, philosophical categories of
political behavior, and it overestimates the domestic causes of external
activism. The first criticism is similar to one made of the analyses based
on security and economic goals: it is necessary yet insufficient in explaining American policy toward reform. It is useful to include current
political thinking among leaders and domestic constraints as dependent
variables, but these analysts deal in broad generalities that provide a
context, yet not an explanation, for decision-making. It is interesting to
note that all of them agree that oscillation occurs, but there is little
consensus on the periodization of the alternation of moods. The number
of analysts who deal with oscillation shows that the phenomenon is real,
but more work has to be done on the categories to make the analysis
more rigorous. The analysis presented in this book will attempt to
overcome this deficiency in two ways: it will combine security and ideological goals to examine the value trade-offs decision-makers feel compelled to make in order to formulate a viable policy, and it will tie a
particular policy (approach to reform in clients) to a party-politics analysis in a systematic manner. This approach will better demonstrate the
complexities of decision-making and produce a framework that allows
for prediction and analysis.

Second, the emphasis on ideological goals overestimates the importance of domestic politics. Many of these analysts accept the concept of

the "pulse" or "rhythm" of internal politics as the main causal connection to the oscillation in external policies. They may criticize reformist intervention as naive, but they rarely criticize bolstering on policy grounds, arguing instead that it is unacceptable to Americans on moral grounds. This leads to the conclusion that internal moralism causes the shift to external activism.

External failure has also played a crucial role in determining shifts in approach toward clients. At this point, an important qualification must be placed on the hypothesis of Democratic reformist intervention versus Republican bolstering oscillation presented in this book: Democratic administrations tend to start off with a reformist approach to instability, and end up with a bolstering approach; Republican administrations tend to start off with a bolstering approach, and end up with a reformist approach. Thus, there is an oscillation *within* as well as among various administrations.

The initial policy choice of a new administration is primarily made because the previous administration's policy choice is viewed as having failed.[68] The subsequent change in policy within an administration comes about because its initial policy choice (either reformist or bolstering) is also perceived as having failed. These shifts often come about in reaction to domestic criticism, yet external factors are equally important. In particular, the losses, or threatened losses, of a nation or nations to hostile forces (especially Communism) have acted as catalysts to policy shifts.

With the incorporation of this qualification into the oscillation hypothesis, the shifts in general policy orientation from 1945 to 1988 can be summarized as shown in Table 1. Two things should be noted about these generalizations: (1) all except the Nixon administration were beginning to shift policy orientation; and (2) Democratic administrations have a greater tendency to begin with a reform orientation (Democrats in Congress are also more likely to press for reforms in aid recipients). Although there is overlap between some administrations, and although Richard Nixon's policy consistency and Lyndon Johnson's initial bolstering approach constitute notable exceptions, the preferred initial policy choices of Democratic reform versus Republican bolstering are useful analytical generalizations.

It is the clash between security goals and ideological goals (the former primarily external, the latter primarily internal) that produces oscillation in reform policy toward client nations. The ideological predispositions of various administrations and national moods offer necessary, but hardly sufficient, explanations for the phenomena these analysts attempt to examine. An emphasis on ideological goals relies on vague categories and broad overviews of history that provide important con-

Table 1 Bolstering and reform during the Cold War

President	Initial policy	Beginning shift to:	Major catalyst in shift
Truman	Bolstering and reform	Reform	Loss of China
Eisenhower	Bolstering	Reform	Loss of Cuba
Kennedy	Reform	Bolstering	Spate of military coups
Johnson	Bolstering	Attenuated reform	Title IX Law, 1966
Nixon	Bolstering	Bolstering	No shift
Ford	Bolstering	Reform	Human rights legislation
Carter	Reform	Bolstering	Losses of Iran and Nicaragua
Reagan	Bolstering	Reform	Successful reform in Haiti and the Philippines

textual variables in the analysis of U.S. policy toward reform in clients. Yet the very breadth of this kind of analysis limits its usefulness as an explanatory and analytical tool.

American policy in dealing with Third World clients has been a matter of some controversy between the political parties, among scholars, and within the body politic. As one might expect in a policy that casts such a wide net, there have been successes and failures. Yet Americans have tended to ignore those successes and dwell on the failures. This fundamental insecurity, perhaps endemic to an achievement-oriented society, has led to an oscillation in policy toward the Third World that satisfies no one and threatens the very goals Americans hope to achieve.

The Politics of Oscillation

2

In this chapter I will analyze the role of domestic politics in creating the conditions that lead to the oscillation between Democratic reformism and Republican bolstering. These policy differences are relative ones: there has been a greater relative tendency for Democratic administrations to call for internal reforms in a client nation in order to fend off the advent of Communists or other hostile groups in periods of intensive political instability, while there has been a greater relative tendency for Republican administrations to call for bolstering existing power patterns and institutions to prevent the advent of radicalism. Though both parties recognize that there are internal and external causes for the instability, the variance in emphasis causes objective differences along party lines in the preferred policy response to the danger of the client government falling.

The oscillation in approach to instability will be examined along three major lines: (1) ideological differences between the parties in domestic politics, which lead to varying views of external approaches to instability in clients; (2) some of the cognitive aspects of decision-making within the context of these ideological differences; and (3) the ideological and psychological reactions, in the form of lessons of history learned or reaffirmed, to external policy failures in the Third World. Special emphasis will be placed on the Truman and Eisenhower administrations because it was during those years that the essential patterns first manifested themselves.[1]

Domestic Politics: Party Politics and the
Role of Government

In the United States, domestic politics has both a direct and an indirect impact on external behavior. The direct impact is the most obvious: the role of public opinion in shaping policy alternatives, the congressional role in determining foreign policies, and the actions of other nongovernmental institutions, such as corporations, labor unions, religious groups, and the like, in lobbying for or against a variety of policy options. The indirect impact is more subtle, but just as important. It includes the role of American ideology and democratic practice at home in shaping attitudes and policies toward other nations. As Cecil Crabb has noted, "As a rule, on the basis of limited interest and knowledge, Americans assume that behavior patterns derived primarily from domestic experience are applicable to the foreign policy field."[2] This tendency is revealed in the different ideological approaches to politics, and therefore to foreign policy, of the Democratic and Republican parties.

Since the New Deal the Democrats have been the party of change, as represented by a vigorous federal governmental role, in the American political system. Democratic administrations are generally perceived, from within and without, as advocating policies that are meant to devolve political and economic power in American society by concentrating power at the federal level in order to redistribute it. The arguments for this kind of change are moralistic and pragmatic: a more equitable system will be a more just and stable one because more people have a stake in preserving existing institutions. Those institutions therefore are legitimized. This was the basic idea behind the New Deal: in order for the system to be preserved, that is, made more stable by increasing participation, it must be reformed moderately in order to fend off more radical reforms.[3] According to this view, the government must become involved in the welfare of society now so that it need not become even more involved later—a sort of inoculation view of political reform.

It should not be surprising that Democrats react to political instability in other societies in a similar fashion. These are deep-seated beliefs that are fundamental to an appeal to the party's constituencies and to the decision-makers' joining the party in the first place. It is not, as Franz Schurmann has argued, that Democratic decision-makers simply want to export the New Deal to other societies;[4] it is, rather, that they tend to react to political instability in other nations by falling back on what they believe they know about politics in their own. The more conservative Southern wing of the party has often disagreed with this view of change, at home and abroad, and has threatened to start an opposition party (for example, the "Dixiecrats" in 1948 and George Wallace in 1968) or has made common cause with the Republicans to block those changes.[5] Keeping this powerful wing on board has been a difficult problem for all postwar Democratic presidents.[6]

The Republicans have been generally viewed, from within and without, as being in favor of the status quo, as the party of normalcy. Beginning with Eisenhower's tenure, the Republicans have not attempted to undo the governmental programs meant to devolve political and economic power domestically; in many cases they have even expanded them, though often at the prodding of Democratic congresses.[7] But the Republicans generally have advocated a slower rate of social change and a more limited role for the federal government in inducing that change. Rather than having a stabilizing effect, "artificially" induced political and economic change is seen as likely to upset established patterns and raise excessive expectations that will ultimately have an unsettling effect on society. It is better, according to this view, to allow society to follow its "natural" course, with the government essentially enforcing established rules. It should therefore not be surprising that Republican administrations have had a greater tendency to adopt a bolstering approach toward client nations. The risk of demands for change getting out of control and leading to more radical solutions is too great to pursue government-induced social change as a conscious policy choice.[8]

Neither of the political parties is quite as cohesive in their leaders' or members' views as these descriptions suggest; nor have their views of foreign policy been as clearly delineated. Both parties have attempted to use power to tip the local balance of power in client nations in favor of anti-Communist, friendly governments.[9] Both have aided in the strengthening of military and police structures within the client state to suppress armed insurgencies. Both agree on the necessity for economic and military reforms in clients. The major difference lies in their respective views of political and social reforms, with the Democrats tending to aim for governmental action for the devolution of power within the client nation in order to gain support for the government. Thus, these abstractions are useful in identifying and analyzing the variance of means that the parties employ in order to promote what are objectively different policies in terms of reformist interventions.

As Clinton Rossiter observed, the difference between the American political parties is based on tendencies, not principles.[10] The cognitive maps of Democratic and Republican leaders, their psychological tendencies toward reform, are fundamentally different and produce measurable variance in their approaches toward clients. As noted, this distinction is a relative one. No President has been completely reformist or bolstering; nor does the United States have the power for him to be so. There is, however, a greater relative tendency for Democratic administrations to react to instability in a client with a call for reforms; Republicans tend to react with a call for bolstering existing governments and patterns of authority. In this sense, Republicans have a greater propensity for cultural relativism in terms of the spread of democracy in the world; Democrats have a greater propensity for a "missionary" approach.[11]

These varying approaches create cycles in some foreign policies. There is a strong correlation between political leaders' views of domestic politics and their attitudes toward political instability in client nations. As one study of the attitudes of American political observers of Japan in the 1940s suggests, there is a correlation between skeptical views of democracy at home and the toleration of anti-democratic behavior abroad.[12] Arthur Schlesinger, Sr., and Louis Bean posited "policy cycles" and "party cycles" respectively.[13] The two are interrelated; as V. O. Key observed: "In a two-party system the answer to the question whether there are political cycles must obviously be in the affirmative unless one of the parties is perpetually out of power."[14] The "Tweedledum-Tweedledee" hypothesis of ideological purists of both the left and the right should not be allowed to obscure the richness of the American political party system.

The Psychology of Bolstering and Reformism

American decision-makers face three competing issue areas (security, economic, and ideological), with the greatest contention often arising from the conflict between security and ideological values. When a value conflict occurs, there are three reactions a decision-maker is likely to experience: avoidance, acceptance, or resolution.[15] These concepts are useful in understanding individual decision-making attitudes toward reform.

Avoidance

A decision-maker may consciously or subconsciously avoid making a decision because the value conflict is too great. Alexander George calls conscious procrastination *rational* and subconscious procrastination *defensive*.[16] This latter problem is not unknown to decision-makers themselves. General Marshall told Dean Acheson "many, many times" that one of the most difficult things for a human being to do is make a decision. The human mind, said Marshall, tends to vacillate between difficult alternatives and "escapes through procrastination."[17]

Rational avoidance occurs when a decision-maker puts off making a decision as a calculated aspect of a political strategy, hoping that the context of the situation will become more manipulable. Marshall's own policy in China for the first few months of 1947 falls into this category; it avoided a decision to bolster Chiang Kai-shek until the situation might deteriorate to the point where the latter would feel compelled to change the nature of his regime. The alternatives of making a potentially limitless commitment to Chiang or abandoning him were so difficult to contemplate that Marshall attempted to manipulate the situation to a point that was more conducive to the acceptance of American entreaties for reforms. He did this by reducing aid to the Kuomintang and, in essence, postponing a final decision one way or the other. This conscious policy of drift failed. In the end, he was forced to abandon Chiang while trying to make it look as if he had not.[18] It was not that the Truman administration would not aid the Kuomintang but could not, given the political coalitions that were the basis of its power, the corruption of the regime, and the actual and potential power of the Chinese Communists.[19]

Avoidance is not the typical response to value conflict in crises. The domestic and international pressures to avoid losing a nation to Communism or other hostile groups have been sufficient to force leaders into decisions even if they are painful and difficult ones.[20] Since the failure of Truman and Marshall's policy in China, decision-makers have not had the luxury of avoidance. They have had to accept or resolve value conflicts in terms of bolstering or reform.

Acceptance

When faced with a situation of intense political instability in a client nation, most American decision-makers have realized that there are underlying and immediate causes for the conflict. The underlying cause has usually been a deep inequality, and a concomitant sense of injustice, in the political, economic, and social structures of the society. These inequalities have generally been present for centuries, though the relative position of particular groups may have shifted precipitously in recent years. The key to understanding why instability has been so prevalent in the Third World lies in the fact that most of these societies find themselves in a transitional period. Traditional and modern societies are relatively stable; modernizing or transitional societies are relatively unstable.[21]

The sense of injustice over traditional patterns of power in society is often clearly articulated by the political left, including Communist parties. This latter development, if it occurs, leads to an especially acute revolution of rising expectations, which comes about when the demands placed on a political system exceed the capabilities of that system to accommodate them.[22] When faced with this situation, government leaders have essentially three options: (1) they can attempt to suppress the demands for change (repression); (2) they can attempt to promote relatively moderate change in order to isolate those advocating radical change (reform); or (3) they can pursue a combination of these two options (reform and repression). The basic value conflict in these situations for American decision-makers is between either promoting order through repression (centralization of power; bolstering) or promoting order through change (decentralization of power; reform).[23]

When determining how the U.S. government should react in these situations, Republicans have had a greater tendency to accept the value conflict and attempt to promote order by bolstering the existing government. If a value conflict occurs, an acceptance of that conflict often leads to an emphasis on one value at the expense of the other.[24] It is not that Republicans do not believe in change; they do. But when that value comes into conflict with something they value more—order—they tend to choose the latter and downplay the relationship between the two. It should be noted that two of the longest-tenured Republican presidents in the postwar era thus far, Eisenhower and Nixon, came into office during unpopular, unwinnable wars in Korea and Vietnam. The tension and uncertainty of the world balance of power in those periods made it more likely that they would choose a less ambitious Third World policy. The emphasis in those years, in the short term, was on holding the line against further Communist advances. Yet the fundamental view of change was also an important determinant in the decisions these administrations made. Thus, initial policy choices are often deeply affected by ideological predispositions and basic views of politics that are formed at home.

John Foster Dulles made this clear as soon as he became Secretary of State. Testifying in executive session before the Senate Foreign Relations Committee shortly after taking office, he set forth his perception of this dilemma:

> I recognize full well that there are plenty of social problems and unrest which would exist if there was no such thing as Soviet Communism in the world, but what makes it a very dangerous problem for us is the fact that wherever those things exist, whether it is in Indo-China or Siam or Morocco or Egypt or Arabia or Iran, for that matter, even in South America, the forces of unrest are captured by the Soviet Communists because they are

smart at that, just as in this country, for a long while they captured the labor unions. When there is a strong labor situation which led to unrest, you would find immediately the Communists had moved in and gotten control, and that makes it very difficult to concentrate on reforms.[25]

Dulles did not want to back dictators like Chiang Kai-shek and Syngman Rhee, he testified, but "in times like these, in the unrest in the world today, and the divided spirit, we know that we cannot make a transition without losing control of the whole situation."[26] The fear of losing control of reform movements left only the repression of them in order to avoid disaster. The value trade-off had been made: a policy aimed at short-term order would prevail over a policy aimed at satisfying internal demands for change in client societies.

Faced with a stalemate in Korea, and convinced that the Truman administration had made crucial mistakes by not fully backing anti-Communists, regardless of their internal policies, Eisenhower and his Secretary of State adopted a clear bolstering policy toward clients. The rising demands for change should be slowed, they argued, lest they get out of control. Thus, they differed greatly from their predecessors on the issue of decolonization. Whereas Truman, Marshall, and Acheson urged the French, British, and Dutch to devolve power to indigenous governments because empires were "things of the past," Eisenhower believed that self-rule could only come after a period of twenty-five years, with a lingering relationship with the colonial power similar to that of the United States and Puerto Rico. Though he and Dulles believed in change in the Third World, they emphasized order.[27] To promote this concept of order, they advocated economic change but also backed "almost any kind of government that was neither radical nor Communist."[28] Eisenhower made this shift in policy immediately clear in his first inaugural address when he warned Americans against attempting to foist democracy on peoples who were not ready for it.[29]

Eisenhower and Dulles saw two crucial mistakes that Truman and his secretaries of state had made in their policy toward Asia. The first was not backing Chiang Kai-shek sufficiently; the second was not making an overt commitment to South Korea in January 1950, thereby "inviting" the June attack by the North. Their policy in the Third World therefore aimed at bolstering clients and making a series of overt commitments to defend nations in Asia, the so-called Pactomania of the 1950s. Pressures to bring about reform through a moderate devolution of power were generally abandoned. With the possible exception of the Philippines, there is not a single example of the Eisenhower administration seriously promoting political and social reforms in a client nation prior to 1958. In Latin America, the President and Secretary Dulles seemed to go out of their way to embrace some of the most brutal dictators in the hemisphere.[30]

Eisenhower and Dulles not only wanted to change policy, but began purging those responsible for reformist interventions during the Truman years. By 1954, twenty of twenty-two China service Foreign Service Officers were driven from government or had their careers ruined. The message to other Foreign Service Officers was clear: reform of client governments was no longer an option. Others concerned with reform in the Third World were also criticized. Wolf Ladejinsky, a land reform expert, was branded a socialist, dismissed as a security risk, and criticized by Secretary of Agriculture Ezra Benson for going too far in promoting land reform in Asia, though he was later reinstated.[31] Thus, a clear bolstering policy was adopted as the initial policy choice.

The shift in thinking in the Eisenhower administration came about after the violent treatment of Vice-President Nixon on his trip to Latin America in the spring of 1958, and after the rise of Castroism. The 1957–1958 recession in the United States had a disastrous effect on Latin America, and political discontent with the bolstering policy was growing. Other areas also showed signs of disenchantment with democracy in 1958. In Pakistan, Burma, Sudan, Indonesia, Thailand, the United Arab Republic, Iraq, Lebanon, Jordan, Ghana, and Guinea, there were unmistakable signs of movement toward more authoritarian rule and, in some cases, anti-Western radicalism. Rupert Emerson was later to call 1958 the year of the "collapse for democratic constitutionalism in the new countries." Though the primary causes were internal developments in those nations, the lack of a forceful, positive American policy was also a factor. The United States was increasingly criticized for consistently siding with reactionary elements in the developing world.[32]

Nor was bolstering successful in producing stable clients. In 1954, twelve of the twenty Latin American nations were headed by military dictators. By 1961, only one was left. Demands for political and social changes had swept away the governments that the United States had been bolstering as stable anti-Communist regimes. Events elsewhere in the Third World also overtook Eisenhower's decolonization policy. In 1960 alone, seventeen African nations gained their independence. The reactive, bolstering policy seemed to be at odds with the forces of change swirling through the new nations.[33] The year 1958 was a time of "Yankee Go Home!" and "The Ugly American."

The problem for the United States was increasingly seen as getting client populations on the side of client governments. Though this represented a more reformist policy than that of the first Eisenhower administration, and provided some of the underpinnings for the sub-sequent Kennedy policy, the depth of Eisenhower's conversion remains unclear. Despite his attempt to take credit for the shift in his memoirs, on his Latin American tour of 1960 he repeatedly told those nations that reforms were a matter of purely internal concern.[34] Thus, the stage was set for the reformist interventions of the Kennedy years, but the policy was never really implemented under Eisenhower. Even when Eisenhower did attempt to shift policy, he was largely prevented from doing so by a coalition of the Republican "Old Guard" and Southern Democrats.[35]

Other Republican presidents have followed a similar pattern of bol-stering as their initial approach to instability in clients. In the Nixon years the reformist approach in Latin America, developed under Ken-nedy and greatly lessened under Johnson, was totally abandoned. And it was not only in Latin America that the bolstering policy was felt. In Greece, for example, the military government was gaining international attention as a result of its increasingly brutal rule. The Nixon admin-istration increased military and economic aid and accepted at face value any assurances by the Greek government that improvements in human rights were being carried out. Nixon also refused to become involved in nations that suffered setbacks in democratic rule. In 1972, President Park Chung-hee of the Republic of Korea declared martial law and jailed much of his political opposition. The U.S. reaction was nonexis-tent. In 1973, Nixon told the Koreans: "Unlike other Presidents, I do not intend to interfere in the internal affairs of your country."[36] Nor was this remark unrepresentative. In April 1969, in criticism of the pressure Kennedy had put on Portugal to dismantle its African empire, Nixon told the Portuguese Foreign Minister: "Just remember, I'll never do to you what Kennedy did."[37]

By the end of the first Nixon administration, recalling the experience of the Eisenhower administration, the bolstering policy appeared to many to have failed. In 1971–1972, South Korea, the Philippines, South Vietnam, Nicaragua, and El Salvador all moved toward more authori-tarian rule, and moderate opposition groups in those nations were increasingly radicalized. An increase in opposition to governments in Chile, Indonesia, Iran, and Uruguay caused a marked increase in hu-man rights violations in those nations.[38] The Nixon and Ford adminis-trations never developed a strategy beyond bolstering to deal with the situation, though Ford was struggling with the political realities when he was voted out of office in 1976.[39]

The reaction in the Democratic Congress was quite different. Begin-ning in 1968, a group of new liberal Democratic members of Congress was elected because of their opposition to the Vietnam War. In 1974 and 1976, legislation was passed linking foreign aid more directly to political and social development. These developments represented a growing desire for a "moral" foreign policy that was not simply based on bolstering anti-Communist regimes.[40]

Thus, by the end of the Nixon-Ford years, whatever domestic support there had been for bolstering had largely dissipated. President Ford and Secretary Kissinger attempted to defuse opposition by publicly declaring the importance of human rights. In practice, however, the policy was not changed. Their "quiet diplomacy" in favor of human rights "involved only the most circumspect protestations."[41]

In a similar vein, Ronald Reagan's administration ran into difficulties with its initial bolstering policies. Though the President gave much fanfare to "Project Democracy," "The Democracy Program," and the establishment of a "National Endowment for Democracy," in practice the administration turned away from the reformism of the Carter years.[42] In terms of the promotion of social reform, the President was extremely skeptical, as the following statement about the Philippines illustrates:

> Years ago, when the Philippine Islands were a territory of the United States, we decided to extend Social Security benefits to the Philippine people. Up to that time families had been extremely close—three generations living together in the home. But Social Security, by removing the dependence of family members on each other, destroyed the family bond. And with it, as we learned later, we effectively destroyed their society. How often that's the outcome of social reform![43]

These views, to say the least, can be debated, but clearly they represented an ideological position resistant to the idea of reformist intervention.

Within a week after Reagan took office, the administration's bolstering policy toward clients became apparent. On January 28, 1981, Secretary of State Alexander Haig publicly stated that the Carter policy would be reversed.[44] Through what it viewed as a policy of "constructive engagement" and "quiet diplomacy," the administration believed it would correct the mistakes of the Carter administration.

By 1984 the policy was running into problems, especially in the Philippines. The Reagan administration was increasingly concerned over the economic, military, and political centralization of power under the Marcos regime, and the resultant demise of support throughout Filipino society, but privately expressed puzzlement over what to do about it.[45] The Aquino assassination became a rallying point for the opposition, but the fundamental problems were already present. In the wake of a massively fraudulent election in 1986 and a growing Communist insurgency, the President was forced to move against his "old friend."[46]

Other areas also showed signs of instability. In Central America, some early assessments expressed concern over the apparent lack of understanding within the Reagan administration of the fundamental forces at work in those nations.[47] When the governments of Haiti and the Philippines both fell, the administration publicly reversed its policy of bolstering and declared that it would move toward the promotion of reform as a general policy prescription.[48] In South Korea, a precipitous increase in political instability, as well as some American prodding, forced the Korean government to hold democratic elections for the first time in more than fifteen years. Thus, once again, an administration began its tenure with one policy and was moved toward an alternative as a result of a perception of policy failure.

This overview of Republican administrations makes it apparent that value conflict has resulted in the general acceptance of one value (order) over the other (change) in initial, short-term policy goals. This has generally led to a bolstering approach which is meant to slow, or even prevent, change in client nations. Over time, however, this policy has often been abandoned because of a perception of policy failure.

Resolution

When a decision-maker is faced with a value conflict of equally held values, the psychological processes of coping with the conflict become more complex. One method of resolving the conflict is by attempting to combine, or integrate, the conflicting values in an attempt to transcend the cognitive dissonance.[49] In this way the two values become part of an integrative whole, each dependent on the existence of the other.

Democratic decision-makers have tended to employ this mechanism when facing the order versus change policy dilemma. This is likely to occur "to the degree two (or more) terminal values imply contradictory courses of action."[50] This has led Democrats, relative to Republicans, to have a greater tendency to follow a reformist policy with clients experiencing instability. It is not order *over* change that presents itself as the best policy choice, but order *through* change. Democrats, since they hold both change and order (ideological and security goals, respectively) equally dear, emphasize the relationship between the values in their policy choices. To the reformer, induced change increases order if it can be controlled; in contrast, to the bolsterer it risks decreasing order and likely cannot be controlled.

When he became Secretary of State in 1949, Dean Acheson adopted a "reform-as-the-best-way-of-fighting-Communism" approach in the Third World that was to last until the advent of the Eisenhower administration.[51] This was especially true in the wake of the fall of China. In his famous speech to the National Press Club on January 12, 1950, Acheson called attention to the need for a more vigorous economic and political reform program:

> It is a mistake . . . in considering Pacific and Far Eastern problems to become obsessed with military considerations. Important as they are, there are other problems that press, and these other problems are not capable of solution through military means. These other problems arise out of the susceptibility of many areas, and many countries in the Pacific area, to subversion and penetration that cannot be stopped by military means.[52]

Communists, argued Acheson, were not the cause of the problem, but a symptom:

> The Communists did not create this condition. They did not create this revolutionary spirit. They did not create a great force which moved out from under Chiang Kai-shek. But they were shrewd and cunning to mount it, to ride this thing to victory and into power.[53]

Thus, the underlying causes of instability, such as poverty and oppression, also had to be addressed. It was for this reason that economic aid began to be justified for security reasons during the Truman administration, partly to facilitate the passage of legislation by conservatives in Congress, but also because the issue areas were seen as increasingly interrelated.[54]

Both Truman and Acheson were resistant to backing extreme rightist regimes and believed that moderate political, economic, and social change was both inevitable and desirable, and, rather than being resisted, should be shaped in a "manner consistent with American interests."[55] The worry was that the failure to achieve reform in China would lead other nations to see Communism as the wave of the future. In contrast to the British, who simply wanted to improve police forces in Southeast Asian nations, for example, the Acheson State Department pointed to that policy's "essentially repressive nature and to the equal importance of pursuing a progressive program which would, in a more positive way, win the loyalty and support of the native populations." The fear of "bandwagoning" for ideological reasons, that is, the view that a particular ideology would appear as the answer to governmental and societal problems in newly independent nations, led to a greater concern with the spread of democratic values in the developing world.[56]

In the summer of 1949, as the Chinese Nationalist regime crumbled, Truman's administration began putting pressure on governments in a number of nations, and on the French in Indochina, Tunisia, and Morocco, to put through political, economic, and social reforms.[57] This was clearly seen as an element of national security policy. The basic idea, as Acheson repeatedly told allies and clients, was to capture the forces of change and nationalism for the Western side in the Cold War. In areas where there was no immediate Communist threat, for example Latin America, there were few such attempts at reform.[58]

The Truman administration began to push even harder for reforms in a number of client states in the aftermath of the outbreak of war in Korea. In Iran, Taiwan, and the Philippines it pushed for land reform, anti-corruption measures, and at least the beginning of representative government. In Egypt, it acquiesced in the anti-monarchical revolution of left-wing reformist officers in order to avoid potential Soviet influence. Though concerned, Acheson refused to intervene to end reformist movements in Iran, Bolivia, and Guatemala. In South Korea, where land reform was accomplished *before* the Korean War, the North Koreans generally failed in setting up effective anti-government guerrilla groups, which was at least partially attributable to a relatively satisfied peasantry that had received the benefits of an American-guided land reform. Though many may only remember the dramatic confrontations of the Cold War, the Truman era also contained classic examples of democratic land reform that saw agricultural production rise and relative stability return in those nations in which it was successfully implemented.[59]

This was the era of men such as Wolf Ladejinsky who roamed from Taiwan to the Philippines to India bringing economic aid and technical assistance, in many cases mixed with high-level American pressure for tenancy reduction and land redistribution, in an attempt to plant the seeds of stability in rural Asia. The Truman administration also often pressed for democratic government. To be sure, the record of success was mixed, and security concerns often overrode ideological ones. But compared to the administration that succeeded it, and others yet to come, the Truman years marked the beginning of a policy of reform and repression as the best way of fighting Communism in the Third World.[60] Thus, the United States began a series of commitments to a variety of developing nations during this period for a mixture of ideological and security reasons.[61]

Other Democratic administrations, with the exception of President Johnson, tended initially to follow the reformist prescriptive tendencies of the Truman years. Psychological integration tends to be strengthened over time if the problem is a particularly insoluble one.[62] By the 1960s, this tendency had manifested itself among many liberal Democrats, especially after the heavy political price they had paid for the loss of

China. Throughout the 1950s, these Democrats had attacked the Republicans for too little military spending, too little economic aid, *and* the backing of right-wing dictators who were alienating their populations. When they again gained the presidency in 1961, the Democrats attempted to integrate the exigencies of order and reform in clients under the rubric of nation-building, a much more ambitious concept than in earlier periods.

Though its record was mixed, to say the least, the Kennedy administration attempted to adopt an integrated program of tough military and security measures, mixed with the promotion of relatively far-reaching political and social reforms.[63] Kennedy saw himself, as he told Khrushchev at Vienna in 1961, as an agent of change at home and abroad.[64] As Arthur Schlesinger, Jr., put it: "Since Democrats had no ancestral hostility to purposeful government and social reform in America, they were less inclined to demand such hostility of foreigners."[65] Though in the wake of Vietnam many only remember the military aspects of counterinsurgency strategy, the political side of those policies was meant to enhance the "will and capacity" of clients "to augment social and political reform programs as a basis for modernization."[66] The framework for that policy included "tough counter-guerrilla action, generous provisions for amnesty, [and] sweeping political and economic reforms,"[67] that is, an integrated strategy of reform and repression.[68]

Lyndon Johnson is an anomaly in the party-politics approach to reform in allies. Though he promoted one of the most widespread devolutions of domestic political and economic power in the history of the United States through his Great Society programs, he generally tended to bolster clients and adopted a clear "Cold War approach" toward the use of aid for political and social reforms—that is, they were matters of internal concern to the client.[69] In the political upheaval of the mid-1960s, which Johnson saw as largely caused in Latin America by the overly ambitious goals of the Alliance for Progress,[70] order was to prevail over change. This led to a marked shift toward a bolstering, military approach in comparison to the policy of the Truman and Kennedy administrations:

> The focus on military assistance helped simplify Johnson's . . . perception of hemispheric affairs. Over and over, particularly in the early crises that occurred in Panama and Brazil, [he] interpreted the problem as one of Communists versus anti-Communists. Except in unusual cases, such as Chile, where Salvador Allende's more radical programs made Frei's agrarian reforms tolerable, top administration officials saw little middle ground between the alternatives of good and evil.[71]

Other Democrats, however, did not agree. Partly in response to Johnson's bolstering approach, congressional Democrats took the initiative in passing the Title IX legislation of 1966 linking foreign aid to "social progress" in recipient nations. President Johnson, a man of the Congress, partially changed his bolstering policies in reaction to this legislation—especially in Vietnam, which led to the fairest national election in Vietnamese history in 1967—but he never really came to grips with the problem.

Jimmy Carter was the first President elected after the spectacular failure of nation-building in Vietnam. He was also the first postwar President who had to formulate foreign policy without the high degree of Cold War consensus of earlier years. Carter was certainly within the reform tradition of Democratic presidents, but his human rights policy differed in two important aspects from earlier Democratic policy. First, Carter's reforms were considerably less ambitious than earlier programs; they were primarily aimed at curbing excesses, rather than attempting to get at the root causes of the problem. Second, his reforms were never clearly integrated with security goals in any systematic fashion. In fact, they were most consistently attempted in areas where there were no immediate security threats to the client government.[72] This made it extremely difficult for him to garner support for these policies under the rubric of the major area of consensus in postwar foreign policy, the containment of Communism. He made the fatal mistake of confusing the temporary disillusionment with containment in the mid-1970s with a fundamental reordering of priorities.

The policy failures in Iran and Nicaragua and the Soviet invasion of Afghanistan in 1979 led to Carter's backing off from the rhetoric and policies of 1977–1978. The human rights policy was not abandoned, but there was a movement toward a more bolstering policy in general terms. When the President's own views changed following the Soviet invasion of Afghanistan, it appeared to many to be a case of too little, too late. Yet in one respect Carter shared the fate of every Cold War president: his initial approach to the Third World was eventually perceived as a failure.

The Perils and Paradoxes of
Reformist Intervention

3

In this chapter I will address the following general questions: What is the American concept of reformist intervention and how relevant is it to the problems of clients? What are the ethical consequences of reformist intervention? What are some of the paradoxical power relationships that are seemingly intrinsic to patron-client interaction? Answers to these questions are necessary in order to create a framework for analyzing the case studies and other reformist interventions.

Definitions and Policy Options

In a general sense, reformist intervention can be defined as the active attempt of one state to alter the domestic politics of other states. There are various types of intervention, usually categorized by the *means* (military, economic, and/or political) used to implement the policy. The *ends* of the policy, however, are always political; they entail the manipulation of the cost-benefit calculations of decision-makers in target states in a future direction preferred by decision-makers in the intervening state.

Reformist intervention is carried out through a mixture of positive and negative sanctions. Positive sanctions are those actions taken by the intervening state that add to the values/goals of target states; negative sanctions are those actions taken that threaten the values/goals of target states. Sanctions can be aimed at altering the foreign or the domestic policies of the target state, but in reformist interventions domestic policies are most often at issue. The two basic characteristics of interventions are (1) they are convention-breaking, that is, they aim at changing the status quo of relations between the intervening and target states, and (2) they are generally aimed at the authority structure of the target states.[1]

Reformist intervention in patron-client relations more generally takes the form of attempting to preserve a precarious ally by affecting the nature of the relationship of the client government to its society. Bolstering does so by utilizing positive sanctions in the hope that this will add to the legitimacy of the client government. Reformist intervention does so by mixing positive and negative sanctions in the hope that the client will alter its policies toward its society. In this sense, bolstering is an intervention on the side of the client government; reform is an intervention on the side of the client society. Both policies have as their initial aim the preservation of the client government. Because of the nature of the intervention, however, the reforming patron at times must search for alternative leadership if the client government will not alter its behavior. This makes reformist intervention a much riskier policy. It is for this reason that reformers, when no alternative leadership can be identified, often fall back on bolstering.

This view is the basis of the famous remark by President Kennedy that in the Dominican Republic in 1961 the United States had three choices, in descending order of preference: (1) "a decent democratic regime"; (2) a continuation of the Trujillo regime; or (3) "a Castro regime." The President stated to aides: "We ought to aim at the first, but we really can't renounce the second until we are sure that we can avoid the third."[2] It is better to have a contentious client than no client.

Yet in extreme circumstances, for example in Vietnam under the regime of Ngo Dinh Diem, the reformer may believe that the risk must be undertaken and support given to alternative ruling groups. Other examples of this phenomenon include Syngman Rhee in South Korea in 1960, Ferdinand Marcos in the Philippines in 1986, and "Baby Doc" Duvalier in Haiti in 1986. Though this course of action is sometimes attempted by a reforming patron, it is used only as a last resort because of the fear that what follows might be even worse.

The Strategic Basis for Reformist Intervention

The primary reason for reformist intervention is strategic, in the broad sense of the term: it is meant to deny a position of influence in the client state to another great power. Economic and ideological goals are normally means to this end. This has been especially true on a global scale in the postwar era, when the United States entered into a direct ideological competition with Communism, but it has long been true in hemispheric relations. Reformist intervention in the Western Hemisphere began with the preemptive logic of the Roosevelt Corollary to the Monroe Doctrine. Secretary of State Elihu Root, for example, defended its application to Cuba in these terms: "We don't want Cuba ourselves; we cannot permit any other power to get possession of her, and, to prevent the necessity of one and the possibility of the other of these results, we want her to govern herself decently and in order."[3] Reformist intervention, then, has been an aspect of U.S. security policy since the United States became actively involved in great-power contention. This is not to say that economic or ideological goals never predominate in these situations, but *typically* they do not.

The United States attempted to break out of the reformist intervention dilemma in the Good Neighbor policy of Franklin Roosevelt in the 1930s. This met with highly uncertain results: first, the United States found that it could not avoid intervention to the degree to which it desired, especially in the policy's early period;[4] and second, the movement away from interventions in the region correlated strongly with a precipitous rise in authoritarianism in the hemisphere.[5] Internal opposition to these authoritarian governments created during the Good Neighbor period was a major reason for the instability of the 1950s. Thus, it is not clear whether the United States can—or should—avoid intervention in the internal politics of those nations in the developing world in which it has major political, economic, and strategic interests.

The American Ideology and the Reformist Tradition

Defining the American concept of reform is a more daunting task than it might seem at first. There are various kinds of particular reforms, and the United States has sometimes promoted one or a number of them in an attempt to broaden the base of the client government. In general, reform has three basic characteristics: (1) it represents a change in governmental policy; (2) it aims at affecting the nature of the relationship between the government and society; and (3) it normally, but not always, aims at a devolution of economic, military, political, and/or social power within society.[6] As used in this book, the term "reform" will encompass all three of these criteria.

The United States at times aims at military, economic, political, and social reforms. Both bolsterers and reformers aim at the former two; reformers are more likely to aim at the latter two. Since intervention is defined as actions aimed at the authority structure of clients, reformist intervention can be further defined as the attempt to decentralize those structures within these issue areas. These reforms fall into two categories: *elite reforms,* those that attempt to alter the composition of the client government through the inclusion or exclusion of particular personnel or groups, and *redistributive reforms,* those that attempt to attract the political support of the masses through an alteration of the distribution of goods.

Elite reforms aim at the decision-making process of the client government and the granting of authority to reformist-minded personnel approved by the patron in order to implement further reforms. Examples of this type of reform are the U.S. attempts to promote the fortunes of the Chinese Communist Party (CCP), liberal groups, and the left wing of the Kuomintang in China; the demand that Ramon Magsaysay be made Secretary of Defense in the Philippines and the political opposition allowed to compete in fair elections; and the attempt to include minority parties in the Diem government in Vietnam. Attempts to exclude the right wing of the Kuomintang, the removal of corrupt officials and generals in the Philippines, and the attempt to get Diem's brother Nhu out of government are also examples of elite reforms. These reforms are also often attempted in the military forces of the client to provide more effective strategy and leadership. In the process of including new elements in the decision-making process, or excluding existing power holders, the composition of the client government is reformed. The reform is in this sense a devolution of power.

Redistributive reforms are those meant to devolve political, social, and/or economic power in society in order to mobilize public support for the client government. Elections, minimum wage legislation, land reform, and the promotion of unions are examples of this type of reform. Anti-corruption measures and the promotion of a free press may also fit into this category in certain circumstances. The purpose of these reforms is to broaden the base of support of the client government, but also to provide accountability and constraints on the arbitrary use of power.[7]

The basic idea for both types of reform is to make the country's leadership more responsive to intra- or extra-governmental groups, as well as to society at large. Elite reforms are seen as a prerequisite to redistributive reforms: if the leadership problem is not solved first, redistributive reforms become a moot point since many in the client government are opposed to them in the first place. Though there were some partial successes in China and Vietnam, generally the United States could not effect elite reforms in those countries, and therefore did not succeed in promoting redistributive reforms. In the Philippines, it was able to effect both.

The ideological basis for these types of reform is that most Americans have a philosophical bias against centralized power. The arguments for this are based on both efficiency and justice. A political and economic system that leaves decision-making at the lowest possible level produces the fewest barriers to individual liberty and economic upward mobility.

This is a basic tenet of liberal democratic thought, and indeed most of those who have immigrated to the United States have come in search of personal freedom and/or economic opportunity (which are viewed as directly related). According to this American ideology, when private groups or individuals gain too much political or economic power, the government has a responsibility to devolve that power (for example, "trust-busting"); when the government is viewed as having too much power, private groups and individuals must work to devolve that power. It is this concept of balance between government and society that is the basis of a good and just society.

This idea underlies the ideological objection to monopolies. It is not the accumulation of power and wealth per se that is the danger (in fact, Americans generally admire this); it is the concomitant ability to dictate to others and erect barriers to competition, that is, the denial of entrance into an economic or political market, that is viewed as the reason for the delegitimization of the status quo. It is for this reason that the plight of the political opposition in other nations has affected U.S. policy to the degree that it has. If this were not the case, Americans would have few ideological problems with dictators as allies in the first place. Reform is not always necessary, and in fact it can be destabilizing in the short term,[8] but when there is a questioning of the institutions of society, governmental or private, in the United States or elsewhere, it is usually assumed that it is based on an excessive centralization of power. Thus, the American idea of reform as a reaction to political instability encompasses the idea of a devolution of power to give other members of society a more equal chance at economic and political participation in order to lend legitimacy to social and political institutions.[9]

It is in this area of the devolution of power, for both elite and redistributive purposes, that the most controversy in relations with clients appears. No client government complains that it has too much power in its hands; the primary problem in getting a client to reform is that these governments fear losing all of their power by giving up some. If the client government wanted to reform, there would be no need to promote this. It is the *resistance* to a moderate devolution of power that presents the diplomatic dilemma to the American reformer.

The Role of the Charismatic Leader in Reform

Though liberal and radical critics often denigrate the relevance of moderate reform to the Third World, the subjective political effects of a moderate devolution of power can be quite profound. Those who propose reform to "get the people on the side of the government" by "getting the government on the side of the people" may be advocating a vague intangible, but not an unimportant one. Peasants tend to react more positively to a charismatic leader than to an efficient one.[10] Because they are not accustomed to a market economy, peasants have difficulty with impersonal relationships.[11] When traditional ties to the lord have been broken, especially by absentee landlordism, a cultural and political vacuum occurs that Communists and other radicals have been very adept at filling by establishing personal, and sometimes beneficent, contact with the villages.[12]

A charismatic reformist leader may also fill this vacuum. In the case of the Philippines, for example, Ramon Magsaysay was the first Filipino leader to visit extensively the barrios of the rural areas, during his presidential campaign of 1953. He promised the rural farmers legal assistance if they had grievances against the government or landlords. If the entire peasantry had taken advantage of this program, the Filipino government could not conceivably have met their demands.[13] The very act of making such a promise, however, convinced them that the government was on their side and could be trusted to protect them from arbitrary treatment by elements that held them in contempt. This is not to say that there was no objective improvement in conditions for the peasants under Magsaysay; there was. But the effects of his political programs were limited.

Magsaysay's Land Settlement program, implemented while he was Secretary of Defense, also had a limited objective effect. The idea was to grant unused land in Mindanao to Huks who rallied to the government cause, thereby relieving the land hunger of the peasants in Central Luzon (a Communist stronghold). Out of more than 600,000 tenant farm families in the nation, however, fewer than 1,000 families were resettled, and fewer than 250 were former rebels. Yet the Communists later admitted that the program had the effect of depleting support for the insurgency.[14] Thus the subjective, psychological advantage that this program provided the government was an important factor in undermining the appeal of radicals. The same might be said of a reformer such as Franklin Roosevelt in an industrialized nation. He never solved the basic economic dilemmas of the Great Depression, but he gave people enough hope to prevent them from seeking more radical and destructive solutions, such as Fascism or Communism. Effective reformers realize that politics is both subjective and objective.

The Recurring Three-Option Diplomatic Dilemma: Opportunities and Constraints

The United States has consistently faced the same policy dilemma in a number of nations: it does not want to go in, but it cannot stay out—

what could be termed, for the Cold War era, the dilemmas of commitment versus containment respectively. In a memo to Dean Rusk, written in 1950 in the wake of the loss of China, the State Department's Livingston Merchant cogently summarized this problem. He also articulated the perceived need for a reformist intervention in order to avoid the advent of Communism in the Philippines, which might have led to a possible American military intervention and far greater costs to Americans and Filipinos:

> The dilemma the United States Government faces is how to force an ineffectual local government to do internally what it must do, without reoccupying the country or otherwise so seriously invading the sovereignty as to cause violent repercussions throughout Asia and Western Europe as well. Drawing on our experience in China, I think that the least unhopeful solution would be to exert all of our pressure, including the cessation of any further economic or military aid, to establish a government which understands its own internal problems and has the political courage to act.[15]

Thus, if decision-makers believe they cannot withdraw from a client nation, the policy dilemma is primarily based in the *extent* and *type* of intervention.[16]

The United States has historically portrayed itself, somewhat hypocritically, as a non-interventionist nation. This is one reason for its oscillating policy toward the outside world. At times its leaders have felt compelled to involve the United States to a greater degree in external affairs, but this has often been controversial. This situation changed considerably following World War II, but the question of how and when to get involved has not been satisfactorily resolved in intellectual or policy terms.[17] Yet as long as the United States is involved in the developing world, Americans must recognize that it is—indeed must be—an interventionist power. The debate should not be over intervention versus non-intervention, but over what kind of intervention, and under what conditions.

Thus, there has been great contention over the question of intervention in the internal affairs of other nations. This is largely based on the spurious argument that aiding established governments in unstable societies is somehow non-interventionist according to international norms. As the international legal scholar Wolfgang Friedman argued: "Any attempt by a foreign power to interfere with internal change by assisting either rebels or the government is probably contrary to international law."[18] Foreign aid *is* a form of intervention. In a poor nation, those who control resources have power. By giving aid to established governments, the United States is intervening in internal politics whether it admits it or not.

This is not just true for rightist regimes in the Third World. By giving aid to the Tito regime in Yugoslavia beginning in the late 1940s, for example, the United States "took sides" against the dictator's internal opposition. Marshall Plan aid to European countries was viewed similarly by Western Communist parties. In fact, this is invariably recognized by the opposition in the recipient society. In China, for example, extragovernmental groups complained bitterly against aid granted to the Nationalist government. As an American official noted at the time: "The Chinese [opposition] also state, with justification, that American nonintervention in China cannot avoid being intervention in favor of the conservative leadership which exists at the present time."[19] This is often the primary purpose of foreign aid in the first place: to prevent the ascendancy of hostile forces to positions in the authority structure.[20]

When faced with this policy dilemma in the Third World, the United States has essentially three policy choices in dealing with clients undergoing intense political instability: withdrawal, reform, or bolstering. The first has been largely negated in the past by the premises of containment. It is sometimes argued a priori that the United States should be less concerned with the spread of Communism in the Third World, especially with the end of the Cold War. This policy choice, however, faces domestic, moral, and geostrategic constraints. As for the domestic constraint, it has been politically devastating to argue this after the fact, as Truman (China), Eisenhower (Cuba), and Carter (Nicaragua/Iran) discovered. The public and congressional reaction to the fall of the Shah of Iran in 1979 and the 1990 Iraqi invasion of Kuwait suggests that this constraint will remain in some form for the foreseeable future, even if the ideological component of anti-Communism is removed.

Concerning the moral dilemma, it is no longer credible, if indeed it ever was, to argue that a radical leftist government will be more progressive than a right-wing authoritarian one,[21] or even progressive at all. Lon Nol, the American-backed client in Cambodia, left much to be desired as a national leader, but his rule was significantly more benevolent than the butchery of Pol Pot. In an imperfect world, choices must necessarily be imperfect.

As for the geostrategic constraint, it might be argued that the United States should withdraw from particular nations, but *at some point* it must become concerned with the internal politics of other nations, even if this involved only Canada and Mexico, in order to deal with its own security.[22] Thus, though withdrawal may be desirable in some situations, it is not in many others. The policy debate should therefore center on where, when, and how the United States should intervene—not if it should do so at all.

The reform option is an extremely difficult enterprise. Over time, this policy is more likely to garner the support of the American people and contribute to stability in clients. In the short term, however, it is a risky policy, and may also threaten longer-term interests by further destabilizing a precarious ally. In addition, it entails an especially intimate involvement in the internal affairs of the client, and, at times, the necessity of fostering a change of leadership. This points to a paradoxical development in the policy debate that has been identified by Samuel Huntington and Henry Kissinger, that is, those who are most concerned with reform in clients (for example, curbing human-rights abuses) are those least likely to support some of the actions needed to bring it about: covert action, or the involvement in internal affairs necessary to identify and support alternative leadership groups that might be more reformist.[23] Americans in general, and reform-minded ones in particular, may have to accept the ideologically unpalatable fact that, at times, ends do justify means. Policy choices should be measured against the costs of their alternatives, not against absolute standards.[24]

The bolstering option is complicated by drawbacks identified earlier: it is unacceptable within the American polity over time and ultimately adds to instability in clients. If the United States were to adopt this as a consistent policy prescription, it would stumble along attempting to stem the flow of change, something that can also entail prohibitive costs in lives and money. Had this policy been more successful in the past, it might be more acceptable in the future. But the recurring instability in clients that have been bolstered suggests that this is a short-term, crisis-oriented policy prescription at best.

Thus, all of the options have serious drawbacks and could court disaster. All of them have moral and ethical consequences that will be difficult for some Americans to accept. If the options are measured against each other, however, reformist intervention may be the least costly for U.S. interests and the client society. Reform may at times seem unrealistic, but it should be viewed as a policy choice in relation to the realistic possibilities of withdrawal or bolstering policies. Within this context, it may often be the least unrealistic of available options.

Reformist interventions are extremely difficult, and at times may turn out to be impossible, but in ethical and policy terms it may be preferable to attempt them in order to avoid even greater costs in the future. Richard Cottam recognizes this problem: "By avoiding a strategy that involves continuing interference, the policy maker does not avoid the necessity to interfere. On the contrary, since little is done to alter dangerous trends while they are developing, avoidable crises occur and, unhappily, a policy of gross interference is commonly employed to deal with the situation."[25] It may be that there are long-term costs to not intervening for reform that may be even more prohibitive than the high short-term risks of that policy.

The Ethics of Intervention

The contradictory impulses of the American ideology are not the only constraints on decision-makers. Americans like to see themselves as a nation of people that obeys international law. Indeed, the United States has been much criticized for having an excessively legalistic approach to the world. If the world is made up of theoretically equal states, each sovereign and inviolable in the internal sphere, as international law and "world opinion" dictate, what gives Americans the "right" to intervene in the affairs of other nations? This is a thorny philosophical and political question, the full examination of which would lead us far afield. There are certain points regarding the policy debate over this question, however, that should be made.

The first point is that there is a double standard in "world opinion" that places the democratic powers, especially the United States as the leading nation of the West, at a distinct disadvantage. Western nations are expected to adhere to the rigorous interpretation of non-intervention, but when Third World nations intervene, there is often a curiously muted reaction from many so-called neutral nations. When the United States intervened militarily in Vietnam there was scathing criticism from much of the world, and even so-called War Crimes Trials in Sweden to protest that war. Similar activities were promoted less successfully in the early 1980s over American policy in Central America. Yet when the Soviets intervened in Hungary in 1956, Czechoslovakia in 1968, or Poland on a regular basis, many of the same circles were strangely silent, though there were relatively mild criticisms over the intervention in Afghanistan. When the United States trained anti-Castro Cuban guerrillas in an attempt to overthrow that dictator at the Bay of Pigs in 1961, there was a worldwide outcry; when Castro sent Cubans to train anti–South African guerrillas in Angola in the mid-1970s, many praised this action. When India intervened militarily in Sri Lanka in the late 1980s, there was virtual silence from the Third World, as there had been when it invaded Goa in 1961. It is not intervention per se that is the problem, but (according to "world opinion") who is intervening and who is the target. The case for a strict interpretation of non-intervention would be greatly strengthened if there were a single standard for every nation. As it is, much of the world is in favor of intervention when they see it as in their interests, and against it when they do not. It is not too much to ask that the West be allowed to view the problem in a similar fashion.

That is not to say that the United States could, or should, completely ignore "world opinion" or international law. But it must be recognized that these are far more restricted concepts than public opinion or municipal law within the domestic realm. As K. J. Holsti has noted, despite an emotional attachment to the concept of absolute sovereignty, the "penetrated" state is the norm, not the exception, in world politics.[26]

Second, a major catalyst in decisions to intervene for reform is requests from opposition groups, and even members of the client government, to do so. Even that vaunted Third World nationalist Mao Tse-tung told American foreign service officers in 1944, with respect to an American reformist intervention in China, that "interference . . . to further the interests of the people of China is not interference."[27] Mao, of course, changed his view when he perceived U.S. policy as pro-Nationalist in 1946. Yet Mao somehow kept his nationalist credentials with leftist critics of American foreign policy, while Chiang Kai-shek and Ngo Dinh Diem of Vietnam were vilified as puppets for doing pretty much the same thing. How does the non-intervention standard fit situations like the military invasions by the United States in Grenada and Panama in the 1980s, which were widely popular with the respective publics in those nations? During the Marshall Plan years, European governments sometimes *asked* the United States to pressure them so that the Americans could take the political heat for unpopular policies.[28] In all three of the case studies discussed in this book, requests for American reformist intervention came not only from extra-governmental groups opposed to the client government, but from intra-governmental ones as well. The basic question that has to be answered is the following: does the United States have responsibilities to abstract standards and particular leadership groups that transcend its responsibilities to the client society at large or to its own interests? If the United States backs an unpopular government, it runs a high long-term risk of alienating the client society; if it responds to the opposition, it runs a high short-term risk of alienating the client government. There is perhaps no definitive solution that would satisfy everyone, or fit every case, but clearly the policy dilemma is more complicated than a simplistic and false dichotomy between narrow definitions of intervention and non-intervention.

Finally, it should be pointed out that the United States itself is the target of intervention in its internal affairs from clients. Lobbyists, public relations firms, business groups, religious groups, ethnic groups, and many other organizations have been mobilized by client governments to affect the internal political climate of the United States. It is true that these efforts do not always work, and often backfire, but they still represent attempts to violate the "inviolable" sovereignty of the United States. The China Lobby is only the most famous example of this kind of activity. As George F. Kennan pointed out at the time, the Kuomintang had "intrigued in this country in a manner scarcely less disgraceful to it than to ourselves."[29] Cottam has pointed out that democracies in general, and the United States in particular, are especially tolerant of this sort of activity.[30] Though many of these actions are legal in open, democratic societies, some are not. Since they are usually banned in authoritarian client nations, they must be carried out through covert action. Thus, if the United States does not want to grant an advantage to authoritarian client governments in an already difficult situation, it must be prepared to intervene in the internal affairs of the client in ways many Americans would rather avoid.

Dictatorship and Societal Transition: Some Causes of Instability

Before analyzing further the diplomatic and policy dilemmas presented by reformist interventions, it will be useful to examine some of the common problems and contradictions in client societies that often cause political instability. I will do this by constructing an abstract model society that incorporates the political dilemmas involved. Each client society has idiosyncrasies: religion, economic groups, historical and cultural traditions, personalities, among others. There are, however, recurring dilemmas based in the objective conditions of various societies that allow for relevant generalizations. An analysis of these commonalities will facilitate comparison and avoid redundancies when the internal causes of instability are examined in the particular cases.[31]

Political Dilemmas of Revolutionary Transitional Societies

Many Third World states are ruled by an oligarchy, military or civilian, often with personal and political ties to the land-owning classes.[32] The military elites are largely composed of or allied with the landowners. The economic foundations of the society are typically agrarian, with a small industrial sector. More than 70 percent of the population directly works the land, with a significant proportion serving as tenant farmers.

The vast majority of the society is desperately poor and illiterate, with high degrees of infant mortality and low levels of nutrition. Many of the landowners have moved to urban areas, creating an absentee landlord problem by destroying the cultural and psychological bonds of the traditional lord/peasant relationship. The lords, no longer present in the countryside, turn to the government to protect their traditional prerogatives and class interests. To accomplish this, the government must centralize power in what has been traditionally a decentralized authority structure.

This process greatly strains the government's capabilities. In order to finance these new responsibilities, the government increases taxes on agrarian production, which are passed on to the peasants. To man a larger army, it forcibly drafts one of the strongest and most productive elements of the poor peasants, young males, further straining the precarious subsistence level in the countryside. These new soldiers (underpaid, underfed, and undertrained) have been ripped from their families and the cultural roots of their villages. Rather than identifying with the peasants of other provinces, they often treat them quite brutally. The peasantry increasingly sees the central government as an outside force, as a negative, repressive element that only takes from them and never gives anything in return.

The only elements in this model society that are educated, and can therefore make a systemic critique, and that are not directly tied to the ruling classes are students, intellectuals, and often journalists. They increasingly attack the ruling classes and the political and economic status quo.[33] The government reaction is often a repressive crackdown and an identification of those wanting any change with those who want total change. Some dissidents are put into prison or killed; some are co-opted into the system; some go into exile; some go into hibernation; some go into the jungle or hills. The latter three groups become increasingly radicalized and convinced of the need for drastic change. If they make common cause with organized dissident or sympathetic groups, often including Communist leadership in an expedient "united front" strategy with other nationalists, they may switch to supporting armed struggle to overthrow the political system.[34]

In the early period of armed struggle, some will become Communists, some will not. Many, however, will become radicalized and convinced of the need for an authoritarian or totalitarian leftist regime to promote rapid social change and prevent the reestablishment of an authoritarian rightist regime. In short, the society becomes deeply polarized, with simultaneous crises in identity, integration, authority, participation, and the distribution of goods. It is under these conditions that the United States usually becomes concerned about a reformist intervention, that is, as an ad hoc response to political instability that threatens the legitimacy of the client government.[35] It is the response of the client society itself, however, that concerns us here.

At this point, the position of the client government is increasingly precarious because of the growing centralization of power in the "modernizing" sense of the term. Barrington Moore points to this problem:

> A highly segmented society that depends on diffuse sanctions for its coherence and for extracting the surplus from the underlying peasantry is nearly immune to peasant rebellion because opposition is likely to take the form of creating another segment. On the other hand, an agrarian bureaucracy, or a society that depends on a central authority for extracting the surplus, is a type most vulnerable to such outbreaks.[36]

Thus, the state becomes the focal point for political opposition of all stripes.

Unfortunately, a typical response for a client government in these situations is to attempt to centralize power through repression alone. This may work if its base of support is broad enough to prevent a coalescence of the opposition. If it is not, however, the government is even more vulnerable, as it excludes groups that were once friendly or apathetic toward the government. In this case, centralization of power creates new opposition, especially in competition among various elites.[37] In China, the Philippines, and Vietnam, for example, those governments were weakest when other anti-Communist nationalists became disaffected from the regime. Though centralization of power may make sense from a security point of view, it may not from a political one. There are trade-offs to be made here between repression and reform, between the centralization and decentralization of power.

Liberalism and the Paradoxical Effects of the Centralization of Power

It has been shown that Americans have a philosophical bias against centralized power. Critics of American policy on both the left and the right have argued that this leads to "naive" crusades to limit power in areas where more government is needed, not less. This criticism may be partially correct, but much of it rests on the false assumption that dictatorships, of the left or right, are considerably more efficient and coherent than liberal regimes in implementing policies. The breakdown of Communist regimes in Eastern Europe and elsewhere in the 1980s, which opened those governments to closer historical scrutiny, suggests that this assertion is wildly off the mark. I will argue that this is generally the case for rightist dictatorships also.

A paradox of power relations in transitional societies lies in the fact that in order for reform to occur, power must be centralized to overcome the intrinsic opposition to change *and* decentralized to mobilize new groups for political support. Those groups that have centralized the power, on the left or right, however, are often those who are the most opposed to decentralization. In short, those that can, will not; those that cannot, will[38] (or at least say they will when they are out of power). While recognizing the need for garnering the power to carry out redistributive reforms, I will argue in contrast to many critics that a centralization of power alone often has the paradoxical effect of making the client government weaker, not stronger. The decentralization of power advocated by liberal democrats is also necessary in some form. Thus, power relations for the purposes of reform should follow a sequence: first centralization, *then* decentralization of power in order to mobilize new groups to the client government.[39] The problem for the United States is that it too often finds itself allied with groups that desire the former, but resist the latter. It is for this reason that it promotes elite reforms.

The necessity for centralizing power first can be illustrated by the case of South Korea in the wake of the fall of Syngman Rhee in 1960. The man who replaced him, Chang Myon, was a democrat who wanted to introduce liberal democratic government to Korea. Because he did not consolidate his own power position, however, he did not have the political wherewithal to overcome the opposition of Rhee conservatives or authoritarian military officers. He was overthrown in a military coup in the spring of 1961 by a group of young officers.[40]

The necessity for decentralizing power is illustrated by land reform policies in a variety of nations. An impressive case can be made for land reform as a substitute for revolution in those countries with a high degree of land tenancy.[41] Very often, however, the client government is reluctant to promote meaningful land reform because it might erode the regime's existing support among landlords. This can be seen in the experience of the Kuomintang in China: that regime was dominated by a coalition of landowners and army officers who had a vested interest in preventing land reform. Once expelled from the mainland, however, the leadership became receptive to American entreaties for land reform. On Taiwan, it was not their land that was being given away, and opposition was much less evident. In addition, some of the elements General Marshall had most wanted out of the government while they were on the mainland were removed following the retreat.[42] This land reform on Taiwan helped create the conditions for a remarkable degree of stability and prosperity by Third World standards.

Thus, shifts in the composition of a government away from those with vested interests in blocking reforms may clear the way for new and stabilizing policies. This is also a reason why bolstering often fails over time: it tends to entrench those most opposed to even minor change.

This may work in promoting stability in the short term, but often does not in the long term. As Edmund Burke observed, "A state without the means of some change is without the means of its conservation."[43]

Critics of U.S. policy have sometimes argued that an authoritarian government is necessary in developing countries to avoid the "inefficiencies" of pluralistic democracy. These nations, it is argued, must forgo political democracy in order to develop economically and foster future economic and social equality. A centrally planned economy is the best way to achieve the latter goals because the government does not have to contend with alternative strategies that would undermine the coherence of economic performance.

There is some reason to question these assumptions, especially in light of the growing popularity in the Third World of market-oriented development strategies in the 1980s and 1990s. Though some developing nations have made progress in the distribution of goods under centralized power relations, planned economies have a dreadful record in the production of goods. Beginning in the 1980s, even countries like the Soviet Union, China, Vietnam, and Yugoslavia moved to decentralize economic decision-making. They did not do so because they had abandoned their political principles, though that may at some time occur, but because the alternative has proved inefficient, devoid of motivation for the average citizen, and incapable of producing sufficient levels of goods to satisfy basic demands. In short, centrally planned economies, especially of the left, have not proved the most efficient means for economic development.

Nor does centralization necessarily bring greater political or military efficiency. As General Marshall discovered in China, military and economic reform would have had to be *preceded* by elite reforms to increase the efficiency of that regime. This lesson was also learned, but not successfully applied, during the Diem years in Vietnam. A regime that will not reform politically because it is afraid of losing its power will often resist reforming economically and militarily for the same reason. Relieved of external pressure for political reform, and ensured that aid will continue regardless of their actions, client governments often attempt to centralize power further in the economic and, especially, military spheres. It is the removal of this external constraint of reformist pressure that often undermines the effectiveness of bolstering as a policy.

The centralization of power also leads to an excessive reliance on personnel chosen on the basis of assured personal loyalty rather than expertise. This often takes the form of placing family members in positions of power: Chiang's brothers-in-law, Quirino's brother Antonio, and Diem's family are examples of this phenomenon. This not only leads to less effective political and military organizations (as in China, the Philippines, and Vietnam) but is a major source of instability in the Third World.[44] It was not for trivial reasons that American policymakers in the Kennedy administration joked that the first criterion for a replacement for Diem was that the new leader be an only child.

The need for loyalty can also lead to the phenomenon of leaders appointing underlings they hold in contempt. Chiang Kai-shek once told General Joseph Stilwell, describing his own officers: "I have to lie awake nights thinking what fool things they may do. Then I write and tell them not to do these things. But they are so dumb, they will do a lot of foolishness unless you anticipate them."[45] The constant interference by Chiang confused lines of command and destroyed what little initiative local commanders had.[46] This led to what Americans called "the world's worst military leadership" during the Chinese Civil War, and was a major reason for the defeat of the Nationalists. Thus, in many respects the process of centralizing power per se involves the particularism and partiality that are contributing factors to instability. Excessive centralization may create new inefficiencies that undermine the effectiveness and legitimacy of government.

Excessive centralization of power has another detrimental effect on political efficiency: what were called "power bottlenecks" by the Americans in Vietnam during the Diem years. Even the most inconsequential decisions had to be made at the highest level. This was a way for Diem to exercise control over the decision-making process, but he barely had the time or energy, certainly not the expertise, to make major decisions, let alone minor ones. At times he would be given proposals that lower-level bureaucrats had already approved, but would then spend months "studying" them to see if it was the right thing to do. At other times he would be given a high-level proposal by the Americans and not have the faintest idea what it involved,[47] though there were lower officials who could have evaluated it. Chiang Kai-shek, at times, would issue orders to his military commanders and then forget that he had given them.[48]

All dictators complain that their underlings are incompetent, but this is as much a means of political control as a real fear that poor decisions may be made. Unfortunately, the only person to whom Diem would delegate authority was his brother Nhu, the worst conceivable choice. Chiang relied most heavily on elements in the right wing of the Kuomintang, those least likely to agree to further change in any form. This not only impeded decision-making at the top, but destroyed initiative at the middle and lower echelons.

The question of political participation and economic development is a complex one. Huntington and Nelson have argued persuasively that participation has different effects in various stages of economic development. In the early stages, increased political participation (to urban and rural middle classes) aids economic development but increases inequality; in later stages (to urban and rural lower classes), it increases equality but hinders economic development.[49] If centralization of power increases in the early stages of development, it may be conducive to economic development,[50] but if it increases too much, and remains centralized, it may retard political development and ultimately become destabilizing. In societies where the basic economic production is agricultural, with the majority working the land, bolstering may mean, in effect, simply supporting the landlords.

Though democracy historically is more strongly correlated with economic development than with economic equality, if the political direction of the client is to be kept out of the hands of radical groups that reject both capitalism and democracy, some trade-offs may have to be made between economic and political development. What may be good long-term economic advice may be very bad short-term political advice.[51] As one business consultant to the State Department jocularly put it in October 1949, to emphasize economic development at the expense of political development is to put the "cartel before the hearse."[52]

Cultural Relativism: A Failed Explanation of Third World Politics

In policy debates, both bolsterers and advocates of withdrawal lean toward cultural relativism in casting doubt on the American capacity to spread democratic values. The questions they raise are important ones. Is the United States attempting to introduce inappropriate solutions to the problems of its clients? Are not autocratic governments more efficient than democratic ones? Do not client governments have a better knowledge of their society than American planners? These questions must be addressed before we move on to the paradoxes of power in patron-client relations.

The cultural relativism argument has often been made for Latin America, where the United States has been involved with reformist intervention for the longest period. The Latins, we have been told, have no liberal democratic tradition. They have instead chosen a "pre-Lockean" view of society based on Rousseau's concept that "community flows from unanimity."[53] Opposition to government in these societies is based on partiality and particularism; it is not a reaction against coercion per se. This view challenges the efficacy of attempting to introduce political reforms in societies where they have no philosophical base.

Presumably this is even more true in Asia and Africa, where liberal philosophical affinities are even more tenuous.

These critics are correct in pointing to the difficulties in implementing such a policy, but do not make a strong case for the *impossibility* of doing so. No nation is insulated from the philosophical and political currents of its times. Edmund Burke criticized the French Revolution for attempting to import ideas from Great Britain that had no philosophical basis in that society. Yet that revolution inculcated the French with the concepts of liberty, equality, and fraternity that are still the wellsprings of most French political life, no matter how imperfectly implemented. Peter the Great's reforms in Russia, and indeed the very idea of the state as something beyond a particular ruler, were borrowed from a study of the political institutions of Western Europe.[54] Following the Republican Revolution of 1911, most Chinese students, intellectuals, and political activists debated the "foreign" ideologies of Democracy and Communism (and later Fascism), not how to return to a Confucianist monarchy.[55] Though ideas and institutions are adapted for local conditions and cultural patterns, they are also shaped by external influences.

In Latin America, the 1990s witnessed Costa Rica, Venezuela, Belize, Colombia, French Guiana, and Mexico as enduring democracies with relatively pluralistic values by Third World standards. In a pattern beginning in the last two years of the Carter administration and continuing for more than a decade, Brazil, Peru, Bolivia, Ecuador, Chile, Uruguay, Panama, Guatemala, El Salvador, Honduras, Paraguay, and Argentina all showed signs of the growth of democratic values, though in varied and uneven forms.[56] Elsewhere, almost all of Eastern Europe, Pakistan, Turkey, Mongolia, Nepal, Burma, the Philippines, and South Korea moved toward democratic institutions in the late 1980s. This astounding spread of liberal democratic values hardly took place in philosophical isolation, and the movement borrowed much from Western political values and institutions.

Following World War II, Germany, Japan, and Italy were forced to base their societies on an ideology that had been largely discredited in those nations during the depression years. Though this ideology was imposed from without, all three nations have remained democratic for more than four decades. The United States does not have the power or authority to replicate this experience anywhere else, but it can indirectly foster democratic values in the world, and can do so directly in some clients.[57] Those values will take varying forms in other societies, but they are democratic nonetheless. In the spread of democracy, form is not as important as substance, though Americans usually overemphasize the former. The argument that non-Western nations will not—

or cannot—establish a political culture that values liberal democratic principles and institutions can certainly be questioned within the context of recent developments in the Second and Third Worlds. Whether they are lasting changes remains to be seen, but the very fact that they occurred seriously challenges the cultural relativism argument.

The Concept of Realistic Appraisal

Samuel Huntington and Joan Nelson, in their work on political partic- ipation in the Third World, have raised the question of cultural relativ- ism in a more practical, less philosophical, sense: does the United States have sufficient knowledge of client societies to intervene for particular political solutions? They state that Americans must realize that the lack of political reforms in client nations is often based on a "realistic ap- praisal" by the client government of its own political position.[58] Other critics, on both the left and right, use the lack of comprehensive knowl- edge of other cultures as a reason for avoiding action altogether.

These critics raise valid points and take aim at the heart of the reformist-bolstering debate. There is a question, however, whether they offer useful advice to decision-makers acting under the internal and external pressures of the real world. Knowledge of other societies is always ultimately superficial. Cultural-relativist critics of American pol- icies, especially academic analysts in regional or area studies, develop a priori standards for levels of knowledge necessary before policy can be made that are often highly unrealistic and unhelpful. This leads to a "paralysis of analysis," as they carefully explicate reasons not to take various actions. As Albert Hirschman has noted, even successful policy choices would often be eschewed if the decision-maker were fully aware of the potential obstacles at the beginning.[59] Yet policy must be made, even if it is based on imperfect information. Therefore, while this criticism is partly correct, some qualifications must be applied to it. It may, in fact, have severely negative consequences if followed faithfully as a prescription.

The first objection to a realistic appraisal argument is that it is often based on opposing perceptions of political position by the patron and the client. When faced with intense political instability, the client gov- ernment is forced to view its position in the short term. The U.S. interest, which has been more involved in the perpetuation of a pro- Western orientation than the existence of a particular government, looks to the long-term political position of the client society. The primary paradox is between the respective views of interests: the client govern- ment sees its political position drawn between short-term power and no power; the United States sees its interest drawn between short-term and long-term power interests of moderate groups of all stripes.[60]

This is the imperative of reform: to protect the long-term power position of the government through the mobilization of mass support. If the situation reaches this point, there are extremely difficult choices to be made by both sides. Although it is impossible to argue absolutely that reform would have "saved" Chiang Kai-shek and Ngo Dinh Diem, it can be argued that a lack of reform was the major cause of their respective downfalls. Unfortunately, the necessity for reforms often can best be analyzed after their absence has caused the government's support to disintegrate. In all three case studies analyzed in this book, the need for reforms was ascertained by the Americans and promoted as a policy choice. This is not to say that Americans have all the answers, but—more often than is recognized—they have some of them.

A second objection to the realistic appraisal argument is that it assumes the client government can make such an appraisal. Dictatorships suffer from what could be called the sycophant syndrome, that is, the tendency to reward loyal underlings who give only good news. As the anthropologist Robbins Burling puts it: "The more centralized the political system, the greater is the danger that the leader will be trapped into a dangerous ignorance by those around him."[61]

Examples of this phenomenon are easy to find. Chiang Kai-shek's generals repeatedly told him that their defeats in Manchuria occurred because of Soviet troops fighting there and reported major battles when there were only minor skirmishes with the Communists in which Kuomintang troops turned and ran. One of Marshall's most laborious chores was attempting to give Chiang a clear representation of the seriousness of the internal situation of the Kuomintang.[62] Speaking about Chiang's most influential advisers, Marshall felt that in terms of "the march of events in the world in relation to people, changes in government, and things of that sort" emerging from World War II, they were "not aware of that, and they are not aware that they are unaware. That is really the serious part of it."[63] One of these men, Chen Li-fu, once told a foreign service officer in early 1947 that he was promoting a moral revival in China because "then it would be easier not to feed the people. And he said it as though he were talking of so many rows of potatoes, even gaily."[64]

Presidents Quirino of the Philippines and Diem of Vietnam also often had no clear idea of the performance of their respective governments.[65] The greater the opposition to their policies, and the longer they stayed in power, the more isolated they became from reality. Centralization of power may be based on a realistic appraisal of the client government's political position, but decentralization may be also.

Third, as has been shown, the effects of centralization are felt throughout the government and seriously affect its relationship with society. Lower officials, because they are dependent only on those above them for their positions, can ignore the welfare of those they ostensibly serve, the public. This exacerbates the problem of relations between rulers and ruled. Officials often tend to form cliques or factions for self-protection, and any change in the status quo is seen by the factions as a threat to their own power positions.[66] Lloyd Eastman describes this process in the Kuomintang:

> The source of the problem was largely structural. Because there existed no effective, institutionalized means to make members of the regime accountable in their conduct of office to political constituencies or forces outside the government, most officials readily lost sight of the larger purposes of government. The attainment of power for its own sake, as well as for the prestige and wealth that accompanied it, became their preoccupation. To reach their goals, they participated in factions, which were the primary vehicles of political activity within the Nationalist regime.
>
> Not policy, therefore, but power and position were the objects of political contention.[67]

These internal struggles rendered the Kuomintang incapable of defeating the highly organized and motivated Chinese Communist forces. It was these factional loyalties that were the basis of the right wing of the Kuomintang's opposition to elite reforms.

Though the United States continuously pointed out this problem to Kuomintang leaders, the advice was ignored. A cultural relativist might argue that this was typical American ethnocentrism and that the Chinese comprehended the situation quite differently. In a Kuomintang postmortem on the fall of the regime, however, the lack of support from outside the government was listed as a major reason. In 1950, the Political Bureau of the Ministry of National Defense declared in a top-secret report: "Frankly speaking, it is impossible to crush the Communist bandits by relying only on the government and the army, without the help of the [common people]. The reason we were defeated on the mainland was precisely because we did not intimately join hands with the [common people]."[68] Unfortunately, this realistic appraisal, despite repeated and resented American advice, was not made until it was too late.

In all three case studies discussed in this book, I will argue that American personnel had a firm grasp of the interrelationship of the problems facing the client. This was so primarily for two reasons: the United States often possesses superior technical expertise, and it often has an intimate contact with the opposition and hears its complaints and concerns. In regard to the latter, all decision-making groups need negative feedback to illuminate potential areas of contention and conflict in their policies.[69] In a closed society, where the government is extremely suspicious of any opposition and is suffering the effects of the sycophant syndrome, negative feedback is absent, or simply viewed as treason.

Fearing the perils of open declarations of opposition, which can include the loss of life, intra- and extra-governmental dissidents see the United States as a conduit for opposing governmental policies. The United States then has the unenviable task of evaluating this information and passing it on to the client government. This development often gives American policymakers a prescience which the client government is structurally, though not intellectually, incapable of attaining.

The Paradoxes of Power: Commitments in Patron-Client Relations

In this section I will examine the paradoxical effects of commitment on patron-client relations. Commitment forms the basis of the diplomacies of bolstering and reformist intervention: the former grants a relatively unrestricted commitment; the latter attempts to reserve commitment as a lever for a quid pro quo. A further examination of the concept is necessary to understand more fully how commitments are utilized by decision-makers.

What Is Commitment?

A commitment is an action or series of actions, including declarations, taken by a state that heighten the predictability of future actions, that is, they are actions and promises that reflect upon the reputation of the initiator.[70] A commitment has four elementary properties: (1) it tries to account for consistent lines of activity; (2) it persists over a relatively lengthy period of time; (3) it consists of activities in pursuit of a chosen goal; and (4) it is extremely difficult to break because it is "morally wrong or practically inexpedient, or both" to do so.[71]

Commitments have both behavioral and psychological properties.[72] *Behavioral* commitments include written treaties, security agreements, declaratory policies, stationing of troops, and/or foreign aid.[73] When added to the psychological consequences of such actions, they lead to "sequences of action with penalties and costs so arranged as to guarantee their selection."[74] In most cases the initiator is making a psychological investment in a future policy, though it may only recognize this over time. Thus, *psychological* commitments deal with promises, intentions, and expectations of behavior.[75]

The patron that makes a commitment is investing in the future existence of the client. The paradox of commitment comes from the differing ways it is used with allies and adversaries. To deter an adversary, and demonstrate resolve that will presumably have consequences in commitments to others, the initiator wants to make an unambiguous commitment to a future line of action (for example, the Truman Doctrine or "drawing the line" in El Salvador or Vietnam). To influence a client, it is better to make an ambiguous commitment so that the patron can threaten to withdraw if certain policies are not pursued.[76] The paradox of power relations occurs because the exigencies of the former largely obviate the possibility of the latter. I will call this situation the "Commitment Trap," using examples from the experience of the United States, though other powers have similar problems in attempting to influence clients.[77]

A commitment from a patron to a client distorts the power relationship and markedly increases the bargaining strength of the latter. The greater the commitment, the greater is the distortion. As Samuel Huntington has noted, "[United States] leverage varies inversely with our commitments."[78] It has often been observed that this is the case.[79]

Nor is this simply a post facto comprehension of the power relationship. General Marshall tried desperately to alter the Chinese view of U.S. commitments. Dean Rusk was aware of the dilemma upon taking office in the Kennedy years: "When I first became Secretary of State, I asked the policy planning staff to give me a memorandum on how a great power avoids becoming a satellite of a small country that is completely dependent on you. They didn't come up with a very good answer."[80]

Though the dilemma became acute in Vietnam, Secretary Rusk was never able to solve the problem. In August 1963, he told Ambassador Lodge that any action taken to convince Diem that the American commitment to him was limited needed "real sanction" or "it is unlikely that it would be taken completely seriously by a man who may feel we are inescapably committed to an anti-Communist Viet-Nam."[81] Yet in 1965, as the crucial decisions for military escalation were being implemented, Rusk would argue at a National Security Council meeting: "We should have probably committed ourselves heavier in 1961."[82]

Why does the United States make such commitments? American policymakers are not stupid or reckless, yet they have seemingly made the same mistake over and over again. The effects of commitment on the patron-client relationship will be examined in more detail in a later section. In order to understand how the United States has found itself in this dilemma so often, however, it is first necessary to explain why the commitments are made.

The Multiple Purposes of Commitment: Signals and Audiences

The theoretical literature on international relations explains that commitments are signals that serve a variety of interests and are aimed at a variety of audiences.[83] There is evidence that decision-makers also view them in this way. Averell Harriman, for example, explained that American policy in Vietnam had to be formed within the context of "conflicting publicity pressures" that had to be balanced: the reactions of the Communist bloc, international opinion, U.S. public opinion, and South Vietnamese opinion.[84] A further analysis of signals and multiple audiences is necessary to understand the Commitment Trap more fully.

The first audience is the systemic and local adversaries. When commitments are made that are meant to deter, they must be made in a manner that leaves no question about the resolve to honor them. This is not an idle or foolhardy concern. According to Milovan Djilas, Stalin told the Yugoslavs to cease aiding the Greek Communists in the Greek Civil War because the United States and Great Britain were committed to preventing a Communist takeover in that nation.[85] Stalin was thus apparently deterred by the Truman Doctrine and other declarations of resolve from further aiding the Greek insurgency.

On the other hand, a lack of clear commitments can embolden adversaries. The Vietnamese Communists incorrectly used the example of America's non-intervention in the Chinese Civil War as an argument that the Yankees would not intervene with troops in Vietnam.[86] Similarly, the Communist insurgents in the Philippines escalated the insurgency and declared a "revolutionary situation" in 1950 largely on the basis of the belief that the United States was unwilling and unable to aid the Quirino government.[87] Thus, the deterrence of systemic and local adversaries may well require a public, unambiguous demonstration of resolve through the use of commitments.

The second audience is made up of allies that may be worried about the political will of the United States to stand up to aggressive expansion. Truman's commitment of troops to Korea in 1950, for example, was partly based on the psychological effects of that action on morale in Europe, as was U.S. policy in other nations in Asia.[88] Even those critical of a universal application of containment recognized the role that commitments play in reassuring other allies. When the State Department's John Carter Vincent warned against a hard-line policy toward Asia in the late 1940s, George F. Kennan, the originator of the containment theory but also a critic of its universal applicability, told him: "John

Carter, your views on Asian policy are quite sound . . . but the immediate problem is to maintain the morale of Europe and its will to resist the Communist challenge."[89] Although the allied desire for American leadership was especially strong during the early years of the Cold War, it remains in the post–Cold War era, as international support for the American response to the Iraqi invasion of Kuwait in 1990 suggests.

The third audience is made up of other clients who will look to actions in one country, or a particular region, in order to determine the intentions of the United States toward them. That American statesmen view it this way is a commonplace insight. Secretary of Defense Robert McNamara stated in an April 1961 meeting on the crisis in Southeast Asia, for example, that he "would not give a cent for what the Persians would think of us if we did not defend Laos."[90] (The United States, of course, did not choose to defend Laos in 1961. As will be shown in that case study, this practically ensured that the commitment to Vietnam would be made. In retrospect, it is apparent that the Communist takeover of Laos rendered South Vietnam indefensible.)

What is sometimes overlooked, however, is that client governments really do view the world in this way. In Asia, for example, it is no coincidence that governments in Singapore, Malaysia, Thailand, the Republic of Korea, the Republic of China, and the Republic of the Philippines were among the strongest supporters of American policy in Vietnam: it demonstrated a continuing commitment to anti-Communism in the region. Moreover, even governments critical of American policy, such as those in India, Japan, and Indonesia, wanted the United States to "do something" to prevent the fall of South Vietnam to the Communists.

The fourth audience is the domestic one. It has long been recognized that in democracies in general, and the United States in particular, there is a perceived need to oversell a problem and its proposed solution in order to garner the support and material means to carry out a policy.[91] In many cases, this need for public support becomes more complicated. In the Cold War period, public opinion often presented decision-makers with two contradictory imperatives that constrained policy: don't "lose" a country, yet don't become too involved. The ambivalence created by these contradictory constraints has been reflected in a confusion and oscillation in policies, or sometimes in a middle-of-the-road policy that is acceptable politically at home, but wholly inadequate to meet the particular challenge abroad.

The combined pressures to satisfy multiple audiences make commitments interdependent, that is, if they are not carried out in one area they will be questioned in other areas.[92] This leads to a strong compulsion among both bolsterers and reformers to make clear, public commitments to particular clients and to attempt to honor them even if the costs of the policies seem prohibitive or irrational.

Commitments are also made to boost morale in the fifth audience, the client. This usually works, however, only in the short term. If dramatic improvements are not made to match the heightened expectations caused by the increase in commitment, this often leads to a pattern in which the morale of the client becomes dependent on still greater commitment and a "let the Americans do it" mentality.[93]

This need to boost morale is further complicated because the signals are being sent not only to the client government, but to the entire client society. In this regard, good-faith attempts to help can actually hurt the client government. In Iran during the Carter administration, for example, the United States tried to demonstrate commitment to the Shah in order to convince the opposition that he retained American backing. This approach backfired, however, as the opposition became convinced that if the United States *really* wanted to back the Shah it would have done even more to support him.[94] Wishful thinking on the part of some opposition audiences in the client society and elswhere creates strong pressures that can lead decision-makers to believe that conspicuous demonstrations of commitments are necessary for effective signaling.

Fate Control versus Behavior Control

How does this process of signaling to multiple audiences distort the power relationship between the patron and the client? Social psychologists offer an interesting analytical distinction through the concepts of *fate control* and *behavior control*.[95] The United States exercises fate control over client governments in the sense that the latter would be compelled to face drastic, painful, and potentially self-destructive developments if the former were to cut off its aid. The United States is usually the "only game in town" for faltering client regimes. As will be demonstrated in the case studies, attempts by client regimes in China and Vietnam to gain leverage with the patron through threats to realign or sign a separate peace failed miserably.

Intuitively, fate control should lead to behavior control: the United States should be able to demand certain behavior from the client. In game theory, for example, the "Protector Game" shows that logically the patron should be able to place demands on the client that the latter can ill afford to ignore.[96] The problem arises when it becomes obvious to the client, and many others, that the patron is so committed to it that it cannot withdraw, that is, the commitment is so unambiguous, or the client perceives it to be, that the patron loses much of its bargaining leverage.

This can be seen in the China and Vietnam cases. President Franklin Roosevelt, in order to compensate for the lack of material commitments to China resulting from his Europe-first strategy in World War II, made excessive verbal commitments to Chiang Kai-shek. He insisted on treating China as an equal power, over British and Soviet objections, when it was obvious it was not, nor would be any time soon.[97] This led to psychological commitments that made Chiang weaker, not stronger: an exaggerated sense of the importance of China; an unrealistic view of what the United States would do to save his government; one more reason to ignore the need for internal reforms; and a dependence on American aid that exacerbated the other problems. It also led to a supercilious attitude on the part of the Chinese concerning American responsibilities toward them. Chiang told Lord Mountbatten at the Cairo Conference, for example: "The President will refuse me nothing . . . Anything I ask, he will do."[98] In the postwar era his brother-in-law, Finance Minister T. V. Soong, openly referred to the Americans as "boobs" and promised Chiang he would secure ever-larger amounts of aid.[99] This attitude toward commitments continued despite countless protestations to the contrary by General Marshall and other officials. When he was in China, the most reactionary elements in the Kuomintang repeatedly told Marshall that the United States would *have* to come to their aid because of the Communist threat.[100] They used this as another excuse to avoid reform and pursue military objectives that were impossible to attain, convinced the United States would have to accept responsibility for the fate of the regime if it collapsed. It did; the United States did not. Even as late as the fall of Peking in early 1949, Chinese officials insisted that the United States would have to send troops to prevent a Communist takeover of China.[101]

Thus, in the case of China, earlier commitments raised excessive expectations in the client about the future intentions of the United States. No amount of denial by Marshall while in China could convince Chiang that American commitments were limited. Schelling recognizes this problem when he observes: "Some of our strongest commitments may be quite implicit . . . Commitments can even exist when we deny them."[102]

A similar situation developed in Vietnam. As early as 1955, Diem was convinced that the United States was so committed to his survival that he could ignore the later entreaties of the Eisenhower and Kennedy administrations for political, economic, and military reforms.[103] In September 1963, in the midst of the bargaining between the Americans and the Diem regime over the Buddhist crisis, the president's brother, Ngo Dinh Nhu, told leaders of the Vietnamese army that the United States was "committed so deeply in Vietnam it cannot stop [its] aid."[104]

This problem increased with escalation. A Vietnamese government official told an American journalist in 1964: "Our big advantage over the Americans is that they want to win the war more than we do."[105] If a psychological commitment reaches this point, the concept of behavior control becomes meaningless. It was only when the United States made known its decision to decrease its excessive commitment in Vietnam after 1968, for example, that leverage increased and real progress was made on land reform.[106] Unfortunately, it appears to have been a case of too little, too late.

The relationships with China and Vietnam are not the only examples of the detrimental effects of excessive commitment to a client government. Nor is the reaction of the Chinese and Vietnamese exceptional, though the degree of perceived commitment was unusual. In Israel, for example, some members of the government have also taken American commitments for granted and as unrelated to U.S. behavior. Golda Meir makes clear in her memoirs that Menachem Begin, when he was a minority member of the Knesset, viewed the United States in this manner. When Meir warned Begin that Israel must coordinate policy with American peace initiatives in 1969–1970 or face a reduction of its commitment to Israel, Begin responded, "What do you mean, we won't get arms? We'll *demand* them from the Americans."[107]

The Bush administration ran into similar problems with the Israelis in the aftermath of the war against Iraq in 1991. When the United States attempted to restrict Israeli settlement policies through vague, implicit threats to aid programs, Prime Minister Yitzhak Shamir remained confident of a continued commitment: "Settlement in every part of the country continues and will continue. [The Americans] try to link the two things, but no one said aid will end. I don't think it will happen." He added later in the interview, "It is inconceivable that our great friend the United States will change its ways."[108]

Similarly, when the United States committed itself to the fate of the Gemayel government in Lebanon in the early 1980s, that government lost perspective in dealing with its adversaries. The Lebanese also displayed a similar degree of superciliousness. One Lebanese official told the Syrians, "I have the United States in my pocket."[109] Though this remark was undoubtedly meant to impress the Syrians, the Lebanese apparently acted as if they believed it. A member of the Gemayel cabinet later observed: "We looked out at all those American ships off our coast and said to ourselves, 'Surely they can't be here for nothing.' In retrospect, I think we as a small power read far too much into the general assurances of a great power."[110] This commitment made Gemayel less willing to deal with the political opposition when there was a chance to do so. European officials later regretted their commitments to the Lebanese government, "which never let us forget them,"[111] strongly suggesting that this phenomenon is not limited to the superpowers in a stark bipolar world. The most detrimental effect of a commitment is that it allows the client to ignore political realities and to pass the responsibility for its fate to the patron.[112]

There is no easy way out of the Commitment Trap. American commitments are often interdependent, and become even more so if the United States declares them to be. As will be shown in the Philippines case study, however, it is not impossible to maintain leverage in a reformist intervention if commitments are kept specific, on a strictly quid pro quo basis, and if their utility in the bargaining process is properly understood by the patron. I shall now turn to the case studies to examine why this has or has not happened in the past, and how it might be accomplished in the future.

CHINA
1946–1948

II

The Marshall Mission, 1946

4

The early postwar policy of the United States in China was based on an attempt to create a viable Chinese government in order to prevent regional instability that might lead to Soviet, or a resurgent Japanese, expansionism. Like much of early post–World War II policy, it aimed at avoiding the mistakes of the 1930s. It had been, in the eyes of many Americans, a weak, disunited China that had "invited" Japanese aggression and eventually precipitated American entry into the war. With Japan defeated and under occupation, the primary concern became the potential for the expansion of Soviet influence. The presence of an armed and politically dynamic indigenous Communist movement in China only increased that concern and gradually transformed it into alarm. Yet the United States did not want China to serve as a source of active contention with the U.S.S.R. The lesson of history most often applied to the Chinese situation was not Munich, but the Spanish Civil War.[1]

The Truman administration desired a non-Communist China but could not fight a proxy war without making a huge economic and military commitment to a corrupt and inept client government. As William Stueck deftly put it, the choice was between the containment of Communism and the containment of a commitment.[2] The United States chose the latter policy; as Secretary of State Marshall later testified: "The real issue was how you would meet this situation without a tremendous commitment of this government on the land area in Asia."[3] Because of the shrinking governmental resource base available for Asia, the only viable option, as perceived by key American decision-makers, was to get the Chinese Nationalist Party, the Kuomintang, to legitimize its rule through reforms. The paradoxical role of commitment in bargaining with the client, the Commitment Trap, was not yet clear. It was only during the latter stages of the reformist intervention, and especially after the fall of the Kuomintang government, that many of these lessons would become apparent and would be applied to the Philippines.[4]

American interest in a reformist intervention in China began during World War II. Chiang Kai-shek's rule was based on balancing a variety of antagonistic coalitions in his party and among his generals. The majority of his forces consisted of relatively autonomous provincial armies, some led by potential rivals of Chiang, that had only a loose allegiance to him. He attempted to control these forces by manipulating supplies from the capital to the provinces, but this was never sufficient to gain their loyalty. As World War II dragged on, he withheld resources from the provincial armies and tried to get them to do the bulk of the fighting, saving his loyal troops to protect his political dominance.

This situation led to a military performance by the Kuomintang that was characterized by lack of cooperation, cohesion, and unity of command. Indeed, much of Chiang's time during the war was spent trying to get his generals to obey his orders. In addition, the conditions for the enlisted men, primarily impressed from the peasantry, were so appalling that desertion rates have been estimated at approximately fifty percent. Given his military weakness, Chiang avoided sustained offensives after the Japanese attack on Pearl Harbor, assured of Japan's eventual defeat with American entry into the war; instead he husbanded his forces to protect his postwar political position. The provincial armies also wanted to protect their postwar position and showed an extreme reluctance to fight for the regime. In view of this lack of military cohesiveness during the war, the "inexplicable surrenders" of the Kuomintang armies during the Civil War that French General Lionel Chassin noted are not that difficult to explain. To treat the armies the Chinese Nationalists had on paper as effective military forces was to treat euphemism as fact. In contrast, the armies of the Chinese Communist Party (CCP), though poorly armed and supplied, grew in strength and expertise during the war.[5]

In the economic sphere, the Kuomintang resorted to deficit spending and high-interest, short-term loans to finance the war. This exacerbated inflationary pressures that were to reach startling proportions in the postwar period, leading to endemic corruption at all levels of society. Food, medicine, and other materials meant for the troops were stolen and sold by corrupt officials; bribes became necessary for even the most fundamental activities of government; the moral fiber of Chinese society was ripped apart. Though the Kuomintang attempted to bring this corruption under control, it invariably failed. An effective crackdown on corrupt officials would have undermined the narrow base of support

of the regime, threatening Chiang's domestic power position. He therefore increasingly looked to increases in American aid as a way out of
his dilemma.[6]

In the summer of 1944, in the face of a possible Kuomintang collapse
due to the successful Ichigo ("At Once") offensive by Japan, President
Roosevelt sent Vice-President Henry Wallace to promote internal reform and unification with the CCP.[7] He followed this failed attempt
with the Hurley Mission, sending General Patrick Hurley to negotiate
unification, and backed Hurley's, and Chiang's, subsequent recommendation to remove General Joseph Stilwell and Ambassador Clarence
Gauss, two men who had lost faith in Chiang's ability to provide leadership.

Hurley replaced Gauss as ambassador, and General Albert Wedemeyer replaced Stilwell, in an attempt at a more persuasive approach
toward the Kuomintang. They were to discover, however, that the more
they backed Chiang, the less they could get him to do. Though personal
relations "improved" with the Kuomintang, no fundamental changes
were brought about.[8] It should be noted that almost everyone, including
such later critics as Hurley, Wedemeyer, and General Claire Chennault,
believed that the only possible options at that point were some sort of
accommodation with the CCP and internal reforms by the Kuomintang
to save Chiang's increasingly precarious hold on power.[9] Negotiations
over unification were still being carried out as the war came to a close.

When the war ended in August 1945, the United States continued its
efforts to effect a coalition government through elite reform, that is,
the inclusion of minority parties into the government. Yet at the same
time, it attempted to bolster the Kuomintang by ordering the Japanese
to surrender only to the government and transporting Kuomintang
troops to north China. It was soon to send U.S. troops to aid in these
tasks.[10] This continued a policy with highly contradictory ends: (1)
bolstering the Kuomintang as the only government in China, which
made it much less likely to accept reforms, and (2) reaching an accommodation with the minority parties and achieving redistributive reforms.
Thus, the commitments of the former aim, and their psychological
impact on the Kuomintang, greatly lessened the leverage for achieving
the latter. The gradual onset of the Cold War during the 1945–1948
period made the control of commitments even more difficult. The worse
the Cold War became, the more Chiang was convinced the United States
would have to give him what he wanted.[11]

While the superpowers claimed to be "staying out of" the internal
affairs of China, each was acting to make sure its favored side would
survive in the fall of 1945. The actions of each alarmed the other,

leading to growing suspicion and eventual political contention in Asia. Within this context, and the resignation of Ambassador Hurley amid his charges that "Communist-influenced" State Department personnel were undermining his efforts, General George C. Marshall was sent to China to effect elite reforms in order to avoid civil war and possible Soviet penetration of China.

In view of the growing hostilities between the Nationalists and the Communists, it was decided to promote the fortunes of the relatively liberal minority parties in China, the so-called "third force." State Department personnel were instructed on November 14, 1945, to "indicate American interest in the increasing activity and sense of responsibility of Chinese minority parties."[12] This policy backfired, as it would throughout the Marshall Mission. Within weeks, the right wing of the Kuomintang physically attacked these elements, further discrediting the Kuomintang with liberals, students, and intellectuals all over China.[13]

Thus, in terms of the three-option diplomatic dilemma, over the following year American policy decisions aimed at avoiding withdrawal because of the growing rivalry with the U.S.S.R. and fear of regional instability if China should again sink into chaos. Yet decision-makers wanted to avoid bolstering commitments that might lead to greater intervention in the future and war with the Chinese and Soviet Communists. They therefore gradually turned toward reformist intervention as a last slim hope. This was not so much a hubristic, naive American attempt at social engineering as it was a choice of reform as the least odious of several dreadful alternatives.

General George C. Marshall arrived in China on December 22, 1945. Like all of the wartime military leaders, he was a man of giant reputation, the man Winston Churchill called the "Organizer of Victory." In contrast to many other men of accomplishment, however, there was not a hint of bombast in his personality. Virtually everyone who met the General was impressed with his integrity and intelligence. He accepted his mission not with enthusiasm and optimism, but as a duty thrust upon him by his nation.

In preparation for his trip, he requested and received almost total control over negotiations with the Chinese government, with a special reporting apparatus in Washington to give him direct access to the President. Truman had an extremely high regard for the General. In a unique way, Marshall's credibility with the President, within the government, internationally, and with the public gave him extraordinary powers in this particular diplomatic instance. For the next year, China policy was to be Marshall's policy. Thus, in contrast to American policy after 1946, domestic politics played only a minor role in decision-making during his mission.

Decision-making: Marshall's Initial Estimation
of the Situation

Upon his arrival in China, Marshall met with American personnel to gather the latest information on the situation. He was not totally unfamiliar with the country, having served there in the 1920s, but he had no recent experience except for his role in the Stilwell affair, in which he had backed the reformist American general against Chiang's objections. He spent his first two weeks in the country hearing testimony from Americans and Chinese of all stripes; this included numerous meetings with Chiang Kai-shek and the CCP representative in the wartime capital of Chungking, Chou En-lai.

Marshall also met with a number of non-governmental Chinese, many of whom asked to see him secretly, which affected his view of the extra-governmental opposition to the Kuomintang. The majority of them were "bitterly hostile" to the government, he later recalled, "though not necessarily friendly to the Communist Party."[14] The extra-governmental opposition elements in China, and their hostility to the Kuomintang, were important factors in shaping Marshall's views.

Marshall decided that bolstering and withdrawal were not viable options. He based this on four major conclusions he had reached early in his stay: (1) neither the Nationalists nor the Communists could win militarily; (2) both were willing to negotiate if they thought they could "win their own objectives" by political means, but the hatred and suspicion existing between the two meant that they could not negotiate a peaceful solution if left to themselves; (3) Truman's December 15, 1945, statement on China announcing the Marshall Mission had an "extremely healthy effect throughout China" and opened the way for an American role; and (4) the relationship between the U.S.S.R. and the CCP was "extremely obscure," which made it imperative to reach an agreement before the Soviets started aiding the Chinese Communists in a major way. These views led to the more general conclusion that the Kuomintang was vulnerable to CCP and Soviet collusion and could not overcome this threat "without full-scale American intervention both in the movement of Chinese forces with American equipment and the use of American personnel, possibly even combat troops." Since this was "utterly out of the question," the only hope seemed to be a united China that would make any Soviet attempts to set up a puppet government in China appear as "overt aggression" by using the force of world opinion to condemn the actions. Marshall therefore told the President that he would aim for a cease-fire, a coalition government, and integration of the Nationalist and Communist armies as preconditions to further American aid.[15]

Bargaining Behavior: Leverage and the
January 10 Agreement

The high hopes raised among many in China by Marshall's appointment seemed to be justified by the military and political agreements reached in mid-January 1946. They were negotiated under extreme diplomatic pressure on the Kuomintang through a quid pro quo bargaining strategy by the United States. Marshall told Chiang the United States could not aid his government unless he made elite reforms and included the CCP and other minority parties in his government. It was this threat of no aid, according to Marshall, that convinced Chiang he had to go along with the agreement on January 10, 1946.[16] The end of the war, the Soviet presence in Manchuria, the dramatic resignation of Ambassador Hurley, and the uncertainty concerning the new administration's views on China apparently signaled ambiguities in the American commitment. If it was not the perceived need to pacify the United States that largely determined Chiang's response to Marshall's plans, it is difficult to imagine why he agreed to share power with a group he had been fighting for twenty years.[17]

Thus, at this point Chiang apparently recognized a dependence on the United States. This provided leverage in gaining his agreement in forming a coalition government. This perception was not to last long, but Marshall was successful in his initial bargaining because both sides needed the United States: the CCP was vulnerable and looked to the Americans to protect it; Chiang was in need of U.S. support.[18]

Decision-making: Marshall and the Political Opposition

Though both sides violated the negotiated cease-fire, and it is impossible, then or now, to identify the side that was most to blame,[19] two points should be made. First, many on the American side, including Marshall, believed that the Kuomintang was more to blame for violations in January and February.[20] This sharply altered their view of the Kuomintang and the entire situation. Second, though the fighting never completely stopped, the cease-fire was not a complete failure. Clashes between the Nationalists and Communists "decreased markedly" after January 20, and "practically ceased" after January 25.[21] Therefore, United States leverage was partially successful in attaining its policy goals.

The Chinese political opposition remained a key determinant in Marshall's view of the situation. He found that he had to deal not only with the three major political groupings, the Kuomintang, the CCP, and the

Third Party Group, but with factions within some of those groups. This necessitated a diplomacy of unusual complexity, as Marshall attempted to manipulate Chinese political forces. Like all reformers, he discovered he had to become involved in internal politics; state-to-state relations would not suffice in achieving the desired policy goals. It was in this area that elite reforms were increasingly seen as a necessary precedent to the broader redistributive reforms planned for the future.

The Kuomintang was split into left-wing and right-wing factions, with the latter being by far the more dominant in numbers and influence. The right wing included the "CC Clique," a group centered around the leadership of the Chen brothers, Chiang Kai-shek's adopted nephews, and the Whampoa Clique, those military leaders trained at the Whampoa Military Academy with a long association with Chiang. The left-wing faction included the followers of Sun Fo, the son of Sun Yat-sen, and small groups such as the Political Study Clique. In general, the right wing was against any and all elite or redistributive reforms; the left wing was in favor of moderate redistributive reforms and more amenable to elite reforms. Marshall attempted to promote the fortunes of the left wing of the party in order to form a centrist political coalition, but he could never accomplish this goal.

The Communists represented the radical left of the Chinese political spectrum. They called for widespread redistributive reform, especially in the rural areas, and were amenable to elite reforms as long as they believed they could not win decisively on the battlefield. Though Marshall wanted to prevent the Communists from taking power, his initial and subsequent estimations of the situation led him to believe that they could not be defeated militarily. If the Communists were included in the government, Marshall believed that they could be isolated from the Soviets and that this would force the Kuomintang to attend to redistributive reform in peaceful political competition for the loyalty of the masses. Since it was generally believed among U.S. personnel in China that a major source of the CCP's appeal was its call for redistributive reform in the countryside, Marshall's policy also increasingly centered on pressuring the Kuomintang into effecting similar reforms to increase its popular support.

The Third Party Group was an amalgam of disparate opposition groups opposed to the Kuomintang and CCP, and included everything from feudal barons to social democrats. The majority of these groups called for political freedoms, and elite and redistributive reforms. Membership included many students, professors, and intellectuals. Their biggest problems were that they were articulate critics of the Nationalists (thereby inviting attacks), numerically small, concentrated in only a few provinces, greatly disorganized, and lacking an army. The more the

United States attempted to promote their fortunes, the more the right wing of the Kuomintang attacked them. When these attacks occurred, some of the most talented and articulate people in China went over to the Communists. Thus, right-wing attacks increasingly radicalized the relatively moderate elements, something Marshall sought desperately— and unsuccessfully—to prevent through elite reforms.[22]

Bargaining Behavior: Marshall Succeeds in Gaining Promises of Reform

Much of Marshall's effort in January centered on getting the Kuomintang to effect elite reforms by granting political concessions to the minority parties in order to offset the military concessions he was asking the CCP to make, and to guarantee the safety of the Third Party Group. He pressed for acceptance through a quid pro quo bargaining approach, refusing to discuss *specific* aid agreements until there was a political settlement. Immediately prior to the January agreement, Marshall requested that Chiang make a statement affirming the freedoms of assembly and press, the allowance of some local autonomy, and the release of most political prisoners. Chiang did this as part of the cease-fire agreement.

A week later, the Generalissimo and Marshall met again. Marshall presented him with a draft constitution he had created as a basis for a political settlement. Chiang studied it overnight, and, in a meeting on January 24, 1946, expressed his reservations over some areas which he believed would give an advantage to the CCP. Marshall did not haggle over what he saw as details (in retrospect perhaps a mistake, because in adversarial bargaining details become quite important), and was most encouraged by Chiang's renewal of the pledge for a bill of rights which would provide for the freedoms contained in his January 14 announcement. The American General felt this was an important point because it would ensure the political survival of the CCP and, especially, of the Third Party Group, and therefore would increase the chances for further elite reforms. He told Chiang it represented a "dose of American medicine" for the ills of China. The Generalissimo was amused.[23]

Since this represented something of a high water mark of Kuomintang acceptance of American recommendations, it is apparent that Chiang continued to believe in his dependence on the United States and perceived a need to pacify its representatives in order to gain commitments. Certainly Marshall stuck to the quid pro quo and continued to state forcefully that the United States could not aid the Kuomintang if there were a civil war.

The CCP reaction to the political agreements was positive, though there were things with which it disagreed.[24] Although this may have been posturing by CCP leaders, their actions for the next two weeks demonstrated a willingness to cooperate. Given their relative weakness politically and militarily, this was not surprising. In any event, Marshall and his staff still assumed that the CCP would align with the U.S.S.R., but were cautiously optimistic over the apparent progress made in the January 10 agreement, Chiang's January 14 statement, and subsequent negotiations.

Truman was pleased. On February 2, he wrote Marshall: "It looks as if the Chinese program is working out exactly as planned." Two days later, Marshall wrote the President that he was in the process of proceeding with arrangements for aid in exchange for the proposed elite reform of a unified government in China.[25]

Bargaining Behavior: Growing Right-Wing Opposition to Elite Reforms

Implementation of the proposed elite reforms ran into trouble from the start. The right wing of the Kuomintang was especially upset at what it viewed as excessive concessions to the CCP. This displeasure was based on their long-standing opposition to all extra-party politics, but particularly on the questions of demobilization, power-sharing, and local autonomy, all of which threatened the right wing's relative political position within the party. In late January and early February, it stepped up secret police attacks on opposition members and newspapers.

The first major break with the spirit of the negotiations, however, came on February 10 when several labor and Third Party Group organizations held a rally celebrating the agreements in the temporary capital of Chungking. The chief Communist negotiator, Chou En-lai, was scheduled to speak at the assembly. An estimated 7,000 to 10,000 people had assembled for the gathering. The meeting was physically disrupted, however, by "organized hoodlums" that were widely believed to be associated with the right-wing CC Clique. Several prominent liberals and proposed speakers were severely beaten. Since this occurred with Chiang out of the capital, the CCP and Third Party Group at this point absolved him of personal blame.[26]

The Americans were dismayed at the attack on the extra-governmental opposition, but there were even greater problems to follow. On February 12, 1946, there was the first major refusal to go along with the cease-fire by a leading member of the Kuomintang military that could not be attributed to misunderstanding or lack of communication. General Chang Fa-kwei publicly claimed that "bandits," that is, a local group associated with the CCP, in Kwantung did not qualify for protection under the cease-fire. On February 13, Chiang ordered Chang to accept an Executive Headquarters truce team to settle the matter. Chang and General Ho Ying-chin, another leading Nationalist general, refused to accept the authority of the truce team.[27]

 With this refusal, a major weakness of the cease-fire agreements was manifested: the United States had powers of sanction over Chiang, but not over his subordinates. As previously noted, Chiang also had only limited control over much of his intra-governmental opposition. Yet, by most indications, he was at this point reluctantly in favor of the agreements in order to ensure continued aid to his government. The United States would not cut off aid to the Nationalists because of the actions of a few commanders. The sanctions had to come from Chiang, but his precarious power position within his party did not allow such an action. Thus, Marshall decided at this point not that Chiang *would* not reform, but that he *could* not. He therefore continued to promise aid to the Nationalists in the belief, mistaken in the event, that Chiang would eventually gain control over intractable elements. The quid pro quo was proving difficult to maintain because of the very weakness of the client government.

Decision-making: Communist Chinese Expansion and Possible Soviet Influence

On February 14, 1946, the CCP leadership in Yenan reacted to these developments by issuing a blistering attack on the Kuomintang and its unwillingness to cooperate within the agreements, especially in Manchuria. It also included a statement that astonished the United States and the Nationalists: the Communists now claimed to have a force of 300,000 troops in Manchuria. This projection, even if exaggerated, represented a phenomenal growth of Communist power in the region and strongly suggested that it had taken place in violation of existing agreements and in collusion with the U.S.S.R., which had been occupying Manchuria since its entry into the Pacific War in August 1945. The Kuomintang accused the Communists of breaking agreements; the CCP argued unconvincingly that the troops had been underground since late 1945. American diplomats, in retrospect, saw this statement as a major turning point in CCP policy, representing a closer coordination of policy with the U.S.S.R. The Soviets also complicated things by repeatedly making heavy-handed demands for economic concessions in Manchuria, as they did throughout early 1946.[28] During the month of February 1946, there was a rising tide of violence on both sides that threatened a political settlement and the reform program.

Bargaining Behavior: Chiang Reneges on His Promises for Elite Reforms

In early March, 1946, Marshall made preparations for a trip home to consult with President Truman. Deep cuts in the military budget had caused the Joint Chiefs to reconsider the plan to turn over surplus supplies in the Pacific to Asian allies such as China and the Philippines. In effect, Marshall had to return to negotiate with his own government for aid to stabilize the situation in China.

A central question to be asked at this point is whether Chiang Kai-shek was simply playing along with the Americans in order to sidestep the quid pro quo and get more aid. Though this may seem a natural conclusion to arrive at given his later behavior, there is good reason to question this interpretation. In fact, one of the leading Western experts on the Kuomintang argues that Chiang was "squarely behind" the agreements made under Marshall's auspices. Indeed, at least four times Chiang met with dissident party factions and urged them to go along.[29]

The Central Executive Committee of the Kuomintang met during March 1–17, 1946, to vote on the agreements. Though it publicly took the position that it accepted them, there was an immediate effort to alter the agreements to a more executive-oriented political system, which would maintain Chiang's (and the right wing's) power position, and a return to the draft constitution of May 5, 1936, that had been superseded by the January 10 agreement. Chiang pleaded with the dissident group, but eventually gave in to them. At a meeting with one group near the end of the session, he promised them, "as long as I am alive, the Communist party will never join the government."[30]

Following his failure in March to bring his own party around, Chiang ventured on a bargaining strategy with the United States that can only be called duplicitous. At the end of the conference he wrote Marshall, then in Washington negotiating within the United States government for the aid package, that he had the situation under control and that the agreements would be passed in toto.[31] He then began systematically breaking them.

Decision-making: The Outbreak of Civil War

The CCP, which had excellent penetration of the Nationalist Government with spies, was aware of the change in Kuomintang plans. Within a few days, it informed its commanders in the field that "peace was hopeless." It then canceled its scheduled March 31, 1946, meeting of the Central Committee that was also to vote on the agreements.[32]

Americans in China noticed a marked deterioration in the political situation after mid-March 1946. Chiang reneged on many basic points of the political agreements (for example, the agreed proportional representation); the CCP reneged on many of the military agreements (for example, the number of Communist armies allowed in Manchuria). Chou En-lai was recalled to Yenan on March 20 and heavily criticized by anti-negotiation factions, lessening his ability to negotiate in the future. With elite reforms no longer a policy of the Kuomintang, the right wing stepped up attacks on the CCP and the Third Party Group. Nationalist military commanders continued to refuse to cooperate with the truce teams. The "irreconcilables" on both sides were now dominant.[33]

A more flagrant violation of the agreements occurred in mid-April when the CCP attacked Changchun, a major transportation and commercial center in Manchuria. This action was initially successful, apparently emboldening the Communist generals; by early May, 1946, they were on the offensive throughout north and northeast China. The Kuomintang launched a counteroffensive which was also initially successful and recaptured Mukden in mid-May. Though Marshall returned to China from the United States and struggled to reach some sort of agreement on a cease-fire, he was unsuccessful. The Kuomintang occupied Changchun with relative ease on May 23, apparently convincing Chiang and his commanders that a quick military victory would be theirs.[34] In early June, 1946, brandishing his declining leverage, Marshall was again able to obtain a cease-fire.

Bargaining Behavior: The Americans Back Off from the Quid Pro Quo

While he was in the United States in March and early April, Marshall negotiated an agreement to transfer war surplus materials to China. He also negotiated a total of $500 million in prospective loans from the Export-Import Bank to be used in the economic reconstruction of a unified China. Though the surplus property agreement was eventually implemented with limitations, the Export-Import loans were "earmarked" but never put into effect because of the outbreak of civil war.

Thus, Marshall negotiated an aid program in Washington even while the January agreements were breaking down. Why did he abandon the quid pro quo approach? At this point, he wanted to use the aid for both reformist and bolstering purposes, goals which were not clearly understood by the Americans given their lack of understanding of the Commitment Trap, the complexity of the situation, and their lack of experience in this kind of diplomacy. The idea was to induce the CCP and the Third Party Group to join the government and to get the Kuomintang to accept a quid pro quo and elite reform; Marshall also wanted the aid, however, to bolster Chiang *within his own party* and to prevent the collapse of the Chinese government. He soon discovered a major paradox in his bargaining strategy: Chiang was politically weak and needed bolstering to gain control of his own party (centralization of power); the more Marshall bolstered Chiang, or the more the latter became convinced of growing American commitments, however, the less likely he was to share power outside the Kuomintang (decentralization of power).

As had been demonstrated in January and February, the more ambiguous the commitment and the more strictly the quid pro quo was adhered to, the more Chiang had to accommodate his behavior to entreaties for reforms; the more unambiguous the commitment, the less he believed he had to do so. Following the breakdown of the agreements in February-March, then, negotiations increasingly centered on the *perception* of the extent of American commitment. Even symbolic gestures took on an exaggerated importance as the Nationalists sought to increase that commitment and the United States sought to limit it.

After Marshall returned with his aid package, many in the Kuomintang argued to the Americans that the party already had a commitment. The right wing did so quite bluntly in private discussions with Marshall, though never in public. By this time, Chiang was telling the American General that it would be difficult to come to terms with the CCP. In March, T. V. Soong, Chiang's brother-in-law and the Minister of Finance, also openly told American officials that they would be forced to give the Kuomintang all the aid it needed to avoid a Communist victory.

Though the United States had declared its aid to be conditional, the promise in March 1946 of bilateral aid in significant amounts ($1.4 billion) undermined the quid pro quo that had been maintained during January-February. It also allowed the Kuomintang to ignore its own internal weaknesses and the politically painful necessity of reform. As one of Marshall's political advisers, Philip Sprouse, later put it, "Once you began to encourage [the Kuomintang] to lean on the external part of the picture [that is, aid commitments] the desirability of their own performance was lessened."[35]

Decision-making: The Cold War and the Loss of Leverage

The developments of the spring of 1946 must be seen within the context of deteriorating superpower relations in February-March, and the increasing bipolarity of the Cold War, a situation that generally enhances the bargaining position of weaker allies.[36] Growing tension between the superpowers convinced the Nationalists not that the United States *would* not withdraw its support, but that it *could* not. This greatly undermined whatever leverage the United States possessed for convincing the Kuomintang to implement elite or redistributive reforms.

In February 1946, as the agreements were breaking down, the U.S.S.R. precipitated the Iranian crisis by raising the specter of breaking off an important province and placing it under Soviet control. This was seen in Washington as a clear example of Soviet expansion and deserving of a strong response. On February 9, Stalin made an anti-Western speech attacking the Anglo-American powers and implied that there would be inevitable conflict between Communism and capitalism in the postwar world. On March 5, Winston Churchill responded, with Truman at his side, in his famous "Iron Curtain" speech at Fulton, Missouri.

These events were not lost on the Chinese, Communist or Nationalist. It was in mid-February that Americans in China noticed a much closer coordination of political positions between the Soviets and the CCP, suggesting that the Chinese Communists also saw the growing East-West hostility to their advantage, though there was scanty evidence of further direct military aid. On the Nationalist side, by late March Chiang was arguing that the United States had to take a harder line against the U.S.S.R. by aiding the Kuomintang; he drew a direct analogy between the strong stand taken by the West in Iran and the situation in Manchuria. The Soviets would back down in the face of a demonstration of American firmness in China, Chiang and his aides argued, as they had in the Middle East. Thus, growing tensions in the Cold War lent credence to the arguments of the "irreconcilables" in both the CCP and the Kuomintang.[37]

As Marshall concluded in his final report:

> In the background there was, of course, the international situation in connection with U.S.-Soviet relations, which was perhaps a major cause for the breakdown of the negotiations in March [1946]. It was a fact that the Kuomintang leaders feared a connection between the Chinese Communists and Soviet Russia and considered the former to be puppets of the Soviets. Accompanying this feeling was the idea that, in spite of the statement of American policy toward China announced by President Truman in December 1945 and in spite of the continued American mediation effort, the United States in the long run must support the National Government against the Chinese Communists.[38]

Thus, the growing perception within the Kuomintang of an implicit commitment due to the onset of the Cold War, despite repeated American denials, led that government to accept the path of least resistance, avoiding the politically difficult options of elite or redistributive reforms.

Several factors that were quite beyond Marshall's control greatly lessened his ability to exert pressure on the Kuomintang. This only became apparent over time, however, as the continued Kuomintang protestations of good faith, the American strategic concentration on Europe and Japan, and the pace of the swirl of events in the Cold War blinded the United States to the effects on its bargaining posture until the summer of 1946. The Americans did not yet realize it, but the Marshall Mission had failed.

Bargaining Behavior: Marshall Begins to Comprehend the Dilemma

By June 1946, Marshall believed that much of the Kuomintang viewed proposed American aid as a form of commitment to Chiang's leadership, which was leading the Chinese to conclude that the United States would come to its aid even without a peaceful settlement. This developed simultaneously with Marshall's view that direct Soviet intervention was less of a threat because of its withdrawal of troops from China in May 1946.[39]

Yet Chiang continued to pressure the Americans for a commitment by implying a possible role for the Soviets in the mediation effort in May 1946. Marshall, recognizing a bluff, told him to give it a try. In their discussions, Marshall complained to Chiang that his right wing would end "any idea of democratic procedures" and that he was following poor advice from his military leaders "as did Japan to her ruination." The Generalissimo responded by launching a successful military attack beyond Changchun which Chiang had promised Marshall would not be undertaken, and which Marshall had promised the CCP would not occur. Thus, the Kuomintang began acting directly contrary to American policy goals at the very time that further commitment was less likely because of a lessened Soviet threat. The lack of sanction likely further convinced Chiang that the United States was not serious in its threat not to back him in a Civil War.[40]

What continued to irritate and confound Marshall the most, and convinced him that the United States had to redefine its policy, was the persistent claim of the right wing of the Kuomintang, especially CC Clique leader Chen Li-fu, that the United States would *have* to come to their aid to prevent Soviet penetration of China. As Marshall stated in later testimony before Congress: "All the time I was out there, I was confronted with the very frank statement, particularly of the Chen Li-fu group, that we would have to [accept responsibility for the civil war and the economy], and that there would probably be a war between the

United States and Russia and we would have to do these various things".[41] Since elite and redistributive reforms were becoming more unlikely, and the drift toward civil war seemingly inexorable, why did Marshall not bolster the Nationalists?

Decision-making: Marshall's Objections to Bolstering

With direct Soviet intervention in China much less likely, the problem facing the Nationalists, as perceived by the Americans, was one of restoring internal stability. Marshall was against the right wing's desire for a purely military solution for military, economic, and political reasons.

In the military sphere, Marshall believed that the Kuomintang's prediction of a victory over the CCP in three months was a "gross underestimate" of the problem and that a "long and terrible conflict" would ensue. He was well aware of the weakness of the Nationalist armies. In addition, he felt that they had no sense of logistics, the basis of all military action and an area in which Marshall was one of the foremost experts in the world: the Nationalist armies simply did not have enough troops or supplies to occupy both Manchuria and north China, or the training facilities to replace the inevitable casualties. They would be dependent on weak lines of communication, vulnerable transportation, and troops that resented the idea of a civil war. As he was succinctly to summarize his view in later testimony: "All [the Communist troops] have to do is be where the Government is not." This would lead to an inconclusive struggle which would further sap the declining strength of the Kuomintang and invite Soviet bolstering of the CCP—"openly or under cover."[42]

In the economic sphere, the lowering of taxes of landlords by the right wing of the Kuomintang in 1945, the increase in expenditures stemming from an oversized military force, which now constituted 70 percent of the budget, and the increased costs of a civil war would bankrupt the government and invite "financial chaos." What aid the Kuomintang was receiving was not reaching the populace or the common soldiers, and there were serious problems in absorbing what seeped through the wall of corruption erected by Nationalist officials. Some of these problems could already be seen in the United Nations relief programs. The United States hardly had the resources available to fund reconstruction, let alone the costs of full-scale civil war.

In the political sphere, Marshall looked to the growing attacks on *all* political opposition, not just the CCP, and the venality and brutality of Kuomintang officials and soldiers in Manchuria and Taiwan. This movement toward total control of all political activity served to increase popular opposition to the Kuomintang markedly, even among some groups that had been previously friendly or neutral. If the Kuomintang was blamed for a civil war that most Chinese believed unnecessary, Marshall believed its base of support would evaporate. Since he believed that such a war could not be won quickly, that it would exacerbate the dismal economic situation of the average Chinese, and that it would entail attacks on liberal as well as Communist elements, he continued to struggle to prevent such an eventuality.[43]

It should be noted that Marshall's predictions all came true. Though he had only a superficial knowledge of the entire Chinese political context, and indeed candidly admitted that he was "puzzled" by it all, his comprehension and estimation of the interrelationship and enormity of the Nationalists' long-term political, economic, and, especially, military dilemmas were quite sound.

Bargaining Behavior: Marshall Attempts to Regain Leverage and Fails

As noted, Marshall became aware of the role of commitment in encouraging the "irreconcilables" in the early summer of 1946. This situation was severely complicated in June when the U.S. Congress, in response to Marshall's trip to Washington in March-April, began debating a surplus property agreement. This entailed the transfer, at bargain rates, of $900 million of wartime materials to China. On June 26, in the midst of negotiations to end the fighting, Marshall wrote Truman that these congressional deliberations were an "embarrassment" to him and that "die-hard Kuomintang elements" were using them as a basis for pressing for a military solution. The prospect of an increase in commitment again threatened to undermine leverage for reform.

Not surprisingly, the CCP objected to the aid package. Marshall attempted to convince Chou En-lai that this aid was long-term and would not be useful for "many months hence." Chou acknowledged this, and said that the CCP was not against aid to the Kuomintang per se, but only "at this moment," stating that he was worried about the psychological effects on the right-wing extremists. Marshall asked for a statement from a high American official that (1) the aid had been planned long ago; (2) the aid was to rid China of the Japanese; (3) the aid aimed to "cement rather than destroy" Chinese unity; (4) the aid was dependent on Chinese unification; (5) it was meant for all of China; and (6) the deteriorating economic situation precluded delay.

On June 28, Assistant Secretary of State Dean Acheson released such a statement to the press, informing Marshall that Truman did not want to do it himself in order "to save the ace for a subsequent deal if . . . called for by you." The primary problem in withholding the aid was that the surplus property materials, which were in "open storage," would deteriorate if not moved quickly. Despite his reservations, Marshall went ahead with the deal rather than dump the materials in the ocean. This was not an idle concern; much of the surplus property material delivered to China arrived in a markedly decomposed condition.

When Acheson's statement failed to have the desired effect, Marshall used his influence to have a second China Aid Bill put into committee in Congress. He then let it be known in Nanking, and to Kuomintang officials in Washington, that it would not pass in the House of Representatives unless there was a personal plea from Marshall himself. He did this in the hope that his refusal would "have a sobering effect upon some aggressive leaders" in the Kuomintang. This tactic also failed, and Marshall let the additional aid bill die in Congress in July. The right wing of the Kuomintang continued to insist that the United States would have to come to the aid of China and used the surplus property deliberations as proof.[44]

In the difficult negotiations of early summer, 1946, there was one minor success for elite reform: under pressure from Marshall, Chiang sent right-wing General Ho Ying-chin, a leading "irreconcilable," on, in Dean Acheson's words, an "innocuous tour or mission abroad" to lessen his influence. General Ho was made Chinese Delegate to the United Nations Military Staff Committee in the United States. Other elite reforms, such as repeated attempts to get the Chen brothers and other obstructionists out of positions of power, were unsuccessful.[45]

Bargaining Behavior: New Emphasis on Redistributive Reforms

With the failure to achieve elite reforms, the redistributive reforms took on even greater significance to the United States. In mid-July a land reform bill was promulgated by the Kuomintang, created with United States assistance, calling for land redistribution, reduction of taxes on peasant households, and an extension of rural credit. It was never implemented. Marshall and the new American ambassador, John Leighton Stuart, a missionary educator with fifty years of experience in China, began exerting unwanted pressure for elections in rural areas to decide the local government impasse between the Nationalists and the Communists. In addition, Stuart tried to convince Chiang of the necessity for redistributive reforms. On July 21, 1946, he told the Generalissimo: "The best and perhaps only way to cope with the Communist movement was to institute agrarian and other reforms that were still more beneficial than those advocated by the Communists and yet were free from the violence, dictatorial methods and possible foreign influence of the Communists."[46] This was presumably something that Chiang did not want to hear. Not surprisingly, he countered that land reform would go forward as soon as order was restored. The Americans argued in turn that redistributive reform was a means to that restoration of order.

Decision-making: The United States and the "Third Force"

In reaction to his lack of success with the CCP and the Kuomintang, Marshall began promoting the Third Party Group as a balancing instrument between those two groups. In the summer of 1946, he later testified, he and Ambassador Stuart made "effort after effort" to increase the "self-discipline and inspiration" of the Kuomintang by promoting the fortunes of the "so-called liberal" groups, "all of whom had come to me" asking for an American reformist intervention on the side of democracy, that is, the "third force" between the reactionaries and the revolutionaries. As in the past, this policy failed for three reasons: (1) these groups were badly divided; (2) they had no mass political base and—what was more important—no army; and (3) the more the United States supported these groups, the more the Kuomintang attacked them.

In mid-July, for example, the Nationalists assassinated two professors associated with the Democratic League, the leading organization in the Third Party Group, in Kunming, and launched nationwide attacks on the opposition press. The garrison commander in Kunming, who was widely believed responsible, was General Ho Kwei-chang, the nephew of "irreconcilable" General Ho Ying-chin. The United States temporarily put some members of the Democratic League under the protection of its consulate in Kunming. When the consulate staff protested the attacks, one local Kuomintang official told them that anyone who criticized the government "must expect to pay with their lives." When Marshall complained to Chiang about the harassment of the liberals, the Generalissimo claimed that they were being followed in order to "protect" them. Marshall snapped: "I'm not so naive as to believe that."[47]

Marshall was deeply disturbed over the assassinations. Killing armed Communists who violently challenged the legitimacy of the government was one thing; killing unarmed liberals, especially since it was in apparent retaliation for his support of them, was quite another. As Chou En-lai himself cleverly argued to the Americans, it was "comprehensible" that the Nationalists attacked the CCP because it was an armed force, but attacks on unarmed dissidents displayed a total unwillingness to compromise with the opposition. The attacks led large groups of students and intellectuals to support the CCP, a development that played right into the hands of Mao Tse-tung, who was actively courting "middle-of-the-road" progressive elements. Ironically, the CCP used the very political strategy the Americans were advocating for the Kuomintang.

This situation was not inevitable. From the best information available, these groups were not pro-CCP, but wanted instead a constraint on the arbitrary use of power by the Kuomintang. The increasing dominance of its right wing virtually drove them into opposition. In the face of American pressure, two junior officers were executed for the murder of one of the professors and Ho Kwei-chang was relieved of command. The attacks did not end, however. At a memorial service for the two slain leaders in August, the chairman of the Democratic League was severely beaten by Nationalist agents.[48]

Bargaining Behavior: The Arms Embargo

The official American reaction to the Kunming assassinations was immediate and negative. On July 30, Marshall told Chiang that the attacks were inexcusable, were leading the nation to civil war, added to the "growing disapproval" of the Kuomintang, and seriously affected American public opinion—the last an implicit threat of a quid pro quo through use of the diplomatic code word for continued support for the Kuomintang. Chiang, as he often did, referred to the traditional Chinese way of dealing with enemies: first harsh treatment, then generous treatment, would cause the ripe fruit to fall into your lap. (Marshall would testify in February 1948, in a sharp exchange with Congressman Walter Judd: "We are still looking for that crop.") These statements had once sufficed, but the events of July drastically altered the American view of the Kuomintang. In addition, the Nationalist armies simultaneously launched a major offensive on all fronts, initiated large-scale looting in areas under their control in Manchuria, and increased the number of executions in Taiwan, leading to large-scale anti-Kuomintang riots in the island province.

Secretary of State James Byrnes wired Marshall that he was correct to protest the "increasingly violent wave of terrorism," and that President Truman would do anything Marshall thought necessary, including making a public statement condemning the assassinations and military movements. Marshall wrote back that a public statement at this point would only make Chiang more intractable, but requested that a private message from Truman be sent through the Chinese Consulate in New York. Marshall drafted the letter to Chiang, which carried an implicit quid pro quo by threatening to "reconsider" American policy in China because of the failure of negotiations, the increase in fighting, and the Kunming incidents. Marshall also separately warned Nationalist officials that he might withdraw from mediation. This threat seriously alarmed Chiang, who was still aware of his dependence on American aid and wary of possible Soviet actions in the northeast.[49]

The situation was further complicated by a CCP attack on a United States Marine convoy at Anping, near Peking. In the face of other minor incidents, Marshall and Navy Secretary Forrestal ordered the Marines concentrated in certain areas to avoid a repetition. The United States began withdrawing its troops at a faster pace to avoid being dragged into the Chinese Civil War.[50]

Chiang reacted to the apparent reassessment of U.S. policy. On August 17, he told Marshall that there was no chance of reaching an agreement with the CCP. Would it be acceptable to the Americans, he asked, if he would accept a coalition with the Third Party Group, but exclude the CCP? Marshall was initially noncommittal on the proposition, but repeated his view that a civil war "virtually invites Communistic expansion and Soviet infiltrations." He added that the situation in China "must be considered in close connection with the negotiations [with the U.S.S.R.] in Paris," that is, the United States did not want China to become an irritant in superpower relations.[51]

What Marshall did not tell Chiang at this meeting was that the United States had already decided on July 29 to place an arms embargo on the Kuomintang in order to force it to end its military attacks on the opposition and avoid civil war. The United States was attempting to focus its commitment at this point by splitting it: economic aid, in the form of the surplus property agreement, would continue in order to prevent an economic collapse of the government, but there would be no military aid that might be used in a civil war. Thus the Americans were attempting to bolster the Kuomintang enough to avoid the regime's collapse, but not enough so that it could ignore American entreaties for elite and redistributive reforms.

This bargaining approach failed because it fogged rather than sharpened the extent of the commitments. If the United States continued to provide aid to prevent economic collapse, was it not reasonable for the Nationalists to assume that it would eventually grant aid to them to prevent a military collapse? Moreover, it was not so simple to separate the two. Though Marshall "reserved out" all military equipment from the surplus property deal, the Kuomintang circumvented this restriction by selling non-military materials and using the funds for military purposes.

Chiang's bargaining ploy also failed. On August 21, the State Department rejected the idea of a coalition with the Third Party Group because many members of the latter were privately telling the Americans that such a move would drive them toward the CCP. The Third Party Group looked to the willingness of the Nationalists to negotiate with the CCP as an indication of its intentions toward other parties.

Again, bolstering the Kuomintang was rejected as an option. In framing an answer to Chiang, John Carter Vincent, the chief China specialist in the State Department, stated that if he thought aid would do any good, he would advocate "all-out support of Chiang." However, he saw only "trouble, trouble, trouble" in backing the Nationalists militarily in a civil war. He put forth the hope that a period of "several months" of fighting would have a "chastening effect" on the extremists in the CCP and the Kuomintang, and would bring "wiser counsels" to the fore.[52]

Marshall had heard this last argument privately from military leaders in both the CCP and the Kuomintang, and he was to accept it only with the greatest reluctance. In a mixture of realism and compassion, he wired Truman on August 30, 1946 that this "somewhat Chinese view" ignored the possibility of Soviet intervention and the prospective suffering of "hundreds of millions of oppressed people." It is perhaps ironic that the greatest concern for the average Chinese in the civil war was being expressed not by Nationalist or Communist leaders, who were understandably more concerned with their relative political positions, nor by professional American diplomats, but by a lifelong American soldier. Marshall had come to believe that he had a personal duty to avoid civil war. As he told one aide: "I probably have not properly represented the interests of the United States. I feel that I am representing the Chinese people." On August 23, he informed the Kuomintang of the arms embargo, though it was not yet told of its extent, apparently in order to exert gradually increasing pressure. On August 30, the Surplus Property aid deal was signed in Washington.[53] The CCP was not informed of the embargo, apparently to avoid encouraging its "irreconcilables," but the information soon leaked in Washington.[54]

Bargaining Behavior: The Final Failure

Marshall saw both the CCP and the Kuomintang as unalterably opposed to an agreement in the fall of 1946. He developed a dual strategy to attempt to overcome this impasse by further promoting the fortunes of the Third Party Group and by moving the negotiations into small groups to discuss the creation of a State Council, which might avoid public posturing.

The chief stumbling blocks remained: a military cease-fire and elite reforms. At Marshall's behest, members of the Third Party Group entered into negotiations with both the Kuomintang and the CCP in September, even while the fighting continued and the Nationalists did well on the battlefield. The Kuomintang's military success, which Marshall saw as temporary, made it less likely that it would compromise because military concessions from the CCP seemed less important.

The situation reached a critical stage at the beginning of October. The Nationalists prepared, and publicly announced, an assault on Kalgan, which the CCP had long said meant full-scale civil war. In June, Chiang had promised Marshall that this city could remain in CCP hands. Marshall desperately attempted to prevent this offensive. On October 1, in yet another attempt to pressure the Kuomintang, he threatened to ask Truman for his recall if the assault on Kalgan were not halted. In an attempt to revive the quid pro quo, he warned Chiang that if the Nationalists captured Kalgan the United States would withdraw all economic and military aid from China.[55]

On October 5, Chiang reacted to Marshall's threat. This development, Chiang told the American, had "caused him more distress than anything that had happened in years." It was "unthinkable" that Marshall could leave China at this time. He promised that Kalgan would be his last military demand. Marshall replied that he would not mediate if the Kuomintang attacked it. The American canceled his recall request and wired Truman: "I think his leaders [that is, the right wing of the party] have carefully played their cards to create this situation believing that, because of Soviet considerations, we would be forced to [go] along with protracted negotiations while the campaign progressed as they desired." Though Marshall believed he had reached an agreement, the Kuomintang armies took Kalgan on October 10. The CCP broke off negotiations, and Chou En-lai left Nanking and traveled to Shanghai.[56]

In the period October 10–17, at Marshall's urging, leading members of the Third Party Group traveled to Shanghai in an attempt to convince Chou to return. For a brief diplomatic moment the "third force" was united in its policy preferences and studiously courted by both the Nationalists and the Communists. But the divisions were too deep, the Third Party Group too weak, and the United States too lacking in influence to stop the fighting.

While the Third Party Group was in Shanghai, on October 11, the Kuomintang officially declared the convening of the National Assembly for November 15, with 1,744 members and representation heavily stacked in its favor. This was the last straw for many in the opposition.

The Democratic League, which had been attempting to get the CCP
back into the negotiations, began to break off from other Third Party
Group organizations and warned Marshall that if he could not get the
Kuomintang to rescind this declaration, he was making a serious error.
At this point, Marshall and Ambassador Stuart further removed themselves from the negotiations in the vain hope that the Chinese parties
could work it out themselves. They could not.

After some ten months in China, Marshall realized that his mission
had failed. He also clearly recognized, perhaps for the first time, the
inverse relationship between commitments and leverage in his bargaining relationship with the Kuomintang, that is, he found himself in the
Commitment Trap. It was a bitter lesson for him. As he told an aide
on October 19, the same day he cut off all American cooperation with
the Chinese secret police: "If you let this bunch [that is, the Nationalists]
know you are for them, you can't do anything with them."[57] Discouraged, the General planned to return home. For all practical purposes,
the Marshall Mission was over.[58]

Bargaining Behavior: Marshall Sticks with the Renewed Quid Pro Quo

With the onset of full-scale civil war in October, Marshall remained
"aloof" from Chiang to display disapproval of Kuomintang policy and
continued his quid pro quo approach to any aid beyond the Surplus
Property Agreement. He cabled Truman and Acheson on November
23:

> I have been very emphatic in stating to [the Nationalists] that it is useless
> to expect the United States to pour money into the vacuum being created
> by the military leaders in their determination to settle matters by force,
> almost 90 per cent of the budget[,] itself highly inflationary, going to
> military expenditures. Also that it was useless to expect the United States
> to pour money into a government dominated by a completely reactionary
> clique bent on exclusive control of governmental power.[59]

Truman wired back on December 3 that he was "relying entirely on
your judgement on all China matters."[60]

In spite of the efforts of Marshall to change Chinese perceptions of
the American commitments, the Kuomintang continued to request huge
amounts of aid, not only without any quid pro quo for reforms, but
also without any accounting procedures that would let the United States
know where the aid had gone. Given the corruption of the regime,

these were ludicrous proposals. American officials told the Chinese Embassy in Washington that the generosity of the past was over; that China could not absorb the aid it had now; that previous aid had not reached the people; that the regime had to overhaul its distribution system to lessen corruption; and that Congress would "examine most searchingly" any further requests.[61]

Decision-making: Domestic Pressure for Bolstering Begins to Build

In late 1946, Marshall began to feel some heat from American friends of Chiang, who wanted a bolstering policy. The conservative press, the War and Navy Departments, and especially Henry Luce of the *Time-Life* publishing empire all began putting pressure on the administration to bolster Chiang. Luce, the child of missionaries to China, made a trip to China in October at the invitation of the Kuomintang. He returned, according to a cable sent to Marshall by former Assistant Secretary of War John McCloy, "freshly imbued with the crusading spirit along the consistent Luce line." Marshall cabled back to McCloy that this was a "most serious complication."

In an evocative phrase which summed up his view of the intractable attitude of the right wing and the increasing demands within China for reform, Marshall wrote that he felt as if he were caught between a "rock and a whirlpool." He then asked McCloy whether he could generate some counter-bolstering viewpoints in the *New York Times* or the *New York Herald Tribune* so that Luce would not encourage the Chinese right wing with his publications and "seriously weaken my hand" through increasing the expectations of greater American commitments.[62]

Though it is impossible to determine the source, on January 8, 1947, the day after Marshall's final statement in China, the *New York Herald Tribune* editorialized: "There is no hope in backing reactionaries in China in the belief that they can stop the Reds. In China, as elsewhere in the world, the United States must stand for democracy and not try to build frail dikes against Communism with worn and useless feudal bricks."[63] The words were not the American General's, but they could well have been.

The Marshall Mission was over. In retrospect, it had been "Mission Impossible" from the very beginning. When the January 10 agreements began breaking down, Marshall's close friend General Joseph Stilwell, remembering his own travails with the Nationalists during World War

II, exclaimed: "But what did they expect? George Marshall can't walk on water."[64] Though it ended in failure, perhaps one of the most important aspects of the mission for the policy that was to follow was the education it gave George Marshall in the chaos that was postwar Republican China.

Reform's Last Hurrah, 1947–1948

5

The American interest in stabilizing China did not end with the failure of the Marshall Mission. Nor did the concern with reform. Rather, during the first several months of 1947 the United States adopted the "wait and see" policy of rational avoidance that had been suggested by the State Department's John Carter Vincent and others the previous summer. The confusion and chaos in China were reflected in the Washington bureaucracy, as the United States government split badly over what to do about the situation—military bolstering versus State Department reformism. The policy disagreements had initially appeared in late 1945. They had remained submerged during the Marshall Mission, but reappeared in even more virulent form as the year 1947 progressed.

Marshall returned to the United States and became Secretary of State in early January, 1947. He faced a difficult dilemma. Pressure was mounting from conservative circles to bolster Chiang, but Marshall viewed bolstering as an impossibility given the corruption and ineptitude of the Nationalist Party, the Kuomintang. Yet he, Truman, and the rest of the administration did not see withdrawal from China as a viable option. Marshall therefore adopted a policy of rational avoidance of a clear decision either to bolster Chiang or to withdraw from China. He saw the only hope in elite reforms that would create a coalition made up of those non-Communist elements allied with the CCP in opposition to the right wing of the Kuomintang, the CCP's alleged "pro-negotiation" faction, the left wing of the Kuomintang, and the Third Party Group. Such a coalition might implement redistributive reforms and avoid military solutions to China's problems. Since the Nationalists were in a militarily preponderant position in early 1947 that Marshall saw as temporary, a few months of a "wait and see" attitude might force the Chinese to realize that the ultimate responsibility for reaching an agreement was theirs, and might chasten the militarist elements of both the CCP and the Kuomintang. The idea was to let the Kuomintang leaders in particular do some "sweating" to convince them that the United States would not automatically come to their rescue because of fear of the Soviets. Marshall was hardly optimistic about such a policy, but he saw the bolstering and withdrawal options as even more odious.

Decision-making: The State Department and Military Policy Debate

The State Department, concentrating on the political problems of China, generally agreed with Marshall's estimation; the military, concentrating more on the military weakness of the Kuomintang armies, began pressing hard for a bolstering policy. This split had remained largely submerged while Marshall was in China because of his prestige and the lingering hope that his mission would succeed. Now that he was formally associated with the State Department, however, it came to the forefront. As Secretary of State Marshall could not expect, nor did he receive, the degree of control over policy that he had enjoyed while in China. He now had to create policies that would be filtered through the bureaucracy. This made internal governmental pressure, especially from the War and Navy Departments, a much more formidable constraint on policymaking. Truman, however, continued to rely heavily on Marshall for China policy because, as he wrote Aubrey Williams, the new Secretary of State was "better acquainted with the situation than anybody in the United States, having just spent a year over there."[1] The attempt to split the commitment on aid (that is, the decision made in summer 1946 for limited economic support but no military support) and the wait for "wiser counsels" were the bases of American policy for the first five months of 1947.

The military's view of the situation was shaped by a deterioration of the Nationalist military position in January 1947. The CCP launched an offensive in Manchuria, led by the forces of General Lin Piao, driving the Nationalist armies back into fortified garrisons in the towns in many areas. From this time onward, American military officers saw a renewal of military aid as necessary for the prevention of a Communist victory in China, though they also recognized the necessity for reforms. They were led in China by Admiral Charles Cooke and General John Lucas, who continuously pressed for an enlargement of the naval and army advisory groups.

In March 1947, Admiral Cooke attempted to get Ambassador Stuart and his chief assistant at the embassy, Walton Butterworth, to press for an immediate expansion of the naval assistance group, an increase in the number of Marines in Tsingtao, and wide-scale publicity for these activities to boost morale in the Kuomintang. When Stuart and Butterworth refused, arguing that this would represent a commitment to the Nationalists in the Civil War, the Admiral started searching for, in Stuart's words, "possible prejudices" against the Nationalists among the embassy staff. Cooke and Lucas were joined by General MacArthur in Tokyo, who stated that the Kuomintang was "not the best" but "on our side."[2]

This marked a growing suspicion of State Department personnel by many in the military that would be used after the Nationalists' fall in the vilification of that department for being infiltrated with "pro-Communists." Though those officers who believed this were undoubtedly sincere, it was a preposterous charge. What critics later overlooked was that many in the military who advocated bolstering also called for sweeping political and economic reforms; at this point it was a difference in emphasis, not kind. The urgency of the military situation, however, led military advisers to believe that a military aid program could not be postponed until political and economic reform agreements were reached.

In Washington, Navy Secretary Forrestal and War Secretary Patterson became the primary advocates of a bolstering policy. Patterson in particular argued that it was risky to withhold economic aid from the Kuomintang until there was an improvement in the political situation, because that aid might be the key to such an improvement.

Marshall blocked the increase in military advisers, arguing that it would have a negative political impact in China, would be viewed as a commitment to the Nationalists, and would inflame Chinese nationalism. He added that the American public had been told that the United States would not intervene in a civil war, and that the troops and advisers would serve no useful purpose since the Chinese had not listened to American military advice in the past, and showed no signs of doing so in the future. The Secretary of State continued to believe that elite reforms would have to be implemented throughout the Nationalist armies before an advisory program would do any good. Despite Marshall's protestations, this lobbying activity by the U.S. military would increase as the military position of the Kuomintang armies deteriorated.[3]

The political program that the State Department was promoting precluded any such commitments because they would encourage the right wing and discourage Chiang from removing its members from decision-making positions. Two days before Marshall returned from China, Walton Butterworth, a man whose judgment Marshall trusted a great deal (he was later to make him the first Assistant Secretary of State for Far

Eastern Affairs), explained the embassy's thinking on the matter and the rationale for the promotion of a "third force." After dismissing the right wing as a group totally against reform who would "dig their own graves," he stated that the United States must promote the fortunes of the liberal elements in China, who "though numerous, are presently weak, badly organized and without armed support." He presented the classic dilemma for the liberal reformer: how to create a "third force" political movement somewhere between the revolutionaries and the reactionaries: "Since neither the Communists nor the right-wing of the Kuomintang is in consonance with American ideals, attitudes, interests or purposes, the pressing problem for the United States is how to help the middle groups to power without provoking a self-defeating chaos. The answer, of course, will have to be found in deeds, not in words."[4] Marshall agreed with this position. With the right wing in charge, he argued, it was impossible to effect elite or redistributive reforms. Throughout the first half of 1947, he was constantly on the alert for any splits in the CCP or the Kuomintang that would show the slightest possibility of forging a centrist coalition, but they never appeared.

Global political considerations also placed constraints on a bolstering policy. In contrast to the situation in Europe in which the United States had relatively self-sufficient allies in late 1946, the State Department argued, it faced the U.S.S.R. virtually alone in Asia. The Soviets had been "relatively quiescent" in China, a fact that State Department analysts found "remarkable." A greater American commitment to the civil war would invite a greater commitment from the Soviets, which would dissipate resources and threaten the American position in Europe. By making Chiang "sweat," the Truman administration might force him to see that the United States would not aid him as long as the right wing was in control of the Kuomintang. If reforms were put through, the United States could then bolster the regime with a relatively modest program that would leave the bulk of its aid for Europe. If there were no reforms, no amount of aid would bail the Nationalists out of a civil war.[5]

The pressure on the Chinese for a reform policy went ahead. This had to be done, Marshall told Forrestal and Patterson, by maintaining a "constructive and sympathetic (as distinguished from exacting)" attitude toward the degree of reform put through by the Kuomintang. Though legislation was promulgated for military aid, Marshall refused to allow any to be delivered and reserved the right to final decision as to "time, type and quantity" to serve as a bargaining chip in dealing with the Chinese. On January 29, 1947, the mediation machinery set up during the Marshall Mission was formally terminated. The United States recalled several thousand troops.[6]

Decision-making: The Situation in China Worsens

If some Americans thought that things could not get much worse in China, they were wrong. In the fighting taking place, the Communists avoided pitched battles, used hit-and-run tactics, and captured large amounts of equipment from the government. The Kuomintang troops increasingly repaired to the garrisons and passed the initiative to the enemy; American military observers in China believed they were incapable of mounting a sustained offensive. When anti-government demonstrations against the fighting broke out in Peking and other cities, the Nationalist secret police brutally attacked anyone even mildly critical of the regime or the Civil War.[7]

In addition to the worsening military situation, the Chinese economy took a drastic turn for the worse in January: the value of Chinese currency went from 7,700 to 18,000 *yuan* to the U.S. dollar in that month alone. The Kuomintang attempted to gain control of the situation by freezing wages, placing ceiling prices on essential commodities, and prohibiting currency speculation and the hoarding of precious metal. These steps were attempted, however, only in the major cities, and the soaring inflation rate undercut price controls. By April, food shortages and labor unrest, even among Kuomintang-dominated unions, forced the government to abandon these programs. Finance Minister T. V. Soong was attempting to apply a monetarist approach to the situation, that is, controlling inflation by controlling the money supply. On February 28, Chiang told him to abandon this policy because he needed more money to pay his rising military costs. Soong resigned. The Kuomintang continued to press the United States for large loans to solve its problems. The "wait and see" policy continued.[8]

Decision-making: The Truman Doctrine and Further Developments in the Cold War

Things were further complicated for the "wait and see" policy and the attempt to return to a quid pro quo bargaining context in early March, 1947, by the enunciation of the Truman Doctrine. The broad rhetoric of the doctrine increased internal and external demands for aid to all non-Communist nations in the world. Though it was not done publicly, the administration made an exception of China, largely because of the military weakness and corruption of the Kuomintang. As President Truman told a cabinet meeting on March 7, in a terse summation of the weakness of the Nationalist armies: "Chiang Kai-shek['s troops] will not fight it out. [The] Communists will fight it out—they are fanatical.

It would be pouring sand in a rat hole [to give aid] under present conditions."[9] Admiral Leahy pointed out that Marshall, who was at the Moscow Meeting of the Council of Foreign Ministers, had hope for China later, but not in the present situation.[10]

In April, Marshall returned from Moscow in a depressed mood. The Soviet reaction to the Truman Doctrine had been most negative, and Marshall was convinced that there was no chance for an early rapprochement between the superpowers. In China, the Truman Doctrine apparently convinced the Nationalists that the impasse was finally over and that aid was on the way, despite frank American denials that this would not be the case unless major reforms were implemented.[11]

Bargaining Behavior: Cosmetic Reforms in China

In mid-February, 1947, as the Nationalists' military and political situation continued to deteriorate, Chiang again promised the Americans that he would reform his government. Cosmetic measures were undertaken. Some members of the left wing of the Kuomintang were included in an April governmental reorganization, with several members of the Third Party Group also included in the government. Chiang bluntly told the embassy, however, that the latter group would be excluded from decision-making positions because they were "incompetent" and wanted too much power. The United States did see the inclusion of members of the left wing as possibly being significant, though Chiang's claim that this action constituted the first coalition government in China's history was discounted because of his remarks over their role. Most other Third Party Group members refused to cooperate with the government.

The most disturbing development that spring was the entrance of the CC Clique into the economic field, something they had largely avoided in the past. Apparently believing that huge amounts of aid were on the way because of expectations raised by the Truman Doctrine, the CC Clique wanted to gain control of the economic institutions of the government to sustain payments to its followers. Thus, the end result of the cosmetic reorganization was a further entrenchment of the right wing in key areas. Though they were not taken in by this charade, and realized that the CC Clique had come out of the shift with an enhanced position, American decision-makers were mildly encouraged at the apparent increase in influence of the left wing, especially the Political Study faction.[12]

Other attempts to make it appear that reforms were being implemented were even clumsier. When asked by the Americans about the state of various elite and redistributive reforms, Kuomintang representatives repeatedly stated they had already been put through. This tactic, claiming that reforms were in fact being carried out, was especially untenable. It was made in the midst of increasing hardship in the rural areas, growing secret police activity and censorship, and a brutal crackdown on students and dissidents in Peking and elsewhere.

In addition, the CC Clique made veiled threats to seek a realignment with the U.S.S.R., another classic tactic for a client. This was not taken seriously by the Americans, and the embassy cabled that it was clearly a ploy by the right wing to scare the United States into giving the government more aid. No apparent serious contacts with the U.S.S.R. were made.[13]

Decision-making: From Bad to Worse in China

In April 1947, Secretary Marshall passed along to President Truman a series of embassy cables from China. They outlined the growing economic, political, and military crises, and the growth of the power of the right wing of the Kuomintang. The litany of problems was serious: the Nationalists claimed to be running low on ammunition in some divisions; they lacked the capacity to repair equipment or replace troops; there was an excessive dispersion and overextension of troops; they lacked competent leadership in the field; the growing economic crisis was affecting soldiers' families, destroying civic morale, and increasing looting; the regime faced major revolts in Taiwan in reaction to the brutal and corrupt rule of Kuomintang officials; and the Nationalists were being blamed by virtually everyone for the unpopular Civil War. These developments were essentially those that Marshall had been predicting since early 1946. Yet the embassy could not suggest anything other than to continue the "wait and see" policy of the previous three months. From the American viewpoint, the Kuomintang was so corrupt, so seemingly bent on self-destruction, and so apparently immune to self-help, that U.S. diplomats saw no alternative to pressing for reforms.

In April, the situation grew even worse. The rice requisitioned for the armies in the north caused shortages in the south, leading to rice riots in a number of southern provinces. Mobs raided stores and demanded food. Student protests and strikes in sympathy with the starving masses rose in number. Chiang's predictions to Marshall of the non-effects of a civil war on the rural areas proved wide of the mark. The Kuomintang reacted by brutally suppressing the demonstrations and arresting thousands.[14]

The reaction in the State Department to the new crisis was one of growing alarm. In early April, 1947, the Far Eastern Division recommended the slackening of the arms embargo in response to the Nationalists' claim in late March that American-trained divisions were running low on ammunition. The United States, they argued, had an obligation to supply these troops because it had trained them during the war and the Chinese had no facilities to manufacture this type of ammunition. The claim of a lack of ammunition may not have been true, but it was believed by the Americans and therefore partly influenced their recommendations.[15]

Marshall rejected these arguments, believing that providing ammunition would represent a commitment to Nationalist policies, could not be kept quiet, and would be widely interpreted in China as a change in American policy, which would encourage the right wing even further. By late April, however, Truman, under heavy pressure from the Navy and Army Departments, and external pressure from Republicans and the conservative press, began pressing Marshall to increase some military aid to the Kuomintang, such as spare parts. On April 25, 1947, in a rare instance of bypassing Marshall's recommendations on China, the President authorized the transfer of limited amounts of equipment to the Nationalists. By May 1947, even strong advocates of the "wait and see" policy, such as the State Department's Arthur Ringwalt and John Carter Vincent, were suggesting increased military aid.[16]

Bargaining Behavior: Marshall Lifts the Embargo

Those who advocated military aid to the Kuomintang, however, had no solutions for the problems with the Chinese military leadership, something that weighed heavily on Marshall's mind. On May 8, Chinese Ambassador Wellington Koo came to see him in Washington, seeking military aid. Marshall, a man not given to hyperbole, told Koo that Chiang Kai-shek was "the worst advised military commander in history." Unabashed, Koo repeated his request for large-scale military aid. Marshall fixed Koo with one of his famous "icy stares" and indulged in a rare burst of irony: "Chiang is faced with a unique problem of logistics. He is losing about forty percent of his supplies to the enemy. If the percentage should reach fifty percent he will have to decide whether it is wise to supply his own troops."[17] To supply an army with this record was to supply, in effect, the Chinese Communists.

The ammunition supply issue was a hotly contested one in the post-"loss" debate in the United States, with would-be bolsterers arguing that shortages had caused Chiang's downfall. Those who later charged this simply ignored the huge losses of equipment by the Nationalists, though

Marshall can be faulted for not making them public for fear that this would undermine the the regime even more. The primary problem was not the provision of military material per se, but the inability of the Nationalist armies to hold on to what they had. The lack of evidence of Soviet provision of large levels of military aid to the CCP after 1945 is pertinent here; with the porous Kuomintang military, such levels were probably unnecessary. Despite strong reservations about the political effects of increasing military aid without reforms, the seriously deteriorating situation in China, internal pressure from the military bureaus and the State Department, the increasing doubts of the President, and domestic pressure from certain circles in Congress and the conservative press led Marshall to lift the arms embargo on May 26, 1947.[18]

Decision-making: The Possibility of Economic Aid Disappears

On the same day he lifted the arms embargo, Marshall requested that the Export-Import Bank grant $500 million in funds to be dispensed at his discretion to the Chinese Nationalists for specific projects. That amount had been earmarked earlier during Marshall's trip to Washington in March-April, 1946, but had never been granted because of the outbreak of fighting. These funds had to be renewed by June 30, 1947, according to law, or else they would be lost to the Chinese.

In mid-June, 1947, the board of directors of the bank turned down Marshall's request. In a strange twist of fate, one of the men on the board most responsible for the refusal was Clarence E. Gauss, the former ambassador to China, a man who was removed from his position along with General Stilwell at Chiang Kai-shek's insistence in the fall of 1944. Gauss was a fiscally conservative Republican, an old China hand, and not in the least taken with Chiang. Now the Generalissimo's machinations came back to haunt him, as Gauss refused to grant the "political loans" because China in the midst of a civil war was a very poor risk.

The bank's refusal to earmark funds for China put Marshall in a real bind. The deteriorating situation in China, and internal and external demands for the State Department to "do something" about the spread of Communism in Asia, put tremendous pressures on him to construct a new policy. Now he would have to go to Congress to get authorization for economic aid. This complicated things in two major ways: (1) congressional hearings might mean a public airing of the corruption of the Kuomintang, something Marshall had been avoiding because he thought it would weaken the regime even more; and (2) Congress would not grant the aid without some accountability and measures of reform from the Kuomintang. Within this context, Marshall struggled for a solution to the problem. He apparently decided to make one last effort to coerce the Kuomintang into reforming.[19]

Decision-making: The Wedemeyer Mission: One Last Try

In mid-June, Marshall began contemplating sending another mission to China. He had previously spurned all such suggestions because of his belief that this would convince the right wing that aid was on the way. In a speech at a dinner meeting of the Business Advisory Council of the Department of Commerce on June 11, 1947, Marshall offered some remarks on China. He pointed to the grassroots support of the CCP, which the Kuomintang lacked; he noted the incompetence of the Nationalist military leadership; he outlined the concept of personal loyalty that determined power within the Kuomintang; and he elaborated on the lack of comprehension on the part of Chiang concerning the actual weakness of his government. He frankly admitted his frustration in seeking a solution: "I have tortured my brain and I can't now see the answer."[20] Yet internal and external political pressures forced him to try something.

Conflicting advice came from a number of quarters. The military argued that a relatively modest military aid program would arrest the deterioration, boost morale in the Kuomintang, and make it more likely that the CCP would come to the bargaining table. The State Department argued that even enormous amounts of aid would do no good without reform, that the political deterioration was far deeper than the military recognized, and that the CCP was unlikely to negotiate while it was in the ascendant and the Kuomintang falling apart. The Nationalists argued that the only problem was the lack of large amounts of aid. Important congressional critics did not have a clue to the real situation in China, largely because of Marshall's silence on the subject, but wanted a policy of bolstering to prevent the advent of Communism in China. Marshall had a good grasp of the problems with a bolstering policy, especially the effects of commitment on bargaining leverage, and wanted some sign of movement toward reform before he would make such a commitment. Sandwiched between the chaos in China and the chaos in Washington, he decided in favor of one last attempt at reforming the Kuomintang.[21]

Historians and political scientists have long puzzled over the exact purposes of the Wedemeyer Mission to China in the summer of 1947. Explanations fall into three categories: domestic pressure, bureaucratic politics, or—the stated purpose of the mission—to get the latest information on the situation in China.[22] William Stueck has recently added the argument that Marshall "probably" sent Wedemeyer to boost morale within the Kuomintang.[23]

Undoubtedly all of the above had an effect on Marshall's decision. With the exception of the last, however, they ignore the psychological effects the decision would have *in China,* something that was clearly on Marshall's mind. I will argue here that Marshall chose Wedemeyer to head the mission in part to increase bargaining leverage for reforms, that is, to raise the baseline of expectations for aid which could then be manipulated in bargaining. The reasons for the puzzlement over why Marshall chose Wedemeyer for the mission are twofold: Wedemeyer was a vocal advocate of bolstering Chiang, and Marshall never revealed his thinking on the subject.

Marshall had become very sensitive to the concept of commitment and its effects on the right wing while he was in China. Clearly he must have realized that sending the man who had replaced the hated, reformist Stilwell in 1944 would be interpreted as a change of policy and an increase in commitment. Indeed, he added Korea to Wedemeyer's itinerary to demonstrate American commitment to that nation. It is safe to assume that Marshall realized that the clear impression would be given to the Nationalists that more aid was forthcoming, without reform.

While offering the carrot of bolstering through the choice of Wedemeyer, however, Marshall simultaneously took actions that emphasized the stick of a quid pro quo bargaining approach. In preparing Wedemeyer's directive, he ensured that the former would make clear that aid would be contingent upon a Chinese willingness to reform and that no aid commitments would be communicated until his report was made to President Truman. He also partly drafted Wedemeyer's final statement in China, leaving in the call for sweeping reforms when others advised removing it. It is doubtful that Wedemeyer would have made such a statement without consulting with Marshall, and there are indications that the latter encouraged such an approach to jolt Chiang into action. His choice for the State Department's representative on the mission, for example, was the reformist Philip Sprouse.[24]

Wedemeyer was briefed on exactly what reforms the United States was seeking from the Chinese. During that briefing session, he expressed the opinion that China would not be a democracy like the United States soon, or even "within a hundred years." John Carter Vincent answered that the United States was not expecting that degree of political development. Yet the Kuomintang needed to "broaden the base" of the government through reforms, though the CCP was now "categorically" left out of consideration for a coalition. Edward Rice, one of the few China hands to escape the purges that were to come, drew up a list of political reforms the United States thought would improve the situation: an end to suppression of the press, guarantees for "freedom of the person," and "some forum in which representatives can express popular feeling and suggest improvement in government." The United States, wrote Rice, was seeking an improvement in "popular approval and popular participation," especially at the village and local levels, though it recognized that China would remain authoritarian and elitist at the national level. Thus, a combination of elite and redistributive reforms was still deemed necessary by the Americans to strengthen the Nationalists by mobilizing elite and mass support against the CCP.[25]

These actions strongly suggest that Marshall continued to have reform very much on his mind when he decided to send Wedemeyer to China. Wedemeyer himself later noted that before he left the United States, Marshall "emphasized and re-emphasized the necessity for concrete evidence that [Chiang and the Kuomintang] are establishing a government structure and are instituting reforms (land, tax and political) that provide a basis for U.S. cooperation and assistance."[26] By concentrating on the concept of commitment in the bargaining relationship with Chiang, the choice of Wedemeyer makes sense as part of a carrot and stick bargaining ploy.

If this was in fact Marshall's purpose, it certainly worked in raising Nationalist expectations of a shift in American policy. The mission, which was not announced either to the Chinese or to American officials in China until Wedemeyer was preparing to leave, was met with delirious joy in Kuomintang circles. The Nationalist press approvingly suggested this might mean that Wedemeyer would be made ambassador to China. It appeared to the Kuomintang that the cavalry was finally coming to the rescue.

Thus, Marshall's earlier fears concerning the effects on the perceptions of commitment by the right wing of the Kuomintang were not unfounded. Ironically, foreign diplomats noted a movement toward self-help in the Kuomintang when it appeared that no huge amounts of American aid were forthcoming with the Truman Doctrine. With the announcement of the mission, however, the Chinese again looked to the United States to solve their problems. Wedemeyer contacted the publisher Henry Luce in early July and asked him for favorable publicity for his mission. *Time* magazine stated that the mission meant increased aid for the Kuomintang. When Wedemeyer arrived in Nanking on July 22, 1947, expectations in China and among bolsterers in the United States were running high.[27]

Decision-making: A Variety of Ideas, but No Solutions, in the Field

Wedemeyer's trip was a depressing one, both for him and for the Kuomintang. He found that the situation had deteriorated markedly since his last stay in China the previous year. Inflation raged on; morale within the Kuomintang had been dropping sharply; attitudes toward the government were uniformly hostile; the cosmetic reforms of the spring had never been implemented; the situation on the battlefield was critical, with the CCP using heavy artillery for the first time, and the "wholesale surrender of [Nationalist] battalions and regiments" in Manchuria; corruption was on the rise; rice riots and workers' strikes were put down brutally by the government, and most of the populace was simply ignoring its many decrees. There was large-scale looting by Kuomintang troops in areas under government control.

Wedemeyer's trip to the northeast was equally depressing: corruption, confiscation, and condescension characterized the behavior of most of the Kuomintang officials in that region. In the south, where the battle conditions associated with the Civil War could not be blamed, the Kuomintang suppressed "even the mildest forms of political disagreement." As officials at the embassy informed him, the Chinese were not pro-Communist, but the Nationalists were literally driving many into the Communist ranks.[28]

American military advisers in China pushed for a bolstering policy, but also emphasized political reforms. General John Lucas said that there had been some recent organizational reforms in the Kuomintang military, but that they would be "of not the slightest use nor will they be possible unless they are accompanied by the political reforms that are so necessary for the nation as a whole." Brigadier General Thomas Timberman, an old friend of Wedemeyer's, described Kuomintang military leaders as "fantastically inept," and offered the opinion that the CCP could not be defeated unless a "third force" political movement appeared. Even Admiral Cooke, though he pushed hard for a bolstering commitment to "boost morale" and prevent a CCP victory, wanted aid made contingent on reforms. Yet the military also argued, especially the Navy, that the United States must come to the aid of the Kuomintang by increasing the numbers and responsibilities of the military advisory group in China. Thus, even most of those advocating support for the Kuomintang were confused about the reform-bolstering paradox. Since the Joint Chiefs had placed China relatively low on a priority list of those nations important to the security of the United States, and the economy-minded Republican Congress had drastically cut the military budget in July 1947, bolstering was a highly unlikely prescription. Those who wanted to bolster the Kuomintang were never able to offer credible answers to the dilemmas posed by the reform and resource questions with such a fiscally conservative Congress and President.[29]

Embassy officials continued to push for elite reforms and a return to the quid pro quo administration of aid. One report suggested a more forceful explanation to non-Kuomintang elements that the United States would not aid the government of China under present circumstances, and an increase in the activities of the United States Information Service to make this clear to the Chinese people in order to create greater domestic pressure for redistributive reform. Another unsigned report clearly called for a search for alternative leadership. Since the Generalissimo and the CC Clique dominated the Kuomintang and believed that the "present international tension" would force the Americans to aid them without reforms, the United States should "cease to consider them as indispensable to our objectives in China." Marshall, however, did not see any alternative leadership that could conceivably galvanize enough support to improve the situation. In addition, this would have entailed a level of intervention in the internal affairs of a client nation that the United States was not yet willing to attempt.[30]

Those Third Party Group elements who had not gone over to the CCP suggested heavy American pressure on the Kuomintang to reform. They uniformly believed that the United States had to play a decisive role in promoting the fortunes of liberal groups. The Democratic League continued to push for elite reforms, that is, a coalition government along the lines of the agreements of January 1946. Its leaders warned that if the United States "endeavor[ed] to bolster the Kuomintang," it would drive the moderates toward the CCP. In general, however, the "third force" in China proved to be a sad illusion. Chiang Mon-lin, a disciple of John Dewey who was connected with the left wing of the Kuomintang, bluntly told the State Department's Philip Sprouse that the CCP would win the Civil War because the moderates in China were "too soft" to lead a revolution.[31]

Bargaining Behavior: Wedemeyer Drops a Bombshell

Wedemeyer was shocked at what he found in China. Even given his previous experience in the country during World War II, the deterioration in conditions was startling. He resented the pressure tactics of the right wing to convince him that things were not as bad as they seemed or that the whole problem was caused by the U.S.S.R.; sometimes Wedemeyer feigned illness to escape the pressure. He believed the Soviets were aiding the CCP, but he wrote Marshall that Nationalist efforts to prove this were "child-like in conception and naive in presentation." The embassy's John Melby wrote a friend that Wedemeyer was filled with "despair, bitterness and anger that any situation could have deteriorated as fast as this one; that any ruling group could pull the obvious and shabby tricks that were pulled on him and that any country could be so apathetic and apparently unwilling to do anything to help itself." Wedemeyer brought his anger and frustration directly to the top echelons of the Chinese government, in Sprouse's words, "to *jolt* them, to *stun* them into doing things."[32]

Convinced that Chiang was not receiving accurate information from his advisers, Wedemeyer had several angry sessions with the Generalissimo. He told Chiang bluntly that he would have to remove corrupt officials and named names, though the top leaders of the right wing were apparently excluded. In yet another attempt to gain a commitment to his government, Chiang asked Wedemeyer to be his "Supreme Adviser." As Wedemeyer's departure from China approached, Chiang insisted that the American give a presentation of China's problems and the conditions for American aid to the top leadership of the Kuomintang. As the date drew near, however, Chiang began to have second thoughts, especially in light of the bluntness he was presented with in private.

On August 22, in contradiction to all sense of Chinese proprieties, Wedemeyer met with the Council of State of the Kuomintang and read them the riot act, pointing to the corruption, venality, and incompetence that characterized the party's rule. Partly because Marshall's ploy had raised expectations of a shift in United States policy to such high levels, the Chinese were absolutely stunned. One elder statesman, Tai Chi-tao, burst into tears at the humiliation involved in this loss of face. When asked whether the criticisms were unjust, however, he replied, "That's just the trouble, what he said was not unjust but perfectly true. I've never been so humiliated in my 26 years of [Kuomintang] service."[33]

Two days later Wedemeyer departed from Nanking. In his final public statement, he again noted the need for elite reforms in the Kuomintang aimed at the removal of "the incompetent and/or corrupt officials that now occupy many positions in the Government, not only in the national organization, but more so in the provincial and municipal structures," the latter a veiled reference to the CC Clique. He therefore concluded that "drastic and far-reaching political and economic reforms" were necessary because "military force in itself will not eliminate Communism."[34]

For the Kuomintang leadership to hear this sort of message from

Marshall or "Communist-influenced" State Department diplomats was one thing; to hear it from a trusted friend who had been a vocal advocate of bolstering was another. The statement was carefully edited by Marshall, who insisted that the call for reforms be included. It was to be America's last-gasp attempt to reform the Chinese government.

Bargaining Behavior: The Chinese Reaction

The Chinese reactions to Wedemeyer's blasts were varied. Many in the left wing of the Kuomintang and in the Third Party Group, though bothered by the embarrassment of the publicity, saw it as a needed burst of candor; the right wing complained, as they had with Marshall, that Wedemeyer had talked to the wrong people while in China and had received a distorted view of the situation.

The reaction of Chiang, however, was one of shock. On the day after Wedemeyer left Nanking, the Generalissimo asked Ambassador Stuart's Chinese secretary, Philip Fugh, whether this meant he had to step down as leader of the government. Fugh was noncommittal. Not too much should be read into this gesture; it was an old tactic of Chiang's to get people to tell him that he was indispensable. Yet his immediate actions suggest that he was badly shaken by this statement by his American friend. He did put through some minor elite reforms that the United States had been suggesting. He removed one of his most loyal and corrupt officials in the northeast and replaced him with an honest and competent general. On September 1, he lifted martial law in Shanghai and informed the United States he would soon name civilian governors south of the Yangtze River. The Americans were cautiously optimistic, though this soon proved to be unfounded.[35]

By mid-September, 1947, Chiang's shock had been replaced with anger. At the Fourth Plenary Session of the Central Executive Committee, he scathingly criticized the party for its incompetence, while totally absolving himself of all blame. He strengthened, rather than lessened, the position of the CC Clique at the expense of the left-wing Political Study Clique which on paper had gained in strength in the April reorganization. In a common tactic for a client, which was taken seriously by virtually no one, he stated that China must never again become dependent on aid from the United States, and he floated thinly veiled rumors that China would pull closer to the U.S.S.R. and appeal to the Soviets for mediation. Ambassador Stuart felt this last tactic was "primarily for effect on the United States" and "reminiscent of similar tactics in the past" when the Kuomintang pressured for aid, as when the Kuomintang had made veiled threats to make a separate peace with Japan during World War II.

Stuart, an old personal friend of Chiang's, was disheartened and dismayed that the Chinese continued to emphasize "overt reliance on [the] *deus ex machina* of American aid" as a substitute for reforms. Most discouraging to American officials, however, was Chiang's reaction to an intra-party movement for elite reform that was meant to throw out "undesirable elements." Chiang's reaction to this movement was, in Stuart's words, "a strong demand that the reform program be dropped." The last attempt at coercion had failed.[36]

Wedemeyer's report, which called for huge increases in aid and an international trusteeship in Manchuria, was rejected and kept secret by Marshall. Wedemeyer seethed in private over this lack of movement on his recommendations. In December, he wrote Chiang that he was sorry he had made his farewell statement public, since it had prevented aid from being granted. For the moment, Marshall returned to the "wait and see" policy of early 1947. Aid continued at low levels; some residual supplies were turned over to private, voluntary American agencies to ensure their reaching the Chinese people.[37]

Decision-making: Domestic Pressure to Bolster Grows

Chiang's reaction to the pressure was also partly a result of his belief that his "friends" in the United States could change policy direction. The Kuomintang counterattacked through friendly elements in the conservative press and the China Bloc in Congress. By mid-October, Marshall began to feel some real heat from military and congressional sources. Navy Secretary James Forrestal, Army Secretary Kenneth Royal, Generals Lucas and Wedemeyer, and Admiral Cooke all pressed for an immediate increase in military aid to the Kuomintang, especially in the face of another effective CCP offensive in Manchuria begun in the fall of 1947. In an important shift, General Lucas and Admiral Cooke, both of whom advocated bolstering but who also realized the need for reforms, were replaced by General David Barr and Admiral Oscar Badger respectively. Barr was a mild advocate of bolstering, though he recognized the need for reforms; Badger was an obsessive anti-Communist who advocated total backing of the Kuomintang. Their reports to the Pentagon reflected the perceived need within the military for an expanded military aid program in the face of deterioration on the battlefield.

Also in mid-October, a group of conservative Republicans and Democrats from the House Military Affairs Committee traveled to China, along with Chiang's old friend, Congressman Walter Judd (R–Minn.) On October 11, they cabled Marshall to "urge extension of immediate aid . . . by meeting [the Kuomintang's] appropriate needs from our available military materials and revising [the] implementation of previous commitments." They had met with Chiang and accepted his argument that "the predicament in Manchuria was an American responsibility" because of the Yalta Agreements. When Judd mentioned to Chiang the removal of corrupt officials, the Generalissimo said, "I cannot make changes now. If I make these changes, the Government collapses and the Communists [will] take over." Yet, according to Judd's recollection, Chiang also said he would remove the "ineffective people" if the United States would commit itself to his government. Chiang also implied that the lack of an aid program to China was due to racism, since the United States was willing to stop Communism in Europe but not in Asia. It was characteristic of Chiang to tell American officials that he could not make reforms, while at the same time promising to make them if they would only increase aid. Marshall had heard all this many times before. Judd told the State Department's Walton Butterworth on November 11, 1947, that the United States must "build on the existing government, bad though it is."[38]

Republicans in Congress, including Senator Arthur Vandenberg and Speaker of the House Joseph Martin, also began pressuring for aid to the Kuomintang. The China Bloc in Congress was not particularly large or powerful in absolute terms, but when added to economy-minded legislators like Congressman John Taber who were against *all* aid programs, the coalition threatened to block aid to Europe unless there was aid to China as well. Their pressure on Marshall to abandon his "wait and see" and reformist policies was especially telling.

Though Marshall and the State Department continued to have deep reservations over aiding the Kuomintang, the deteriorating conditions in China, bureaucratic pressures, and domestic forces that threatened containment in other areas of the world finally overcame those reservations. In late October and early November, decisions were made to push ahead with the implementation of past programs blocked since the Marshall Mission and the addition of new programs of military aid.[39]

Decision-making: The End for Reform

The political situation in China worsened. The intra-party struggles of September resulted in the greater dominance of the CC Clique. On October 28, the Kuomintang banned the Democratic League as a legal political party, claiming it was a Communist front organization. Members of the left wing of the party were not informed in advance of this action, and told American officials that it greatly disturbed them. Some professors were arrested and executed, though the League was allowed to dissolve itself. News of this latest move reached Marshall in Washington on November 3, 1947. On that day, he told a meeting of the Committee of Two that the United States must aid China to "boost morale" in the Kuomintang and "accept the fact that [the Chinese] do things differently and less efficiently than ourselves." He continued, "We must recognize that we have the problem of prolonging the agonies of a corrupt government, and that we probably have reached the point where we will have to accept the fact that this government [that is, the Kuomintang] will have to be retained in spite of our desire to change its character." A week later he requested that Congress give aid to China. For the United States, the attempt at reforming the Kuomintang on the mainland was over.[40]

Epilogue: Aid to China to Save Europe

The domestic pressure on the Truman administration to aid China grew throughout the winter of 1947–48. Military aid had been increasing throughout the autumn, and was increased even further after Marshall's November 3 decision. Yet leading Republicans such as Senator Vandenberg, Speaker of the House Martin, and Governor Thomas Dewey continued to call for aid programs for China before they would support aid programs for Europe, though Vandenberg did so in private. Especially in the House of Representatives, pressures for bolstering Chiang grew intense.

Caught between those who would bolster Chiang or deny aid to Europe, and those who wanted *no* aid programs anywhere, the administration reluctantly gave in to these pressures. Walton Butterworth later recalled that the China legislation was introduced because of pressure from Vandenberg and was in reality "a sop to certain circles." The publicity from the conservative press and the Luce publishing empire also had a growing effect on the public. In a special poll on China taken by the State Department in December 1947, a majority of the public was, for the first time, in favor of loans to China.[41]

In November, the administration attempted to separate European and Asian policies by putting forth an aid bill that included France, Italy, and Austria but not China. The bill passed the Senate, but was blocked in the House. Marshall then went to Congress with a request for $570 million in economic aid for China, and the Senate appropriated an additional $100 million for military aid. The House pushed for a Greek/Turkish–style bill with the involvement of American military advisers; the Senate defeated this attempt at bolstering. A conference bill was passed on April 2, 1948, with $338 million in economic aid and $125 million in military aid to China, though the final totals included only $275 million in economic aid.

The State Department never had any enthusiasm for this aid in the absence of internal governmental reforms in China. Marshall, in his testimony before the Senate Foreign Relations Committee in executive session, stated that in his opinion the Kuomintang could not defeat the CCP. The United States could not stop the approaching debacle unless it took over the Chinese government to "administer its economic, military and government affairs." It could not do this, Marshall stated, for the following reasons: (1) Chinese nationalism would not allow it; (2) the United States did not have sufficient personnel; (3) the economic costs might be limitless; (4) it would entail an extremely long-term commitment; (5) once committed, the United States could not withdraw; and (6) it would make China the focus of United States–Soviet contention and might lead to a repeat of the Spanish Civil War on a larger scale. Making such a commitment, he argued, would dissipate American strength and render it ineffective everywhere. Yet to not help the Nationalists would make the United States vulnerable to the charge that it was responsible for the demise of the Chinese government—"a death blow, almost." To give the Nationalists one last chance, to fulfill a perceived moral commitment, and to save the European aid program, the administration decided to aid the Kuomintang despite the slim chance that it would do anything but "prolong the agony."[42]

Though there were sincere attempts to arrest the decline of the Kuomintang, especially by Chiang's son, Chiang Ching-kuo, its problems multiplied. Inflationary pressures increased, destroying the savings of the wealthy and the small middle class, many of whom backed the Kuomintang. Widespread rice riots broke out in the summer of 1948, as rice that sold for 6.3 million *yuan* in May jumped to 63 million *yuan* in August. Even in this critical situation the Chinese resisted any and all attempts by the United States to get them to provide accountability for aid, thereby slowing the implementation of American programs.

In November 1948, with his armies in the north crumbling around him, largely through wide-scale defections, Chiang Kai-shek prepared to leave the mainland. The first "domino" had fallen. Henceforth withdrawal from a client would become virtually impossible because of the domestic finger-pointing over blame for the loss of China. American foreign policy would never be the same.[43]

Conclusions

The Truman administration has been much criticized for its promotion of inappropriate political institutions in China. This charge has some truth in retrospect, but the reformist intervention was not simply based on a blindly idealistic attempt to remake that nation in the American image. There was a pragmatic aspect to the promotion of pluralistic values: the United States was seeking the inclusion of alternative leadership groups in order to constrain the arbitrary use of power by the Kuomintang, which was alienating the populace, and the promotion of mass mobilization through redistributive reforms that were being blocked by the party's right wing. Those who argue that the United States should have concentrated only on technical and economic reforms ignore the leadership problem in the Kuomintang: right-wing dominance and the failure of elite reforms also blocked technical and economic reforms.

The Kuomintang was not against these reforms because they were Western ideas per se, but because they called for power-sharing with other groups and economic and political participation for the masses, concepts that were alien to the dominant faction's fundamental view of politics. Other Chinese, however, including the left wing of the Kuomintang and the Third Party Group, favored such changes, though in widely divergent forms. The CCP also adopted a similar short-term political strategy, picking up disaffected elites and mass support in the process. The Kuomintang did not just passively exclude much of Chinese society; it actively alienated it. This created a political vacuum that the CCP filled, but if it had not, it is probable that some other group or groups eventually would have done so. One thing is clear, however: the liberal groups in China were not numerous, powerful, or ruthless enough to fill the political vacuum of the chaos of Republican China, even with American help.

The most glaring weakness in the American approach to China in the 1940s, for both bolsterers and reformers, was that it assumed a potential coherence and effectiveness of Chinese governmental institutions that did not even approximate the reality of the Kuomintang. That party had all of the disadvantages of a totalitarian regime and none of its alleged short-term advantages in efficiency in decision-making. For the most part, Chiang simply could not get his orders obeyed with any regularity. His own separation from the political and economic realities of his government's policies reinforced his inclination to crush all dissent with force. Despite all the talk of its "great leader," "revolutionary spirit," and grandiose aims, in the aftermath of World

War II the Kuomintang was basically an amalgamation of antagonistic groups in which personal, family, and factional gain was the primary basis of political activity. Though there were honest and talented *individuals* in the Kuomintang, they were incapable of creating effective political organizations or factions. Those most organized, the right wing, were those least likely to effect the changes necessary to garner support outside of the party and the most likely to create extra-party opposition.

Chiang stayed in power in the short term by balancing off these mutually exclusive forces. He lost power in the long term because this approach to leadership left him with an impotent government incapable of providing legitimate authority or hope to the average Chinese that the admittedly huge problems facing China would be solved. No reasonable amount of U.S. aid without reform could ever have overcome this fundamental weakness.

It is impossible to escape the conclusion that Marshall was in over his head in attempting to manipulate Chinese domestic forces toward acceptance of American policy goals. With withdrawal considered impossible in the immediate postwar years, and bolstering made impossible by the corruption and incompetence of the Kuomintang, Marshall saw no reasonable possibility for U.S. policy other than a reformist intervention. When it became apparent that reforms would not be implemented in 1947–1948, he reluctantly advocated withdrawal, while covering that policy with minimal aid.

The reluctance of the United States to withdraw because of the burgeoning bipolarity of the Cold War, and the Nationalists' recognition of this, undermined American leverage. Yet the careless use of commitments also had a deleterious effect. Clearly the attempt to split the commitment by granting economic but not military aid fogged the extent of potential U.S. intervention and convinced the Nationalists, correctly in the short term, that the United States would not withdraw. But it also apparently convinced the Chinese, incorrectly in the long term, that the Americans were more willing to bolster the Kuomintang than was the case. Thus, unclear and incoherent commitments did not serve the interests of either the patron or the client well.

Bureaucratic wrangling and domestic elements in favor of bolstering also seriously undermined leverage. Yet this was but a reflection of the incoherence of American policy goals: the United States did not withdraw because it could not, given internal and external pressures, and Chiang came to realize this; it did not bolster because it could not, given the inefficiencies, incompetence, and corruption of the regime, and still follow higher priority goals in other areas. Unable to withdraw or bolster, the United States aimed for a middle policy of "staying with the situation" which, given the weaknesses of the Kuomintang, meant a reformist intervention so that it could *eventually* bolster the Chinese government. This the United States could not do, partly because it could not credibly threaten to withdraw. This was the essential policy dilemma that was never solved in terms of leverage.

Though the Americans, especially U.S. political officials, came to understand this dilemma, they largely felt there was nothing they could do to arrest the situation. In retrospect, it was a major mistake for the State Department, and especially Marshall, not to have explained the situation to the American people. If the China White Paper of August 1949 had been released in August 1946, some of the political volcanoes of the McCarthy period might have been avoided, or at least attenuated. But that would have involved American officials' washing their hands of the problem, something they refused to do because of the fear of Soviet expansion, a concern over possible regional instability, a perceived moral commitment to alleviate the chaos and suffering of the Chinese people, and an excessively optimistic belief that something could be done about the situation.

It is the curse—and the charm—of an American to believe that there is always a solution to every problem. United States officials continued to believe, long after there was much evidence to the contrary, that *at some point* the Kuomintang would adopt the pragmatic, pluralistic American point of view. Marshall might have done better to act in a more ruthless manner with the Kuomintang and the CCP, and worry less about the suffering in China. That he did not, however, says much for his essential humanity. If there was any American naiveté in China in the 1940s, it was that Marshall believed that if the Chinese, Nationalist or Communist, told him something they meant it. But for these two groups, acting in their own interests, the American was an unwelcome intrusion that both attempted to manipulate for their own purposes.

Perhaps the best postmortem of United States China policy was made by John Carter Vincent, one of its architects and most tragic victims. Writing to his brother in 1951, in the midst of defending himself against various charges from the political right in seemingly interminable congressional hearings, he offered a succinct overview of the fall of Republican China:

> There never was a time when we could have saved China for Chiang Kai-shek without going into the country with a large army and literally establishing a protectorate. The historical tragedy is that the rise of Communism coincided with the complete deterioration of the Nationalist Government. Revolution there would have been. We tried to make it a liberal one but the odds were against us.[44]

THE PHILIPPINES
1950–1953

III

Saving the Philippine Republic, 1950–1951

6

The Philippine Islands were America's only official colony. When independence came on July 4, 1946, United States decision-makers were well aware that events in the Philippines would be seen, in Southeast Asia and elsewhere, as indicative of American intentions throughout the developing world. Therefore, in addition to sentimental, moral, economic, and historical attachments, there were Cold War considerations in that country that included American prestige in a unique way. Policy choices must also be seen within the context of the American desire that its European allies (Great Britain, Holland, and France) divest themselves of their colonies in Southeast Asia in a peaceful manner to prevent growing nationalism in that area from turning toward Communism. In late 1945, some within the U.S. government counseled postponing Filipino independence because of the chaotic conditions resulting from an especially harsh Japanese occupation, and the fierce fighting that ensued in that nation during the final months of the war, but the regional and ideological context created strong pressures to go forward.[1]

These fears were not unfounded. In those areas of Southeast Asia where decolonization went fairly smoothly, relatively moderate nationalist groups dominated; where it did not, despite efforts to convince the French of the need for such action in Indochina, the extreme left eventually dominated. The Philippines thus became a linchpin for much of U.S. policy in Asia primarily for a mixture of security and ideological reasons. It was to be, in the phrase of the day, a "showcase of democracy" in that region.

American colonial policy in the Philippines aimed at "attraction," that is, a relatively benign colonial rule leading to gradual democratic development, and ultimate independence. This policy offered new opportunities for political participation for Filipinos in comparison to

Spanish rule, but these opportunities were carefully circumscribed and were limited, in effect, to the economic elite. Yet, relative to other colonial powers, the United States also brought progress to its colony. This created difficulties for Filipino nationalists attempting to stoke the fires of anti-American sentiment. Manuel Quezon, leader of the Nacionalista Party and advocate of independence, once exclaimed in frustration: "Damn the Americans, why don't they tyrannize us more?"[2]

Democratic development under American tutelage was gradual. In 1907, the United States set up the first popularly elected legislature in Southeast Asia, though it retained a veto power over legislation until 1913. In 1916, suffrage was extended to all literate males. In addition to these political reforms, which should be viewed within the context of the ethnocentrism of the times, the United States modernized and extended public education, secularized the state, built roads, bridges, and other elements of infrastructure, and also created health and sanitation facilities to improve the conditions of the common people. In the economic sphere, Filipino products were given preferential treatment by the United States, especially sugar and coconuts. Although this policy was well-intentioned, it allowed for the perpetuation of the agrarian elite and a growing concentration on commercial rather than subsistence agriculture that plagues the Philippines to this day.

The policy, moreover, was filled with contradictions: the political structures were dominated by an economic elite who were largely averse to a greater expansion of social and political reform. Thus, the Americans were involved enough in Filipino politics to make a difference, but not enough to transform that society.[3] These trends were only exacerbated during the Great Depression, and rural unrest was rampant by the mid-1930s. Quezon, partly inspired by the New Deal, put forth moderate reforms that were imperfectly implemented.[4]

The Philippines were crippled during the Japanese occupation in World War II. Since resistance to Japanese rule was the strongest in Southeast Asia, Japanese atrocities were also among the worst there. Most of the active resistance, however, came from the common people, not the elites, many of whom collaborated with Japan. The most active resistance centered around two groups: those who served exclusively with the United States in creating an intelligence network and performing sabotage, commonly referred to as "Guerrillistas"; and those who served with the Communist-led guerrillas based primarily in central Luzon, the "People's Anti-Japanese Army," or, in its Tagalog acronym, "Hukbalahap"—the Huks.[5] Both groups fought bravely and faced death on a daily basis. In the early 1950s, they would become powerful political forces: the former rallying around the reform movement of Ramon

Magsaysay, who was one of them; the latter rallying around the leadership of the Philippine Communist Party (PCP).

The United States set up various commissions to determine postwar financial needs and assess claims, and passed the Philippine Rehabilitation Act of 1946 to aid in the restoration of public property and basic public services. It granted relatively large amounts of military supplies in order to aid in the maintenance of internal order, to pave the way for post-independence armed forces capable of protecting the republic, and to free U.S. troops for occupation duty in Japan. The United States granted $120 million for the repair of roads, port and harbor facilities, and other infrastructure projects, $100 million to aid "existing governmental units," and $400 million for the restoration of private property destroyed in the war. Payments were also made to the Guerrillistas for services rendered during the war.

Two points should be made about these arrangements: (1) the U.S. Congress tied them to passage of the Bell Trade Act of 1946 by placing a limit on overall payments of War Damage unless the act was accepted; and (2) some unscrupulous Filipinos and Americans took advantage of the programs for their own undeserved profit. The Bell Trade Act was, to say the least, a most ungenerous treatment of a battered ally. American exports to the Philippines were to be duty-free and of unlimited quantity for eight years, followed by a gradual implementation of a tariff. Filipino exports to the United States, however, were subject to absolute quotas, including the most important agricultural products. Given the economic disparity between the two nations, this was an exploitive arrangement.

In the case of Filipino misuse of the Guerrillista payment program, huge numbers of Filipinos claimed to have been fighting the Japanese throughout the war, whereas there was no conceivable way they all could have done so. Some Filipino officials were later convicted of misuse of War Damage funds. These developments convinced many U.S. officials that the Filipinos were ungrateful; they convinced many Filipinos that the Americans were ungrateful. The War Damage and corruption issues would remain alive through much of the postwar period, exacerbating tensions on both sides.[6]

Decision-making: Bolstering and Growing Postwar Instability

From 1945 to 1949, U.S. policy was primarily aimed at bolstering the prewar political institutions of the Philippines. There was only a limited

American concern, for example, with the 1946 election between the Nacionalista and Liberal parties. The elections were characterized by sporadic violence as the Liberal party won a majority in the congress. Liberals Manuel Roxas and Elpidio Quirino were elected president and vice-president respectively. Following the election, the Liberals passed legislation revising the constitution to allow for the Bell Trade Act, but excluded, illegally and quite probably on the basis of false charges, ten opposition members for vote fraud.[7]

On April 15, 1948, President Roxas died while touring Clark Air Force Base. He was succeeded by Vice-President Quirino, a man with little support within the Liberal party or with the populace. Quirino's first approach to the growing insurgency was to attempt a negotiated settlement. When this failed, widespread, open fighting between insurgents and the Filipino government spread. A situation developed similar to that in China: the Huks demanded political reforms, *then* military concessions; the government demanded military concessions, *then* political reforms. On September 13, 1948, Quirino declared the Huks in a "state of rebellion."[8]

In light of the growing instability, it appeared that the extra-governmental opposition was being radicalized. As the insurgency grew throughout 1949, the Philippine Constabulary (a national police force), the Civilian Guards (loosely trained militia, sometimes complemented by so-called "private police," the latter usually paid by large landowners), and the armed forces increasingly alienated the populace. There were increasing reports of cooperation between the Filipino people, rich and poor, and the Huks. Growing numbers granted the Huks sanctuary and monetary support in order to be left alone. There were also reports of some Constabulary units reaching similar agreements with the Communists.[9] As if this were not enough, there was a series of corruption scandals within the Liberal party, greatly increasing intra-party strife. The United States, adhering to its generally bolstering policy through 1949, watched in dismay as the Liberals publicly struggled over control of the party and the government, which seriously lowered civilian morale.[10]

Decision-making: The China Analogy

Many in the State Department began applying analogies from the fall of China to the Filipino context in 1949. Growing instability in the Philippines, and throughout Southeast Asia, created pressure on the United States to do something to prevent the rise of Communism in the region. Early in 1949, President Truman instructed Secretary of

State Dean Acheson to construct an aid plan for the Philippines that avoided the corruption of the War Damage claims.

The lessons of China and the paradoxical role of commitment in the bargaining relationship had begun to take hold in official Washington, especially in the Far Eastern Division of the State Department. Diplomats were increasingly skeptical about bolstering as a prescription for faltering client governments. As early as March 1949, the Southeast Asian desk at the State Department had argued that "[the American] experience in China has shown that the extension of external assistance [alone] . . . is not an effective means for encouraging a country to face squarely its problems with the determination to help itself."[11] Various meetings through the spring and summer were therefore dominated by discussions of ways to promote elite and redistributive reforms in the Philippines through a quid pro quo use of commitments.

Despite the China experience, these plans were as yet only vague outlines. In mid-August, 1949, Secretary Acheson ordered further study of the problem.[12] Plans were also made that summer for greater levels of military aid within the context of growing alarm over the growth of Chinese-inspired Communist movements in Southeast Asia.[13]

Decision-making: The 1949 Election

As the fall 1949 Filipino election drew near, American alarm increased. "Extraordinarily heavy" deficit spending, growing Huk activity and general lawlessness, abuses of the populace by the Constabulary and Civilian Guards, and continued factional strife among Liberals contributed to a sense of pessimism. On October 21, the State Department's Richard Ely, the head of the Philippines and Southeast Asia desk, wrote to a colleague: "A serious situation is developing."[14]

As their political position deteriorated, Quirino and his Liberal loyalists turned to physical attacks on the opposition to ensure victory in the election. Throughout the late summer and early fall of 1949, the American embassy received constant reports of violence. The advantage rested with the Liberals, since Quirino had broad police and patronage powers that the others lacked. In September, he replaced Constabulary commanders in the provinces who were considered neutral with party loyalists. He then set up paramilitary organizations comprised of newly released criminals, under the control of his brother Antonio, who were given arms and promised presidential pardons. In addition, Quirino promised each loyal congressman 400,000 pesos in "pork barrel" projects (money the government did not have), manipulated the distribution of election inspectors to his benefit, and promised the Guerrillistas further payments from the United States, though he had been specifically told this was not possible by the Americans.[15]

Violence and corruption in the 1949 election were heaviest in Cebu, Negros Occidental, and the provinces of central Luzon, where Quirino's forces were closely aligned with large landowners. The rural areas suffered the most; roving bands of Constabulary, Civilian Guards, and government-armed criminal elements randomly fired into many barrios to intimidate the populace. In many areas polling places were moved to distant points at the last moment in order to make it harder for people to vote. Registration lists were padded to comic proportions; in some districts the number of votes equaled the total population. Entire warehouses of valid ballots were openly set afire. According to reports from the southern provinces, voters were asked upon entering polling stations for whom they intended to vote. If they answered the Nacionalistas, they were told to leave. If they persisted, they were beaten. Some provincial newspapers were closed down. The voting in Manila was observed by the United States embassy and was considered generally fair—Nacionalista presidential candidate Jose Laurel won the city. In the provinces, however, violence and fraud were much the rule. Twenty-four people were killed and eighteen wounded on election day, but the widespread beatings and intimidation are not reflected in these statistics. Quirino won the election by 450,000 votes; the Liberals dominated both houses of congress.[16]

Both Americans and Filipinos were shocked at the events surrounding the election. Former President Sergio Osmena resigned his position on the ceremonial Council of State in protest, calling the election a "terrible travesty of the democratic process." One of the leading members of the Commission on Elections said simply, "There is no more democracy in the Philippines." The obvious fraud and violence bred a deep cynicism among the people, especially those in the provinces. In Lanao, the people wisecracked that even the birds, the trees, and the dead had voted for Quirino. The embassy noted a marked demoralization throughout Filipino society.[17] The United States had thus far followed a generally bolstering policy with the Filipino government following independence. This was about to end.

The political fallout from the 1949 election was even worse than predicted. By making false promises to virtually everyone, Quirino had raised expectations among important groups. The Guerrillistas were frustrated at the lack of promised payments from the United States; the released criminals were frustrated at the lack of employment and pardons that had been promised, though some were incorporated into the Constabulary and Civilian Guards; Nacionalista partisans were frustrated at their lack of a fair chance at the polls; and the general populace was frustrated at the lack of progress in reconstruction, the violence of the election, and increasing reports in the press of growing corruption in their government. Simultaneously, there was an armed uprising among the Moros in the Sulu archipelago, noted the embassy, that within a few weeks after the election had "gotten out of hand." All of these groups were armed to various degrees, and they took out their frustration and growing anger through increasing violence. Groups of roving bandits and angry dissidents sacked and looted the provinces. The position of the Filipino government grew increasingly precarious.[18]

Bargaining Behavior: Toward a Quid Pro Quo

The government in the Philippines reacted to the growing crisis by urgently requesting increased military aid. The State Department was in favor of granting it, given the growing violence, but it wanted an agreement for a joint military program with some decision-sharing with U.S. personnel serving with the Joint United States Military Assistance Group (JUSMAG).[19] On December 8, 1949, the Filipino government agreed in principle, and delivery was expedited throughout early 1950. Ambassador Myron Cowen, however, warned against a strictly military answer to the growing violence. The dissidents were too broadly based to handle with police methods, especially since the Constabulary and Civilian Guards were causing many of the problems.

Again, the experience in China appeared to provide a relevant analogy. The Filipinos, Cowen argued to Washington, had to learn the lessons of China and aim their policies at gaining the support of the people. He recognized that the situations were not exactly the same— there were "many heartening differences"—but the parallels were "too numerous for comfort." By March 1950, he was arguing that the United States must convince Quirino to implement elite and redistributive reforms through a quid pro quo or the chances for democracy would be destroyed in the Philippines.[20]

Within this context, President Quirino announced that he would travel to the United States for a physical examination at Johns Hopkins Hospital. He left for the United States on January 7, 1950. Before departing, however, he publicly stated that he was going to push for Guerrillista recognition and more veterans' benefits, presumably to lessen the dissident violence among those groups.

This was a sore point with the Americans. Truman had personally told Quirino in August 1949 that the Guerrillista issue was closed as far as the United States was concerned. The administration's growing irritation with Quirino over his public misrepresentation of this issue led to a policy review. The Treasury Department promoted the harshest view and pushed hard for a quid pro quo policy, especially in the economic field, and recommended that Truman "firmly advise" the Filipinos that no more aid would be forthcoming until a comprehensive reform program was under way. The Philippines, it argued, was relying too heavily on American aid.[21]

Quirino was given a cool reception in the United States, something that clearly upset him. After receiving negative responses to every request for aid in a meeting with President Truman, the Filipino president brought up an idea that had been proposed to him by Ambassador Cowen on Christmas night, 1949. Apparently to the surprise of the Americans, since he had been resisting the idea in Manila, Quirino suggested a United States economic mission, along the lines of the Dodge Mission to Japan, for the Philippines. Truman stated that he was "most interested" in this and that he would give it "the deepest and most sympathetic consideration." Plans were made to carry out negotiations with Ambassador Cowen. The final discussion was over Quirino's request for increased War Damage payments; Truman refused to consider them "at this time."[22]

Clearly Quirino was depressed over his lack of success at the meeting and his failed attempts to gain further commitments from the Americans. He had been telling friend and foe alike at home that he would garner greater aid to end the dissidence and solve his political problems. Though military aid was beginning to flow, the Americans had successfully demanded a say in the use of the funds and in the subsequent military planning through a quid pro quo bargaining approach. Following his meetings with Truman, Quirino went to Johns Hopkins Hospital, where he was told he was a sick man. The doctors told him to keep away from pressure and tension to the greatest possible extent. Unfortunately, the pressure at home was only beginning.

Decision-making: A "Revolutionary Situation"

American entreaties for elite reforms grew throughout early 1950. This was in direct relation to the growing insurgency and lawlessness in the Philippines. The embassy reported increasing Communist influence in labor unions and among peasant groups, and an apathy among groups previously friendly to the government. The most serious development, however, was the linking of the Huks with other armed dissident groups, including disaffected Nacionalista partisans and the government-armed criminals used in the election.

The embassy received reports, later confirmed by captured Communist documents, that leading members of the PCP were leaving Manila and joining friendly forces in the provinces to coordinate anti-government activity. The PCP, seemingly in conjunction with the call of the newly established People's Republic of China in November 1949 for the overthrow of non-Communist nationalists, enlarged its politburo and "confirmed the existence of a revolutionary situation." The Huks in Central Luzon began a series of attacks in coastal provinces, apparently, as the embassy reported, in anticipation of clandestine foreign aid from the Chinese Communists. The Filipino government's reaction was an increase in indiscriminate attacks by the Civilian Guards, Constabulary, and armed forces in relatively uncoordinated and large-scale military maneuvers. This strategy, as is often the case, served to create more dissidents than it destroyed through the inevitable excesses of the undisciplined troops, undermining support for the government even further.[23]

The situation deteriorated precipitously at the end of March 1950. On March 29, the eighth anniversary of the founding of the Huks, large-scale attacks occurred, including some within forty miles of Manila. For the next two days, they grew in scope and scale, placing the armed forces on the strategic defensive. On March 31, the embassy began seriously considering the evacuation of nonmilitary personnel. On the same day, San Pablo in Laguna Province, a city of 50,000 residents, was temporarily under the control of the insurgents. Acheson wired the embassy that Washington was "deeply concerned" over the turn of events and requested policy recommendations.[24]

On the following day, Quirino, who had declined to admit publicly the full seriousness of the situation, told a press conference that the Huks aimed at "the downfall of this country with the end in view of placing it under Communist influence." By mid-April, the situation had reached such a state that Secretary Acheson briefed President Truman on the economic and political deterioration. He told Truman that the United States would have to undertake a reformist intervention or risk "a rapid decline into chaos" in the Philippines, and possibly in the region.[25]

Bargaining Behavior: The Filipino Reaction and Initial Attempts at Elite Reforms

The Filipino reaction to American pressure for military reform was swift. Army General Mariano Castaneda, who was the Chief of Staff of the armed forces, and Defense Secretary Ruperto Kangleon bitterly complained of American attempts to tie increased military aid in a quid

pro quo to a planned reorganization of the armed forces and Constabulary. A cosmetic reform was carried out in April: the Constabulary was
again placed under the administrative control of the armed forces. This
reform was less than complete, however, because operational control
was placed in the hands of Interior Secretary Sotero Baluyot, an ultra-
conservative landowner and advocate of a military solution to the uprising.[26]

The activities of the armed forces and Constabulary were a growing
problem; the abuses of the populace had reached such a point by April
that Senator Tomas Confesor threatened to join the insurgents himself
if the indiscriminate repression in his province was not ended.[27] Because
of their obstruction of military reform, General Castaneda and Secretary
Kangleon became the objects of elite reform attempts by the United
States.

There was also an elite reform attempt by the United States at a
higher level. Though there had been a temporary reconciliation among
Liberals following the 1949 election, the deteriorating situation of early
1950, revelations concerning the activities of President Quirino and his
brother Antonio during that election, and new corruption scandals
revealed in the spring led virtually all of Quirino's party to abandon
him politically. Vice-President Lopez, a respected and relatively honest
politician, publicly broke with the president and, at the behest of the
Americans, privately asked him to "retire" for six months to allow
effective reforms to be put through. This clumsy attempt at elite reform
failed. When Quirino refused to leave, there was serious talk of impeachment among much of the Filipino political elite.

By late April, the embassy judged that an impeachment action would
pass in the Senate; the House, however, remained under Quirino's
control, largely because Speaker of the House Eugenio Perez was reportedly deeply involved in a Chinese Nationalist immigration scandal,
and Antonio Quirino had evidence of such involvement. Perez was a
powerful politician who was surrounded by a group of loyalists in the
House, including a young Liberal congressman, Ferdinand Marcos. As
long as Quirino retained the Speaker's support, he could not be forced
out through impeachment.

The Filipino government was paralyzed. The widespread disenchantment with the president made it unlikely that he could gather enough
support, even within his own party, to react effectively to the crisis
facing his society. In an attempt to overcome his loss of support in the
Senate, Quirino had Speaker Perez promulgate a bill in the House
giving him "limited extraordinary powers" in early May. He accompanied this request with a promise of a 100,000-peso "pork barrel"
project for every Liberal senator and congressman who voted for the

bill. Despite the fact that Quirino floated rumors that he would declare martial law if the bill were not passed, it was defeated in the Senate in June. The public and press reaction to this move, given the present abuses of the government, which was also approaching bankruptcy, was one of shock. A major impasse had been reached between the Senate and House. In the face of this apparent breakdown of legislative authority, the State Department decided to move.[28]

Decision-making: The United States Moves Further toward a Reformist Intervention

In early April, 1950, Ambassador Cowen was recalled to Washington for consultation. As noted earlier, the United States was showing new concern over Southeast Asia throughout late 1949 and early 1950. Within this context, a policy review was again undertaken in another inter-agency meeting in Washington.

The Americans saw the main problem as the leadership of Quirino, whom Cowen described as "incompetent, vain, stubborn, and unwilling to listen to his close advisers." The present government probably could not long survive with Quirino at the helm, he argued, since he had lost much political support even within his own party. Cowen recommended that "this Government undertake no further programs in the Philippines" until a time in which it was possible to determine "whether the growing discontent will lead to the necessary reforms or to chaos."[29]

The general consensus among those at the meeting, including the military, was that a strict quid pro quo approach toward aid was necessary to force the Filipino government into action. Aid granted under present conditions would be perceived as bolstering Quirino, an eventuality the United States wanted to avoid because it would further alienate the non-Communist opposition. At the same time, the deteriorating security situation demanded a greater response. It was decided that the United States must intervene for reformist purposes in the Philippines. Any commitments had to be met with assurances *and* demonstrations that U.S. aid would be well spent.[30]

The embassy in Manila agreed with the "get tough" approach and strongly backed a quid pro quo, reformist approach. On the day of the meeting, First Secretary Vinton Chapin wrote Cowen that the United States had two options with Quirino: (1) a "hands off" approach (bolstering); or (2) making aid conditional on actions that would be clearly and publicly specified "to force him into less suicidal paths" of behavior (reform). Chapin wrote that the embassy had learned that the United

States had recently "laid down the law" to the Greek and Korean governments on reform. He suggested having the State Department send a "similar riot act . . . to be read to Quirino." Secretary Acheson passed on this grave prognosis to President Truman on April 20. The actions of the United States after this date strongly suggest that Truman accepted the State Department's reformist prescription.[31]

Bargaining Behavior: Problems in Implementing the Quid Pro Quo

Following Ambassador Cowen's return to Manila on April 24, 1950, heavy pressure, including the threat of reduced aid, was put on Quirino to agree to a variety of reform measures: the acceptance of the Bell Mission to determine economic policies; a meaningful reorganization of the armed forces; measures to balance the budget; movement toward ending corruption; and additional elite reforms to replace individuals within the Filipino government who were considered incompetent and/or corrupt. At this point, the reforms were still largely aimed at political elites; the military leadership was temporarily spared. The problem was, as is often the case in patron-client bargaining over reforms, that the changes would hurt those members of the government who were still loyal to Quirino. The Filipino leader, not surprisingly, balked at carrying out the reforms in such an unstable political atmosphere.

The bargaining between Cowen and Quirino continued throughout May and June, with notable success for the United States only in the acceptance of the Bell Mission in mid-May in reaction to the threat to withhold all economic aid without such an agreement. This was an important point for the United States; the State Department's John Melby stated that Truman was "very insistent" that the mission get under way. Only after the most blunt and unbending quid pro quo diplomacy was it accepted by the Filipinos. As one indication of how difficult and tense the negotiations were, Quirino, a proud and emotional man, burst into tears when he told Cowen of his acquiescence. He promised he would call a special session of the congress on June 15 and that he could get any reform measures the United States wanted. Given Quirino's political weakness, the State Department labeled this statement "sheer nonsense." To deal with corruption, Quirino named an "integrity board," but then announced that it could only offer suggestions, not make policy.[32] Implementation of the reformist intervention was proving more difficult than originally expected, as the Filipino leadership generally held its ground and stalled for time.

Decision-making: Dealing with Domestic and International Pressures

It was demonstrated in the China case that domestic and international political pressures had a great effect on American decision-making. The Truman administration, therefore, felt compelled to relieve some of its domestic criticism in the wake of the fall of China. It continued the high-level pressure on the Filipinos, making further aid contingent on acceptance of reforms. In contrast to China policy, however, the administration kept Congress informed of the seriousness of the situation and the actions it was taking. Acting Secretary of State James Webb briefed Senator Tom Connally, for example, and told him that the Philippines was crucial to American policy in the entire Far East. Quirino, he stated, wanted a "blank check and no questions asked" bolstering approach to aid, which would lead to disaster. If the Philippines did not become a "showcase of democracy," the British, French, and Dutch would not listen to American advice on capturing nationalist movements for the West. The "Philippine experiment must succeed," said Webb, "at any cost." This approach worked. In contrast to the China experience, Congress was generally supportive of the Truman administration's policy decisions in the Philippines.[33] Thus, domestic constraints were not as evident as they had been in the earlier case.

Though the United States was making plans for a reformist intervention, it did not yet have the internal consensus or political will to do this in the early summer of 1950. International events, including the rise of armed Communist insurgents in most of the countries of Southeast Asia, led to a growing consensus that there was a regional threat to American interests. The State Department became even more alarmed in early June when, for the first time, the Soviets devoted an entire article in a propaganda journal to the Huk insurgency. An American diplomat in Bangkok noted that this particular journal did not comment on such developments until the Soviet Union believed there was a good chance of success for its favored side.[34]

The event that galvanized United States policy toward the region, however, was the outbreak of the Korean War on June 25, 1950. Any doubts over the importance of Southeast Asia to American security were whisked away with the outbreak of war, and Congress became more amenable to providing the resources necessary for more ambitious economic and security programs in the region. Within weeks, the Bell Economic Mission (to the Philippines) and the Melby Military Mission (to all of Southeast Asia) were dispatched to devise programs to avoid the advent of Communism in friendly countries. The United States, however, was not going to expend scarce resources unless the recipient government had the capacity to utilize them effectively.[35] Reform in the Philippines took on even greater importance. It seemed to many that drastic changes were necessary, and soon.

The alarm over the security of the region that arose from the Korean War was increased in early July when an American deserter fighting with the Huks, Private Ronald Dorsey, surrendered to the Filipino government. Dorsey informed his American interrogators that the Huks were growing in strength and receiving funds and sanctuary from local officials and wealthy Filipinos. He claimed that the rebels not only made tacit agreements with the Constabulary to avoid combat, but knew of armed forces and Constabulary plans well in advance. The Huks were having no problems in recruitment because of the abuses by the various military forces. More ominously, Dorsey claimed that the Filipino Communists were in direct contact with both Moscow and Peking, and had Chinese Communists advising them in the field. Though there was no hard evidence of these latter claims, the possibility that a concentrated, international Communist movement was sweeping Southeast Asia added to the growing sense of urgency. On July 18, Acheson instructed Cowen to grill Dorsey most closely on the Soviet and Chinese roles in the Filipino insurgency,[36] though no further information was apparently forthcoming.

Bargaining Behavior: A Quid Pro Quo and a Reformist Intervention

The outbreak of war in Korea also created a war scare in the Philippines, especially with the initial losses of the allied forces in July. This caused the opposition to rally around Quirino temporarily. In order to take advantage of this renewed coalescence, and to attend to some of the problems that came to light through the Dorsey disclosures, the United States exerted intense pressure on Quirino in July through a quid pro quo to force him to incorporate the Constabulary and Civilian Guards fully into the armed forces in order to increase organizational efficiency, stop intelligence leaks, and end abuses of the populace.

In a new bargaining approach, in contrast to the China case, the United States did not split its overall commitment between economic and military programs. Instead, it broke down its commitments into component parts—that is, the overall commitment remained, but specific reforms were directly tied to specific aid programs in a quid pro quo. This approach quickly bore fruit. On July 26, 1950, Quirino ordered the Constabulary incorporated into the armed forces; on July 27 the United States delivered a major shipment of military supplies it had made contingent on this reform.[37]

This close association of aid and reform established a pattern for future agreements: commitments for aid were not implemented until commitments for reform were implemented. By breaking down the overall reform requests into increments, and placing them on a priority basis, the United States could get Quirino to go along without seeming to hand over the reins of government to the Americans. Pressure was usually administered privately to avoid loss of face. In addition, the fears raised by the Korean War, and reports of links between the Huks and the Chinese Communists, even if not true, apparently underscored to Quirino his dependence on further American aid. Within this context, U.S. pressure for reform and quid pro quo bargaining were beginning to work.

Decision-making: The Filipino Government Nears Collapse

Because of the increased Cold War tensions in Asia, the United States began to analyze more systematically the problems facing the Quirino government. Military reforms that would lessen abuses of the populace were only one part of what was envisioned as a comprehensive program. On August 10, for example, the CIA issued a secret report calling for widespread political, economic, and social reforms to prevent a Communist insurgent victory. With the Bell Mission studying the economic problems, however, the United States concentrated on military reforms during July and August of 1950. Because the alienation of the public was so deep, a major overhaul of the entire Filipino defense structure was deemed necessary.[38]

A major crisis arose in August 1950, when Secretary of Defense Kangleon began to criticize President Quirino and General Castaneda publicly because of some promotion scandals and continuing widespread reports of extortion by the Constabulary and Civilian Guards even though they were now under armed forces control. As in China, the Filipino army was promoting ineffective, corrupt, and inefficient officers because of their personal relations to important political figures and local officials, not because of their expertise on the battlefield. When it became obvious that Kangleon would be fired, Quirino moved to name Teofilo Sison, a notorious collaborator during the war who had been convicted of treason, to the post of Secretary of Defense.

The United States vigorously protested the prospective appointment of Sison; Speaker of the House Perez, who had presidential ambitions for 1953, also objected strenuously because Sison would be totally dependent on Quirino. Quirino reacted to Perez's objections by publicly calling for an investigation of the Speaker's finances, strongly implying they had been greatly improved in the Chinese immigration scandal of 1949, in which visas had been sold to fleeing supporters of the Kuomintang during the collapse of the Chinese Nationalist regime. When word reached Perez of this, he called for a recess, and then eventual postponement of the congressional session.

Perez was, noted the embassy, "fighting mad." The Filipino diplomat Carlos Romulo told the embassy that Perez had warned Quirino on August 21 that if he did not step down he would be impeached. On August 23, Cowen wired Washington that intelligence sources suggested that Quirino would likely soon fire Secretary Kangleon and assume the Defense portfolio himself in order to defy any impeachment attempt by the congress. A few days later, the Huks launched major offensives in some provinces, with reports of attack forces of 1,000 men. In Tarlac, they attacked the Constabulary camp and hospital, raping the nurses and slaughtering them along with doctors, patients, and attendants. In a public argument over responsibility for the attacks, Secretary Kangleon resigned. Within the context of these dramatic developments, and to preclude, in effect, a military coup, the United States decided to act.[39]

Bargaining Behavior: The Quid Pro Quo and Elite Reform: Enter Ramon Magsaysay

American officials, in both Washington and Manila, had been promoting the fortunes of a young Liberal congressman from Zambales, Ramon Magsaysay. At the end of August, they strongly pressured Quirino to accept Magsaysay as Secretary of Defense. The congressman was a Guerrillista, chairman of the Defense Committee in the House, and a popular figure among Liberals. Though Quirino was friendly toward the young man from the countryside, he argued that he was not cabinet timber.

Yet Quirino came under intense pressure to appoint Magsaysay as Secretary of Defense from internal and external sources: a quid pro quo on military aid from the United States, and political threats from his own party loyalists, led by Speaker Perez, who told Quirino that they would block military appropriations if it were not done.[40] Thus, Quirino's political weakness, together with internal and external pressures within the context of regional tension, dissuaded him from an appointment that might have meant the end of civil government in the Philippines.

The appointment of Magsaysay was a turning point in the insurgency.

The new Secretary of Defense was an energetic, efficient, honest, and, in his own way, charismatic leader who rejuvenated the Defense Department through wide-scale reforms. A week after his appointment, CIA agent and Air Force Colonel Edward Lansdale returned to the Philippines. This marked the beginning of one of the most unusual relationships in the history of American diplomacy. Lansdale and Magsaysay became the closest of friends (they literally lived together at Camp Murphy following death threats against the latter and his family) and worked together in a symbiotic collaboration that led to a creative approach to the military and political problems in the Philippines.

The respective roles of Magsaysay and Lansdale remain shrouded in controversy. Though it was believed within the CIA, and by later critics of American policy, that Lansdale "invented" Magsaysay, this is an incorrect, ethnocentric, and rather arrogant interpretation. Though Lansdale was not, at times, above exaggerating his own role in the successful counterinsurgency, he was also willing to apportion the credit, decrying those who seemed "to describe a mysterious role for me which I don't deserve. Magsaysay and I were as close as brothers . . . but he was more than able to make up his own mind, do his own planning, and do battle for the things he believed in." Lansdale also chastised those Americans who "simply cannot conceive of an Asian being a real man in his own right."[41] D. Michael Shafer has made the equally unfounded, opposite argument that it was Magsaysay alone who devised and carried out the reforms—against American advice![42]

Lansdale contributed an imaginative approach to psychological warfare and intelligence-gathering; Magsaysay contributed a knowledge of and sympathy for the common people that led him to take actions to curb the arbitrary and abusive practices of the armed forces, Constabulary, Civilian Guards, and the "private police" of the large landlords. Benedict Kerkvliet's interviews with former Huks make it clear that the key factors in their defeat were the *combination* of the charisma of Magsaysay, the attractiveness of American aid programs, the popularity of the reform of military abuses, and the resulting improvement in the effectiveness of the armed forces.[43]

Magsaysay's military reforms were numerous and profoundly changed the organizational structure and performance of the armed forces. In part because of continuing pressure from Lansdale, the new JUSMAG Chief General Leland Hobbs, and Ambassador Cowen, Quirino gave the new Secretary of Defense impressive powers of promotion and court martial. Magsaysay flew around the country on surprise inspections, firing officers on the spot if they seemed lax or ineffective. He submerged the Constabulary under armed forces control, lessened the power of the Civilian Guards, and reorganized the army into Battalion Combat Teams, which were enlarged infantry battalions with artillery, heavy weapons, and service units.

This last development was a most important one; the Battalion Combat Teams were self-contained, mobile units of 1,000 men who did not have to forage or steal from the peasants to survive. They also spent the majority of their time in the field, not in the garrisoned towns. Patrols were carried out not by large, cumbersome, and ultimately unwieldy military forces, but by smaller, more efficient units that were much less likely to scare or alienate the local populace. Magsaysay and his team also initiated the widespread use of Scout Rangers, five-man squads utilized to locate the base areas of the enemy.

In addition to organizational reforms, Magsaysay established a ten-centavo rate for telegrams to his office telling of armed forces abuses; created free legal assistance for poor farmers; offered rewards for turning in firearms and the provision of intelligence; and created the organizational machinery for the resettlement of Huk defectors. The social reforms were never completely implemented. The psychological advantage they gave the government, however, seriously undercut support for the Huks. This can be seen in the reduction of Huk military strength over the next five years: almost as many surrendered as were killed or captured. Though it would take months for the full effects of the military reforms to be felt, effective elite reform meant the military problems of the Philippines were on the way to solution.[44]

Decision-making: The Bell Mission and Planning for Redistributive Reforms

The Bell Economic Mission had arrived in Manila in mid-July, 1950. On August 31, Daniel Bell, the head of the mission, wired Washington, in anticipation of his full report, that the Quirino government would collapse if it did not receive an immediate loan of $20–30 million. He reiterated the nearly unanimous belief among mission members that widespread redistributive reforms were necessary to produce a stable society in the Philippines. In view of the dangerous situation in Asia, wrote Bell, the United States must grant the aid, but those funds must be placed on a strictly quid pro quo basis in order to effect needed economic, political, and social reforms. Secretary of State Acheson briefed President Truman on Bell's telegram on September 1. The following day, the President told Acheson that he agreed on the need for aid and reform, and said: "We will discuss it as soon as we have further information and see if we can't arrange to save the Philippine Republic."[45]

Daniel Bell reported to the President in person on September 11, 1950. He outlined the depressing details of the inefficiency, corruption, and antipathy toward the common people that characterized the Quirino government. He set a priority list of reforms that he believed would have to be carried out that included "competent and vigorous military action" along with redistributive reforms, that is, an integrated political and military strategy of reform and repression. Bell also told Truman that there was little hope of further high-level elite reforms, and that therefore Americans would have to assume key positions in the Filipino government. He recommended granting $250 million over five years, "supervised and administered" by American personnel. Truman was "most interested" in the report and "horrified at the situation" Bell described. The decision had been made at the top of the United States government, rather than within its bureaus, to reform the government of the Philippines.[46] In the event, the United States did not have to assume direction of Filipino affairs. Because of the success of the reformist intervention, to the surprise of many Americans, the Filipinos quickly learned to fend for themselves.

Within weeks, the administration received further support for reform with the report of the Melby Military Mission on September 29, 1950. The choice of John Melby, a foreign service officer with recent experience in the China debacle, to head a military mission was an important one. He and Ambassador Cowen saw to it that the military members of the mission were well-briefed on the interrelationship of the political, military, economic, and social elements of the insurgency. The Melby Mission's report, therefore, reflected a political component that otherwise might have been missing, and concluded: "The military problems of the country are complementary to the [economic and political] problems."[47]

Melby and his colleagues advocated an increased military program in the Philippines, but in conjunction with other reforms to get at the underlying causes of the insurgency. In contrast to the China case, the necessity for military *and* political reforms was emphasized by both the American military, which had previously been advocating a more bolstering policy, and the State Department. Thus, the client government was not confused over American resolve in maintaining the quid pro quo.[48] In addition to the Treasury, State, and Pentagon consensus on the need for a reformist intervention, the CIA was also strongly in favor of such a program.[49] This united front within the bureaus of the U.S. government was a key to the successful reformist intervention in the Philippines.

Truman's decision of September 11 culminated in NSC Document 84/2 on November 9, 1950, which called for a major overhaul of the armed forces, adoption of the redistributive reforms recommended by the Bell Mission, and increased aid levels "contingent upon the institution of . . . reforms by the Philippine Government." Recognizing that "extreme care" must be exercised in persuading the Filipino government to take necessary action, the report called for "the reassertion of U.S. influence to the extent required to eliminate prevalent corruption, provide efficient administrative services, and restore public faith in the concept of government in the best interests of the people."[50]

Bargaining Behavior: The Quid Pro Quo of the Quirino-Foster Agreement

The Filipinos were aware of and apprehensive about the Bell Mission's recommendations, and the likelihood of future pressures for reform. The Filipino government complained publicly about the charges of corruption and objected to any U.S. supervision of aid programs. In a particularly bitter outburst, Quirino's private secretary, Federico Mangahas, publicly complained of American hypocrisy on October 25, 1950. The Filipinos were "mere pikers" when compared to "the stink familiar and now taken for granted in Washington," said Mangahas. The United States must accept that the Filipinos "cannot be bullied to accept that their friends, however well-meaning and altruistic, have cornered all the stock there is of efficiency, competence, vision and integrity in the world."[51] Though Quirino disavowed the statement, it was clear that he agreed with its message.

The Filipino government also made contacts with the American Legion in the United States to lobby for military aid. This attempt at counter-pressure failed; the virulence of the Mangahas statement caused widespread criticism of Quirino in the Filipino press and Congress. The United States, far from deterred, saw that the quid pro quo was already beginning to show results, especially in the area of elite reforms: at the end of September Quirino reshuffled his cabinet, making new appointments partly at the behest of Ambassador Cowen.

The security situation also remained serious. Though Magsaysay was going forward with his military reforms (he court-martialed nine officers in November 1950 for extortion, illegal confiscation of rice from the peasants, selling arms, and falsification of public documents), the United States received reports of wealthy Filipinos withdrawing funds and depositing them in the American banks. Despite Filipino resentment, the United States went ahead with its pressure for reform.[52]

In November 1950, Truman sent William Foster, the head of the newly created Economic Cooperation Administration (ECA), to negotiate with Quirino. After intense quid pro quo bargaining, an agreement was reached on November 14. The Quirino government committed itself to balancing the budget with a more equitable tax code, establishing a minimum wage to raise the standard of living for the average industrial and agricultural worker, and carrying out the redistributive reforms outlined in the Bell Report. In return, the United States committed itself to provide technical assistance (especially in tax collection, social legislation, and economic reform), to provide advisory personnel for the various programs, and to grant $250 million in economic assistance over "several years" as proposed in the Bell Report. The United States continued to make its commitments contingent on Filipino actions; funds were to be released only when the Filipino government kept its end of the bargain.[53]

Decision-making: The Security Situation

At the end of 1950, the United States could take some satisfaction from the programs it had promoted in the Philippines: military reforms were quickly putting the Huks on the defensive; Filipino governmental commitments to redistributive reform were relieving some of the underlying causes of the insurgency; and the basic organizational machinery had been created for a reformist intervention in Filipino affairs. Despite this progress, however, the security situation remained serious. On October 18, Lansdale and Magsaysay, acting on the defection of the Huk leader Taciano Rizal, the grandnephew of the Filipinos' greatest nationalist hero, Jose Rizal, raided PCP headquarters in Manila. This action delivered a heavy blow to the Huks: a total of 105 persons, including some politburo members, were arrested; five tons of documents were captured; and military supplies and propaganda materials were destroyed. The documents indicated that the Huks had been in contact with Chinese Communist representatives overseas and that they expected aid from them in the near future. The documents seriously alarmed the Quirino government because they showed a huge expansion of Huk organizations since January, and demonstrated that they had had contacts with government officials, including, the embassy suspected, Speaker of the House Perez.

Quirino was so shaken by these disclosures that he issued Proclamation 210 on October 21, which suspended the writ of habeas corpus under his emergency powers. The embassy was initially alarmed over this development, given Quirino's past performance, but acquiesced when Magsaysay assured the embassy that there would be no abuses of these powers by the armed forces. Most members of the congress agreed with the action, though they too were nervous about possible abuses.

The reaction in the United States, however, was highly negative; on October 24, the *Washington Post* editorialized: "The ugly truth is that the Quirino regime is bankrupt both morally and financially." In retaliation for the arrests of the politburo in Manila, the Huks struck back at Magsaysay's barrio in Zambales province by murdering twenty-two residents (men, women, and children), kidnapping ten, and burning thirty-four houses. The Secretary of Defense redoubled his efforts to invigorate the armed forces and put them on the offensive.[54] Things were improving, but there was no room for complacency.

Bargaining Behavior: A United Front for Implementation

Many of the decisions made and deals struck in the last half of 1950 had yet to be implemented. In the bargaining over implementation of the reforms, the United States decided on setting priorities: first, military reforms; then economic/social reforms; finally, political reforms. Though agreement had been reached in Washington as to the coordination of the activities of JUSMAG, the newly created ECA office in Manila, and the embassy, there was some rough sailing in the early months of 1951 among those bureaus in Washington. In general, the military played a relatively passive role, being understandably more concerned with the war in Korea; the ECA took the hardest line with the Quirino government, vocally protesting any aid delivered before reform legislation was passed and programs implemented; the State Department, which was given wide control over policy direction, oscillated between a hard and a soft line based on its perception of the political consequences of either approach.

Unlike the China case, the American policy debate in the Philippines therefore centered on the pace of the reform program, not whether or not to reform. This meant that less time was spent within the bureaucracy debating over the merits of reform versus bolstering, and a united front was created in dealing with the Filipino bureaucracy. Thus there was a comparatively high degree of consensus, and therefore coordination of policy, in the Philippines, with military and economic considerations decided within the context of their political consequences. In the following sections I will describe these areas according to the sequence of priorities given them by the United States, though it is important to remember that many reforms occurred simultaneously or in close succession.

Bargaining Behavior: Military Reforms and the Quid Pro Quo

The Americans were quite pleased with the reforms that Magsaysay had put through since September 1950. Some of the most glaring examples of armed forces corruption and alienation of the citizenry had been curbed. Magsaysay's surprise inspections and policy of promotion according to military performance rather than political connections shook up the local commanders and let them know they would be judged on their military expertise and ability to establish good relations with the local populace. His reorganization of the armed forces further submerged the Constabulary and Civilian Guards, which were quickly purged of criminal elements, into military units under a unified command. The Battalion Combat Teams proved to be quite successful in positioning and targeting Huk units, with a minimal disruption of normal life in the countryside. In Cebu and the Moro areas, Magsaysay moved to disband the "private police" forces of the large landowners that had been instrumental in alienating the local people. In response to these improvements, the embassy recommended $10 million for a further expansion of these Battalion Combat Teams. By late January, 1951, the military outlook had measurably improved.

Yet the United States stuck to its quid pro quo bargaining approach in terms of overall commitments in order to keep the desired programs on track. On January 22, 1951, Cowen told Magsaysay that George Marshall, then Secretary of Defense, had warned Carlos Romulo that "he did not wish to have the same experience that he had had in China in supplying arms to an Army which was guided by political interests." Magsaysay agreed and promised to do everything possible to depoliticize the armed forces. On January 30, 1951, Ambassador Cowen informed the State Department that Magsaysay was "doing a really brilliant job" as Secretary of Defense.[55]

With military programs going forward, the question arose within the administration concerning the relationship of military commitments to other aspects of U.S. policy. While maintaining the stick at the higher levels, the embassy argued that the United States must go ahead with the carrot of its military program before reaching agreement on many outstanding economic and political issues. The ECA office in Manila balked at this proposal, agreeing instead with the hard-line directives from Washington. Although Cowen agreed there should be "no commitments pending performance," he argued that to delay on the military program might mean that Magsaysay's position within the Filipino defense establishment would be threatened. In effect, the embassy argued that it had used the stick to get Magsaysay appointed and that it was now time to use the carrot to ensure he would remain. This milder approach would presumably spill over into the economic and political spheres and create a less confrontational bargaining context with Quirino.[56]

The possibility of threatening the reforms by taking an excessively hard line with the Filipinos was a real concern for American diplomats. Quirino was distressed over the lack of speed with which the United States was fulfilling its commitments on military aid. In January 1951, he sent Carlos Romulo to Washington to push for the implementation of military aid programs, arguing, with some justification, that he was putting through difficult reforms and had little to show for it. In April, he angrily recalled Romulo to Manila, telling the latter there was no use in leaving him there because American aid was but "a trickle." Romulo returned on April 23 and informed Quirino that "not one centavo" of further military aid would be forthcoming unless a major elite reform was put through: the removal of armed forces Chief of Staff General Mariano Castenada and Constabulary Chief General Alberto Ramos. Cowen brought this requirement directly to Quirino, and the latter's reaction was, in Cowen's words, "an explosion."

Cowen kept up the pressure, telling Quirino that some abuses of the armed forces and Constabulary were continuing, despite Magsaysay's reforms. American aid, he argued, could not go forward unless changes were made. The problem, said Cowen, was that Quirino was surrounded by aides who were afraid to tell him the truth about the security situation. He told the Filipino that he needed a "hatchet man" to inform him of true conditions, strongly implying that Magsaysay was the man for this position. Quirino agreed that his aides were less than forthcoming and that he would consider such a move.

The quid pro quo worked. In a clear victory for elite reform, Castaneda and Ramos were removed; as soon as this was done, military aid again began to flow. This represented a new bargaining approach toward Quirino that proved successful: a hard line in terms of commitments; a soft line in terms of blaming his underlings for mistakes and praising any and all movements toward elite or redistributive reforms as his personal triumphs. This approach "drew the line" as far as overall commitments were concerned, yet positively reinforced behavior the Americans approved. By early May, the State Department was congratulating Cowen for his "fine work" in developing "an understanding relationship with President Quirino."[57]

Magsaysay's reforms, and the removal of Castaneda and Ramos, had a great impact on the military situation throughout the summer of 1951. With the elite military reforms in place, redistributive reforms could go forward. The Secretary of Defense then began the sensitive tasks of turning military prisoners, who had a way of "disappearing," over to civilian officials, pushing a land resettlement program for Huk defectors in Mindanao, acquiring American payments for non-Guerrillista Filipino veterans, and expanding the Battalion Combat Teams with the aid that began to flow.

By early August, the reforms began to show concrete results. In a major action against the Huks in Zambales Province, in retaliation for their November 1950 attack on Magsaysay's barrio, the new Battalion Combat Teams performed excellently. This raised morale in the armed forces precipitously; as the embassy reported, the soldiers were "jubilant" over this "tremendous success." As the Filipino government proved itself more capable of decisive military action, the United States placed fewer controls on its use of military aid. On August 21, 1951, Cowen reported enthusiastically that it "appears likely" that the Huks would soon "disintegrate" militarily if the pressure were kept up. In early September, the State and Defense departments agreed to fund an expansion of the armed forces by 6,000 troops (to some 60,000 men— roughly a 4:1 numerical advantage for the government troops over the insurgents, though the Constabulary and other police forces would increase this ratio) upon the recommendation of Magsaysay. By the end of 1951, the military problems were well on their way to solution.[58]

Bargaining Behavior: The Quid Pro Quo and Redistributive Reforms

With the military reform program going forward and the Huks on the defensive, the United States turned its attention to economics and other areas where it was believed redistributive reform was needed. The reforms had been outlined in the Bell Report and consisted of a lessening of luxury consumer imports, a minimum wage law, and the creation of independent labor unions. Before these could go forward, however, there were policy disagreements between the State Department and the ECA office in Manila, especially over how to use the money provided by the Quirino-Foster Agreement.

One area in which the State Department and ECA agreed was on the need to make the $50 million proposed aid in the form of grants, not loans. If the aid was offered in loans, they argued, it would undermine Quirino's political position considerably and lessen American leverage. In addition, it would be more difficult to hold loans to the quid pro quo criteria that were producing results in the reform program.

The problem was that the Treasury Department was concerned over the balance of payments, and had adopted as policy the refusal to grant aid to nations that themselves had a positive balance of payments. The economic situation in the Philippines had improved considerably since it had balanced its budget at American insistence. In essence, the Quirino government was in danger of becoming a victim of its own success.

The embassy fought to have the aid remain in grant form. As Ambassador Cowen pointed out to Washington, the United States had made aid contingent on a balanced budget; now that this was being accomplished, Treasury was saying that the Philippines did not need grants but could afford loans because it had a balanced budget. This was unfair, argued the ambassador, and would make the Filipinos much less likely to follow through in other areas since they could credibly argue that the United States was "welshing on at least implied commitments." The ECA program, he explained, was a lever to gain acceptance of the Quirino-Foster agreements; to cut the amounts now would endanger the whole reform program. A compromise was finally reached whereby, for the first year of the program, $45 million would be in grants and $5 million in loans. The quid pro quo approach was continued. The day after the minimum wage legislation was passed on April 4, 1951, the aid agreement was completed, and delivery began soon thereafter.[59]

By June 1951, much of the essential legislation of the Quirino-Foster Agreement had been passed in the Filipino congress, and implementation had begun. Other tasks lagged behind the success of the military reforms. The goal of truly independent labor unions was a redistributive reform that the Americans took very seriously. The politburo raid of October 1950 showed that the Huks had made great inroads into Filipino labor unions, many of which were "company unions" that were used to prevent workers from real collective bargaining. After the passage of the minimum wage law in April, the United States began to put pressure on the Quirino government to pass legislation to promote collective bargaining among unions and management, especially agricultural workers.

The program really got under way in early 1951 when the embassy and the Filipino government placed more public emphasis on the growing Communist influence in labor unions. In response, the Filipinos' National Confederation of Trade Unions called for the abolition of any unions that were Communist-dominated. In addition, the United States sent representatives of the American Federation of Labor (AFL) and the Congress of Industrial Organizations (CIO) to the Philippines to help organize non-Communist, independent unions. The Free Trade Union Committee in Manila was formed to accomplish this task.

Finally, a major elite reform was implemented when the embassy demanded that the Secretary of Labor be relieved of his position for abuse of office, threatening that the aid would not go forward until this was done. Quirino announced this change in July. Though the attempt to promote the fortunes of organized labor would grow in intensity over the next few years, the program had its origins in the reforms of the Quirino-Foster Agreement. In 1953, the Filipino government passed a major Collective Bargaining Law, with the support of Filipino and American corporations in the Philippines, which had been partially written by the embassy.[60]

On August 11, 1951, Ambassador Cowen informed the State Department that the reform program was on track in two of three phases: military and economic, but not yet political. He also asked to be relieved of his post, arguing that his job was essentially completed. Ten days later, he wired Assistant Secretary of State for Far Eastern Affairs Dean Rusk with a scorecard of American accomplishments during his two years of tenure. These included (1) a renegotiated military base agreement; (2) a military aid agreement that was on its way toward implementation; (3) Filipino acceptance of the Bell Mission; (4) Filipino acceptance of the ECA program and the essentials of the Quirino-Foster Agreement for redistributive reforms; (5) Filipino involvement in the Japanese Peace Treaty; and (6) a mutual defense treaty between the United States and the Philippines. Whereas it had appeared that the Filipino government was going to collapse in 1949, this was now unlikely. The reasons for its new stability included its balanced budget (and possibly a surplus), rising production indexes, stable and gradually receding price levels, internal monetary reserves well above the safety level, the successful military initiative against the Huks, and a lessening of military and police abuses attended by a corresponding rise in civic morale.

The ambassador also commented on the quid pro quo tactics necessary to accomplish these goals: "We feel we have just cause for satisfaction . . . but must recognize that, without exception, [the reforms] were made possible only by continuously applied pressure." The United States, he argued, must show "firm patience and sympathetic understanding" in dealing with the Filipino government if it was to retain its "ideological bridgehead" in Asia; if not, the nations of Southeast Asia would look elsewhere for world leadership.[61]

The problem was that in preventing a collapse of the Quirino government, the United States had improved the political position of the Liberal Party at the expense of the Nacionalista opposition, and, if given a chance, Quirino would destroy the two-party system. Now that collapse was unlikely, and the Communists on the defensive, the United States must undertake "the strengthening and encouragement of [an] opposition party devoted to constructive criticism of domestic issues" to establish "a broadened bipartisan base for Phil[ippine]-American relations." This could only be done, Cowen stated, if all American aid, economic and military, were channeled toward this objective.[62] With the military and economic reform programs going forward and leading to greater stabilization, the United States turned its attention to political reforms.

Bargaining Behavior: The Quid Pro Quo for Political Reforms

Political problems had not been ignored in the first half of 1951, especially selective elite reforms that brought more energetic and honest people such as Magsaysay into office, but military and economic programs had taken precedence. As early as May 1951, however, opposition members had come to the embassy asking for American intervention to prevent a repeat of 1949 in the 1951 election. The State Department was convinced that the United States had to assure the fairness of the 1951 election to prevent the opposition from becoming permanently alienated from the electoral system, to base the entire reform program on a bipartisan basis, and to prevent a descent into the violence and corruption of 1949.[63]

Conditions were favorable for such a development for various reasons. For one thing, Quirino was angry over the disloyalty of local Liberal officials during the preceding year and saw no reason to use his powers to protect their political positions. Quirino was also not personally involved in the election, and his aides convinced him that he could not win in 1953 if there was a repeat of the violence of 1949. In addition, Vice-President Lopez had entered into a temporary political alliance with the Nacionalistas to ensure a fair election. Magsaysay assured the United States and Filipino citizens that, in contrast to 1949, the armed forces would remain neutral, and the United States and Filipino politicians put pressure on Quirino to restore the writ of habeas corpus in most provinces. American pressure also played a role. Beginning in June 1951, the United States informed Quirino, every major political leader in the congress, and local officials that it was "most interested" in a fair election and that violence would threaten the entire American aid program.[64]

In addition to domestic political pressure and American warnings, there was a split in the important sugar bloc in congress. A thirty-year agreement over the share of profits going to millers and planters had expired in early 1951, and Quirino had sided with the millers, who were demanding a greater share. This caused a three-way split among the Liberals: the planters rallied around Vice-President Lopez; the millers rallied around Jose Yulo; the remainder of the party rallied around Speaker Eugenio Perez. This disunity among Liberals made Quirino less likely to intervene on the side of any particular group; he apparently hoped to keep all factions within the Liberal camp for 1953.[65]

The role of the United States, however, was not confined to expressing displeasure over possible violence. Sometime that summer, the CIA sent a liberal Republican from New York, Gabriel Kaplan, to the Philippines to establish with CIA funds the National Movement for Free Elections (NAMFREL), an organization that played a crucial role in the elections of 1951 and 1953. NAMFREL carried out propaganda activities promoting democratic values, distributed U.S. Information Agency voting materials emphasizing the importance of a free election, and contacted Filipino editors and journalists to suggest a role for them in policing the polls. American journalists were also enlisted for such a task. In addition, the United States got the Commission on Elections to ask Magsaysay formally to ensure electoral rectitude. These actions were all ordered from Washington.[66] When added to the role that Magsaysay and the armed forces promised to play in protecting the electoral results, these measures greatly improved the chances for a fair election.

These and other activities were facilitated by the removal of Quirino from the scene in late summer, as he made a trip to the United States for medical treatment. After a stay at Johns Hopkins Hospital, he met with Truman on September 14. Although he told the Americans he had received a clean bill of health, the Truman administration acquired his hospital records (probably through the FBI), which showed that he had an enlarged heart and kidney disease. Melby informed the State Department that another active political campaign at that time would "kill him." With Quirino incapacitated and out of the country, the United States stepped up its activities to ensure a fair election.[67]

The election was expected to be a close one by the embassy. It was wrong. Despite the improved civic morale associated with the reform program, the Nacionalistas won an overwhelming victory in the election, a development that took the Americans, and the Liberals, by surprise. The election was honest according to the standards of 1949: the Chairman of NAMFREL declared that while the former election had been 30 percent fair, 1951 had been 75 percent fair.[68]

The aftermath of the 1951 election was as positive as the aftermath of 1949 had been negative. Having seen that political change was possible without violence, the populace generally demonstrated greater cooperation with the Filipino government and the armed forces. Huk surrenders rose precipitously, and the PCP found it much more difficult to recruit new members. The Nacionalista leadership met with embassy officials and American congressional representatives in Manila, thanked

them for the American role in the election, and promised more cooperation in the future. They immediately muted their objections to the
Japanese Peace Treaty, with the exception of Claro Recto, the Treaty's
harshest critic, who argued that to change his public position so soon
would make him appear "insincere." The party now publicly claimed it
was no longer simply an opposition organ but part of the leadership of
the Filipino government, which would require a "great measure [of]
maturity and sobriety."

The embassy opined that the goal outlined by Cowen in August of a
more balanced, bipartisan approach to Filipino politics had been accomplished by a combination of Filipino public opinion, U.S. pressure, and
the actions of Magsaysay. An unexpected positive side development
of the election was a French request, in view of the improved security
situation in the Philippines, for a copy of the 1936 Philippine Independence Act, apparently in consideration of a possible similar action in
Indochina. The United States Consulate in Saigon requested a French
translation in reply to the "titillating request." Unfortunately, nothing
apparently came of this.[69]

Two ominous trends developed following the election: Liberal dissatisfaction with the military reforms, and party regulars' demands for the
removal of Magsaysay. Speaker Perez complained to Quirino that the
Constabulary again had to be separated from the armed forces, arguing
that there was danger of a military coup and that Magsaysay had presidential ambitions. The embassy believed this pressure was in preparation for the 1953 election, in which Perez was expected to be a candidate
for president, and was quite alarmed at the prospect. Liberal party
officials were now arguing that Magsaysay should be relieved because
of "partisanship" in the 1951 election. The embassy responded by convincing American and Filipino journalists to heap lavish praise on both
Quirino and Magsaysay for the fair election practices. These measures
aimed at undermining the reform program did not work, so others
were tried. Within a month, the threat to Magsaysay's position had
reached the notice of President Truman. On December 6, Assistant
Secretary of State James Webb warned the President of "certain influences" that were now out to destroy Magsaysay for his role in the
election.[70]

In response to these developments, public diplomacy was attempted.
Secretary of State Acheson made a public statement congratulating
Quirino and Magsaysay; Truman sent a congratulatory message
through the embassy. Stronger measures were also implemented: the
quid pro quo was again wielded in the area of military assistance.
JUSMAG informed armed forces officers that a separation of the Constabulary from Filipino Defense Department control, which was being

promoted by the Liberal regulars, would mean a reduction of military aid. These combined pressures worked: the armed forces retained control of the Constabulary (for the present); Cebu Governor Rafael Lacson, one of the worst offenders in the 1949 and 1951 elections, was temporarily suspended by Quirino; Magsaysay remained in office. The consolidation of the reforms of the 1951 election, cabled the embassy, demonstrated "tremendous strides" toward democracy in the Philippines.[71]

On the day after the election, Ambassador Cowen left for the United States. After considering, among others, former Connecticut Governor Chester Bowles and Undersecretary of State Ed Foley, Truman and Acheson selected retired Admiral Raymond Spruance as the new ambassador. Spruance was a hero of World War II, the former head of the Naval War College, and a believer in the theories of the American land and tax reformer Henry George. He also believed in the use of commitments as levers in promoting reforms in the Philippines. His choice as ambassador turned out to be a most propitious one for the American program of reform.[72]

A New Government, despite Washington, 1952–1953

7

The events that transpired in United States–Filipino relations after 1952 should be seen within the context of the advent of the bolstering Eisenhower administration in January 1953. As noted in earlier chapters, the new Republican administration brought into office a more conservative view of the promotion of change and a bolstering approach toward developing allies undergoing intense instability. Even a program that had made vast improvements in the security situation in the Philippines was deeply distrusted by the new Secretary of State, John Foster Dulles, and the new Assistant Secretary of State for Far Eastern Affairs, Walter Robertson. The reformist-oriented officials in Manila, however, maintained quite a different view. There is evidence that suggests the embassy team kept programs going, and created others, in defiance of their superiors in the United States.

Decision-making: The Opposition after the 1951 Election

The opposition Nacionalista Party won all nine senate seats up for election in 1951 and greatly increased its representation in the House of Representatives. The embassy attempted to get the Nacionalistas to cooperate with Quirino for reforms, many of which they had generally favored in the past. Party leader Jose Laurel told the embassy that he thought Quirino was "mentally ill," but that the Nacionalistas would try to work with him. The opposition party then introduced a bill to ensure a fair election in 1953 by strengthening the powers of the Commission on Elections, outlawing the creation of Civilian Guards and "private police," and putting forth measures ensuring the speedy publication of election results. It followed this by introducing a bill that would have ended Quirino's emergency powers. In late February, 1952, the Nacionalistas initiated another ploy with 1953 in mind: they informally approached Magsaysay to be their presidential candidate. Though no deal was made at the time, the Filipino Secretary of Defense began to consider the possibility of this arrangement.[1]

All of these Nacionalista moves met with covert approval and support from the embassy. Thus, American backing of an opposition party aided in creating important constraints on the arbitrary use of power by the client government. Though this was a limited success in the promotion of pluralistic political values, it was a success nonetheless. These new developments, added to the U.S. role in the election of 1951, meant that the political reform program outlined earlier by Ambassador Cowen and his staff was on track.

Bargaining Behavior: The Reformist Pressures Continue

Though Quirino told the United States that he was in favor of economic and social reforms, his actions belied this. Magsaysay publicly stated that some political and economic reforms were not being implemented and that this was lessening the effectiveness of the anti-Huk military programs. Yet reforms on the labor front went forward because the Nacionalistas and the so-called "progressive," anti-Quirino bloc in the Liberal Party combined to push through major legislation. Ordinarily, these actions would have been blocked by Speaker Perez in the House, but his absence on a trip to the United States, and the estrangement of many party bosses from Quirino, gave the opposition coalition greater power in passing legislation. In late February, 1952, the Filipino congress, urged privately by the embassy, moved toward passing an omnibus labor law, in part drawn up with American help and based on the National Labor Relations Law of the New Deal, though it was not passed until 1953. Actions against Communist influence in unions went forward, as well as against abuses by non-Communist labor leaders. In March 1952, eleven former labor leaders were imprisoned for rebellion, murder, arson, and robbery.[2]

Decision-making: Quirino Begins to Move Away from Reform

In light of the lack of apparent political benefit accruing to him from the election of 1951, Quirino moved to regain the support of his party stalwarts. The political infighting in the Liberal Party remained fierce in early 1952. In April, recognizing that he was virtually without political support, Quirino began mending his fences with Liberal Party bosses. On April 4, he ordered the Armed Forces of the Philippines (AFP) out of Negros Occidental, which facilitated the eventual return to power of Governor Lacson, one of the worst offenders in the 1949 election, and he also effected a rapprochement with Speaker of the House Perez. As his price for the rapprochement, Perez began pressuring for the removal of Magsaysay and the reappointment of General Castaneda as Chief of Staff of the armed forces. Aiming at the reform programs, Perez also pressured for land resettlement to be taken away from the armed forces, the merger of intelligence and police organizations in a civilian agency, and a cut in the defense budget to undermine Magsaysay's influence. The United States reacted negatively to all of these actions. If they succeeded, the embassy noted, the 1953 election would make 1949 look like "a Sunday school picnic."[3]

Magsaysay's position became increasingly precarious. In order to "strengthen [Magsaysay's] hand as far as possible," the United States invited him to Washington in June 1952 and pointedly arranged a meeting with Truman, who showered him with lavish praise. This apparently convinced Quirino, who was under intense pressure from Speaker Perez to remove the Secretary of Defense, that this action would threaten American aid.[4] Magsaysay was safe for the time being, and the military reforms were kept on track.

While government-to-government negotiations continued, other programs were also initiated. The Philippine Rural Reconstruction Movement was created in 1952 under the direction of Y. C. "Jimmy" Yen, who had created a similar program in 1948 in China, and later on Taiwan. The Movement was funded by the CIA, CARE, Inc., and Filipino and American corporations in the Philippines.[5]

There was, moreover, a consensus among the embassy team that redistributive reforms also had to keep pace in order to keep the Huks on the defensive and garner support for Filipino social and political institutions. In anticipation of further action, the Americans prepared a plan for a land reform program as the key to alleviating some of the underlying causes of the political instability.

In April 1952, Robert Hardie, an agrarian expert and former colleague of Wolf Ladejinsky in Japan, issued a preliminary report on land tenure problems in the Philippines. After reading the report in Washington, former Ambassador Cowen wrote a long letter to his replacement as ambassador, Admiral Raymond Spruance, expressing his support for Hardie's conclusions. If the Philippines was to become a "stable outpost" of democracy in Asia, argued Cowen, redistributive reforms that lessened the social and economic disparities of Filipino society had to be implemented. These included the abolition of absentee landlord-ism and its replacement by owner/cultivators with adequate credit systems provided by American aid, the creation of non-Communist labor unions, and the development of an "efficient, honest, and sufficiently well paid" civil service. Cowen warned Spruance that Quirino would pay lip service to reforms but would have to be coerced into implementing them. Cowen also recommended using the Hardie Report as the basis for a further land reform program by presenting it to Quirino as a list of American policy goals.[6]

Though there apparently is no available record of Spruance's reply, there is evidence that he agreed with Cowen's analysis and prescription. He later wrote his daughter: "If the shackles of the landed aristocracy are not loosened, there will be a revolution in the Philippines when we get off the lid—and it will not be a peaceful and bloodless one. Our best hope is for a free election in 1953 and a candidate who wants to effect the much needed reforms and who has a Congress that will cooperate with him in doing so."[7] That candidate was about to emerge in the person of Ramon Magsaysay.

Decision-making: The Opposition Moves; A Political Deal Is Struck

Magsaysay's position within the Filipino government changed drastically throughout 1952 because of the resentment of Liberal Party bosses and provincial officials over his role in the election of 1951. Ironically, his reform program in the armed forces and success against the Huks greatly lessened the necessity of keeping him as Secretary of Defense. By mid-1952, it was increasingly apparent that Quirino was going to run for president in 1953. He was caught between two conflicting political pressures: the United States, which made it clear that it wanted Magsaysay to stay in office; and his own party, which made it just as clear that Magsaysay had to go. In August, Quirino made peace with his party: he made a deal with Liberals in congress, exchanging their support for his veto of some anti–Emergency Powers legislation for his support of them in the 1953 election. These developments made Magsaysay's position increasingly untenable, since it was obvious that Quirino could not retain the support of Liberals and still allow him the same freedom of action in 1953. Though Magsaysay had been approached by the Nacionalistas as early as February, surreptitious meetings between its representatives, Magsaysay, and independent opposition leader Lorenzo Tanada began in earnest in August 1952.[8]

By the end of September, the embassy was receiving reports of the contacts between the Nacionalistas and Magsaysay. The latter originally planned to run for president as an independent, with Tanada as his running mate. He tested the political waters with Guerrillista groups and the Junior Chamber of Commerce. Encouraged by Lansdale and other advisers, Magsaysay was appealing to younger, less traditional political groups who felt increasingly frustrated over the existing leadership.[9] These groups had become more active in the election of 1951, and Nacionalista Party chief Jose Laurel was anathema to them because of the "collaborator" label he had retained from the war. Added to Magsaysay's widespread popularity among the common people, the support of these forces made him a formidable candidate. Since it was well known that he was also a favorite of the United States, the Secretary of Defense became a lightning rod for the anti-Liberal opposition.[10]

American officials were again losing patience with Quirino. A major development occurred in mid-October, 1952, when the Liberals attempted to exact campaign contributions from American businessmen in the Philippines. The basic idea was that in exchange for export licenses, U.S. business interests would give large contributions to Quirino and withhold advertising from anti-Quirino newspapers, especially those owned by Vice-President Lopez, who was estranged from the president. The State Department reacted sharply to this ploy, telling Spruance that "positive steps" must be taken to avoid the "exaction of contributions" from Americans. The United States was further alarmed at the passage of a Emergency Powers Resolution in the House under the leadership of Speaker Perez, demonstrating the restoration of a political alliance with Quirino. At the same time, Quirino double-crossed Magsaysay by publicly questioning his authority to arrest a Moro leader, something he had in fact been ordered to do by the president. This was widely interpreted, by Americans and Filipinos, as a slap in the face of the Secretary of Defense.[11]

For Magsaysay, this series of actions was the last straw. It appeared that the pro-Quirino Liberals were planning a repeat of the 1949 election. He and the Nacionalistas began meeting in earnest to create a political alliance. The deal was consummated in a November 16, 1952, meeting of Laurel, Tanada, Senator Claro Recto, Magsaysay, and another leading Nacionalista, Eulogio Rodriguez. Following some discussion of a possible military coup led by Magsaysay, in which the latter refused to cooperate, a written agreement was produced to prevent a double-cross. The Nacionalistas requested the right to name the cabinet in exchange for their support; Magsaysay considered going along until talked out of it by Tanada, Lansdale, and others. This plan was changed to the naming of a cabinet "upon the recommendation and with the consent" of the Nacionalistas and Tanada's tiny Citizens' Party. Recto, Laurel, and Tanada pledged not to run for the presidency. In addition, Magsaysay strongly implied that he could easily get American political and financial support. In response, Laurel told him: "Let's face the facts. In this country the sympathy of the Americans is a factor to be considered in winning. Well, you have that sympathy. You have the friendship of the Americans. Use it for the benefit of the country."[12]

The written agreement was passed by Lansdale to Ambassador Spruance for safekeeping. This later caused problems for the United States during the 1953 election, when it became known that the document was in the embassy safe. Thus, the battle lines for the 1953 election were drawn in November 1952—a set of popular leaders with few powers of physical coercion, against a discredited administration which had plenty. American policy would increasingly concentrate on preventing the use of those instruments of coercion.[13]

Decision-making: The Liberals Move: Land Reform Deferred

Filipinos from both parties attempted to gain American support for the campaign. Throughout December 1952, Liberal political allies of Quirino visited Spruance and told him the United States must stay out of the upcoming election, threatening to criticize the Americans publicly for interference in Filipino politics. At the same time, opposition politicians, including some dissidents from the Liberal Party, came to the embassy and pleaded with the United States to intervene to ensure a free election. Spruance told both sides that the United States would remain completely neutral in the election, but that the American Congress would cut off aid to a government not freely elected by the Filipino people.

The embassy was disturbed at reports that Quirino had ordered the armed forces to end the activities of NAMFREL. In response, Spruance suggested that Secretary Acheson make a public statement demonstrating United States interest in a fair election, which was done. The Filipino press gave wide coverage to the statement, and to articles appearing in the American press about similar concerns.

In addition to the concerns over the upcoming election, redistributive reform programs began running into problems. Quirino told Spruance, for example, that the idea of land reform was "distasteful" to him. In response, Spruance leaked parts of the Hardie Report to the Filipino press in December 1952, something Quirino had specifically asked him not to do, and it was much discussed, usually favorably, in various Filipino editorials. The Liberals reacted angrily, commenting on possible "Communist influences" in the State Department (it might be recalled that the Republicans had just won the 1952 election in the United States using similar charges).

Though Spruance remained convinced of the necessity of land reform, the growing danger of a repeat of the 1949 election diverted
American attention to political problems. The assistant director of the
Mutual Security Administration (MSA), which had replaced the Economic Cooperation Administration, in Manila stated that the United
States would have to use all its influence to assure a fair election in 1953
and, given Quirino's opposition to redistributive reform, he "would hate
to see us use up our ammunition in what would probably be a futile
attempt to get an adequate land reform program at this time."[14] Once
again, the problem of elite reform in a client government prevented a
concentration on needed redistributive reforms.

Decision-making: The Opposition Coalition and the Magsaysay Campaign

Though it was apparent to many that Magsaysay had broken with
Quirino and made a deal with the Nacionalistas, he continued to claim
publicly that he was disinterested in politics. He had wanted to resign
as Secretary of Defense in November of 1952 but was talked out of it
by Lansdale and Spruance, who feared a lessening of military pressure
against the Huks and a movement away from the depoliticization of the
army. This was apparently a realistic concern. In January 1953, Magsaysay told the embassy that Quirino planned to separate the Constabulary from the armed forces in order to use it in the election. The United
States protested this proposed action through JUSMAG, and, if indeed
it had been actually planned, it was avoided for the present.

By late February, 1953, speculation over Magsaysay's defection from
the Liberals was widespread. On March 2, he resigned from the Filipino
government, claiming in his public letter of resignation that Quirino's
idea of dealing with the insurgency was "just to go on killing Huks."
This would be futile, stated Magsaysay, "while the Administration continues to breed dissidence by neglecting the problems of our masses."
Quirino, after considering taking over the Defense portfolio himself,
named Secretary of Justice Oscar Castelo as Magsaysay's successor.[15]

This development, however, recreated the dilemma the United States
faced in the aftermath of the 1949 election. If the opposition, which
was now led by the most enthusiastic and notable reformer in the
Philippines, and the symbol of American policy to many, became alienated from the democratic political process, the entire reform program
would be in jeopardy. It might also lead to a resurgence of the Huks.
The embassy watched with keen interest as Magsaysay made his appeals
to the general public.

Magsaysay began campaigning immediately and in the process introduced something new to Filipino politics: a personalized, populist campaign. Previously, politicians had largely made symbolic visits to the rural areas but generally relied on the mayors of the villages and provincial cities, mostly appointed by the president and controlled through "pork barrel" politics, to deliver the votes on election day. The Liberals were therefore relying on traditional local political bosses to deliver the vote.

Magsaysay, given his barrio origins and recent experience as the champion of Juan de la Cruz (the Filipinos' John Q. Public), recognized that a word-of-mouth campaign such as that used for psychological warfare against the Huks was an effective way to mobilize support among the masses. It was here that Lansdale's psychological warfare and propaganda techniques were most helpful. In essence, Magsaysay repeated his actions as Secretary of Defense, but now utilized them in the political arena. He used an airplane to visit a relatively large number of barrios in a flurry of campaign activity. He also adopted a folksy— some said corny—campaign style, in part suggested by Lansdale and other Americans, that sought to identify him with the average Filipino. But it is a mistake to reduce Magsaysay's campaign and candidacy to nothing more than a slick advertising campaign masterminded by Lansdale, as left-wing critics often do. Magsaysay attracted a youth movement coalition of Guerrillistas, young professionals, businessmen, and various reform elements by claiming credit for reforming the armed forces, ensuring a free election in 1951, and promising increased prosperity through economic development and American aid. His populist campaign involved the common people in electoral politics in ways that would not be matched again until the 1980s.

The Quirinos and the Liberals had not a clue to understanding all of this. To give some idea of the overconfidence of the Liberals, when Magsaysay pointed to the scandals of the past, one party spokesman stated that corruption was "natural" since mankind had been corrupt since Adam and Eve. The Liberals generally remained unable to grasp the changes in Filipino public opinion since 1951. Given the immediate popularity of the new campaign style, and the creation of hundreds of "Magsaysay for President" clubs, the embassy noted that he would win easily in November *if* there was a fair election.[16] By the early summer of 1953, this was becoming much less likely.

Bargaining Behavior: The Liberals Counterattack

The Liberal politicians reacted to the electoral threat posed by Magsaysay through a series of actions that demonstrated a desire to return to the political climate of 1949. They would discover, however, that it would not be as easy as in the past. First, aroused public and press opinion constrained those kinds of blatantly violent tactics. Second, other political institutions, especially the Supreme Court, had been invigorated by the changed attitudes in the wake of the 1951 election. In January 1953, for example, Quirino attempted to suspend Manila Mayor Arsenio Lacson on trumped-up libel charges because he was vehemently opposed to the Liberals. The Supreme Court, however, struck this down as unconstitutional. When this new willingness to challenge Quirino was demonstrated, the opposition increasingly looked to the Court to place limits on the arbitrary use of power by the executive. Third, the United States, even with the bolstering Eisenhower administration, continued to declare publicly and often its interest in a fair election. Thus, as a result of internal and external pressure, the Liberals found it much more difficult to gain control of the electoral process than had been the case in 1949.[17] This was not for want of trying.

The Liberals devised a campaign strategy composed of four elements: mobilization of support; harassment of the opposition; negation of the instruments and organizations used to ensure the free election of 1951; and the neutralization of U.S. influence. In terms of the mobilization of support, Quirino first moved to consolidate control over his own party. He was not a very popular figure among Liberals. He kept potential defectors in line by threatening to expose corrupt practices. Since he and his brother Antonio, the latter becoming much more politically active with the president's worsening health, had control over the intelligence services in the Philippines, they had dossiers on all of the Liberal leadership. In the rough and tumble of Filipino politics, the threat of disclosure is a standard tool for enlisting loyalty, and the Quirinos used it extensively.

The Quirinos also turned to mending fences with disaffected elements, as they had already done with Speaker Perez, especially provincial politicians. When a typhoon hit the Philippines, causing extensive damage, the Quirinos used "pork barrel" to aid Liberals in order to enlist their support in the election. Evidence was later disclosed showing that pro-Liberal provinces that had not even been hit by the typhoon received huge amounts of money while pro-Nacionalista provinces that were badly damaged received none. Taxes in pro-Liberal provinces were also lowered. By the spring of 1953, Quirino was again in the driver's seat of the Liberal Party.[18]

The second campaign tactic for the Quirinos was harassment of the opposition. Though Quirino initially refrained from attacking the popular Magsaysay, he launched constant attacks on the "collaborators" Jose Laurel and Claro Recto. This was not an effective tactic, however, because collaboration was pretty much a dead issue by this time, and, after all, Quirino himself had served in Laurel's wartime puppet cabinet during the Japanese occupation.[19] Quirino then had the Internal Revenue Service give notice to Laurel, Recto, and Nacionalista leader Eulogio Rodriguez that they had been investigated, were in arrears, and had until April 15, 1953, to pay back taxes. They appealed this decision to the Supreme Court and were eventually successful. Quirino then publicly attacked Laurel for being "afraid" to run against him, in an attempt to goad him into abandoning Magsaysay, apparently believing his chances would be better in an election against the older politician. Laurel calmly stated that it was time for a new generation of leaders.

The Nacionalistas became increasingly nervous over these attacks, and on May 7 Recto informed the embassy he had information that he, Laurel, and Magsaysay were to be arrested as "pro-Communists." Although this did not happen, the following day Recto was arrested on trumped-up bigamy charges. In retaliation, he attempted to get Secretary of Defense Castelo disbarred by investigating some of his previous activities which were widely believed to be illegal. On June 17, 1953, the key witness against Castelo, Manuel Monroy, was murdered. The harassment had reached such a point by the end of the month that members of the tiny, newly formed Democrata Party and Nacionalista candidates in Manila asked the embassy for asylum in the event of assassination attempts during the campaign by Antonio Quirino's secret police. By the summer, the violent ghosts of 1949 seemed to be back to haunt Filipino politics.[20]

In their attempt to neutralize or negate extra-Executive institutions, Quirino and Speaker Perez tried to regain "emergency powers" because of the "special wartime" situation. The timing of the efforts in an election year, and the lessened Huk threat by 1953, however, caused a negative reaction in congress from the Nacionalistas and the "progressive" bloc (Liberal dissidents and independents) which remained opposed to Quirino. Perez was forced to put the legislation into committee to await possible future action. In April, following his rapprochement with Quirino, Perez again attempted to separate the Constabulary from the armed forces and to appoint the brutal and corrupt General Mariano Castaneda as Secretary of Defense, assuring the public and the United States that this was not being done for political reasons.

Following a meeting in the embassy, JUSMAG protested this action and warned that military aid programs would be cut off if it took effect. On June 18, Perez visited Spruance and told him that if the United States had lost faith in Quirino, a development that was becoming increasingly obvious, it should not worry because he would personally guarantee that the Constabulary would not be used for political purposes. Given Perez's past, the embassy was hardly reassured by this promise. Since overall separation of the Constabulary and armed forces might threaten military aid, the Quirinos did so only in some remote provinces.

Perez also told Spruance that the Liberals would win easily in 1953 because people in the barrios did not read newspapers, but voted as told to by their mayors. This proved to be a gross underestimation of the changes that had taken place since 1951. The Liberals also attacked NAMFREL and the newly formed Committee for Free Asia (CFA), which had also been created with CIA funds. Quirino stated publicly that these organizations' demands for more democracy in the Philippines were "ridiculous" since the Filipinos already had "too much" democracy and had abused it. NAMFREL and the CFA continued to operate, with the embassy warning the Filipino government about attacks on personnel from these organizations.

Apparently viewing the burgeoning independent labor unions as possibly undermining Liberal influence by destroying the power of the "company unions," Quirino attempted to "nationalize" all unions, a move that was prevented by yet more American pressure in the form of a threatened aid reduction. In addition, Antonio Quirino created several new Guerrillista groups through promises of the reopening of the payment question in order to undercut Magsaysay's popularity with them. These were generally unsuccessful, especially since the United States publicly stated that the payment question remained closed. Given the difficulties in manipulating internal factors to their satisfaction, in large part because of U.S. pressure, the Liberals turned to a fourth tactic—the neutralization of the influence of the United States.[21]

Bargaining Behavior: American Policy and Liberal Attacks

As in 1949 and 1951, the election campaign of 1953 in part centered on the attitude of the United States. The Liberals and Nacionalistas both attempted to elicit American support. In contrast to the 1949 and 1951 elections, however, the positions of the parties on the role of the United States were now reversed: the Nacionalistas discounted foreign "meddling"; the Liberals bitterly attacked it. As is usually the case, the perception of U.S. intervention was based on which groups were its beneficiaries.

The United States did not want to be put in a public position of favoring one group over the other, but it cannot be denied that the embassy team wanted Magsaysay to win the election. With the new administration in Washington, which made clear it had no preference between the parties, though it strongly favored a fair election, the most significant development in American policy in 1953 was the extent to which the embassy in Manila, convinced of the need for further elite and redistributive reforms, exceeded its instructions from Washington.

Liberal machinations against U.S. influence began in early 1953. Quirino announced in mid-January that he would head a mission to the United States to renegotiate the unpopular Bell Trade Agreement and reopen the Guerrillista payment program. He was publicly informed that the United States would not do either in an election year. When this occurred, the Liberals began verbally attacking the United States for interference in the Filipino election.

Throughout March and April, the interference issue dominated Filipino politics. Pro-Quirino Liberals openly called for Spruance's recall, and the prevention of Lansdale, who had returned to the United States for a short period, from reentering the Philippines. In another attempt at intimidation, Defense Secretary Castelo publicly stated that foreign journalists who wrote stories unfavorable to the Filipino government would be arrested and deported. He quickly had to withdraw that threat because of American and domestic press reaction.[22]

Tensions were increased in March by the activities of Adlai Stevenson, who was on a fact-finding trip to the Philippines in the wake of his loss in the 1952 American presidential election. At the behest of Ambassador Spruance, Stevenson publicly expressed his concern over American public reaction to a possible repeat of 1949 in the coming election. This infuriated Quirino and precipitated further condemnations of American intervention just when the issue seemed to be receding. The Filipino president again called for the removal of Spruance, adding William Lacy, Lansdale, and the entire MSA agrarian staff, especially Robert Hardie, to his list of villains. United States–Filipino relations reached the lowest level since the spring of 1951.[23]

Decision-making: Secretary of State Dulles Softens the Quid Pro Quo; The Embassy Reacts

With the controversy over U.S. actions in the Philippines and the relative indifference toward reform in the new administration in Washington, the embassy turned to greater use of covert action to protect what were perceived by the embassy team as American interests. It was at this point that the policy of the Eisenhower administration and the embassy in the Philippines diverged. Though it is difficult to ascertain just how much Washington knew of the actions of the embassy, there is some evidence that it was relatively uninformed. Having learned a bolstering lesson from China, many key officials of the Eisenhower administration were decidedly hostile to reformist interventions.

President Eisenhower, Vice-President Nixon, and Secretary of State Dulles were the leading bolsterers in the new administration. In addition, the Assistant Secretary of State for Far Eastern Affairs in 1953 was Walter S. Robertson. Robertson was the cousin of China Lobby favorite General Albert Wedemeyer, had served on General Marshall's staff in China, and strongly believed that the United States should have bolstered Chiang Kai-shek. He later described the American concern with reform in China as "stupid, blundering idiocy." The idea that peasants might be attracted to the programs advocated by Communist revolutionaries was "idiotic nonsense."[24] With such a bolstering group of people now in power in Washington, the embassy team could no longer count on high-level support for the programs they had been espousing for several years.

On March 13, 1953, the date of Quirino's initial call for Spruance's removal, Dulles wrote a top-secret policy directive to the ambassador stating he was confident that the embassy would "maintain in fact as well as in appearance [an] absolutely impartial and correct position" in the election. Spruance was ordered to make clear the American interest in a fair election and the Bell Report recommendations, but the Eisenhower administration wanted it known that it would approve of either Magsaysay or Quirino as president of the Philippines. The fact that this was a top-secret communication suggests that it accurately represented Dulles's thinking on the matter.[25]

Spruance reacted by making several public statements in favor of neutrality, but there was after this point a shift to increased covert actions to weaken Quirino's chances in the election. Whether this was ordered from Washington is unclear, but there were subsequent cables from Dulles reiterating his disinterest in the outcome of the election as long as the procedures were reasonably fair. Communications between the embassy and Washington at this point show a clear reformist policy from the former, and bolstering from the latter. As I will show, there is further evidence that the embassy team exceeded its mandate from its superiors in the United States.[26]

Bargaining Behavior: The Liberal Search for Counter-leverage

The Liberals did not confine their counter-leverage pressure to public statements condemning American intervention. In mid-March, 1953, a group of young Liberal congressmen loyal to Speaker Perez, including a subsequent president of the Philippines, Ferdinand Marcos, introduced a resolution calling for the withdrawal of the small Filipino military force from Korea. Since this was proposed during sensitive peace negotiations in that nation, it was clearly an embarrassment to the United States. The reaction in the Philippines was extremely hostile, and it served to weaken the Liberals further in the congress and among the public. Filipino press reaction was uniformly negative. Quirino quickly disavowed this move, but Speaker Perez and his loyalists refused to back down. General Albert Pierson, the new head of JUSMAG, publicly stated that the United States could not be expected to fight Communism alone in Asia. The legislation was allowed to wither in House committee.[27]

Though the government of the Philippines ended its call for the removal of Ambassador Spruance after Joaquin Elizalde, former ambassador to the United States and a confidant of Quirino's, convinced the president that the more he pushed for this action the less likely it would be that the United States would acquiesce, the Quirino government continued to demand the removal of agricultural expert Robert Hardie, and the prevention of Lansdale from reentering the Philippines.

In the case of Hardie, whom the Quirinos charged with "embarrassing" the Filipino government with his "Communist-influenced" call for land reform, the government was eventually successful. With the Huk insurgency largely under control, the incentives for such rapid changes in the socioeconomic structures of Filipino society were viewed as unnecessary by the bolstering Eisenhower administration. The ad hoc nature of American reform policy again took hold. Hardie was removed in August, and his report was repudiated by the State Department.

In the case of Lansdale, following recommendations from Washington that he be kept in the United States until after the election, it was only with the most insistent requests from Ambassador Spruance that he was spirited back into the country with orders to refrain completely from dealing in political affairs. He did not, and disobeyed those orders by acting as a conduit for private and official support of the Magsaysay candidacy. This gave Lansdale a reputation for "free-wheeling" behavior that in part prevented him from attaining high position in his next assignment, Vietnam.

General Pierson, generally in favor of a less active reformist policy in the Philippines than his predecessors had advocated, reacted to the pressure of the Filipino government by removing Lansdale from JUSMAG. Ambassador Spruance, possibly with a straight face, then had Lansdale assigned to the Office of the Historian of the 13th Air Force in Manila. Within a short period of time, General Pierson would be relieved of command of JUSMAG upon the recommendation of Spruance and reformist military officers. He was replaced by General Robert Cannon, a man with CIA connections, and one much more amenable to a reformist policy. Lansdale's return and future actions did not escape the notice of the Quirinos. That summer Antonio sent a "hit squad" that nearly assassinated the CIA agent.[28]

Decision-making: Washington Backs off Further; The Embassy Team Persists

Throughout the summer of 1953, the Quirino forces constantly complained about United States interference in the electoral process, while they simultaneously attempted to gain commitments for themselves in order to bolster their position in the coming election. Washington reacted to pressure for non-interference by warning the embassy to stay neutral in the election. The embassy team was informed that American policy was to do its "utmost [to] keep U.S.-Philippine relations above [Filipino] domestic politics." Thus, commitments were only indirectly used to attempt to influence the behavior of the Filipino government, and then only in preventing a blatantly unfair election.[29]

The Filipino counter-pressure was enhanced by the reaction of Senate Republicans, who launched a campaign to refrain from undermining "America's friend" Elpidio Quirino. In contrast, Democratic Senator William Fulbright informed the Undersecretary of State for Congressional Relations, Thruston Morton, that he and congressional Democrats would join in any action to pressure for reforms. In partial reaction to these intra-governmental, contradictory pressures for bolstering and reform, the State Department again instructed Spruance to inform Quirino that it wanted a fair election, but could live with either party's victory. Given the attempts by the Liberals to use physical force to manipulate the results of the election, this was considered among the embassy team as a prescription for disaster.

Ambassador Spruance, possibly stalling, did not so inform Quirino because, he claimed, the Filipino president's deteriorating health and another trip to Johns Hopkins Hospital in July prevented it. Assistant Secretary of State Walter Robertson warned Spruance once again on June 16 that the administration wanted to avoid intervention on behalf of any particular candidate. If, however, it appeared that there was to be a repeat of 1949 and "more drastic" action was necessary, he recommended Spruance's return for consultation so that Quirino would know that Spruance spoke for President Eisenhower. Spruance advised waiting to see if Quirino was too ill to be a candidate, because if he was, the probable Liberal candidate would be the vice-presidential candidate,

Jose Yulo. If that occurred, said Spruance, "our problem [would be] over" because Yulo, Democrata Party candidate Carlos Romulo, or Magsaysay would never cheat in the election. If Quirino ran, however, he would recommend his return for consultation since a violent, illegitimate election would be almost a certainty.[30]

The Quirinos' fear of American intervention on the side of their political opponents was not unfounded. In the summer of 1953, Magsaysay's campaign began to run into financial problems. Since the Nacionalistas had agreed to the coalition with him partly because of a belief that he could secure American monetary and political backing, they pushed for greater United States support for their candidate. Though it is unknown how much financial backing was extended to Magsaysay— estimates range from $50,000 to $3 million—it is clear that the CIA in Manila provided funds during the crucial months of June and July, at the same time the embassy team was being ordered to stay out of the campaign. Much of this money apparently came from American corporations in the Philippines, funneled through the ubiquitous Ed Lansdale.

Though the Liberals got wind of these contributions, the embassy officially reiterated U.S. neutrality. Lansdale continued his covert actions in favor of the Nacionalistas and against the Liberals, in disregard of his previous orders. Partly in order to restrict his activities in the Philippines, Washington began sending him on sporadic trips to what turned out to be his next assignment, Vietnam. Throughout July, the Nacionalistas continually attempted to gain public United States approval and support.[31] They could not do so, though covert aid was continued by the embassy team.

Bargaining Behavior: The Liberals Attempt to Repeat 1949—and Fail

President Quirino traveled to the United States for medical reasons in June 1953. Before leaving the Philippines, however, he and his brother Antonio issued a number of orders that revealed their desire to repeat the violence and corruption of the 1949 election. They printed bogus ballots and shipped ink eradicator to some provinces, created "goon squads" consisting of newly pardoned criminals, denied use of public facilities to Nacionalista candidates, replaced neutral Constabulary commanders with Liberal loyalists, threatened the supply of newsprint for opposition newspapers, physically threatened advertisers of opposition newspapers, allegedly attempted to assassinate Magsaysay at one point, and created a shortage of affidavits in order to restrict voter registration in many provinces. The violence aimed at opposition candidates rose markedly in July and continued throughout the summer and fall, and leading Nacionalistas again inquired about possible asylum in the United States embassy. The embassy received reports that the increase in tension was leading to a revival of unrest in the rural areas.[32]

Yet 1953 was not 1949. The reforms of 1950–1952 had taken hold in a way that the embassy, and certainly the Liberals, did not yet realize. First, informed Filipino public opinion was a much greater force to reckon with than in 1949. The popularity of the Magsaysay campaign in many barrios, the aroused press, and important arbiters of public morality such as the Catholic Church all combined to place constraints on the Quirinos and made much more difficult the gross and blatant violence of the earlier election.

Second, Filipino institutions, including those created with American money such as NAMFREL and CFA, as well as indigenous institutions such as the Commission on Elections, the Church, and the Supreme Court, were much more difficult to manipulate or ignore in 1953, and acted as deterrents on especially outrageous behavior. NAMFREL and the Commission on Elections repeatedly developed programs to counter the more obvious attempts to stuff or alter ballots. The Church came out strongly for a fair election, and in September 1953 six bishops issued a letter to all parishes, in an obvious reference to the Quirinos, stating that every citizen must vote "under pain of mortal sin, when there is danger of evil men obtaining control of the government." Quirino would later apportion a major part of the blame for his defeat to the Church (Quirino was a Protestant, which was unusual for a Filipino politician; Magsaysay was a Roman Catholic).

Finally, the Supreme Court, enjoying an unprecedented popularity and prestige, repeatedly struck down attempts by the Liberals to restore full "emergency powers" to Quirino, to extend the suspension of the writ of habeas corpus to all provinces, or to replace unfriendly mayors in key provinces. The vitality of American-supported organizations and indigenous Filipino civic and religious institutions, and their dedication to democratic ideals, was a pleasant surprise to the embassy.[33] There were other actions taken by the embassy team, however, which were also important in preventing an electoral disaster and ensuring the ultimate electoral victory of Ramon Magsaysay in 1953.

Bargaining Behavior: Covert Action against Quirino

Though the entire record of American covert action during this period remains unclear, it is evident that the embassy team acted, at times independently, to ensure a fair election. It had been instructed by Washington in March 1953 to aid NAMFREL, CFA, CARE, and other organizations publicly dedicated to achieving this goal. These groups also worked covertly to aid Magsaysay's campaign, although the extent of Washington's knowledge of their activities in this regard is unknown. In addition, the embassy encouraged indigenous Filipino organizations such as the Commission on Elections, the Church, and various business groups.[34] As noted above, however, this was as far as its mandate extended.

Many actions of the CIA in this period remain shrouded in secrecy. Yet some information has reached public examination. Lansdale's close relationship with Magsaysay led him, in apparent collusion with the CIA's Manila Chief, General Ralph Lovett, to act on the Nacionalistas' behalf during the election. The CIA wrote speeches for Magsaysay during his campaign, helped plan election strategies, funneled funds from the Agency and private sources to the campaign at crucial times, arranged favorable treatment from Filipino and American journalists, allegedly infiltrated the Liberal Party and drugged some of its speakers on the campaign trail, and provided the Nacionalistas with crucial campaign intelligence.

The CIA also carried out other covert actions to ensure a fair election. When the Quirinos succeeded in obtaining a warehouse of fake ballots which they were about to distribute to Liberals in the provinces, for example, Lansdale and his team burned it to the ground. JUSMAG Chief General Robert Cannon later recalled that the CIA was "furnishing money, furnishing political advice and in some cases I think a little strong arm." It is unclear whether this was the full extent of the activities, but when these actions were uncovered in Washington, key decision-makers in the Eisenhower administration complained about them. In an interview years later, Lansdale would only admit that he and his team "got into a lot of trouble with the top brass" for "going too far" during the election.[35]

This was not, however, a case of the CIA as "rogue elephant." Clearly State and JUSMAG personnel were also aware of, supported, and participated in these actions, and they were closely coordinated with other activities in an integrated plan. The lack of communication with Washington can be seen in the activities of Ambassador Spruance, who led the entire effort. After being recalled to Washington for consultation in October 1953, he told the embassy team that his superiors in the State Department again made it clear that they wanted a fair election, but wanted no preference shown to either candidate. Eisenhower and Dulles were generally familiar with the situation. Yet he also told the CIA's General Lovett that he had not been entirely forthcoming with his superiors in Washington, afraid that their disapproval might threaten the embassy's attempts at reformist intervention.[36]

Since there is no way to determine the full extent of embassy team activities, there is no way to analyze completely their effectiveness. It should be noted, however, that they clearly kept the Quirinos, and the Liberals in general, off balance. This presumably made it more difficult for them to gain coercive control of the electoral process. The ethical and moral ramifications will be left for the reader to determine, but they should be judged within the context of the potential losses of life and long-term suffering for the Filipino people if the Liberals or the Communists had been in power after 1953, at least as the problem was viewed by the embassy team, as well as against abstract standards or codes of conduct.

Bargaining Behavior: The Embassy Team Continues the Quid Pro Quo on Its Own

The embassy team was busy trying to ensure a clean election in 1953. In September, the embassy received reports that President Quirino was once again considering naming General Castaneda as Secretary of Defense. Quirino's action was in response to the highly negative publicity that Secretary Castelo had received that summer for abuses by the Constabulary in some provinces, which precipitated his being sent to the United States. In addition, Quirino attempted to replace officers who were considered neutral, and who had played key roles in the fair election of 1951, with corrupt loyalists. The ambassador and the new Chief of JUSMAG, General Cannon, went directly to Quirino and complained about this attempt to politicize the armed forces, warning that it would adversely affect the American military aid program. The personnel changes were again avoided.[37]

In mid-October, 1953, the activist policy of JUSMAG under General Cannon created more controversy. Cannon told Chief of Staff General Calixto Duque that the Filipino armed forces should send officers to polling stations to ensure that voting was fair and voters were not coerced. General Duque, already under intense pressure from the Quirinos to avoid doing so, refused JUSMAG's request. When this occurred, General Cannon, under dubious authority, announced that he would position JUSMAG officers at the polls to ensure fair voting procedures. Quirino vigorously protested this, and launched an anti-American campaign to appeal to nationalist sentiment, with a notable lack of success. The State Department also protested this action to the embassy and wired Cannon that it "did *not* approve" of the plan, arguing that it wanted to stay out of the internal dispute. Secretary Dulles followed up this protest with an order to desist from going ahead with the JUSMAG plan in order to prevent Filipino domestic politics from entering into the diplomatic realm of American-Filipino relations.

In a characteristic development, General Cannon ignored the orders from the State Department and stationed JUSMAG troops at the polls on election day. Ambassador Spruance assured Secretary of State Dulles on November 6 that American personnel were being kept out of the provinces where the most trouble was expected, something that was not true. It should be noted that most observers, Filipino and American, cited the presence of JUSMAG troops at key spots as a major reason for the relative fairness of the voting in those areas.[38]

Other, less dramatic actions were also taken. In October, at the behest of the Eisenhower administration, a group from the U.S. House Armed Services Subcommittee visited Quirino in Manila and warned him of its concern with the fairness of the election. Approximately forty American journalists were sent by the United States government and, along with Filipino journalists, acted as an added constraint on the Quirinos. The attention afforded the elections helped prevent the widespread fraud and violence of 1949, and presented the Filipino government with further costs in public and international opinion that were apparently too high for it to pay.[39]

Epilogue: Success and Failure in the Philippines

With the exception of certain provinces and isolated incidents, the election of 1953 was judged by the embassy as "generally fair and clean." One last controversy was created, however, over the presence of the *U.S.S. Wasp* and its destroyer escorts in Manila Bay on election day, which some Filipinos saw as a warning aimed at the Quirinos. This was complicated by Magsaysay's retiring to the barge of Admiral Richard Cruzen on the same day to await the election results.

Though Quirino complained of American interference, and some officials in Washington were infuriated, the issue became moot with the magnitude of the Nacionalista victory. Magsaysay outpolled Quirino by more than two to one, carried twenty-five of twenty-eight cities, and won forty-eight of fifty-two provinces. Since the candidate the United States wanted to win did so, there were few who were going to nitpick about the means used to achieve this end. Thus, little post-election analysis was carried out to determine how the successful reformist intervention was accomplished. In any event, Eisenhower and Dulles congratulated the embassy team, the President reportedly saying, "This is the way we like to see an election carried out."[40]

Magsaysay brought something new to the Filipino political process: a coalition of landed interests, young professionals, Guerrillistas, and common people. The contradictions inherent in this coalition, however, became manifest after the election. Magsaysay attempted a variety of socioeconomic reforms and met with limited success, yet he was blocked in the Filipino congress, especially by the entrenched landed interests. By attempting too much, he actually accomplished much less than he might have.

Though Magsaysay was a reformist president, the degree of United States support for land reform and other redistributive reforms was markedly lowered during the Eisenhower administration, and this support would have been necessary to overcome the intrinsic opposition to reform within Filipino society. The land reform specialist Robert Hardie was replaced by John L. Cooper, a much more conservative analyst of the social and economic problems facing the Philippines. Though Spruance stayed on as ambassador until 1955, the high-level pressure for reforms was a thing of the past. The conservative Republican Homer Ferguson, a leading member of the China Lobby, replaced Spruance as ambassador, and clearly did not approve of the redistributive reforms advocated during the Truman administration.

Thus, the "monumental importance" of finally attending to the endemic inequities of Filipino society as envisioned in the Truman administration, in the face of the end of the Huk revolt, was seen as unnecessary, and possibly harmful, by the new administration. The purge of the Far Eastern Division analysts of the Roosevelt-Truman era in the wake of the fall of China left State Department representatives who were relatively hostile to this approach to a client nation, especially when stability had returned to its political life. Though the United States backed Magsaysay's land reform of 1954–1955, the lack of enthusiasm was obvious. Yet again in the history of the American-Filipino relationship, at the very time when the United States might have made fundamental changes in the existing patterns of socioeconomic relations in the Philippines through redistributive reforms, it was not interested in doing so. Magsaysay repeatedly complained to his aides that the United States was too slow to support his reform plans. When the Filipino president asked for American help in overcoming Filipino congressional obstructionism to his reform program, he was informed that this was impossible.

On March 16, 1957, Magsaysay's presidential airplane crashed into the side of Mount Manungal in Cebu. The American reformist intervention, for the present, was over. It was not to return as a general policy approach until its brief resuscitation during the Kennedy administration.[41]

Conclusions

The reformist intervention in the Philippines was a success. Even in a society in which the United States had great influence, however, it took constant use of its commitments as leverage to achieve its policy goals. There are some obvious differences between the China and Filipino cases: the scope and range of the problems facing the Philippines were less complex than those of China; the United States had a long history of interdependence with the Philippines, and both the Filipinos and the Americans had a greater level of understanding of each other's political systems; there was no sanctuary or direct military aid for the Huks as there had been for the Chinese Communists; the Korean War made a greater level of resources from Congress available to the Truman administration than had been the case during 1945–1948; and there was a greater tendency for the Filipinos to emulate American political ideals. Within this context, it was simply more likely for the reformist intervention to succeed in the Philippines than in the chaotic morass of postwar Republican China.

It would be a mistake to conclude, however, that a successful policy was a foregone conclusion or that the Filipino case is so distinctive that it does not offer lessons for reformist interventions in other societies. There was much tough bargaining and political interaction between the two governments. There were also aspects of American bargaining behavior that differed significantly from the Chinese case and that made it much more likely for the policy to succeed. Thus, the historical relationship between the United States and the Philippines is necessary yet insufficient to explain the policy outcome.

The first change in bargaining behavior was that American officials, especially in the Truman State Department, had learned and absorbed the lessons of China in regard to leverage and the Commitment Trap, and devised ways to circumvent the latter. Though the United States was committed to the Philippines, and the Filipinos recognized this, Quirino and his colleagues were never exactly sure of the extent of this commitment. The embassy team was very successful in bringing home the fact that commitments were limited and contingent upon actions of the Filipino government through a consistent quid pro quo bargaining approach. Thus, ambiguities over ultimate American intentions were maintained during the implementation of U.S. aid programs. This was also made clear by the actions of the top levels of government, at least during the Truman period.

By implementing its aid programs on a strictly quid pro quo, priority basis, the United States was able to defuse the inherent Filipino oppo-

sition to elite and redistributive reforms and to prevent it from coalesc-
ing. The military reforms brought about by Magsaysay undermined the
power of the Liberal Party to gain coercive control over the electoral
process, but the party did not realize this until the success of those
reforms changed the political climate to such an extent that the Liberals
could no longer act as they had in the past. If the reforms had been
implemented as a "package deal" in the Philippines, as had been tried
in China because of the intensity and scope of the problem, as well as
lack of experience by the Americans in asking the client virtually to
transform itself overnight, the opposition to them might have been
much more widespread and intense. This proportional approach also
made it less likely that the Liberals could appeal to nationalistic sentiment that would have been aroused through such a comprehensive
intervention.

As the American pressure at the highest levels receded in the Eisenhower administration, however, an increase in covert actions was
deemed necessary by the embassy team in Manila to prevent authoritarian retrenchment in the election of 1953. As in any policy, the attitudes at the top levels of the American government are of paramount
importance. The lack of follow-up after 1952 to the redistributive reforms envisioned by the Truman administration is unfortunate. In
many ways, the Filipino people are paying for that, and subsequent,
inattention to the present day.

Second, the lessons of China learned by the Americans in presenting
a united front of unfettered resolve to the client in the quid pro quo
also had a great effect on United States policy. The reformist policy
prescriptions of the State Department's Edward Rice (a reformist advocate in China in the 1940s; later a reformist advocate in Vietnam in
the 1960s), agrarian specialist Robert Hardie, Ambassadors Cowen and
Spruance, and John Melby are notable in this regard. At the tactical
level, Edward Lansdale was instrumental in implementing the reformist
policies through his imaginative approach to counterinsurgency. President Truman, Secretary of State Dean Acheson, and Secretary of Defense George C. Marshall also demonstrated an understanding of the
need for a cohesive, coordinated policy, and the paradoxical relationship
between commitments and leverage. In contrast to the China case, or
later in the Vietnamese context, this cohesiveness made it less likely for
the client to attempt to sidestep reformist American agencies and appeal
to more bolstering ones. Thus, the cohesiveness of the United States
effort was a key to the successful bargaining outcome.

Third, the Filipino political system, which unlike that of China had
pluralistic aspects, was easier to penetrate than the Chinese system.
Though he proved himself capable of violent action against his fellow

citizens, Quirino could not attack unarmed dissidents, political opponents, and critical journalists in the manner of Chiang Kai-shek. This
made it easier for the United States to influence the Filipino political
system. The Americans proved themselves capable of dealing surreptitiously with the political opposition and channeling its frustration with
the existing government into constructive, responsible action rather
than blind obstructionism. The existence of relatively independent political and societal institutions was extremely important in penetrating
another political system. For that reason, among many others, the promotion of pluralism in client nations should be a primary policy goal.

Fourth, the leadership of Ramon Magsaysay as Secretary of Defense
must be mentioned. Though hardly "invented" by the United States,
Magsaysay was an American liberal reformer's dream come true. A
dynamic, charismatic, honest, and compassionate leader dedicated to
democratic values is a rare commodity in any country, not just in the
Third World. He provided a key element in the reform program that
was lacking in China: an effective alternative leadership to which the
Americans could turn. His legacy is not American, though he was one
of the best allies the United States ever had in the Third World, but
Filipino. It is not surprising that organizations in the Philippines are
dedicated to preserving his memory.

Finally, a major share of the credit for the reforms should go to the
Filipino people themselves. In the face of brutal violence, they were
capable of acts of incredible bravery in challenging the right of their
government to suppress democracy. Though much of the credit for the
relative fairness of the 1951 and 1953 elections rests with Filipino institutions and United States policy, it should not be forgotten that the act
of voting in the violent atmosphere following the election of 1949 was
an act filled with danger.

The Filipinos, like the Chinese, wanted change along peaceful, democratic lines following the devastation of World War II. United States
policy consisted of providing a means of bringing this about, something
it could not accomplish in China. The Filipinos, like the Chinese, were
not pro-Communist, but were pushed in the direction of the radicals
by the active alienation of the populace by their government. When the
successful reformist intervention ended the most glaring examples of
government corruption and abuse in the Philippines, the Maoist "water"
(support from the people) dried up, leaving the "fish" (the guerrillas)
high and dry. By 1953 the insurgency was no longer a major problem,
and by 1955 most of the Huks had surrendered. In his summary of the
election of 1953, Ambassador Spruance mentioned Filipino institutions
and United States policy as "important factors" in the preservation of
democratic values. In the end, however, he stated: "The Filipino people

deserve the most unreserved congratulations."[42] To that, democrats everywhere can only agree.

Reformist intervention may not be the only, nor even the best, means to avoid the advent of hostile forces in a strategically placed Third World client of the United States. In the Philippines, however, it was an effective means to avoid the loss of a strategic asset, improve the lot of the average Filipino citizen, and prevent the possibility of greater intervention in the future. The use of American troops, which had been recommended by some in the State Department and embassy in 1951, for example, was happily unnecessary when they became available in 1953 with the end of the Korean War. Reform had helped the Filipinos handle the military situation largely on their own, with the United States providing the economic, military, and political tools for a successful counterinsurgency.

This is one of the ironies of reformist intervention. Though Americans like doing things on a grand scale, it was the relatively small effort in the Philippines that was a key to helping the Filipinos solve their own problems. The costs of the policy, therefore, were modest, and the benefits great.

It would be impossible to replicate the exact conditions of United States–Philippine relations during the early 1950s in any other context, or even in the Philippines today. There is no magic formula that can be applied to every instance with similar characteristics. If the United States decides to pursue a reformist intervention in a client nation in the future, however, there are valuable bargaining lessons to be learned from the Filipino case. This will not ensure a successful policy, but it may mean that it will be less likely to fail.

VIETNAM
1961–1963

IV

The New Commitment
to Diem, 1961

8

The advent of the New Frontier in 1961 signaled a return to reform as a general policy prescription toward instability in clients following the bolstering Eisenhower years. Eisenhower had begun the shift toward a more reformist policy after 1958, but it was the Kennedy administration that implemented it most consistently in the postwar era. As is typical with reformist periods, it was carried out by a Democratic administration following a period in which bolstering by Republicans was perceived by many to have failed in creating stable clients. The integrated military, economic, and political reform programs of the Truman years were thus resurrected within the context of the changing conditions of the 1960s.

These conditions were both internal and external. In domestic politics, the loss of China and the stalemated war in Korea, and the use of those situations for partisan political purposes by the Republicans, left Democratic leaders with reputations for softness in dealing with Communism. This domestic context is important in understanding the toughness with which the New Frontier seemed obsessed. Thus, according to the State Department's Lucius Battle, Republican, congressional, and public Cold War pressures—the "whole realm of the past [decade]"—weighed heavily on the Kennedy administration: "everybody was a little afraid at being called too liberal."[1] Within this context, withdrawal would have been difficult for any president; for a Democrat, it bordered on political suicide. This is not to say that the New Frontiersmen did not believe in a tough approach; they did, as had Truman. But in the wake of China, Korea, and McCarthyism, the fear of failure in the Third World, especially Asia, was particularly acute during the Kennedy and Johnson years.

The external pressures were the same as those facing the Truman and Eisenhower administrations, but the situation had worsened considerably in the late 1950s. The Kennedy administration was quickly presented with a number of crises (Laos-Vietnam, Cuba, Berlin, and the Congo) that had been festering late in the second Eisenhower administration, and for which there were no easy solutions. Though Vietnam was not *the* important crisis in the Kennedy years, as many in retrospect tried to portray it, neither was it a sideshow. The region was viewed as a weak link in the chain of containment that had to be held. Since withdrawal was not perceived as a viable option, and the bolstering of the Eisenhower years had failed to create a stable regime in South Vietnam, the Kennedy administration gradually adopted reformist intervention as its basic approach toward the government of Ngo Dinh Diem.

United States policy toward Diem[2] had been largely one of bolstering in the years 1954–1960.[3] This is not to say that no reforms were implemented. The training of indigenous military, police, administrative, and economic officials, limited land reform, and civic action programs were initiated, though they were seen by the United States as only first steps in mobilizing domestic and international support for the regime. The American military began the task of training a Vietnamese army to enable it to repulse an attack across the seventeenth parallel, and to aid in restoring domestic order.

It is also incorrect to assume, as many did because of subsequent events, that the bolstering policy completely failed. In fact, Diem was a relatively popular leader from 1955 to 1958, especially following the withdrawal of the French, as even the party history of the Communist regime in the North today admits. Relatively sophisticated observers such as Ellen Hammer were impressed by the progress that had been made in the early years.[4] In response to the successful attacks on the Communists in the South by the Diem government, the People's Republic of China and the U.S.S.R. began granting larger amounts of aid to the North in July 1955.[5]

Though the bolstering policy of the Eisenhower administration seemed to be working on the surface, problems that later would become acute were already beginning to appear by 1959. This was especially true of the American support given to Diem's brother Nhu and his semi-secret Can Lao Party, as well as his secret police, a policy that backfired on the United States. The repression that was the result of this policy worked in the short term to nearly destroy the network of the Communist cadre left behind by the North Vietnamese in 1954: the Government of the Republic of Vietnam (GVN) killed 2,000 Communists and arrested 65,000 "suspects." Communist party membership dropped from 5,000 to 2,000 members. It was, stated a later party history, "the darkest period" for the insurgency in the South. Diem's policies also alienated many non-Communist Vietnamese in the long term, however, through the excessive and arbitrary use of force. In addition, Diem, still wary of autonomous dissident groups in the countryside, made what in retrospect was a major error by abolishing elected village councils and replacing them with appointed officials loyal to the GVN. These officials, who were resented by many peasants, would become targets of assassination by the Communists throughout the late 1950s and early 1960s.[6]

The more alienation with the regime spread during 1957–1959, the more Diem appointed civilian and military personnel according to their total loyalty to his family, the more resentment spread among non-Communist Vietnamese, the more he personally took over decision-making for even trivial matters, and the more he relied on his brother Nhu for advice. By 1958, the promising start made on land reform and civic action in the countryside had virtually ended. Though Diem retained a relatively strong power position through 1957, by 1958 the facade had begun to crack.[7]

The regime, as it had evolved within the context of constant challenges to its authority in the late 1950s, was increasingly totalitarian in attempting to gain control over virtually all elements of life in South Vietnam. With potential and actual enemies everywhere, Diem relied on his family for advice to an extraordinary degree. Decisions were made by the president, then communicated to the government and populace. Position and promotion in the army and government were apportioned according to loyalty to the Ngo family. Eschewing U.S. advice for increased development in the private sector, the government attempted to gain control over the economic life of the nation. Elections were held, but were strictly controlled by the secret police apparatus. Though this allowed for control of military, political, and economic organizations in the short term, it also created increasingly violent opposition to the regime.[8]

Alarmed at the growing opposition to the regime, the Eisenhower administration abandoned its bolstering policy and in 1959 began putting pressure on Diem for reform. This policy entailed consistent pressure from Ambassador Elbridge Durbrow in the last year of the Eisenhower administration for elite and redistributive reforms to broaden the base of the regime. Following a coup attempt by dissident young military officers in November 1960, this pressure increased. The Ngos, apparently convinced of continued U.S. commitment, moved in the opposite direction toward further control of political life.[9]

Decision-making: President Kennedy's Initial Estimation of Vietnam

In late 1960, the Eisenhower administration sent the ubiquitous Edward Lansdale to Vietnam for an estimation of the deteriorating situation. Lansdale was something of an anomaly in the wrangling over reformist intervention versus bolstering: he recognized the necessity for elite and redistributive reforms as a central part of counterinsurgency policy, yet he was against the quid pro quo diplomatic approach, arguing instead that bolstering was necessary to beget agreement on reform. He saw solutions to the problem with the client government in cross-cultural, personal bonds created through shared sacrifice and subtle persuasion. Lansdale argued, with verve and insight, that these types of friendships are particularly important in non-Western cultures, where impersonal political and economic relationships have not yet taken hold. Yet he also recognized the futility of bolstering a client regardless of its actions. Such views often placed him outside the mainstream arguments over bolstering versus the quid pro quo: bolsterers were put off by his constant references to a need for political, economic, and social change as an integral part of counterinsurgency strategy; reformers were put off by his frequent references to a need for friendly persuasion rather than coercive diplomacy.[10]

Upon his return to the United States, Lansdale wrote a report emphasizing the need to regain the trust of the Ngos in order to prevent a Communist takeover. Characteristically, he bluntly criticized American officials who bolstered a client with little or no thought given to the long-range consequences of their actions. After pointing out that it had been the State Department that had promoted the creation of the Can Lao Party and the secret police under Nhu, against the advice of many (including Lansdale) in the CIA, a situation that State was now lamenting, he pointed to the contradictions in this kind of bolstering. The benefits were, he stated, "extremely short-term" and had inevitably driven other non-Communist opposition groups underground: "I cannot truly sympathize with Americans who help promote a fascistic state and then get angry when it doesn't act like a democracy."[11] Having skewered U.S. policy for the previous four years, Lansdale was surprised when told to report to a meeting with the new President in late January, 1961.

President Kennedy was more knowledgeable about the situation in Vietnam than many other members of Congress. He had been a founding member of the "Friends of Vietnam," a group dedicated to avoiding the advent of Communism in that nation, but he had also been extremely critical of the French role. Now that he was President, however, he perceived the U.S. commitment unsentimentally. A bellicose January 1961 speech by Soviet leader Nikita Khrushchev challenging the United States in the Third World had focused attention on hot spots in the developing areas. After reading Lansdale's report, Kennedy commented to aide Walt Rostow: "This is the worst one we've got, isn't it?" He met with Lansdale and key advisers on January 28.[12]

Lansdale argued that elite reforms would have to wait until Diem was reassured of American support and that the seriousness of the situation in Laos and Vietnam precluded placing increases in aid on a quid pro quo basis. Kennedy asked whether it was possible to initiate action against the North to relieve the pressure in the South. He was informed that it was Diem who blocked such action, preferring to concentrate on his internal security problems. Kennedy noted that military aid alone was not enough and asked "whether the situation was not basically one of politics and morale." Secretary of State Dean Rusk, perhaps remembering his experiences in the Truman State Department, noted the difficulty in supporting and pressuring Diem simultaneously. President Kennedy said he would write to Diem, and ordered National Security Adviser McGeorge Bundy to set up "task forces" on the crisis areas of Vietnam, the Congo, Laos, and Cuba.[13]

Bargaining Behavior: Toward a Quid Pro Quo?

A counterinsurgency plan that had been drawn up under Eisenhower was put forward on January 30, 1961. It consisted of $28.4 million for the expansion of the Army of the Republic of Vietnam (ARVN) by 20,000 men, $12.7 million for a 32,000-man expansion in the Civil Guards (paramilitary groups based in the villages), and $650,000 for psychological warfare and covert action. Kennedy also ordered the Pentagon to create training facilities for American soldiers/advisers schooled in the political and social aspects of war, as well as military strategy. The impetus for the "new" counterinsurgency doctrine, which was actually a reiteration of many of the ideas developed in the Truman administration, came from civilian advisers such as Walt Rostow, Roger Hilsman, and Robert Komer, not from the career military, who often resented this intrusion into their areas of expertise. This was the beginning of a bureaucratic split over the relative emphasis to be placed on military and political factors in Vietnam that was to explode in 1963.[14]

With the counterinsurgency plan approved in Washington, the problem remained of how to approach Diem. Secretary of State Rusk initially agreed with those advocating a quid pro quo. He wired Ambassador Durbrow on February 3 that the counterinsurgency plan had been approved to deal with the immediate crisis, but there was also a long-term need for "liberalization to retain [the] necessary popular cooperation." Domestic politics in the United States were also a concern for the secretary of state. The current funding, he stated, was for fiscal year 1961; in the future, congressional approval would be necessary, and Congress would watch most closely for progress on elite and redistributive reforms. If Diem did not cooperate, Durbrow "should inform Washington with recommendations, which may include suspension [of the] U.S. contribution."[15]

In apparent response to this pressure, three days later Diem announced major elite reforms, which the United States had been urging for months: a new Department of Civic Action, a new National Economic Council, a new Department of Rural Affairs, and other lesser councils at the provincial and village levels to increase participation in the Vietnamese government's programs.[16] As the United States repeatedly discovered, however, having Diem's promises for reform did not mean that they would be implemented. Throughout February, employing classic tactics for a client, he stalled over the elite reforms. Ambassador Durbrow consistently pressured for implementation of the "package deal," but the Vietnamese leader would not be moved.

By mid-March, Kennedy was displaying growing frustration over the impasse. He peppered National Security Adviser McGeorge Bundy with "repeated questioning" over Vietnam and was "really very eager indeed that it should have the highest priority for rapid and energetic action." With a Vietnamese presidential election scheduled for April 9, it was decided to wait until after that date to approach Diem more forcefully.[17] There were intervening events of the Cold War, however, that undermined the ability of the United States to pressure Diem through a quid pro quo approach to commitments.

Decision-making: The Cold War in the Spring of 1961: Drawing the Line

The importance of Laos to the defense of a non-Communist Southeast Asia had been emphasized to Kennedy by Eisenhower during their meeting in the transition period. In August 1960 a CIA-trained Laotian army officer, Kong Le, had carried out a coup that split the anti-Communist opposition and turned power over to the neutralist Prince Souvanna Phouma. These events led to an alarming increase in armed activity by the Communist Pathet Lao. In the following month, the

North Vietnamese made the decision to push for military victory in South Vietnam. Intense fighting in Laos broke out in mid-December, 1960, with the American-backed forces performing badly—in fact, in many cases, simply running away. Within this context, Eisenhower told Kennedy that the United States might have to intervene unilaterally with troops to prevent the advent of Communism in that nation. As Press Secretary James Hagerty told one Kennedy transition team member, the United States "may be committed to war" in Laos. In mid-March, 1961, the crisis worsened as the U.S.-backed forces were routed on the battlefield in the Plain of Jars. This precipitated a crisis that threatened the whole of Indochina.[18]

With the American-backed troops faring so badly, Kennedy moved toward a negotiated solution. He did not, however, want to appear to make a deal from a position of weakness. The Soviets appeared to be intransigent, with their preferred side doing so well on the battlefield. As Secretary of State Rusk wired the embassy in Moscow, the United States had offered a carrot of a negotiated settlement in January, but had been rebuffed. It now must offer a stick. The U.S.S.R. had responded to the offer to negotiate with a large airlift to the Communist forces in Laos through Hanoi. Though the Soviets had warned that an "extension of U.S. aid to [the] rebels would greatly increase [the] dangers in Laos," it was a risk the Kennedy administration was willing to accept.[19]

The increase in aid was given to precipitate negotiations over Laos, but key advisers also argued for a show of force in Thailand and Vietnam to deter the Communists from replicating the Laotian success in those nations. Kennedy sent 500 Marines to the Lao-Thai border, moved a fleet into the Gulf of Siam and the China Sea, and put U.S. troops in Okinawa on alert. The CIA was sent into Laos to arm and train Meo tribesmen, who were meant to replace the disintegrating Laotian army as effective anti-Communist forces. The President then sent clandestine messages through India to the Chinese that threatened military intervention in Laos if the Communist offensive were not ended, but that also promised to seek a negotiated solution if the Soviets stopped their airlift. A few days later, the Soviets and the United States began negotiations for a ceasefire.[20] Over the next fifteen months, the "neutralization" of Laos was negotiated by Ambassador-at-Large Averell Harriman.[21] It would remain, however, as a backdrop for United States–South Vietnamese negotiations through 1962.

The Cold War pressures were not only coming from the Soviets; domestic criticism of Kennedy was also increasing. Republicans publicly attacked the President for "appeasement" in seeking a negotiated solution in Laos. Some of the most publicly hawkish members of Congress, however, told the administration privately that they were against military intervention. One of the biggest problems was Eisenhower, who was apparently still smarting from Kennedy's criticisms in the 1960 campaign.

Democrats also pressured the President to hold the line in the region. Senator J. William Fulbright wrote to Kennedy: "The thought occurred to me that the extent to which you might be willing to go in defending Laos could possibly be influenced by the stability in Viet-Nam. It would be embarrassing, to say the least, to have Viet-Nam collapse just as we are extended in Laos."[22]

In an effort to fend off right-wing and intra-party criticism, Kennedy convinced British Prime Minister Harold MacMillan to send a letter to Eisenhower asking him not to "encourage those who think that a military solution in Laos is the only way of stopping the Communists in that area." In addition, the influential columnist Walter Lippman publicly took to task those who criticized in this vein: "You can't decide these questions of life and death for the world by epithets like appeasement." Though these statements temporarily eased the domestic calls for military solutions to every Cold War crisis, this domestic political pressure continued to shape the administration's policies.[23]

More bad news was in store. In mid-April, 1961, the disastrous Bay of Pigs invasion ended the honeymoon some had had with the New Frontier. Though the President's popularity with the public actually rose, many leading observers began to question his competence. A week prior to the Bay of Pigs, Soviet Cosmonaut Yuri Gargarin made the first manned orbital space flight, which, though it did not have the effect of Sputnik in 1957, underscored growing Soviet power to many in the West. In addition, Soviet Premier Khrushchev was publicly berating Dag Hammarskjold following the death of Patrice Lumumba in the Congo, on the heels of his tough speech in January proclaiming Soviet support for "Wars of National Liberation." Adolph Berle noted in his diary that Kennedy had more crises thrust upon him in his first months of office than any president since Lincoln.[24]

In light of the Laotian and other Cold War crises of the spring, the United States decided to take a tougher line against the Communists in Vietnam. Three days after the Bay of Pigs debacle, Kennedy told a cabinet meeting he wanted a coordinated plan to prevent the fall of the Diem government, giving Lansdale and Roswell Gilpatric of the Defense Department one week to produce a report. The President again personally pushed the idea of covert actions against the Northern regime. At an April 29 meeting, the Joint Chiefs of Staff suggested a military, rather than negotiated, solution in Laos. In the aftermath of the Bay of Pigs, however, both the President and Attorney General Robert Kennedy were most reluctant to intervene militarily in that nation. Robert Kennedy and Secretary of Defense Robert McNamara agreed that the best place to "draw the line" in Southeast Asia was through Vietnam and Thailand. Since this was what General Douglas MacArthur also advised in an April 28 meeting with President Kennedy, the decision was made to establish an American troop presence in Vietnam to deter the Soviet and Chinese from attempting to repeat the Laotian crisis in that nation. Plans were made to send Vice-President Johnson to Southeast Asia to signal American resolve through the commitment to Diem.[25]

Bargaining Behavior: Ambassador Durbrow Fails in Arguing for a Quid Pro Quo

Following his guaranteed election victory on April 9, 1961, Diem continued to demonstrate an unwillingness to agree to the elite and redistributive reforms called for in the American counterinsurgency plan. On April 12, in an interview with the conservative columnist Joseph Alsop, he accused the United States of denying him crucial aid since 1958 and not taking his problems seriously enough. The only American Diem had anything positive to say about was General Lansdale, and he implied that he should be sent to Vietnam as ambassador.

Ambassador Durbrow cabled that this was an obvious tactic to get more American aid, that the insurgency had not grown because of a dearth of resources but because of many of the actions of the Diem government, that the South Vietnamese could not absorb much of the aid they already had, and that elite and redistributive reforms were also necessary to defeat the insurgency. Since it was the Vietnamese government that was stalling on the counterinsurgency plan, and those negotiations were secret, Durbrow stated that Diem was using Alsop to counter U.S. pressure for reform. He advocated calling his bluff: "I recommend [that State] send me strong instructions to [the] effect that [the] GVN should start implementing [the integrated counterinsurgency] plan or we cannot give M[ilitary] A[ssistance] P[rogram funds] for [a] force increase."[26]

While this response was being contemplated, Lansdale strongly objected, pointing to the "personality clash" between Diem and Durbrow. Lansdale often reduced complex matters to problems of cross-cultural, interpersonal relationships, an area in which he excelled. With the situation deteriorating in the countryside, and Cold War considerations pressing on all sides, Lansdale's prescription was adopted, and the new ambassador, Frederick "Fritz" Nolting, was instructed to take a more persuasive approach with Diem to assure him of United States support.[27]

Though the American objective remained "to prevent Communist domination of South Vietnam and to create in that country a viable and increasingly democratic society," Cold War pressures to demonstrate resolve, the weakness of the client regime, and an increase in infiltration from the North in May 1961 led to a temporary policy consensus. With Nolting's arrival in Saigon, the United States again began bolstering the government of South Vietnam.[28]

On April 29, President Kennedy approved a 100-man increase in the Military Advisory and Assistance Group (MAAG) and 110 CIA personnel. Though the United States was later criticized for keeping its allies in the dark over these moves, in fact the British, French, and Canadians were informed of this secretly in mid-May, 1961. The allies agreed with the necessity of the buildup, but wanted to avoid the embarrassment of a public disavowal of the Geneva Agreements. The government of India was informed in July.

The State Department was also considering a bilateral treaty with the Diem government and the public rejection of the Geneva Agreements, though the concerns of the allies prevented the latter. Some advisers, such as Undersecretary of State Chester Bowles, Ambassador Durbrow, Ambassador Kenneth Young, and Theodore Sorensen, attempted to convince Kennedy of the necessity for a quid pro quo, but the seriousness of the situation and the perceived need to establish a presence in Southeast Asia precluded delay. Though there was concern over possible military intervention by the Chinese if the United States sent troops, the CIA discounted that eventuality because China had serious economic and political problems in the aftermath of the disastrous "Great Leap Forward."[29]

The sense of urgency was increased in early May, with a spate of reports of coup planning among a variety of groups, especially in the ARVN, who were all asking for U.S. support. Even Dr. Tran Kim Tuyen, the head of Ngo Dinh Nhu's secret police, was plotting against the regime. Within this context, elite reforms were considered necessary in the long term to mobilize support and increase organizational efficiency. In the short term, however, Diem was considered irreplaceable. With coup plots brewing everywhere, it was decided to bolster the Diem government domestically and internationally, and send U.S. troops to deter the Communists from expanding the war.[30]

Bargaining Behavior: The Johnson Trip and Managing Commitments

Vice-President Lyndon Johnson traveled to Southeast Asia in early May, 1961, accompanied by President Kennedy's sister and brother-in-law, to signal American commitment and resolve. He suggested to Diem the introduction of American combat troops, the entrance of Vietnam into the Southeast Asia Treaty Organization (SEATO), and a United States–Vietnamese bilateral defense treaty. The Vietnamese leader, to the surprise of the Americans, rejected the troops, though he accepted United States advisers to accelerate the expansion of the ARVN. He told Johnson that he would later consider a bilateral treaty.

Diem's argument, which embassy officials upon reflection thought sound, was that to carry out these measures would automatically abrogate the Geneva Agreements, causing the dissolution of the International Control Commission that was supposedly policing the agreements. Diem had absolutely no faith in the Agreements or the International Control Commission, nor should he have had, but he argued that they had a certain deterrent value on the North Vietnamese. If the Agreements were abrogated, this would probably cause further outright aggression by the Communists.

When presented with this new development, Kennedy again rejected the advice of reformist advisers for a quid pro quo, and that of the military Joint Chiefs of Staff for pressing further for the introduction of U.S. combat troops, and expanded the advisory effort without reciprocal commitments for reform from Diem. On May 11, 1961, Kennedy issued NSAM 52, calling for "military, political, economic, psychological and covert" action to prevent the overthrow of the government of South Vietnam. Though the creation of "an increasingly democratic society" remained a goal, it moved to the background. In essence, Diem had won the waiting game; the counterinsurgency plan aid went ahead without reform.[31]

When Diem rejected most of the reforms in the counterinsurgency plan, the State Department began to have doubts about the offer of a bilateral treaty. This occurred in reaction to a change of attitude in the Vietnamese government in the wake of Johnson's trip. There were a number of economic issues that had been negotiated for some two years, and the negotiations had reached their final phase when Johnson arrived to demonstrate the commitment to Vietnam. After the trip, United States personnel noticed a distinct unwillingness on the part of the Vietnamese even to discuss these agreements. Once again, it appeared that a demonstration of commitment had undermined American leverage in Vietnam.[32]

In light of this development, the State Department immediately withdrew the offer for a bilateral treaty until an economic mission had determined what actions were necessary to place the economy of South Vietnam on a sound fiscal basis. On May 29, 1961, the administration announced an economic mission under the leadership of Dr. Eugene Staley, a distinguished Stanford University economist. On the same day, the embassy helped arrange for a British advisory mission to be sent to Saigon under the leadership of the experienced counterinsurgency specialist Sir Robert Thompson.[33]

Decision-making: The Cold War Again

In early June, 1961, President Kennedy traveled to Geneva for a summit with the Soviet Premier, Nikita Khrushchev. Though initially hopeful that summit diplomacy would engender a modus vivendi with the U.S.S.R. in a number of areas, Kennedy was disappointed with the bluster and ideological harangues that he was subjected to by the Communist leader.

Subsequent actions by the Communists suggested that they were not bluffing. Within weeks of the meeting, the United States received intelligence reports that the Soviets had conducted a massive airlift of supplies to Hanoi and that the North planned increased infiltration of officers and cadre into South Vietnam through Laos and Cambodia. In an important intelligence stroke, the United States "turned" a member of the North Vietnamese delegation to the International Control Commission in Hanoi, and was told by the informant that the North Vietnamese intended to infiltrate 30,000 personnel in July and August, many of whom were originally from South Vietnam but had been trained in the U.S.S.R. and China for a year. Though the number turned out to be excessive (this might, in fact, have been "disinformation" to discourage an escalation by the United States), a precipitous increase in infiltration did occur in preparation for a September Viet Cong offensive. United States actions should be seen within this context. Unfortunately, the United States, as is so often the case, could not release the information without threatening the loss of its source. In response to the threat, however, it made plans to outline publicly the control of the Viet Cong by the North, and the latter's training of the Pathet Lao.[34] This culminated in the issuance of the *Vietnam White Paper* in the fall of 1961.

Khrushchev continued to bluster over Berlin following the Geneva summit meeting. Kennedy responded with a major military buildup, including a doubling of the number of draftees, the reactivation of some reserve units, and a $3.25 billion increase in military appropriations. In reaction, the Soviets acted to solve the Berlin crisis unilaterally with the construction of the Berlin Wall in mid-August. Khrushchev also announced the resumption of atmospheric nuclear testing in late August; Kennedy resumed underground testing in early September. The need to demonstrate resolve in the wake of the Bay of Pigs, Laos, and the Berlin Wall was to dominate United States policy in Vietnam until the Cuban missile crisis of October 1962. In reaction to the Soviet performance at Geneva, Kennedy told James Reston of the *New York Times:* "Now we have a problem in making our power credible, and Vietnam looks like the place."[35]

Bargaining Behavior: Cosmetic Political Reforms in Vietnam

The bolstering approach to Diem in the late spring of 1961 seemed to bear fruit at first. On May 26, Diem's closest adviser outside his family, Secretary for the Presidency Nguyen Dinh Thuan, told Ambassador Nolting that the elite and redistributive reforms promised since February would be implemented. They turned out to be extremely limited in scope, and essentially cosmetic. At the time, however, they appeared to be indicative of a positive response to bolstering. Ambassador Nolting, a man of seemingly boundless optimism in dealing with the Ngos, said the changes made were "primarily organizational rather than political" but still represented a positive movement toward elite reforms. The political opposition in Vietnam, however, was not so easily convinced. On May 31, six South Vietnamese diplomats, including two ambassadors, resigned in protest over the cosmetic cabinet reorganization. Dang Duc Khoi, the chargé d'affaires in Bangkok, stated to the Americans following his resignation that the reorganization proved "Diem intends no real change in his method of governing." Resignations of some of the most talented members of the South Vietnamese government were a growing problem for Diem, reinforcing his belief that he must rely on Nhu and his own judgment.[36]

This set the stage for the spiral of poor relations between the Americans and the Vietnamese over the next two years. The more Diem resisted elite reforms, the more dissidence spread among intra- and extra-governmental elites. The greater the opposition to Diem became, the more the United States pressed for elite reforms.

Decision-making: State Support for Reform; Pentagon Support for Bolstering

The security situation continued to deteriorate. On June 9, Diem sent Kennedy a private letter requesting additional military aid, arguing that increased Communist infiltration from Laos was dispersing his troops.

If he did not receive increased aid, he warned, he would be forced to begin withdrawing from northern provinces and his government might collapse. To train the new troops, he urgently requested a "considerable expansion" of MAAG. Though he reiterated his dedication to the political and social goals envisioned by the counterinsurgency plan, he stated that he must first restore order. A growing number of American political and economic advisers, however, viewed reforms as a sine qua non for the restoration of order. Even Ambassador Nolting saw a "cause and effect relationship" between the growing insurgency and the "overcentralization" of the government of South Vietnam, though he continued to advocate a bolstering approach. This chicken-and-egg disagreement over order and reform would last until the end of the regime.[37]

Diem's request for additional aid, while placing secondary importance on the elite and redistributive reforms of the counterinsurgency plan, exacerbated a growing bureaucratic split over bolstering and reform. The military pushed for a bolstering approach to meet the new situation on the battlefield. When the United States moved toward a negotiated settlement in Laos, Kennedy's military advisers viewed the security of Thailand and Vietnam as gravely threatened. They therefore believed that military aid could not wait for the slow process of an overall settlement of the controversial areas of elite and redistributive reforms. The Pentagon argued for immediate military action to gain the initiative on the battlefield and to deter the enemy from increasing its commitment to the Communist insurgents in Vietnam, as they had done in Laos.

State Department advisers agreed that the military situation was serious, but were worried over the negative effects of military bolstering on Diem before settlement of outstanding political and economic issues. In reaction to Diem's request, State argued that military commitments would further undermine leverage for economic and political reforms.

Despite grave doubts voiced among his political advisers, Kennedy ordered an immediate increase of funding for 20,000 ARVN troops (to a total of 170,000) under the counterinsurgency plan, but deferred the question of further increases until he received the report of the Staley Economic Mission.[38]

Dr. Eugene Staley headed an economic survey mission to Vietnam during June and July, 1961. On July 22, Staley delivered a preliminary report proposing an agreement that included a quid pro quo bargaining approach for elite and redistributive reforms. This set the negotiating agenda for the rest of 1961 and created new American pressures for reform. This series of developments gave hope to reformist agencies, especially the State Department.

The reformist agencies continued to press their case for a comprehensive reform program. The State Department, the Budget Office, and the International Cooperation Administration argued that the United States "ought to insist upon much more in the way of political and economic action as a condition for additional aid." In the event, President Kennedy, in consultation with Secretary Rusk, Walt Rostow, and George Ball, leaned toward the reformist position, emphasizing a list of redistributive reforms that the Americans believed should be taken as "emergency actions" to "strengthen the vital ties of loyalty" between the government and the people, especially in the rural areas. These consisted of land redistribution, rural credit to small farmers, road construction, educational programs, medical services, and improved relations between rural administrators and the peasants. Also included was yet another request for elite reforms and the delegation of authority. If these actions were taken, Kennedy wrote Diem, a "Free Vietnam" would be "among the highest priorities" of the United States government.[39]

Bargaining Behavior: The United States Splits Its Commitments

President Diem's reaction to Kennedy's quid pro quo was not encouraging. When Nolting met with him on August 8 to obtain his reaction, Diem displayed his irritation over the strings attached to the aid offer. Nolting explained that reading between the diplomatic lines would show a major commitment to the South Vietnamese government, and that the United States was resolved to aid him in his struggle against the Communists. Diem indicated his objections to elite reforms, because, in Nolting's words, they "might take out of his hands the detailed planning and direction for which he has such an appetite." In light of these objections, Rusk instructed Nolting to go ahead with a joint communiqué that announced the economic and military aid programs, but to remove the political and social provisions for the present, stating that they would be negotiated separately. He also ordered the removal of vague promises of commitment to avoid the appearances of further "contractual undertaking[s]" and "executive agreements that do not exist," stating that he feared the South Vietnamese would use them as a "negotiating gambit" in future bargaining.[40]

   In the bargaining over reform in the summer of 1961, Diem did rather well. He received a major commitment from the United States to his government and diluted its entreaties for joint planning and elite reforms to such an extent that no firm commitments were obtained from him. The only major concession he made was the devaluation of the *piastre*, one of the recommendations of the Staley Mission, and something he had been planning to do in any event. Although President Kennedy, Secretary Rusk, and others were aware of the dangers of making commitments without receiving any in return, the Cold War events of the summer and the deteriorating security situation in Vietnam itself prevented them from taking a hard line with their client. Events were about to occur, however, that would alter this situation markedly.

Decision-making: The September 1961 Viet Cong Offensive

In spite of his success in bargaining with the United States, Diem's position in the early fall of 1961 remained precarious. He was especially concerned about the reports of increased infiltration from Laos. The United States was also concerned about these reports in light of the intelligence information it had received that summer. Further evidence was not long in materializing.

On September 10, the Viet Cong mounted a major offensive that MAAG believed represented a "significant increase in Viet Cong capabilities," especially in the Cambodian border areas. By September 15, there were reports of a doubling of North Vietnamese officers and cadre in South Vietnam (from 1,500 in July to 3,200 in September), an increase of some 7,000 members of the Viet Cong since January, attacks involving 1,000 troops or more in some areas, "large scale military movements" in Laos, Cambodia, and North Vietnam, an increased use of Soviet and Chinese military tactics that suggested the infiltration of trained cadres from the north, the increased use of terrorism against noncombatants (for example, the mutilation of women and children in some provinces, something not previously done to a significant degree), and devastatingly effective attacks on the South Vietnamese irregular militia forces in the provinces. By September 20, 1961, a Joint State-Defense Message from Saigon stated that emergency military aid must be granted to Diem within thirty days "if [the] GVN [Government of Vietnam is] to retain [the] capacity to defend itself."[41]

On September 22, 1961, State's Chester Bowles wrote Nolting that the Diem government should request increases in military aid including increased training of the provincial militia, those worst hit by the attacks, and more technological means for dealing with the infiltrators. On September 25, President Kennedy made a speech at the United Nations on subversion in Vietnam; as Bowles later wired Nolting, this was done to "underline [the] importance with which [the] matter [was] regarded" in Washington. Kennedy expressed his own "urgent" interest in reports of any substantial infiltration into Vietnam from Laos and Cambodia.[42]

Decision-making: The October 1961 Policy Review

The September offensive alarmed both the Diem government and opposition elements in Saigon. On September 15, Diem declared a national emergency based on the perception that the Viet Cong were no longer a guerrilla force, but were engaged in a full-scale war against the government. He then suspended civil liberties to a large degree and pushed through legislation in mid-October giving him extraordinary powers to meet the crisis. The increased infiltration from Laos, and the continuing negotiations over that nation's fate without South Vietnamese participation, worried Diem. When Souvanna Phouma was named the leader of a provisional government in Laos on October 8, raising the specter of the growth of neutralist sentiment in Vietnam, he reacted with a sharp crackdown on the opposition. Madame Nhu's so-called Public Morality Law, though not passed until 1962, was introduced in the National Assembly and banned, among other things, divorce, adultery, contraception, all forms of public meetings without government permission (even weddings and funerals had to be approved), and dancing in public. To make matters worse for the regime, a major flood occurred in the Mekong Delta in early October, which stretched the government's resources to the limit. Under pressure from the Ngos to do something, the United States faced a deteriorating military and political situation in Vietnam that precipitated a policy review within the U.S. government over how best to meet the crisis.[43]

The options open to the Kennedy administration were not numerous. In regard to withdrawal, Kennedy never seriously considered the possibility in the fall of 1961. A main reason had been pointed out by Senator William Fulbright that spring: the potential effects of a collapse of South Vietnam on the delicate negotiations over Laos. If the United States withdrew from Vietnam, its diplomatic position in Laos would be virtually untenable, raising the specter of falling dominos. In addition, the decision had been made earlier in the year to "draw the line" in Vietnam and Thailand, and pulling out of the former under the pressure of a Communist offensive would be viewed, it was believed, as a serious defeat for the United States. Finally, Republican pressure over containment was an added constraint. When Ambassador John Kenneth Galbraith discussed the dangers of becoming overly committed to Diem in November, the President told him: "There are limits to the number of defeats I can defend in one twelve-month period. I've had the Bay of Pigs and pulling out of Laos, and I can't accept a third." The policy review therefore centered around the bolstering-reform dilemma in Vietnam.[44]

In general, the military continued to promote the bolstering option.

Though military advisers recognized the need for reforms, they argued that the exigencies of the battlefield precluded delay. They advocated a precipitous increase in materials, training of troops (especially for the reeling militia), and the deployment of American combat troops, preferably in Laos but, if that were politically impossible, then in Vietnam. Though they acknowledged that the Viet Cong could recruit sufficient troops locally, they tended to emphasize the role of infiltration in the deteriorating security situation. The Joint Chiefs rejected the use of multilateral forces from other nations as unlikely to solve the problem. Thus, bolstering continued to dominate the military's advice to President Kennedy.

In reaction to this advice, on October 7, National Security Adviser McGeorge Bundy told Kennedy that the United States must discover "a way of acting much more vigorously in South Vietnam." Four days later, the President partly accepted the arguments of the bolsterers and increased the number of advisers in MAAG, ordered preparations for sending combat troops, appealed to SEATO for support, and announced that he would send General Maxwell Taylor to survey United States options—all without asking for anything in return from the Diem government.[45] Again, in deference to allies, who were generally in favor of the U.S. response but preferred that any buildup be carried out surreptitiously, American embassies were ordered to deny the increases until they were already in effect.[46]

Those in the State Department and the International Cooperation Administration who advocated reform were not against the military buildup advocated by Defense. In fact, some in State accused the military of dragging their feet in the training and equipping of the ARVN and the militia. They worried, however, that Diem had not kept his promises made earlier in the year to implement elite and redistributive reforms. Sporadic but insistent reports were received from the United States Operations Mission, which had programmatic responsibility for the social and economic efforts in rural areas, that ARVN troops were alienating the peasantry and ignoring the civic action pronouncements from Saigon. Concentrating on the failure of political and economic programs, these agencies advocated a quid pro quo approach. Though they recognized that increased infiltration from Laos was a serious problem, especially in the Central Highlands, they tended to concentrate on the local recruitment capabilities of the Viet Cong, something the CIA also emphasized.

The redistributive reforms advocated by the civilian agencies were meant to alleviate the underlying causes of discontent, rally support to the government, and make such Communist recruitment more difficult. If the reforms were carried out in conjunction with a vigorous military

program, which the agencies also saw as obviated by the Ngos' centralized leadership, the South Vietnamese government might have a chance
to overcome its military and political problems. If combat troops were
sent to Vietnam, argued Secretary Rusk, leverage for reforms would be
lost; if Diem did not reform, American troops would be inadequate to
handle the deteriorating situation.[47]

This reformist argument was strengthened through surreptitious
meetings with opposition figures who told the United States that the
war would be lost if reforms were not put through. The intra-governmental opposition's proposal for reforms, however, did not include the
broad-based elite reforms the United States was suggesting. Secret Police
Chief Tuyen told one CIA operative: "There should be no yielding to
pressures for liberalization. Democracy was not what was needed in
Vietnam's extremity, but leadership."[48]

The extra-governmental opposition, however, was also extremely ag-
itated in the wake of the September Offensive and the subsequent
government crackdown on dissent, and the need to rally support for
the Vietnamese government remained a critical concern. In addition,
many in the ARVN were now openly criticizing the regime. If these
elements were to form an anti-Ngo coalition, cabled Nolting, there could
be "real trouble." In the midst of what the ambassador labeled "insecurity, uneasiness and emergent instability," the United States was not
about to make a greater commitment to the regime without reforms.[49]

Decision-making: The Taylor Mission

In mid-October, 1961, General Maxwell Taylor led a team of military
and political analysts to Vietnam to assess the situation and generate
policy options. Much of the discussion there centered on the introduction of American combat troops to aid in the military effort. The Joint
Chiefs and Secretary of Defense Robert McNamara advocated sending
as many as six divisions. Many in the State Department remained wary,
though they felt this might become necessary at some time in the future,
and advocated taking a hard line with Diem in terms of reforms. Ambassador Harriman wrote Arthur Schlesinger that he feared the Defense
Department saw military action as a cure for the political problems of
the Ngo regime and drew a loose analogy with the loss of China: "Our
experience with Chiang Kai-shek may not be quite applicable, although
it has some applicability."[50] Virtually everyone, however, was in favor
of increased aid. Although there were widely divergent policy recommendations in terms of bolstering and reform, there was little sentiment
for abandoning the situation.

In early November, 1961, General Maxwell Taylor delivered his report to President Kennedy. He called for an increased logistical task force, increased military and economic aid, an increase in covert operations, and the deployment of the 8,000 troops recommended by Ambassador Nolting and the MAAG chief, General McGarr. He left open the possibility of direct attacks on the North if ground troops and increased training did not turn the tide. In addition, the report called for widespread elite and redistributive reforms as part of a joint effort by the United States and Diem's government to capture the loyalty of dissident elements in Saigon, and to mobilize the rural populace to the government's cause.

To ensure actual implementation, rather than the empty promises of the past, Taylor advocated a "limited partnership," with United States personnel sharing in all decisions pertaining to security. Though the main emphasis was on the military problems, the political and social aspects were included. In addition, mission member Walt Rostow, who was worried about Diem's isolation, recommended that Lansdale, who was also a member of the mission, be sent back to Vietnam to help convince Diem of the need for changes. The issuance of the report brought to the forefront the bureaucratic split over bolstering and reform.[51]

Defense Secretary Robert McNamara and the Joint Chiefs reacted to Taylor's recommendations with a reiteration of their view that 8,000 troops were not enough to turn the tide in Vietnam. They posited that a minimum of six divisions were necessary to offset infiltration and have a real impact on the performance of the ARVN. On November 8, the Secretary of Defense sent a memo to President Kennedy making these points, and strongly suggested that the larger troop commitment be made. A precondition for such an action, however, was a general, public commitment to securing a non-Communist Vietnam.[52]

The State Department, including Secretary Rusk, was more circumspect in its recommendations for troops. On the day Taylor sent his initial memo from Baguio in the Philippines, Rusk, who was attending meetings in Tokyo, told State to give "special attention" to whether Diem would take the "necessary measures to give [the] U.S. something worth supporting." If the Vietnamese were not willing to delegate authority to military commanders and incorporate extra-governmental nationalists, argued the Secretary, a "relative handful" of American troops would not be decisive in solving the crisis. While "attaching [the] greatest possible importance" to the defense of Southeast Asia, the United States could not make an "additional commitment" of its prestige to a "losing horse." He instructed State to review carefully "all measures we expect from Diem if our assistance forces [the] U.S. to assume de facto direction [of] Vietnamese affairs." Ambassador-at-Large Averell Harriman agreed. On November 11, he wrote Kennedy a memorandum stating the need for a Laotian agreement acceptable to the United States, and noted that the most such an agreement would accomplish in Vietnam would be to "buy time" for Diem. The United States, said the Ambassador, must "make it clear to Diem that we mean business about internal reform."[53]

The perception of allies and other clients was also an element in the deliberations of November 1961. The governments of Thailand, Great Britain, Malaya, Singapore, Australia, and the Philippines, that is, those nations that believed they would be most directly affected by a collapse of South Vietnam, were in favor of sending American troops to arrest the deterioration in the security situation. The governments of Burma, India, Japan, Canada, and France were against an introduction of U.S. combat troops, though they were in favor of some American response, and suggested more pressure on the Diem government for internal reforms. Since the allies tended to split along the same lines as the bureaus within the U.S. government, it is unclear whether they were a crucial factor in the decisions reached, but the perception that the response to the crisis would have consequences beyond Laos and Vietnam was reinforced. In addition, those nations that questioned the use of combat troops did not protest the policy decision, even those on the International Control Commission that was supposedly policing the 1954 Geneva settlement. Rusk cabled Nolting, in the wake of a visit from Prime Minister Nehru in early November, 1961, for example, that India was "winking an eye on our side" over the escalation of the American commitment to a non-Communist Vietnam.[54]

Bargaining Behavior: Reform and a Quid Pro Quo: NSAM 111

Recognizing the growing split between the Pentagon and the State Department, the Secretaries of Defense and State attempted to overcome the underlying disagreements. A joint State-Defense memo was sent to Kennedy by Secretaries McNamara and Rusk advocating an integrated approach: (1) an increased commitment in aid and advisers, but no combat troops; (2) a quid pro quo bargaining posture when dealing with Diem; (3) preparing contingency plans for the introduction of larger numbers of combat troops and possible attacks on the North; and (4) a broad, public commitment by the United States to the defense of South Vietnam.[55]

On November 15, Kennedy reached a decision. In National Security

Action Memorandum 111, he adopted three of the four points in the
Rusk-McNamara memo, excluding only a broad, public commitment to
the defense of South Vietnam, which was considered unnecessary in
the wake of Vice-President Johnson's trip. The task remained, however,
of getting Diem to agree.

From the Vietnamese perspective, the Americans were asking a lot.
In return for its increased commitment, the United States requested a
"prompt and appropriate" mobilization of the populace for war including "a decentralization and broadening of the government so as to
realize the full potential of all non-Communist elements," the devolution
of power "to appropriate governmental wartime agencies" to increase
effectiveness and avoid "power bottlenecks," and an organizational overhaul of the military command structure for a more effective, mobile,
and offensive army. As State's Roger Hilsman put it, the United States
felt "an obligation in Vietnam and elsewhere to bolster the civilian
components of the government." In addition, there was to be a reform
program aimed at improving relations between the rural populace and
the ARVN through curbing repressive measures in the countryside and
increasing civic action programs. It was hoped that the elite and redistributive reform programs would galvanize the war effort and make
the use of American combat troops unnecessary.[56]

This all depended, however, on the reaction of Diem to the plan. As
Rusk noted in his telegram to Nolting: "You should bear in mind that
a crucial element in [the] U.S. government's willingness to move forward
[with increased commitments] is [the] concrete demonstration by Diem
that he is now prepared to work in an orderly way with his subordinates
and broaden the political base of his regime."[57] The "whole package,"
wrote Rusk, should be viewed as the "first stage in a partnership" to
defeat the Communist insurgency in Vietnam.[58]

Bargaining Behavior: The Ngos Balk:
Client Bargaining Tactics

Nolting presented the package in general terms to Diem on November
17, pointing to the "far-reaching and difficult measures" the United
States was willing to take if assured that the government of South
Vietnam would make similar tough choices. Diem was stunned by the
scope of the American role in the plan and told Nolting "he presumed
I realized that our proposals involved the question of the responsibility
of the Government of Viet Nam. Viet Nam, he said, did not want to be
a protectorate." Nolting responded that the United States also did not

want a protectorate, but he believed that if this was to be avoided in the common fight against Communism, Vietnamese nationalists "now sitting on the sidelines" must be included in the struggle through elite reforms. Diem answered, as he often did, that he must first restore order, that reforms were going on all the time but were ignored by the Americans. A lack of experienced personnel meant that he and his family had to take on the leadership responsibilities themselves. The first meeting on the new decisions thus ended in a stalemate.[59]

Once the potential consequences of the American proposals had sunk in, the Ngos responded sharply by attempting a number of counter-leverage ploys. First, they reacted to a slowing down of United States military shipments during the October policy review by turning to the French for the purchase of military equipment. Though this tactic would not work as effective counter-pressure in the long run, since it was largely paid for with American aid dollars, it was apparently meant to bring home to U.S. officials that the South Vietnamese had alternatives to the plan.

Second, Diem attempted to make arrangements with the Republic of China on Taiwan for military advisers to replace the Americans. This was blocked by the United States, which also would have had to pay for that program, and the Americans suggested Korean troops in addition to U.S. advisers, something that had been discussed during the Taylor Mission. The leader of the Republic of Korea, General Park Chunghee, had offered a Korean contingent earlier in the year, and discussions about possible deployment were carried out with Admiral Felt, the Commander-in-Chief of Pacific Forces based in Hawaii, in late November.

Third, the government-controlled press, under Nhu's direction, began a virulent anti-American campaign, questioning the United States' relationship with Vietnam and bitterly complaining about the conditions placed on aid. This ploy especially irritated the State Department because it had wanted to keep the quid pro quo secret to avoid handing the nationalism issue over to the Viet Cong, something for which the Ngos in fact were pleading. One Saigon daily, *Thoi Bao*, ran a headline on November 24 that was representative of Nhu's press campaign: "Vietnam is Not Guinea Pig for Capitalist Imperialism to Experiment on—Is It Time to Reexamine U.S.-Vietnamese Cooperation?" When Rusk complained to the Vietnamese ambassador in Washington, and Nolting to Diem in Saigon, they were told that this was not a government policy but a spontaneous outpouring of resentment against American interference. On November 27, *Thoi Bao* compared the Taylor Mission to the Marshall Mission, which, it alleged, "resulted in tying the feet of Mao's enemies." The United States, it editorialized, always misunderstood the question of authority and believed its style of leadership was best for small nations. Another daily, *Le Song,* also compared Vietnam to China in 1947. The Vietnamese demonstrated that they could utilize alternative lessons of history. Under intense United States pressure, the propaganda campaign was called off by the end of November.[60]

Bargaining Behavior: The Americans Persist

Though Diem had not made his final position known, Secretary Thuan told Nolting on November 22 that the Ngos thought the concessions in the plan were too great and would hand the Vietnamese government over to the Americans. Three days later, Nolting again met with Diem. The Vietnamese leader told the American that the quid pro quo of the U.S. proposals gave "a monopoly on nationalism to the Communists," that power-sharing outside of the government was putting the political cart before the security horse, and that he had already reformed his government to the greatest extent possible given the shortage of qualified personnel.

Nolting backed off from his instructions of November 15, stating that the United States was "not seeking a quid pro quo as such," and apparently took Diem's claims of reform at face value, something others were reluctant to do. He cabled Rusk that the United States "should . . . put [its] major stress on efficiency in [the] GVN [Government of Vietnam] rather than on [the] more nebulous concept of 'political reform.'" On November 27, Kennedy met with McGeorge Bundy and Alexis Johnson to discuss the problems and Diem's reaction. Though plans had gone ahead for an increase in aid, it was not being delivered, and military aid had been slowed. Some non-military aid already destined for Vietnam was held back in Subic Bay in the Philippines.[61]

In order to overcome the impasse, the United States sweetened the offer with an additional $160 million in Commercial Import Aid as a positive sanction, but stuck to the quid pro quo bargaining approach. Nolting was instructed on November 28 to hold "sustained conversations" with Diem in order to gain his acceptance. He was also to search for concrete measures the United States could pursue, and if agreement could not be reached, to return for consultations to ensure that Diem realized the importance the United States placed on the entire "package deal" of elite and redistributive reforms. In reaction to the renewed emphasis on a quid pro quo, Diem asked to see Nolting on December 1. The latter cabled Rusk that a "cool and unhurried approach" was needed in dealing with the Vietnamese, and that the United States could not be impatient in such a delicate situation.[62]

Bargaining Behavior: A Deal Is Struck and Promises Are Made

Though contemporary and subsequent accounts of the bargaining in late 1961 suggest that the United States abandoned reform as an important goal in dealing with Diem, and received nothing in return for its commitment to his regime in late 1961, this is not the case.[63] Kennedy adopted the State Department's arguments on the need for reform and ordered Nolting to continue to press the Ngos to accept American guidelines. On December 1, 1961, the Ambassador did just that. After a "marathon discussion" with Diem, in which he adamantly stuck to the quid pro quo, agreement was reached over a comprehensive, joint program. In the joint memorandum approved by Diem on December 4, the United States agreed to increase its levels of aid, to participate through "uniformed personnel in operational missions with [Vietnamese] forces," and to provide the organizational machinery for "closer consultation with U.S. advisors, as agreed, in planning the conduct of the security effort." The memo plainly spelled out the quid pro quo: "Before taking such far-reaching steps, the U.S. has sought, and the [government of Vietnam] has given, assurances that the [government of Vietnam] will take measures to increase its efficiency and to increase its public support in Viet-Nam and abroad."[64]

In order to improve efficiency, the Diem government agreed to a series of elite reforms: to "reactivate and use" the National Internal Security Council, to create "a secretariat to formulate decisions and directives," and to allow the Council to oversee implementation of its edicts. It also agreed to reorganize and decentralize the military command structure and to "consult with the U.S. on specific measures to this end." The Vietnamese vowed to centralize intelligence gathering (this section of the memo is largely sanitized and therefore presumably aimed at some sort of coordination with the CIA), and to allow joint surveys with American personnel in the provinces to ensure implementation of the reform package. Diem pledged to create a 5,000-man border ranger force in the northwest, allow the "closest coordination" with American officers in all activities involving United States military units, and accept American advisers "in certain [Vietnamese] administrative organs" upon agreement between the two governments.[65]

In the area of redistributive reforms, the Diem government promised to improve support for the regime by giving "a broader sense of participation in the war effort to the people of South Viet-Nam." Additional reforms aimed at developing "more contacts between officials of the [government] and the people," improving the government's public information service, bringing non-Communist prisoners to trial "promptly," and "develop[ing] . . . an amnesty policy for Viet Cong defectors." In addition, the following passage summarized the purpose of the reforms as far as the United States was concerned:

> While continuing vigorously to develop the infrastructure of democracy in Viet-Nam—in which the United States will do its utmost to help—the Government of Viet-Nam recognizes also the importance, in relation to its fight with international communism[,] of developing at all levels its democratic institutions, and will take all practical and feasible steps to this end. While the determination of such steps rests of course with the GVN, the GVN will continue to consider suggestions of the U.S. government in this regard in the spirit of the new partnership.[66]

Once again, the Ngos had only reacted meaningfully to quid pro quo bargaining. It would become quite obvious in the coming months, however, that "democratic institutions" would be construed in widely divergent ways by the two governments.

Since the entire United States program was being held up awaiting Diem's acquiescence, the agreements gave the green light to going forward with the new aid programs. By mid-December, 1961, sophisticated military equipment and United States military advisers began to arrive "in country." On December 22, 1961, U.S. Army Specialist 4th Class James T. Davis of Livingston, Tennessee, became the first American soldier to die as a direct result of engaging in combat operations in Vietnam.[67] The United States was committed to a government it believed would reform. It would discover that it was tragically mistaken.

Successes and Failures, 1962–1963

9

The year 1962 began with a good deal of optimism in Saigon and Washington over the prospects for a joint, coordinated program to prevent the fall of South Vietnam. Throughout 1962, this optimism was justified by the short-term results. Even skeptics, and indeed the Northern regime itself, admitted that it was a good year for the government of South Vietnam. This progress, however, proved to be a temporary illusion, a shadow of success rather than real substance.

The introduction of American troops and materials, especially the use of helicopters, gave Diem the time he needed to implement the elite and redistributive reforms necessary to mobilize support for his regime. Because of the very nature of the regime, however, the time was wasted, and many of the political and social programs went largely by the wayside. This political failure, contrasted with real military progress, caused the American bureaucratic split over policy between the State Department and the military, begun in earnest in the fall of 1961, to break wide open in 1963. During 1962, however, it would remain largely submerged as a result of progress on the battlefield. The varying approaches envisioned by the respective bureaus, however, are keys to understanding the incoherent policies that followed in 1963.[1]

Decision-making: The Military and State Department Points of View

The American military, especially its senior officers, resisted the new counterinsurgency doctrine of the civilian theorists of the New Frontier. The civilian doctrine was an integrated "political" approach based on "clear and hold" tactics and the "oil blot" strategy. The "new" doctrine, actually the reintroduction of the lessons learned in the Truman years, aimed at dispersing the insurgents through military operations to clear important provinces, followed by positive civic action to hold territory for the government and mobilize support from the populace. The oil blot strategy aimed at gaining control of the countryside in an incremental fashion, placing maximum emphasis on ensuring secure areas rather than attempting to pacify all of the rural areas simultaneously. The Thompson Advisory Mission from Great Britain advocated a similar approach, though the Americans placed more emphasis on systematic governmental reforms.

The problem was that this approach ran against the conventional organizational and battlefield concepts of American military doctrine. These concepts, at least since the American Civil War, were based on the concentration of force to overwhelm the enemy. The political approach, in contrast, aimed at a dispersion of force through the use of light weapons and small patrols. In organizational terms, the major thrust was for a decentralized structure with a great deal of flexibility in the field, with equal emphasis placed on a variety of nonmilitary civic actions. Resistant to this civilian meddling in their area of expertise, the military wanted to maintain a conventional organizational structure with maximum emphasis placed on technology. Small units fighting guerrilla style were viewed, at best, as complementary to the more standard military missions. The military was never comfortable with nor fully accepted the equal necessity of the civic action programs. Since the military hierarchy viewed the war in more conventional terms, they resisted the political approach and thought the political and social reforms envisioned to be of secondary importance.[2]

Not all military personnel advocated a narrow military approach; nor did everyone in the State Department advocate an integrated political approach.[3] The varying views of counterinsurgency, however, tended to split along bureaucratic lines. Though this was to become an even greater problem with the introduction of large numbers of troops in 1965, it caused great difficulty in formulating a program in the early 1960s also.[4] Thus, in contrast to the Philippines, and in congruence with the China case, the military and civilian bureaus of the U.S. government fought bitterly over policy in Vietnam throughout the period examined.

The contrasting positions held by the State Department and the military affected their respective views of whether the counterinsurgency program was succeeding. Though both recognized the real military progress made during 1962, State increasingly saw that success as temporary if the promised elite and redistributive reforms were not included to consolidate the military victories. Although at the beginning of the year the military also called for reforms, they became increas. sanguine in this regard during 1962. By November, General Ea Wheeler, later the Chairman of the Joint Chiefs, stated in a speech: ". is fashionable in some quarters to say that the problems in Southeast Asia are primarily political and economic rather than military. I do not agree. The essence of the problem is military."[5] The differing views of counterinsurgency virtually ensured that the military and political/economic/social programs would be implemented largely independently of one another.

Yet President Kennedy apparently believed that the political approach was going forward. On March 31, 1962, he told Stewart Alsop: "What they're doing at Fort Bragg [that is, the Special Forces training] is really good, but, in the final analysis, what is needed is a political effort."[6] It was not until late 1962 that the State Department would fully realize that the political effort was not going forward.

Bargaining Behavior: Commitments and Leverage Lost

Despite the reservations of reformist civilian officials, the United States rushed ahead with its aid programs, especially the military. This was based on the arguments of bolsterers that the battlefield dictated the pace of implementation. As General Maxwell Taylor later observed, the Pentagon did not want to hold back the military programs "to the pace of the slowest civil program."[7] William Colby, at the time a leading CIA operative in Vietnam, notes that the American military had been arguing at least since 1960 that the exigencies of the military aspects of the insurgency should take precedence.[8]

This is entirely understandable from a military point of view; military officers are responsible for the lives of their men, and, after all, people are getting killed in areas of their responsibility. Given this fact, should deliveries of ammunition, for example, be held up until the client government puts through, say, a bridge-building or rodent eradication program? Political, social, and economic programs are at best slow to demonstrate their value; military programs have a much greater immediacy. This asymmetry in programmatic responses led to commitments that undermined American leverage through an abandonment of the quid pro quo so carefully crafted in late 1961.

In February 1962, Diem agreed to the creation of an enlarged military advisory organization, the Military Assistance Command, Vietnam (MACV). Shortly thereafter, Army General Paul Harkins arrived to take command. The Joint Chiefs of Staff followed this agreement with concrete proposals for "Operation Beef Up" to increase the levels of materials and numbers of advisers. Helicopters, light aircraft for surveillance, transport aircraft, ships and boats for coastal and river patrols, communications equipment, and defoliation programs were increased prodigiously throughout 1962. The numbers of personnel also increased in order to implement the counterinsurgency program. The military half was going ahead, though the centralized military structures of the Army of the Republic of Vietnam (ARVN) remained in place.[9]

Diem did inaugurate some cosmetic elite and redistributive reforms aimed at the rural areas. On paper, these reforms were impressive. On January 8, he announced that his government would put through economic reforms, for example, higher taxes on business and imported luxuries, which were never implemented, and the creation of an Economic Council, which was given no authority. In addition, an impressive array of redistributive reforms was announced. These included the following: an increase in pay for militia cadre; increased training for rural officials to improve government-peasant relations; public health programs; the construction of new primary schools; the construction of radio stations and the provision of receivers to the villages; expanded road construction programs; a United States–funded rural credit extension program; an insect, rodent, and cattle disease eradication program; the inclusion of the Montagnards (minority tribes in the central highlands) in the reforms; and public works programs to reduce growing unemployment.

Though the United States had committed itself to funding these programs, the problem still remained of how they were to be implemented, especially the organizational arrangements. Though Diem had agreed to American representation to oversee the projects, he now proceeded to renege on that promise. In order to maintain control over decision-making and implementation, he stalled on the creation of the joint committees, refused to allow American administrators in the rural areas, and kept decision-making in his own hands. Through the effective tactic of delay, the government of Vietnam prevented the redistributive reforms from going forward throughout much of 1962, even while economic and military commitments went ahead.[10] Though the quid pro quo approach had worked in obtaining promises for reform, the lack of a threat of negative sanction during the implementation process allowed the Vietnamese to ignore protests from the United States.

Elite reforms became even more unlikely when dissident officers from the Vietnamese Air Force attempted to assassinate Diem and his family by bombing the presidential palace on February 27, 1962.[11] The reaction of the Ngos was predictable. Rather than seeing the attack as a symptom of the exclusive nature of their system of rule, they viewed it as yet another reason why they could not share power with anyone but their most trusted aides. Although this attitude was understandable, it was most unfortunate for the long-term stability of the regime. Though the extra-governmental opposition had made attempts to coalesce in early 1962, these movements collapsed in the face of the Ngos' determination to maintain political power at any cost. As Robert Shaplen later put it: "The inability of the opposition elements to get together and present a united front [to the Ngos in early 1962] admittedly had hurt their chances, but by the middle of 1962 there was no longer any point in even trying."[12]

Bargaining Behavior: The Shadow of Success: Implementing the Strategic Hamlet Program

Though the Ngos were ever more wary of losing control in the wake of the February assassination attempt, they realized that something had to be done to gain support in the rural areas. Under pressure from the United States to implement a coordinated program to benefit the people, they latched on to an attenuated version of the political approach. In a resurrection of the *agroville* scheme of the 1950s, which had been borrowed from the French, the Strategic Hamlet Program was agreed to on March 19, 1962. Diem picked his brother Nhu to head the program—a most unfortunate choice. Prior to this time, Nhu had been a feared and powerful "unofficial" leader of the government of South Vietnam. The Strategic Hamlet Program allowed him, in his own phrase, to step from the shadows.

The basic idea was to gather villagers into fortified hamlets to provide defense against Viet Cong attacks and separate the populace from the insurgents. The program was based on the successful use of such villages during the Malayan Emergency, which had officially ended only in 1960. In contrast to that program, however, and in contradiction to the advice of American and British advisers, the Strategic Hamlets were promulgated over huge areas in ludicrously swift fashion and with little follow-up on the redistributive reforms that were an integral part of the plan. By September, the government was claiming that over four million peasants were secure in Strategic Hamlets, or more than one-third of the rural population. The appearance of a comprehensive rural program was accepted by bolsterers and reformers alike, and apparently by the Ngos themselves, as evidence of progress on the social and political front. Added to the real progress on the battlefield, this created the illusion of a general improvement. In May 1962, Defense Secretary Robert McNamara, in a visit to Saigon, claimed that "every quantitative measurement . . . shows that we are winning the war." In September 1962, Ho Chi Minh revised his timetable for the overthrow of the Ngos from one to twenty years.[13]

In reality, however, the Strategic Hamlet program was a resounding failure and may have even done more harm than good, though this would only be ascertained over time. First, the program was implemented far too quickly. In contrast to the "oil blot" concept of gradual "clear and hold" operations through coordinated military and civic action, the program was used as a security measure to manipulate and control the populace and was implemented in large areas that had not, in fact, been cleared of Viet Cong. Though the Americans and Thompson constantly counseled against this rapidity, the Vietnamese went ahead anyway. As is now known, but was hardly suspected at the time, the Viet Cong infiltrated the government of South Vietnam at high levels by getting one of its operatives, Colonel Pham Ngoc Thao, appointed as Nhu's chief administrator in the program. It was Thao who advocated the rapid approach which seriously strained the government's resources and ensured the failure of the program. (Thao was also one of the major participants in the anti-Diem coup of 1963.) Second, the cadre sent to implement the program were largely city-bred. They misunderstood the peasants and took a condescending attitude toward them; their main goal was to impress their superiors in Saigon rather than really helping the peasants. Third, the geographic and cultural patterns of Vietnam's villages were especially resistant to this type of concentration of the populace. Fourth, many of the rural administrators were corrupt, and what few funds found their way to the villages usually did not find their way to the peasants. Fifth, the government never followed through on funding for many of the programs (for example, payment for forced labor from the peasants or militia), instead exhorting the populace on the value of Nhu's "personalist" self-sufficiency. Finally, the hamlets were quickly infiltrated and undermined by the Viet Cong.[14]

Though it succeeded in initially physically separating the peasants from the Viet Cong, the program utterly failed in gaining their allegiance to the government and alienated many apathetic peasants who resented the uprooting of traditional ways of life without replacement with an equivalent, let alone more beneficial, socioeconomic environment. As a result, many of the hamlets became "Potemkin Villages," that is, showfront projects to impress visiting Vietnamese and American officials from Saigon and Washington. Robert Thompson would later comment: "No attention was paid to their purpose. Their creation became the purpose in itself." With the military successes of 1962 and the resultant temporary confusion within the insurgent movement, however, the gross exaggerations of Nhu were taken at face value, perhaps even by himself. The more the military succeeded against the insurgents, the more the government envisioned the Strategic Hamlets in strictly security terms.[15]

As in China under Chiang Kai-shek, the Ngo regime believed that moral exhortation, an appeal to tradition, and military programs alone would turn the tide. As in China, they were wrong. Though many would later criticize the Americans' integrated, political approach to counterinsurgency in Vietnam during the Diem period, it was in fact never even close to being implemented.

Decision-making: The Rise of the Harriman Group

Signs of serious political problems began to arise in the redistributive reform programs by mid-1962. Within the State Department and the National Security Council staff, there arose a group of skeptics centered around the leadership of the new Assistant Secretary of State for Far Eastern Affairs, Averell Harriman. With the conclusion of an agreement leading to the supposed "neutralization" of Laos in July, which the Communists promptly violated, and which Harriman had negotiated, this group increasingly turned its attention to the problems of Vietnam. This reformist group included Roger Hilsman, Michael Forrestal, Ted Heavner, and many middle-level State Department, Agency for International Development (which had replaced the International Cooperation Administration), United States Operations Mission, and CIA officials in Vietnam. These officials increasingly questioned the military orientation of policy and the lack of implementation of the civic action programs.

Further complications arose in March 1962, as General Ne Win carried out a bloodless coup in Burma and turned that nation away from the West. In light of these developments, more attention was given to Vietnam in Washington in late 1962 than at any time since December 1961. Averell Harriman believed that the best that could be expected from the Laotian settlement was to buy time for Diem to reform. With the conclusion of those agreements, he and his colleagues concluded that the Vietnamese government was not utilizing that time wisely. They therefore began pushing for the implementation of the program agreed to in December 1961.[16]

In September 1962, Diem finally agreed to "joint sign-off" programs, in which Province Rehabilitation Committees, made up of Vietnamese and American officials, would oversee the redistributive programs in the villages and Strategic Hamlets. This was done in reaction to intensive pressure from the United States, including a threat of a reduction in aid for the Hamlets. Thus, nine months after the South Vietnamese government had promised a joint program in the rural areas, the policy was finally being put through.[17] This development was to have important consequences for the rise of the Harriman group in the State Department.

The reformist factions in State, the CIA, and the National Security Council began to have serious misgivings over the direction of policy even before they began receiving the negative reports from the middle-level officials sent to the countryside in the fall of 1962. As early as August 6, Michael Forrestal informed the National Security Council's Carl Kaysen that he believed that the United States had been "pussy-footing" around with Diem. In light of the growing military success on the battlefield, and a lessened danger of collapse of the government, the Harriman group believed Diem now had no excuse not to go forward with the political side of the program. Two days later, Forrestal advised McGeorge Bundy of the problem and commented that "our pressures on Diem . . . need to be stepped up even at some risk."[18]

Forrestal then brought his case directly to the President and received his approval. On August 18, he wrote Kaysen and Bundy that Kennedy was "very anxious to push on with the civilian side of the counterinsurgency program as fast as possible." A month later, it was decided that the President would personally pressure Secretary of State for the Presidency Nguyen Dinh Thuan, who was traveling to Washington on an official state visit, for more redistributive political reforms, including village elections and other democratic processes in the Strategic Hamlets.[19]

Decision-making: The Rise of the Critical Press

When the middle-level American officials and some military officers went to the countryside in the latter half of 1962, they were alarmed at what they found, especially in the Mekong Delta. In contrast to the cheerful reports from the Vietnamese government on the conditions in the villages, which were often passed on verbatim by Ambassador Nolting and General Harkins, the lack of effective political, economic, and social programs in the Strategic Hamlets was worrisome. Though certain showplaces were passed off as representative by the Vietnamese, most of the hamlets were in organizational, social, military, and political disarray. Forced labor that took the peasants away from their farming chores without compensation, maltreatment from government officials, corruption that prevented American aid from reaching the peasantry, and the disorganized security apparatuses of the villages were among the conditions that worried the American advisers.

These concerns were reflected in the advisers' increasingly harsh reports on the government's performance in the rural areas. Though they passed these grave conclusions on to the embassy, the reports were rarely sent on to Washington by Ambassador Nolting. The bolsterers' viewpoint is summed up in a representative public statement by General Harkins, the head of MACV: "I am an optimist, and I am not going to allow my staff to be pessimistic."[20] As is often the case when middle-level officials become disgruntled with policy and believe the system is not responding to these criticisms, they turned to the press to communicate their discontent.

The American press in Vietnam had grown increasingly restive over the lack of forthrightness by the Kennedy administration during the escalation of the commitment after December 1961. In addition, the Diem regime, which never understood the crucial role played by the press in a democratic political system, literally believed that many U.S. journalists were "pro-Communist." The Ngos, especially in reaction to the criticisms leveled against them in the fall of 1961, began to harass the foreign press in a clumsy attempt to control the content of their reports. When middle-level American officials became embittered and privately more forthcoming, the press printed their complaints wholesale. Since it was increasingly obvious that the best-case pronouncements emanating from the embassy were excessively optimistic, the press jumped on every worst-case assessment issued by disgruntled junior officials. When the embassy and the Vietnamese pressured for more "positive" reporting, this only confirmed in the journalists' minds that they were correct in their judgments. Beginning in mid-1962, many of the press reports from Vietnam increasingly showed a pessimistic and critical bent. The more critical they were, the more the embassy, MACV, and Vietnamese officials attempted to control their reporting. This vicious spiral of poor press relations was to break wide open in 1963.[21]

This situation was most unfortunate. Though there was some truth to these critical analyses, a worst-case approach was as biased as the best-case assessments of the embassy and MACV. All of a sudden, at least in comparison to previous reporting, the South Vietnamese could do nothing right. This "incompetence" became *the* story that was to be reported, with individual journalists, especially the younger ones, largely competing with one another to gather further "proof." Thus, balanced reporting by American journalists, some of whom tended to split along bolstering (for example, Marguerite Higgins) and reformist (for example, David Halberstam) lines, though reformist journalists far outnumbered their bolstering colleagues, was not a hallmark of the press reports emanating from Saigon after mid-1962. This split in the press tended to exacerbate the confusion over what the United States should—or could—do.[22] Though American journalists would later become fond of quoting Rudyard Kipling about pitying the fool who tries to "hustle the East," this is what many of them, whether they knew it or not, were asking their government to do.

Decision-making: Growing Opposition to Bolstering in the State Department

By November 1962, the combined criticisms of the middle-level officials and critical journalists were sufficient to create doubts in the minds of many in the Harriman group over the direction of policy. Though they had brought these doubts directly to the President, he was consumed with the complexities of the Cuban missile crisis and its aftermath in October and November of 1962. Forrestal therefore turned to Robert Kennedy, who was optimistic and hawkish, as an important official who had the ear of his brother. On November 7, he wrote the Attorney General:

> I became concerned about the kind of information you seem to be getting on South Vietnam. Both Averell [Harriman] and I feel that the war is not going as well out there as one might be led to believe . . . The reports we get indicate that the political problem is growing relatively worse. There has been very little indication to date that Diem's Government has been able to follow up the military operations with the type of social and economic programs which would convince the people whose security has been assured that they are better off with Diem than with the Viet Cong.[23]

Following this report, Robert Kennedy was kept abreast of the doubts of the Harriman group, and presumably informed the President.

At the beginning of November 1962, in reaction to the conflicting reports of rural progress from its middle- and high-level officials in Vietnam, the State Department sent Ted Heavner to Vietnam to conduct a survey on the progress of redistributive reforms in the counter-insurgency program. Heavner, who had a relatively extensive background in Vietnam and spoke Vietnamese, spent the six weeks of his trip in the villages interviewing peasants, as well as American and Vietnamese officials. His prognosis upon his return confirmed the doubts expressed by the Harriman group and was reported to the President.[24]

Increasingly aware of the growing doubts in his State Department, Kennedy also sent Senator Mike Mansfield to Vietnam to survey the scene and assess the conflicting reports from the field. Mansfield was an old friend of Diem's and a founding member of the Friends of Vietnam in the 1950s. His report gave a gloomy prognosis on the counterinsurgency program and the chances of the regime to survive. Even though the United States had made a major commitment to the Ngos over the previous eight years, Mansfield reported, "substantially the same difficulties remain if, indeed, they have not been compounded." If Diem continued to refuse elite reforms, there was nothing the United States could do to save his government.

After reading the report offering this unwelcome news, a version of which was made public, Kennedy attempted to rebut it, using the arguments passed on by the embassy. Mansfield responded sharply: "You asked me to go out there." The President replied: "Well, I'll read it again." Kennedy knew that Mansfield was not viscerally anti-Diem, nor a man with naive expectations of what could be accomplished in developing nations. His background as an early and strong supporter of Diem's regime gave him a particular credibility within the policy debate.

After a second reading of Mansfield's report, the President told an aide: "I got angry with Mike for disagreeing with our policy so completely, and I got angry with myself because I found myself agreeing with him." This was a characteristically ironic Kennedy statement that can be construed in a number of ways. Yet, for apparently the first time, doubts had been implanted in the President's mind concerning the possibilities of success for American policy.[25]

Decision-making: The Hilsman-Forrestal Report

As he often did when he was receiving conflicting advice over policy, Kennedy dispatched two officials, Roger Hilsman and Michael Forrestal, both strong critics of Diem, to Vietnam in late 1962 to gather further information on the situation. Hilsman and Forrestal returned from Vietnam in late January, 1963, filled with dismay. Their doubts concerning the political side of the program had been confirmed. Hilsman termed the Strategic Hamlet Program "a fraud, a sham." The shooting war seemed to be shifting to the enemy's advantage. There was a dire lack of overall coordination and planning as well as a continued lack of competent intelligence gathering, and there was no sign from the government of South Vietnam that things were ever going to change. In their official report, Hilsman and Forrestal pointed to the lack of coordination between civilian and military planning, the lack of effective implementation of the civilian programs, and the absence of long-range planning for what kind of society the United States was attempting to help construct. In a reflection of the dissatisfaction of civilian officials with the direction of the war, they criticized the military for using relatively large operations, especially extensive use of airpower and artillery, that were having an adverse political effect in the villages.[26]

In criticizing the American relationship with the Diem government, they pointed to a lack of pressure from the embassy in favor of the "policies which we espouse," arguing that the United States had far too little contact with "meaningful opposition elements and we have made no attempt to maintain a U.S. position independent of Diem." They advocated the appointment of a new ambassador, a "more outspoken" attitude toward policies of which the United States disapproved, increased support for extra-governmental leaders such as the union leader Tran Quoc Buu and less for the Nhus, and pressure for "gradual liberalization" to mobilize support for the war effort. In addition, Forrestal, in a separate memo to the President, advocated a more forthcoming treatment of the American press in Saigon. The report, flying in the face of the optimism prevalent since early 1962, hit the administration like a thunderbolt.[27]

The Hilsman-Forrestal report was not the only source to reflect growing doubts over the efficacy of the military approach. On January 11, 1963, the CIA issued a report questioning the entire program and the reliability of Vietnamese statistics concerning progress on the battlefield. The Vietnamese government was claiming 30,000 enemy casualties in 1962. Yet current insurgent strength was estimated at 22,000 to 24,000 (compared to 17,600 in June 1962), which meant that either body counts were grossly exaggerated, or there was a "remarkable replacement capability" by the enemy (which suggested that the use of greater firepower begun in early 1962 might actually be *creating* insurgents), "or both." The political programs, the report stated, were blunted by the Diem government's "political modus operandi." This was also true in the military field as Diem's appointments of officers on the basis of personal loyalty "hobbled" ARVN combat effectiveness and an excessive centralization of authority bred a fear of acting without direct orders, thereby destroying initiative on the battlefield. All of these criticisms were within the context of a widespread perception of a gross insensitivity to popular grievances and local interests by government officials. Though the North continued to infiltrate cadres into South Vietnam, the thrust of the report blamed the growing problems on the Diem government itself.[28]

Two days later, in reaction to similar reports within the State Department, Secretary Rusk cabled Nolting that President Kennedy and other officials in Washington were "greatly disturbed" by recent reversals of the Vietnamese military on the battlefield, especially their miserable showing at the battle of Ap Bac. The Viet Cong had adjusted to the new technology, especially improving their ability to shoot down helicopters, and were again on the strategic offensive. Criticizing Diem for failing to carry out the sweeping social and political reforms promised in late 1961, the Secretary demonstrated the diminishing patience within the United States government over the Vietnamese government's lack of implementation of the counterinsurgency program: "Acceptance of change will mean a showdown with President Diem." Remembering his own experiences during the Truman administration, Rusk added darkly that the present problems with the Ngos were "alarmingly reminiscent" of the loss of China and the power relationship with Chiang Kai-shek.[29]

Bargaining Behavior: General Harkins Tries His Hand at Reform

In response to the increasing criticism within the State Department which he viewed as threatening the entire effort in Vietnam, General Harkins wrote a letter to Diem on February 23, 1963, pleading for reforms. Citing the military progress of the previous year, he also bluntly stated that "logistical operational functions" had to be improved through elite reforms in the military by the "delegation of authority and appropriate transfer of personnel." "Operational control," he continued, "must be decentralized to the corps and division commanders who have the responsibility, the means and the tactical knowledge to do the best job possible." Though Harkins was telling Washington and the American press in Saigon that the Strategic Hamlets were a great success, he offered a very different opinion to the Vietnamese leader, heavily criticizing the program for its lack of redistributive reforms:

> The civic action phase of the Strategic Hamlet Program often lags behind the military effort. The military clear and hold operations, the construction of defenses and the training and arming of defenders is often complete long before effective public health, education and agricultural assistance is provided in the Hamlets. This situation in many cases disappoints the people, who have neglected their crops and families to build the Strategic Hamlets and train for their defense. I urge that all agencies of your entire government cooperate to maintain the momentum of this program so that we do not lose the support of the population. We must insure that once the Strategic Hamlets are constructed that the other programs to improve the lot of the people are not neglected.[30]

The Vietnamese government's response to this entreaty for the implementation of the 1961 agreements was extremely harsh. From this time onward, Nhu added middle-level and junior American military officers to his list of villains and threatened to reduce their numbers. Chastened by his attempt to get the Ngos to change, and convinced that more pressure for political reform would threaten the military program, Harkins joined with General Wheeler and Admiral Felt to convince the Kennedy administration to bolster the Diem regime.

Decision-making: The Bolsterers Mount a Counteroffensive

On March 9, 1963, Admiral Harry Felt, the Commander-in-Chief in the Pacific based in Hawaii, sent a long rebuttal to the Hilsman-Forrestal report that gave the official bolstering line. The lack of overall planning, he averred, was "not [repeat] not relevant to [the] military situation." Misjudging the effects of commitments on bargaining leverage, Felt and Harkins remained optimistic because of the "inescapably evident fact" of continuing United States support and military aid, and the "obvious fact" that the military and civil efforts were improving. The Strategic Hamlet Program, they believed, was a great success and had captured the loyalty of the populace "regardless of standards or location." Though they acknowledged that there was no adequate amnesty program as yet, this was because Diem refused to implement one. The political programs had not kept pace with the military successes, but the "Vietnamese personality" and modus operandi of the Ngos prevented rapid improvement. They suggested continuing the present policy and hoping that Diem and Nhu would come around; in effect, they advocated bolstering.[31]

On March 20, 1963, Admiral Felt answered a query from the Defense Intelligence Agency over whether the war would be lost "unless there [is] a change made in the government" with a negative reply: "I disagree. Diem's government is making reforms and has a record of progress[,] slow though it may be." Six days later, Nolting passed on a request from the Diem government for more aid and recommended that it be granted, even as anti-inflationary economic reforms continued to be blocked by the Ngos.[32]

On the same day that Nolting's request for more aid was sent, Admiral Felt forwarded a summary of a discussion he had had with Sir Robert Thompson, the British counterinsurgency specialist, in Saigon. Thompson asserted that the Diem government was winning the war, that the Strategic Hamlet Program was succeeding, and that the Viet Cong were on the defensive. Though Thompson would later admit he had been wrong—note his retrospective comment on the Strategic Hamlets

Even Thompson giving Kennedy wrong idea.

quoted earlier—his optimism had a reassuring effect on President Kennedy. In early April, on a trip to the United States, Thompson met secretly with the President (to avoid giving Diem the impression that he was reporting to Kennedy) and gave him a similarly upbeat appraisal. Thus, the analyses of those who believed that the situation was improving, or that the entire effort would be threatened by reformist pressure, temporarily prevented the United States from taking a hard line with its recalcitrant client.[33]

Bargaining Behavior: The Ngos Attempt Counter-leverage

Though Diem was upset over what he considered unfair criticism of his government and interference in Vietnamese affairs, the sharpest reaction emanating from the Mansfield Report, the criticisms of Hilsman and Forrestal, the Harkins letter, and the CIA criticism came from Diem's brother, Nhu. Apparently convinced that he must obtain counter-leverage in the relationship with the United States, Nhu began making indirect contact with the North Vietnamese regime, using the French ambassador and the Polish member of the International Control Commission as intermediaries. He also secretly informed the Americans through the CIA operative Lucien Conein.

Though this ploy was undoubtedly undertaken to gain leverage with the United States—if he were really thinking of making a deal, why tell the Americans?—it had a chilling effect on various ARVN officers and convinced some of them that Nhu had to go. As Conein later put it: "If he had told this to me, the generals knew of this also and they considered this as a danger because what in the devil were they fighting for if the Central government was negotiating behind their backs." Though this was not taken too seriously in Washington at the time, it did lower the American opinion of Nhu even further.[34] It is not clear if Diem was fully informed, or informed at all, about these machinations by his brother. The more Nhu attempted to use this ploy, however, the more adamant the Americans became that he must leave the government. Thus, the patron-client relationship was already strained at the onset of the Buddhist crises of that summer.

Decision-making: The Buddhist Crises: May–August, 1963

The story of the multiple crises of the Diem government with the younger leadership among Buddhists in Vietnam is well known and will only be sketched in this section. In short, there was a spiraling deterioration in relations with the Buddhists that began as a local crisis in the traditional capital of Hue, soon reached national proportions, and finally became an international crisis of major dimensions. The growing opposition to the Ngos was a major aspect of American decision-making throughout the second half of 1963.

The local crisis began on May 8, 1963, when local police and ARVN troops attacked a group of Buddhist protesters in Hue, the traditional capital of Vietnam and the diocese of Diem's older brother, Archbishop Ngo Dinh Thuc. Though Catholics had been given permission only a week earlier to fly papal flags to commemorate Thuc's twenty-fifth anniversary as a priest, the Province Chief, under orders from Saigon, forbade the Buddhists to fly their flag in celebration of the 2527th birthday of Buddha. When a crowd of several thousand gathered peacefully at a radio station to hear a protest speech by Tri Quang, a young Buddhist bonze (priest), the Province Chief dispatched five armored cars to disperse the crowd. A hand grenade was thrown by an ARVN soldier. In the ensuing confrontation, the troops opened fire, and one woman and eight children were killed. These events, and the Diem government's reaction, precipitated a spiraling confrontation between the Catholic Ngos and the younger Buddhist leadership.[35]

Though there was no systematic persecution of Buddhists under the Ngo regime, there had been discrimination.[36] Though many Vietnamese were only nominally Buddhist, the bonzes and their followers became lightning rods for opposition to the Ngos. In response to further demonstrations, the government banned all public meetings in Hue.

The crisis reached national proportions on June 2 and 3 with a series of nonviolent demonstrations by Buddhists in Hue. The June 3 demonstrations were dispersed by ARVN troops using "mustard" or "blister" gas; three people were killed and sixty-seven hospitalized. The civilian population in Hue, reported the State Department representative in that city, was in a "state of extreme anger." It was widely believed that Nhu was responsible for these recriminations, with or without Diem's knowledge, and for similar preceding actions in Quang Tri on June 1 and 2. Under American pressure, Vice-President Tho, himself a Buddhist, was appointed to head a commission to investigate the incidents. The government offered some conciliatory gestures such as a mutual moratorium on propaganda and the legal equality of Buddhism and Catholicism. Just when the situation seemed to be defused, however, the Nhus once again altered the equation by publicly calling the Buddhists Communist-inspired traitors.[37]

The crisis reached international proportions, however, with the first dramatic demonstration of discontent in Saigon. On the morning of June 11, a bonze sat in the lotus position in front of a prominent

Buddhist pagoda in Saigon surrounded by 350 chanting bonzes and nuns. He was doused in gasoline and set on fire. The journalist Malcolm Browne had been alerted the previous evening. The self-immolation was duly recorded by Browne's camera and flashed around the world. The Buddhist crisis in Vietnam became an overnight scandal of the largest proportions, placing intense internal and external pressure on the Kennedy administration to "do something" about its client in Saigon. The radical Buddhist leadership sent bonzes to rural areas to agitate against the government. Over the next few months, six more Buddhist martyrs would die in similar fashion. Madame Nhu exacerbated the situation by making crude remarks about "bonze barbecues" and offering to supply gasoline and matches for any further immolations. American policy in Vietnam was in deep trouble.[38]

A more serious development in retrospect, however, was a trip made in June 1963 by ARVN Generals Duong Van "Big" Minh and Tran Van Don to Thailand for SEATO exercises in that nation. While there, they were shocked by the international outrage reported in the Thai press over the treatment of the Buddhists in their nation. Upon their return to Vietnam, they began gathering support for a coup.[39]

Bargaining Behavior: The American Response

The U.S. response to the early Buddhist crises had been quiet but persistent pressure to reach an amicable solution with the bonzes before the unrest affected the war effort and the legitimacy of the Ngo regime. With Nolting on a well-deserved vacation, the embassy was headed by his assistant and close friend, William Trueheart. He met with Diem on June 9, 1963. In strong and blunt terms, Trueheart told Diem that the United States would not stand for such repressive measures against the Buddhists. If an agreement were not reached with the bonzes, he said, "my government would very likely consider that [the Vietnamese government] was at fault and would have to dissociate itself from [its] actions." At this meeting Diem displayed traits, or perhaps tactics, that were to become more evident over the ensuing crisis period—he did not seem to know, or at least denied that he knew, that his government was taking certain provocative actions. The Vietnamese president then stated that he could not reach an agreement with the Buddhists until they were politically "isolated." He blamed the crisis on inept officials in Hue, though not because of their actions of May 8 and after but because they had "given too much encouragement" to the Buddhists previous to that incident.[40] Thus, Diem believed that his government was in trouble not because it had been too harsh, but because it had been too lenient.

Trueheart left the meeting disheartened and discouraged with Diem's reaction. On the following day he met with the Secretary of State for the Presidency, Nguyen Dinh Thuan, expressed his dismay over the government's handling of the crisis, and formally protested against the temporary police detention of four American journalists covering the Buddhist crisis. He warned against a reported government-sponsored ceremony mourning the recent death of Pope John XXIII, and again warned against Madame Nhu's statements, which had inflamed passions in the Buddhist religious community. Thuan agreed with Trueheart and expressed dismay that the government could not seem to come to grips with the problem. Rusk wired the embassy that the State Department "fully endorsed" the approach to Diem and Thuan and congratulated Trueheart on his "initiative and vigor."[41]

On June 14, 1963, Secretary Rusk wired Trueheart that he should surreptitiously contact Vice-President Tho and explain to him that if Diem could no longer act, and only under that condition, the United States would support Tho as a successor if he could achieve conciliation with the dissidents. Trueheart replied that this would not be a viable plan since Tho did not have the backing within the government to take control. In addition, he stated that he was "not rpt [repeat] not impressed" with the political opposition. Trueheart counseled further pressure on Diem to make conciliatory gestures, though he acknowledged that this was "certainly the longest of shots." If Diem was "in a mood to freeze up," then "his days are indeed numbered." Though there was much talk about a coup among the intra- and extra-governmental Vietnamese opposition, it seemed unlikely at that point. If the approach for conciliation failed with Diem, then the United States would move toward supporting an alternative leadership. In the face of intense American pressure, which included the threat of an aid cut, Diem reached a conciliatory agreement with the Buddhists on June 16, including the important issue of equality of legal status with Catholicism. The problem, as always, was whether Diem would keep his word.[42]

Bargaining Behavior: Nolting Applies Pressure

In mid-July, Fritz Nolting arrived back in Saigon. Although he was a "lame-duck" ambassador (Henry Cabot Lodge had been named ambassador to Vietnam in mid-June, in part to fend off Republican criticism of Kennedy's policy), Nolting labored to convince Diem to take a more conciliatory line with the Buddhists and other opposition groups to ease the crisis and save the American commitment to his regime. It was, in retrospect, the last chance for the bolsterers.

On July 17, shortly after Nolting's return, the Vietnamese government made a large number of arrests of Buddhists allegedly suspected of being Viet Cong. In his discussions with Diem, Nolting emphasized the changed mood in Washington and spent the entire day of July 18 "urging, encouraging, [and] warning, trying to get [him] to move in [a] constructive manner."[43]

In response to the pressure, that night Diem made a conciliatory speech aimed at the Buddhist leadership promising to loosen flag restrictions and to create a government committee to listen to the grievances of the Buddhists; he called on both sides to work toward a peaceful solution. The Buddhists publicly thanked the Americans, not Diem, for the gesture. This was probably a critical mistake on their part. In their discussions with American officials, the Buddhists recalled that each conciliatory verbal gesture made by the Ngos in the past had been followed by escalating violence by the secret police and special forces. They suggested greater concessions from Diem to assure them there would not be a repetition of that pattern. Nolting wired the State Department that Diem was amenable to all of the conditions, but local officials were undermining their implementation.

The apparently conciliatory approach by Diem temporarily defused the unrest in the cities. Nolting then exacerbated the tense atmosphere by making a public statement to the effect that there was no religious persecution in South Vietnam. Though this was technically true, it gave the appearance of a lack of interest in the problems of the Buddhists by the United States. The bonzes bitterly condemned the ambassador in a public statement passed to eager American journalists on August 1.[44]

The spectacle continued. The Nhus launched a counterattack on August 1, with comments by Madame Nhu in a CBS television interview again referring to "bonze barbecues." On August 3, a speech by Madame Nhu accused the Buddhists of being anti-religious, pro-Communist, and treasonous for inciting "foreign intervention" in Vietnam. On August 4, another bonze died of self-immolation in the coastal province of Binh Thuan, suggesting that the unrest was spreading to rural areas. In fact, it would later be ascertained that the government's popularity fell drastically in some rural areas beginning in late July. A few days later, the Vietnamese ambassador to the United States, Madame Nhu's father, publicly attacked his daughter for her intemperate remarks about the Buddhists, causing further embarrassment in Washington and an international reaction.[45]

On August 14, Diem told Nolting that he could not make any more conciliatory gestures because of the growth in unrest in recent days and the resulting criticism in the American press. Nolting told him "bluntly" that "we could not accept this." When Diem complained that the American press did not understand the contributions made by each Ngo family member to the cause of anti-Communism, Nolting warned that the United States might not be able to "continue our present relationship to him and to his government" if he did not separate himself from the Nhus, or at least from their public positions. Diem promised to do so before Nolting left for the United States the following day. He also promised Nolting that he would follow a policy of conciliation with the Buddhists.[46]

This implicit threat of a quid pro quo brought some limited results: on August 14, Vice-President Tho publicly stated that the Nhus' position was not that of the government. The next day, Diem made a public gesture of independence from the Nhus, especially Madame Nhu, at the same time as he was requesting a short-term increase in aid from the United States. He also made conciliatory gestures toward the Buddhists. The Americans again believed they had a promise of reform from their client. Once again, they were wrong.

Bargaining Behavior: Nhu Attempts to Neutralize American Pressure

The Ngos were increasingly wary of their relationship with the United States, which now seemed to be abandoning them in the face of serious challenges to their rule. In mid-August, large-scale student demonstrations broke out in Hue and other cities in support of the Buddhists. In light of these demonstrations, as well as reports that the protests were spreading to rural areas and affecting morale among the ARVN troops, the Ngos decided to move before the arrival of the new United States ambassador, Henry Cabot Lodge.[47]

Nhu's plan was quite ingenious. He would gain the support of the ARVN, whose leaders were already planning a coup and who thought Nhu's plan might further consolidate their power, by promising it a new and greatly expanded role in the government through the declaration of martial law. He divided power within the ARVN by setting up three separate commands under General Tran Van Don, General Ton That Dinh, and Colonel Le Quang Tung, the head of the special forces. Since the latter two officers were considered completely loyal, he would co-opt the potentially disaffected officers by including General Don. In addition, Nhu must have realized that what was to come would seriously strain relations with the United States. By including the ARVN in his scheme, he was directly connecting that area of American commitment that is most difficult to threaten—the military—to the Ngos. After reaching agreement with the ARVN over martial law, he ordered Colonel Tung to attack the main pagodas in Saigon and Hue and arrest Buddhist leaders on August 20.

The plan, which was personally approved by Diem, seemed to solve all of the Ngos' problems: the ARVN would be divided at the top echelons, preventing the cohesiveness of opposition necessary for a coup; American pressure would be neutralized by including the army in the attacks; and the Buddhist problem would finally be removed from center stage by the blanket arrest of its leadership.[48] Unfortunately for Diem and Nhu, they seriously underestimated the negative reaction of all three groups.

Fed up with the duplicitous behavior of the Nhus, under pressure for a response from domestic critics, sensitive to international protestations over religious persecution, especially in Asia, and fearful of the consequences of the newest crisis on the war effort, the Kennedy administration was jolted into action.[49] It initially reacted to the pagoda raids of August 20–21 by publicly dissociating itself from the actions, protesting to the Diem government, and waiting until its new ambassador arrived on August 22. It was not entirely clear to the administration, which was clearly taken completely by surprise by the attacks, who exactly was in charge of the Vietnamese government. After the dust settled, however, it was apparent that Diem was still in power, but that the Nhus had emerged from the newest crisis in a greatly enhanced position. This was deemed unacceptable by the United States and, increasingly, by many in the Vietnamese government.

After a brief initial period of defending the martial law edict, the ARVN generals soon realized that they had been outfoxed by Nhu. This development led to more coup plotting among senior officers, and overtures to the United States for aid in overthrowing the Ngos.

In a very important development for what followed, Secretary Nguyen Dinh Thuan, who had also initially defended the pagoda raids, told Rufus Philips, an old colleague of Lansdale's in the 1950s as well as an operative of both the United States Operations Mission and the CIA, on August 24 that he wanted to resign and leave the country but could not do so because he feared for the life of his family. In dealing with the Ngos, Thuan stated that, as difficult as it might be, the United States must try to separate the Nhus from Diem. The Americans must be "very firm" on this point or expect a descent into "chaos." The present growth in power of the Nhus was "disastrous," and "under no circumstances should [the] U.S. acquiesce." He stated that the ARVN had not known of the pagoda attacks in advance, did not support Nhu, and would turn against the Ngos if given a clear sign by the United States. In a series of remarks that coincided with the growing frustration in the State Department, Thuan "also said that the U.S. must not be afraid of leaving the door open to the Communists, by withdrawing support from the government as long as it contained the Nhus. He reiterated that the U.S. had to be firm. If it was, the army would respond." This kind of advice, coming from a longtime loyal subordinate of the Ngo family, and one of the most respected members of the Vietnamese government, had a significant effect on United States policy. It was, in fact, brought straight to President Kennedy.[50]

Decision-making: The Initial Decision to Promote a Coup

As fate would have it, the Harriman group was more or less in charge of the State Department in Washington on the weekend when the messages from the ARVN generals and Secretary Thuan arrived, with most of the principal decision-makers of other departments out of town or unavailable for immediate consultation. Harriman, Hilsman, and George Ball drafted a pro-coup telegram to be sent to Saigon, received the President's approval by implying that there was a consensus on the move, and then gained acquiescence from the other principals, who were convinced to go along largely because they believed that the President was in favor.[51]

The cable was sent to Saigon on August 24 ordering the Voice Of America to dissociate the ARVN from the pagoda attacks. By mistake, a second policy directive threatening to cut off aid unless the Diem government changed policies, which was meant for the embassy but not the public, was inadvertently also broadcast over the Voice of America.[52]

Given the tension in Saigon, Ambassador Henry Cabot Lodge, who had just arrived, was absolutely furious at the Voice of America announcement on an aid cutoff, telling Washington that he feared "a violent reaction" from Nhu. Lodge was initially against fomenting a coup because of an apparent lack of consensus and will among the dissident Vietnamese generals who were contacting the CIA. In light of the August 24 cable, however, he saw no turning back on the road to overthrow the Diem regime. These developments set forth two basic splits within the administration, the first between anti-coup bolsterers and pro-coup reformers in Washington, which created great ambivalence and ambiguity in policy directions, and the second between anti-coup bolsterers (for example, General Harkins) and pro-coup reformers (for example, Ambassador Lodge) in Saigon. These disagreements over policy reached startling proportions in the coming weeks.[53]

On August 26, 1963, the principals in Washington convened and discovered the manner in which the Harriman group had received permission to go ahead with the August 24 cable. General Taylor, Secretary McNamara, and CIA Director John McCone were especially angry at having been left out of such an important decision. Having believed that his administration had reached a consensus on the cable, the President was also quite irritated at the Harriman group and issued a severe tongue-lashing to its members. When Michael Forrestal offered to resign, Kennedy snapped: "You're not worth firing. You owe me something, so you stick around." At the meeting that morning, Kennedy asked for information on what the Vietnamese thought of the pagoda raids. He was soon informed that many Vietnamese were blaming the Americans for the attacks and calling for U.S. pressure to get rid of the Nhus. Since the United States was publicly committed to the pro-coup policy enunciated in the cable, it was decided that it should stand for the present.[54] President Kennedy was shocked at the intensity of the disagreements in the bureaucracy. He soon confided to a journalist friend: "My God! My government is coming apart!"[55]

Decision-making: The Bolsterers Counterattack and Prevent a Coup

The bolsterers in the Kennedy administration were adamant about allowing Diem to stay. This was especially true of the military. On August 28, the same day Saigon CIA Station Chief John Richardson wired Washington that the United States had reached the "point of no return" in promoting a coup, General Taylor wired General Harkins in Saigon through "back channels" that the decision to promote a coup was now being reconsidered in Washington. Lodge was not informed.[56]

General Harkins, who was as much of a bolsterer as Nolting, had reluctantly gone along with the coup plans following the August 24 cable. After receiving the Taylor cable, however, he took the position that Nhu must be made to leave government as a result of pressure on Diem to relieve him of his authority, but Harkins was vehemently against Diem's leaving. From this time onward, he would steadfastly work against the promotion of a coup.

The following day, August 29, Harkins called in CIA Station Chief Richardson and agent Lucien Conein and told them that the pro-coup policy was no longer in force. Later the same day, Conein met with General "Big" Minh and informed him of the policy "change." Minh was deeply disappointed with the shift in sentiment and wanted an aid reduction to demonstrate U.S. displeasure with the regime and gain support within the army for the coup planners. In response to this request, however, Secretary Rusk, convinced that Ambassador Lodge had not yet "come to grips" with the situation, wired that an aid reduction might precipitate a violent reaction from Nhu and that it was now considered excessively risky in Washington. Since it had already been publicly announced that the United States would reduce aid, Lodge, having no knowledge of the Taylor-Harkins cable, was furious at the refusal to initiate an aid cut, and wired that there was no turning back from the August 24 cable. When Lodge found out what Harkins had told Conein and Richardson, and through them the Vietnamese generals, he exploded. He had been complaining to Washington that trying to prod the generals into initiating a coup was like "pushing spaghetti." Now he knew what had created their apparent change of heart. From this time onward, Lodge only told Harkins what he believed was absolutely required for him to know. The embassy and MACV were now following two different policies. When Kennedy discovered what General Taylor had done, he called him into his office for a private chastisement. The President then wired Lodge that the ambassador had the power to initiate an aid reduction at his discretion.[57]

But it was too late. The mixed signals coming from Harkins and Lodge had scared off the Vietnamese officers. On August 31, one of the leading coup plotters, General Tran Thien Khiem, told the United States that the coup plan was no longer operational. For the moment, there would be no coup in South Vietnam. The generals and their cohorts had backed off.[58]

Decision-making: Elite Reforms: Getting Rid of the Nhus

When it became obvious that the coup plotters had abandoned their plan, decision-makers in Washington turned to two new short-term goals: regaining leverage with the Vietnamese through selective aid "slowdowns," and forcing the Nhus from positions of influence. These goals were the result of increasing domestic and congressional pressure to pursue elite reforms and end the attacks on the Buddhists. As Assistant Secretary Hilsman told the press in an off-the-record briefing, the United States did not want to "play God" in Vietnam, but it could no longer fully support a government in which the Nhus were influential. The United States, he stated, would not instigate a coup in Vietnam, but would make increasingly clear that it was fully committed to Vietnam, but not the Ngos.[59]

Nhu's plan with the pagoda raids aimed at dividing the army to prevent a military coup, neutralizing the possibility of an American aid reduction over the Buddhist crisis by symbolically linking the ARVN to the Ngos through the declaration of martial law, and solving the Buddhist problem in one stroke of swift repression. None of the goals were achieved. A growing percentage of the ARVN now supported a coup. The Americans, though confused as to their ultimate intentions, had made it clear that the raids represented a real turning point in their relationship with the Ngos. Though many of the bonzes had been arrested, other groups, especially students, joined in the anti-Ngo protests. Thus, the actions of Nhu had alienated the ARVN, the United States, and much of the urban population of Vietnam.

There were other reasons to object to the presence of Nhu in the government, including his increasingly mercurial behavior. Secretary Thuan and other officials told the Americans that Nhu had been an opium addict for the past two years.[60] To growing numbers in the administration, including President Kennedy, it appeared that the regime could not survive with the Nhus sharing power with Diem.

Bargaining Behavior: The President Gives Public Warning

On September 1, 1963, President Kennedy himself decided that he would have to address the crisis in Vietnam as part of the campaign to induce the Nhus to leave the government. On September 2, he told Walter Cronkite in a television interview that the Vietnamese regime needed "changes in policy" and "perhaps personnel" or it would probably lose the war. Though he coupled that remark with a defense of the American commitment, it was clearly meant as a signal to Diem about the Nhus. Lodge was informed by Rusk that the comments represented "the U.S. Government's attitude toward the situation and should be followed as the official U.S. public position." Coming directly from the President, the threat to the commitment to the Ngos was clear.[61]

To avoid any possible misunderstanding, Kennedy's signal was followed by limitations placed on aid programs. On September 3, Rusk ordered Lodge to put a good portion of the nonmilitary aid to Vietnam (including the crucial Commercial Import Program) on "maximum administrative delay," which meant that any new aid would be painfully slow in arriving. This was an additional signal meant to demonstrate U.S. displeasure and to complement the President's verbal warning.[62] The Americans, at this point, would not initiate a direct aid reduction as a threat, but they were stepping up the pressure.

Bargaining Behavior: Nhu's Bargaining Tactics

Nhu had been intermittently flirting with the North throughout 1963. He again ostentatiously raised the specter of a deal with the Communists in response to the American action. President De Gaulle of France severely complicated things on August 29 by calling for the simultaneous unification and neutralization of Vietnam. In late August, Nhu increased the number of veiled threats of a separate peace with the Viet Cong and North Vietnamese, and was in actual contact with the enemy through the French ambassador. As in the spring of that year, this was undoubtedly intended to gain counter-leverage against the United States, but it was impossible for American diplomats to know Nhu's actual motives because of his highly unstable personality.

There is no evidence to suggest that American officials ever took the threat of a separate peace seriously, and there is some evidence to the contrary. When reports of contacts between Nhu and the North Vietnamese reached Washington, the State Department argued that Diem would never allow a separate peace and was not "personally capable of any deal with Hanoi." This might have added one more reason to get rid of Nhu, but it does not appear to have been an important factor in the ultimate decision to get rid of Diem. Thus, contrary to some accounts, Nhu's flirtation with the enemy was accurately viewed by the United States as bargaining behavior to fend off reform attempts, which now included the exclusion of Nhu himself.[63]

In the broader scheme of things, neutralization was not perceived as a viable option by the administration. President Kennedy noted at a meeting on September 3 that the French suggestion for neutralization resembled the Laotian model of the previous year. If neutralization was not working in Laos, he wondered, why were some so anxious to try it in Vietnam? Since both withdrawal and neutralization were considered impossible, and bolstering increasingly unfeasible, the United States stuck with elite reforms to replace those believed most responsible for the problems of the Vietnamese government—the Nhus.[64]

On the day following President Kennedy's public signal, Nhu at first reacted in a conciliatory manner. He visited Lodge and agreed to various American policy suggestions. He claimed he would leave the government and move to Dalat, and he promised that Madame Nhu would leave the country on a speaking tour. The government, he added, was willing to express a policy of conciliation toward the Buddhists, and the cabinet would be broadened by elite reform to include opposition members.

State Department officials worried that Nhu was stalling, but the Department decided to use the opportunity to press for specific measures of reform as its "optimum position" to obtain as much out of the Ngos as possible. This might have been a tactical error, since it may have convinced the Ngos that American demands for reforms were virtually unlimited. These demands included the release of the bonzes and students, the end of press censorship, the restoration of the damaged pagodas, the end of martial law, and a resumption of negotiations with the dissident Buddhist leadership. Secretary Rusk wired Lodge that the United States would closely monitor the Ngos' behavior, but there was not a high degree of optimism in Washington. Like the boy who cried wolf, the Ngos' credibility was wearing thin. None of these reforms was ever implemented, although Madame Nhu soon left on a speaking tour that, to the horror of the Kennedy administration, included the United States.[65]

Nhu followed his suggestions to Lodge of renewed cooperation with a new crackdown on intra- and extra-governmental dissidents. Secretary Thuan told General Harkins that most members of the government were under heavy surveillance from Nhu's secret police. The situation was made worse when Nhu again ordered attacks on a series of peaceful student demonstrations against the government, and arrested much of the political leadership of the extra-governmental opposition. Many of the students arrested were the sons and daughters of upper- and middle-level government officials and military officers. Because of these arrests, the degree of loyalty of these groups to the Ngos was increasingly suspect.[66]

Decision-making: The Search for Leverage

Realizing that it could not immediately instigate a coup or implement elite reforms, the administration moved once again toward regaining its leverage with the Vietnamese government. The Americans, however, were rediscovering the inverse relationship between commitments and leverage. Demonstrating this frustration, Secretary of State Rusk suggested to Ambassador Lodge that the Ngos "may feel we are inescapably committed to an anti-Communist Viet-Nam."[67] Further aid reductions were necessary to convince them that this was not the case, and to return United States–Vietnamese relations to a quid pro quo basis.

As a first step toward this goal, nonmilitary aid programs had been slowed. Since there had been no movement toward agreement in Saigon, the State Department began making plans for specific cuts in aid to pressure the Vietnamese. It first wanted to know, however, the degree of opposition to Diem and the chances for his political survival. To that end, Kennedy dispatched another mission to Saigon to "get the facts."

The widely disparate presentations on September 10 by Marine General Victor Krulak, for the bolsterers, and John Mendenhall of State, for the reformers, only served to highlight the extreme disagreements within the government. The President, wearied over the constant infighting and widely divergent accounts of the political situation in Vietnam, quipped: "You two did visit the same country, didn't you?" At the same meeting, however, Rufus Philips, a CIA operative with long experience in Vietnam, argued forcefully that things were deteriorating seriously for the Diem government in the countryside and affecting the war effort. This appraisal was soon followed by a similarly pessimistic report by Sir Robert Thompson, in direct contrast to his upbeat assessment of spring 1963.[68]

At an interdepartmental meeting later the same day, Hilsman was ordered to draw up a plan to regain leverage by reducing the aid programs to the Diem regime; the CIA was asked to produce a report outlining possible alternative leadership to the Ngos; Forrestal was asked to write a report on what would likely happen if the United States postponed a decision. The meeting ended with Harriman and McNamara disagreeing, the former negative and the latter positive, over whether the war could be won with Diem in charge. The next day, the President ordered all aid programs delayed until further notice.[69]

Decision-making: The McNamara-Taylor Mission

The Kennedy administration continued to struggle with the problem throughout September. Late in the month, the decision was made to send yet another mission to Saigon to gather more information on the political and military situation. The group was led by Secretary of Defense McNamara and General Taylor, both known as skeptics in terms of promoting a coup, but it also included reformers such as Michael Forrestal. In a discussion of the trip's purpose, the President emphasized that he wanted to know why his political and military advisers were so divided on Vietnam. Secretary McNamara offered the explanation that the political reformers were thinking of the long-term political effects, while the military bolsterers were thinking of short-term military effects. The President stated he had reached the same conclusion.[70]

Though the military views of the mission's report were unduly optimistic in light of subsequent events and knowledge, the widespread political turmoil and pessimism in South Vietnam raised new doubts in many previously optimistic minds over whether the Ngos could hold on. Though Taylor generally stuck with his bolstering advice, Mc-Namara apparently altered his views of the situation.

The report of the mission reached President Kennedy in early October, and aimed at reaching a policy with which both reformers and bolsterers could live. Though it gave a nod to "great progress" in the military effort, it was pessimistic in the political sphere. The report offered three policy prescriptions that became the basis of United States policy until the overthrow of the Ngos. First, the United States would take no direct role in fostering a change of government. Second, the United States would "seek urgently to identify and build contacts with an alternative leadership if and when it appears." Third, selective aid reductions in areas not directly tied to the war effort should be initiated. Within this context, the aid to Colonel Tung's Special Forces, including those units involved in the pagoda raids, for example, would be cut off until they were utilized on the battlefield. In other words, the United States would not actively induce a coup, but would remain alert for one while pressuring the Vietnamese government for reform.

This policy was something of a compromise solution to the splits between the reformers and the bolsterers. It avoided the objections of the bolsterers to getting rid of Diem; it avoided the objections of the reformers to excessive commitment to the Ngos. Though it appeared to be a long shot, the use of selective aid cuts just might make Diem reform.

On October 2, the President personally had George Ball inform Saigon: "No initiative should now be taken to give any covert encouragement to a coup." If it looked as if a plot was gathering support, however, the United States should move to establish contact with its leaders.[71]

This policy, however, was full of contradictions. There is a difference between promoting a coup and preparing to react should one occur, and the Kennedy administration attempted to draw that line in early October. The problem was that by the very act of preparing to manage the consequences of a coup, the administration made it more likely that one would occur. Contacts with coup planners, no matter how circumspect, and selective aid reductions encourage such plots. The administration discovered what the Americans had learned in China and the Philippines: it is difficult to dissociate yourself from a client government when you are perceived to be responsible for its existence.

Some in the administration, however, understood the dangers inherent in such a policy. At an October 3 interdepartmental meeting, Secretary of Defense McNamara, who was much less supportive of the Ngos after his trip to Saigon, warned that the United States "cannot stay in the middle much longer." The policy of selective aid cuts suggested in his report "will push us toward a reconciliation with Diem or toward a coup to overthrow Diem." The Americans could live with either of these outcomes, but they could no longer live with the status quo.[72]

On the other hand, the long shot of inducing reform just might work. The administration went forward with aid reductions "to indicate to the Diem Government our displeasure at its political policies and activities and to create significant uncertainty in that government and in key Vietnamese groups as to the future intentions of the United States," and "to produce movement in the Vietnamese Government towards liberalization that will gain the popular support necessary to win the war." On October 14, the President personally wrote to Lodge asking him to monitor closely the effects on the Ngo regime of the reductions in aid, especially in the crucial Commercial Import Program.[73]

Bargaining Behavior: The Reaction in Saigon

It is clear that the American reduction in aid was carried out partly in response to renewed coup planning in Saigon. Though the coup plotters in the ARVN had backed off from a coup in late August, they had not given up their plans. According to General Don, it was difficult for them to convince the crucial elements in the field to join their group in light of the mixed signals from the United States on its commitment to the Ngos. By late September, the coup plotters again contacted the United States surreptitiously. On October 2, Don held a meeting with the CIA's Lucien Conein. Don told him that the plotters needed some sign, such as an aid reduction, to use in convincing wavering elements. On October 5, Conein met with General "Big" Minh, who asked once again about the attitude of the United States. Though Conein was noncommittal, the aid reductions began on the same day.

By October 10, it appeared that the coup was on once again. The aid reductions were not the only signals sent to the opposition; it became increasingly clear that the United States and the Vietnamese government were on a collision course. The Nhu-controlled press attacked the Americans for the aid reductions and accused them of undermining the government. This played right into the hands of the coup plotters, however, because it was a clear demonstration that there were deep divisions between the Ngos and the Americans. In addition, Madame Nhu arrived in the United States and proceeded to destroy whatever public and congressional support remained for the Ngos through her outrageous statements. Finally, the first results of the aid reductions began to be reflected in speculative markets, especially the reduction in the Commercial Import Program. Though the first concrete effects were not expected for two to four months, the knowledge that they were forthcoming had a negative impact on the popularity of the Vietnamese government and an important psychological effect on the regime's supporters. By October 21, Michael Forrestal, after a trip to Saigon, could write to McGeorge Bundy about the "growing political effects of our aid cut-off."[74]

Unfortunately, the Diem regime's behavior toward its own people did not change for the better; it in fact got worse. Reports were received by the Americans that ARVN soldiers had been ordered to rape female students who had been arrested, in order to deter other students from demonstrating. Even if these were only rumors meant to scare the students into submission, they had the effect of seriously undermining morale in the ARVN and throughout Saigon. Student groups from Saigon began going to the countryside to organize dissent and avoid the widening military draft. Government personnel were so intimidated by the activities of Nhu's secret police that they abruptly broke off old friendships with Americans. The arrests "at all levels" of society continued, including a mass arrest of labor leaders. The Ngos were so afraid of popular unrest at this point that they even closed down the elementary schools. This campaign of terror and intimidation was meant to make people fear the regime; instead it made them angrier. By mid-October, the civic demoralization throughout Vietnam had begun to affect more seriously the war effort.[75]

Bargaining Behavior: The Policy Splits Send Mixed Signals to the Plotters

Though there appeared to be a growing consensus in Washington, the policy splits between the embassy and MACV in Saigon had not disappeared. The bolsterers, led by General Harkins, accepted the "no direct involvement" policy direction as an indication that the United States did not *favor* a coup. The reformers, led by Ambassador Lodge, accepted it as an indication that the United States should not *participate* in a coup. These varying perceptions were well known to the coup plotters and acted as a constraint on their willingness to act.

Things were further complicated on October 22 when General Harkins, unaware of the full extent of contact between the CIA and the plotters, drew General Tran Van Don aside at a reception and told him he had heard rumors of Don's involvement in a coup plan. Harkins made it clear that he was against any such move.

Don was confused. He had been told on October 17 that aid to Colonel

Tung's Special Forces in Saigon would be reduced unless those troops were sent to the field, a move that was already occurring. John Richardson, the CIA Station Chief who was close to the Ngos, had been sent home at the plotters' and Lodge's insistence. Conein, under orders from Lodge, had told Don and others that the United States would back a coup. Now Harkins was saying something quite different. Did these mixed signals mean that the Americans would attempt to play both sides, as they had in the past? When Don met with Conein the following day, the CIA agent assured him of American support for the coup. Still dubious, on October 28 Don drew Lodge aside at a ceremonial affair and asked him whether Conein spoke for the United States. Lodge replied that he did. That night Don again met with Conein and confirmed that the coup would now proceed. Conein asked for an exact date, since Lodge planned an imminent return to the United States for consultation as an additional means of pressure on Diem. Don was noncommittal at this stage. On October 29, he visited General Ton That Dinh, a key defector from the Ngos who was acting as a covert double agent for the plotters in dealing with Nhu. They decided that the coup would go forward on November 1.[76]

Decision-making: The Bolsterers' Last Gasp
Is Thwarted by Lodge

As the coup plotters made their final plans, General Harkins realized that he was being systematically left out of the information flow of the dealings with the plotters. In his cables to Washington, he remained adamantly opposed to a coup. In late October he began sending messages raising the question of whether General Don was a double agent who was attempting to snare the United States into an embarrassing trap.

The White House had already gotten cold feet over the prospects of a coup. Because of this anxiety, and in response to the possibility of a double cross, there was an emergency meeting on October 29. It was decided that the generals did not have sufficient backing to carry out the coup successfully. National Security Adviser McGeorge Bundy wired Lodge that the administration wanted to cancel the coup, since it seemed it would likely fail. He was ordered to tell Conein to so inform the ARVN plotters. Lodge wired back angrily on October 30 that this was impossible. The only way the United States could stop the coup was to inform on the plotters, he argued, which would mean that no group in Vietnam, including the Ngos, would ever trust the Americans again.

Bundy cabled back on the same day that this was unacceptable to the

President and that the administration wanted the ability to end the coup plot at any time that it appeared it would not succeed. General Harkins sent off three long, angry telegrams complaining about being left out of the formulation of policy. The White House ordered Lodge to share information with the general. Later that day, October 30, 1963, the imminence of a coup was again communicated to Lodge by the plotters. He postponed his visit to the United States for consultations and *never informed* Conein of the ordered change in policy.[77]

Lodge doesn't share info and creates disunity.

Bargaining Behavior: The Ngos' Last Ploy to Regain the Commitment

The Ngos had one last scheme for holding on to power. The plan called for their agents to stage a fake coup in Saigon. Nhu and Diem would repair to a predetermined hideout; the real coup plotters would then reveal themselves and could be identified for liquidation. Nhu's agents were to assassinate several prominent American officials in Saigon including, rumors had it, Ambassador Lodge, to demonstrate to the United States that the regime was necessary to maintain stability. Diem and Nhu would then return triumphantly to Saigon, blame the real coup plotters for the deaths of the Americans, and recapture the American commitment by restoring order.[78]

In order to stall for time, however, the Ngos first attempted to neutralize United States influence with the ARVN plotters. They did so by signaling a softening of their resistance to reform. They sent Secretary Thuan, now reconciled with the Ngos, to visit Lodge to suggest that Diem was beginning to "come around" on the reform program. This was followed by an invitation to Lodge for a trip to Dalat aboard Diem's personal airplane. These gestures were taken seriously by the United States. Despite their contacts with the coup plotters, many Americans continued to believe that some rapprochement with Diem might be possible. On October 30, Lodge even cabled a draft of a conciliatory presentation he would make to Diem in the event that the United States renewed its aid. The planned agreement allowed Nhu to stay in a minor cabinet position, but again called for widespread elite and redistributive reforms. Lodge also averred, however, that "I can think of no way whereby the execution of such a plan could be guaranteed or how we can protect ourselves against foot dragging and evasions."[79]

The facade of conciliation created by Diem to gain time for the fake coup was continued literally right up to the outbreak of the real coup. On the morning of November 1, at a meeting produced by a surprise visit to Saigon by Admiral Felt, Diem asked to see Lodge privately. The major problem facing his government, said Diem, was "bad publicity." The elite and redistributive reforms would be implemented, he promised, but on an incremental basis—"au fur et à mesure."

Lodge was apparently hopeful, or at least he tried to appear that way in dealing with his superiors in Washington. He cabled Rusk: "If [the] U.S. wants to make a package deal, I would think we were in a position to do it." He continued: "In effect, [Diem] said: tell us what you want and we'll do it." As they parted, Lodge told Diem that the rumors of assassination plots against the ambassador had not altered his admiration for the Vietnamese leader. It seemed that Diem might finally change, though by all indications Lodge remained convinced that a coup was necessary. On the surface, however, the quid pro quo seemed to have finally worked.[80]

We now know, however, what United States officials at the time could not have known. The Ngos' conciliatory approach was a smokescreen for the fake coup plot which was meant to renew the U.S. commitment to their regime. The Ngos knew that the United States was too committed to Vietnam to withdraw, but they also increasingly recognized in the fall of 1963 that it could withdraw its commitment from a *particular government*. In the pagoda raids of August and the fake coup plot of November, the Ngos were desperately attempting to regain that commitment for themselves.

But time had run out. Twenty-four hours after the beginning of the assault on the presidential palace by dissident officers, Diem and Nhu were assassinated after surrendering to the coup forces, apparently under orders from General Minh. Three weeks later, President Kennedy was assassinated in Dallas. The ordeal in Vietnam for the Ngos was over. For the United States, it was just beginning.

Epilogue: The Substance of Failure

Unlike much of what the ARVN did in Vietnam, the coup was carried out with clockwork precision. The reaction to the coup was ecstatic among much of the population. The CIA reported "popular jubilation in the provinces as well as Saigon." Symbols of the regime were unceremoniously destroyed. Leading members of the regime were arrested, and some shot. The patrician Lodge became an unlikely Vietnamese folk hero, at least for a few weeks, as a symbol of the overthrow of despotism, personalistic rule, and the unbridled, arbitrary use of power. General Minh promised a return to civilian government "within two or three days." U.S. diplomats in Hue described Vietnam's mood as "happy and relaxed" and noted that the "feeling is frequently expressed that U.S. policy has been vindicated."[81]

But it was not to be. American officials soon received reports that ended the euphoria, discovering in the next few weeks what Hilsman later called "the underside of the rock." Not only had security in the countryside been deteriorating since the beginning of the Buddhist crisis in May, it had been doing so since late 1962. The rot was quite deep: the ARVN had been attacking areas where they were sure there were no Viet Cong; peripheral areas with no major political or strategic significance were being held to "show the flag"; the Strategic Hamlet Program was even more of a fraud than the American reformers had realized; the Ngos had manipulated statistics to demonstrate "progress" to their patron; there were reports of some of the populace making deals with the Viet Cong, and even supplying them with ammunition, in order to be left alone.[82]

The enemy took great advantage of the confusion brought on by the coup. The first week following Diem's death was later labeled the "bloodiest seven days of the war" until that time, with more than 1,000 incidents of Viet Cong attacks. The generals never seemed to be able to move beyond their own petty jealousies. Though the United States might have used its post-coup leverage of diplomatic recognition and aid to attempt real change, it made the conscious choice not to do so in the face of the growing instability. On November 3, Rusk wired Lodge that the administration would not "use [a] delay in resuming aid as summary leverage on [the] Generals." On the next day, Lodge told Generals Don and Minh that the aid would again flow.[83]

By mid-1965, after eleven years of largely failing to get the Vietnamese to fend effectively for themselves, the United States decided to accomplish its goals through a massive military commitment to South Vietnam. But the paradoxical lessons of the inverse relationship between commitment and leverage had not been sufficiently learned. When those crucial decisions were being made in 1965, Secretary of State Rusk would lament at a National Security Council meeting: "We should have probably committed ourselves heavier in 1961."[84] The United States was to discover once again after 1965, however, that the more commitments it granted its various client governments in Vietnam, the less it could get them to reform.

Conclusions

The American involvement in Vietnam from 1954 to 1963 is a classic case of how not to deal with a client government. Unlike Chiang Kai-shek and Elpidio Quirino, Ngo Dinh Diem was largely chosen as leader under American auspices. The problem was that Diem never learned to do anything but attempt to defeat domestic enemies. Since he and his family refused to share power with other groups, and those groups increasingly demanded a share of power, he saw virtually his entire society as actual or potential enemies. He reacted to this pervasive threat in ways that allowed him to remain in power in the short term. In the long term, however, this system of governance rendered him incapable of mounting an effective *political* response to the challenge posed by the Communists.

As various groups in South Vietnamese society formed but continued to be excluded from the government, the ARVN became increasingly politicized. By the time of the attempted coup in November 1960, the alienation of the Ngos from much of the rest of their society was affecting their ability to mount an effective *military* response to the Communists. They reacted by removing relatively independent officers and replacing them with sycophants, many of whom displayed not a jot of initiative, or even comprehension, on the battlefield. Those who did were constantly rotated to different command positions so that they could not mount a coup against the regime. The Vietnamese military's—and the Americans'—dissatisfaction with these arrangements was the eventual, and one is tempted to add inevitable, cause of the fall of the regime.

The Kennedy administration attempted to regain leverage in late 1961 by placing its increasing commitment to Vietnam on a less personal, more programmatic basis through the use of a quid pro quo bargaining approach. It was rewarded with the only significant specific agreements to reform ever obtained from the Ngos. Instead of following through with a quid pro quo during implementation in 1962, however, the administration went forward with its programs to aid the regime. It is small wonder that the Ngos protested so bitterly about American observers in the countryside. This was something new in the relationship: actual demands for implementation of previously empty promises. After eight years of previous bolstering, Diem was not prepared to acquiesce to the "limited partnership" the New Frontier offered. Indeed, he was not willing to institute a partnership with anyone outside his family. Thus the American reformist intervention must be considered a policy failure, despite some limited and ephemeral short-term successes.

Conclusion:
Bargaining in Chaos

The United States has had an oscillating policy toward the Third World since 1945. In general, as I have noted, Democratic administrations have tended toward reformism, at least in their initial policy choices, and Republicans have tended toward bolstering, at least in their initial choices. The global reform policy of the United States was greatly expanded in 1949, to a large degree because of the perceived regional threat in Asia in the wake of the fall of China. In addition, three major lessons of history were learned from the demise of the Kuomintang on the mainland that had global consequences for American foreign policy throughout the Cold War era. The first was accepted by both political parties; the second and third were contrary lessons accepted along party lines.

The first lesson was that the United States should not withdraw from nations bordering the U.S.S.R. and China or, by extension, those deemed strategically important to containment. Once the China issue got caught up in the domestic political debate over containment policy, neither party would accept withdrawal as a viable solution to the dilemma presented by intense political instability in clients, at least until the fall of the Batista regime in Cuba in 1959. When Castro announced his Marxist orientation and subservience to the foreign policy goals of the U.S.S.R., however, that case only reinforced the lesson drawn from the fall of China. It was learned again by many in Nicaragua and Afghanistan in the late 1970s. With withdrawal an impossibility, only bolstering and reformist intervention were left as viable policies in the situation of saving a tottering client government. The debate over these lessons has led to the oscillation according to party lines in U.S. policy toward the developing world.

Republican decision-makers drew a bolstering lesson from the

Chinese case. The main problem, indeed many argued the *only* problem, had been a lack of commitment to Chiang Kai-shek. The Republican party has therefore tended initially to bolster unstable allies and, to a relatively greater degree than the Democrats, to let political and social reform go by the wayside. This position is partly due to the lesson drawn from China and partly to the relatively conservative nature of the party's constituencies and ideology.

Democratic decision-makers drew a reformist lesson from the fall of China. Whereas many Republicans argued that the United States had not backed Chiang sufficiently, many Democrats argued that Truman had backed him too long, and had not taken a tough bargaining approach to promote democratic reform. The Democratic party's general policy approach toward instability in clients has been initially to promote reforms aimed at alleviating the underlying and immediate causes of the disaffection with the client government. This position is due partly to the lesson drawn from China and partly to the relatively liberal nature of the party's constituencies and ideology.

Since withdrawal was no longer viewed as a viable option in the wake of the Kuomintang defeat, partisan decision-makers have tended to oscillate between Democratic reformist interventions and Republican bolstering of clients. Neither policy has lived up to the expectations of proponents. Yet reform seems to have a relatively more positive record in the long-term promotion of stability, but a more modest record in the short term. Bolstering seems to have a relatively more positive record in the short term, but a more modest record in the long term. Primarily for this reason, reformers have often eventually turned toward bolstering and bolsterers toward reform.

This also reflects the essential dilemma of the reform-bolstering dichotomy. If the United States promotes democratic political development, this may lead to long-term stability, but it may also threaten the short-term viability of precarious client governments. If the United States bolsters, it may save those governments in the short term but runs a higher risk of losing them in the long term.[1] In the crisis situations analyzed in the case studies, the grievance-producing actions of the client government were so broad and acute that bolstering was not perceived as a viable option.

The most distressing feature of American policy in this area is that both reformist interventions and bolstering are perceived as failures, if success is defined as the achievement of political stability. Because of the short-term risks inherent in reformist intervention, it has generally not lasted very long as a policy orientation. In overall terms, reform has been a central feature of U.S. policy toward unstable clients during approximately 33 percent of the Cold War era. The Kennedy and Carter administrations were backing away from their reformist policies by the end of their tenures. The Truman administration, despite some setbacks, was not. But Truman and Acheson paid a tremendous political price for this policy. The Republican charge that Democrats were "soft on Communism" was a major constraint on the Democratic administrations that followed.

Bolstering, however, does not seem to offer an effective alternative. The failure of that policy to aid in securing stability in clients—and in many cases its strong correlation with an *increase* in instability over time—led the Eisenhower administration to grope toward a more reformist policy in the late 1950s. The Johnson, Nixon, and Ford administrations never adequately changed their bolstering policy, but domestic support for bolstering had dissipated by the mid-1970s, and instability in clients ultimately increased. The Reagan administration faced similar dilemmas in its second term and moved toward reformist interventions.

These policy failures highlight the dilemmas facing decision-makers. The contradictory impulses in the American ideology (cultural relativism/bolstering versus "missionary" approach/reformist intervention) place constraints on leaders that prevent a consistent U.S. policy toward the Third World. Given this ideological milieu, either policy eventually will be viewed as failing if a nation is "lost" to the United States (for example, China, Cuba, Iran, and Nicaragua): bolstering fails because the rest of the world is not "becoming democratic"; reformist intervention fails because "we cannot expect the rest of the world to copy us." It is apparent that the United States, even in the post–Cold War era, must develop a more consistent policy orientation toward clients if it is to satisfy its own security goals, retain the support of the American people, and avoid the extreme policy disputes of the past.

This intellectual and policy incoherence has meant that American policymakers have had great difficulty in satisfying both security and ideological goals. One might ask, then, what policy can the United States follow if both reformism and bolstering are perceived as failing? One way out of this "damned if you do, damned if you don't" dilemma has been implicitly posited by Samuel Huntington, who defends reformist intervention by questioning the premises by which it is usually evaluated. If reformist intervention is judged according to the high standards of American ideology, the degree to which American-style democracy is exactly replicated, or the rhetoric necessary to garner support for the policy, the usual criteria for doing so, it is obvious that the reality in client nations does not measure up to this standard (nor does it in the United States).[2] Reformist interventions, according to this standard, will always fail.[3]

Huntington replaces this unrealistic yardstick with two alternative criteria for analyzing policy: (1) an examination of the actual effects of reformist interventions, which are inevitably partial, relative, imperfect, and dissatisfying, but generally progressive; and (2) an informed speculation about what would occur *without* American promotion of reform, which, given the dismal empirical record of bolstering, would be an even more disappointing result. Judged by these standards, the record of reformist interventions has been fairly good. If global trends in a more democratic direction are correlated with reformist and bolstering periods, it becomes clear that reformist interventions do have an effect in general policy terms.

Huntington has identified those periods in which there was a relative movement toward greater democratization in the Cold War era. When they are correlated with the periods identified as reformist in this book, patterns of influence become apparent. In the late 1940s and early 1950s (approximately the Truman years), movement toward democracy was at a high point. During the mid-1950s (the first five years of the Eisenhower administration), democracy on a global scale was lessened. In the late 1950s and early 1960s (the late Eisenhower period and the Kennedy administration), it again gained the ascendancy. From the mid-1960s to the mid-1970s (the Johnson, Nixon, and Ford administrations), democracy was again on a downturn. Beginning in the late 1970s (the Carter years), democracy again gained momentum.[4] The Reagan administration's belated turn to reformist interventions in 1986 also correlates with movement toward democracy in the Philippines, South Korea, Chile, Taiwan, and potentially Haiti, as well as other nations where the United States has had influence.

These categories are relative, of course, and there are overlaps among administrations. Though democratic development is not monocausal, and the internal politics of a society remain the most important variable, external influences can also play a crucial role, for example, as in the "demonstration effect" of the democratization of Spain and Portugal in the mid-1970s on South American nations struggling toward democratic development. Among these external influences, American policy at times has been an important factor, especially in those nations in which the United States has directly intervened. Though this idea is often disparaged by academics, especially cultural relativists and regional specialists who are viscerally anti-intervention and who concentrate on the uniqueness of every society, people in other nations recognize this fact. For example, when Jimmy Carter traveled to South America in October 1984, he received a hero's welcome from civilian officials in Peru, Argentina, and Brazil for his human rights policy, which they felt had been partially responsible for greater democratization in their respective societies.[5] There can be, therefore, a strong correlation between the direction of United States policy and the attractiveness of democracy in the world, especially in client nations.

The evidence suggests that American reformist interventions have led to a limited yet positive influence in the Third World: when the United States has promoted reforms on a mass scale, things have often gotten incrementally and relatively better for client societies than if it had never done so; when the United States has not promoted reforms, things have gotten considerably worse, with ultimately negative consequences for the stability of clients. These reformist interventions have also had important residual effects in other Third World nations.

It would seem, then, that reformist intervention is a highly imperfect policy choice, but one that is preferable to bolstering in client nations that are deemed strategically important and are undergoing intense political instability. But it must be understood that even tremendous efforts will bring about only imperfect results and inevitable short-term "failures." There will be steps forward and steps back. The United States can bring a client only to a certain point, and then that nation must fend for itself. The perils of attempting to do too much, especially in light of the paradoxical consequences of excessive commitments, are now too evident to ignore in the future.

Periods of reformist intervention by Democratic administrations have tended to occur under four general conditions: (1) when a period of intense political instability has emerged in a client or region; (2) when the political, economic, social, and/or military policies of the client government are perceived as exacerbating, rather than alleviating, the instability; (3) when previous bolstering seems to have failed in the promotion of stability; and (4) when either withdrawal or bolstering is considered impossible.

Though reformism may be viewed by some as reflecting characteristic American naiveté, it is seen by its proponents as a realistic policy response to alter the political character of ineffective client governments that threaten U.S. security goals through their possible collapse. This book suggests that reformism was not an unreasonable response, even granting that China and Vietnam were policy failures, because bolstering was properly deemed impossible within the internal and external policy constraints faced by American decision-makers. After the failure in China, so was withdrawal.

Competing Perspectives on the U.S. Role in the Developing World

Three descriptive and prescriptive paradigms for the American role in the developing world—liberal, conservative, and ideological—were presented earlier.[6] Liberal critics promote reform as a policy choice, but contend that the United States generally has not promoted reform. Conservative critics promote bolstering, but contend that the United States has naively promoted reforms. The ideological perspective correctly identifies the oscillation between reformism and bolstering, but offers very little in prescriptive terms. What is the relevance of the three paradigms for American policy in the developing world? These perspectives will be reexamined here in light of the analysis presented in the case studies in previous chapters.

The Liberal Critique: The United States Should Reform

This book has made it apparent that the United States has intervened for reform to a greater extent than has often been previously recognized. In descriptive terms, when one views the relatively far-reaching reforms *attempted* by the Truman and Kennedy administrations, it is clear that the charge of liberal critics that the United States has consistently backed reactionary dictators without attention to the promotion of political development along democratic lines is largely incorrect. A clearer distinction must be drawn, in general policy terms, between reformist and bolstering administrations.

The United States, especially during reformist periods, has in fact been an actively progressive force in developing countries. By concentrating on failures in the *implementation* of these reforms, while ignoring limited but real progress, and portraying bolstering periods as the norm, liberals have added to the imbalanced view that the United States is a status-quo power in terms of the internal politics of its clients. Though their critique has value in pointing to the salience of the internal causes of instability as an important aspect in the defeat of insurgents, it views the necessary changes as too easily implemented and too potentially popular among important groups in the client society. In short, like the other perspectives, the liberal critique prescribes a policy without constraints, something that does not—and cannot—exist.

In prescriptive terms, the United States would have to intervene in the internal politics of the client nation to an extraordinary degree to promote the more humane programs that liberals critics espouse. It is simplistic to believe that all the United States has to do is back the morally correct side, even if it could be identified, and its policies will succeed. The lack of an alternative leadership able to gain power and govern by itself is such a consistent policy dilemma in these societies, and withdrawal such a commonly odious option, that massive political intervention may the only possible manner in which the fortunes of a non-totalitarian, reformist, and progressive "Third Force," politically somewhere between the violent brutality of the reactionaries and the revolutionaries, can be promoted.

Thus, although the liberal perspective is partially correct in descriptive terms, it is woefully inadequate in prescriptive terms. Successful reformist interventions require policies that this group is unlikely to support. Liberal critics often play the unhelpful role of holding the client government, and United States policy, to unrealistic standards that may actually undermine the possibility of the changes they support. The promotion of change in the world is neither as simple nor as possible, within the tremendous security, economic, and political constraints of the policy process, as this group tends to assume.

The Conservative Critique: The United States Should Bolster

The conservative view that the United States has unnecessarily and naively promoted reform in clients is largely incorrect in descriptive terms, especially in dealing with the dilemmas of the promotion of stability in clients. The almost total concentration by this group on the external, Communist aid given to insurgents, thus conveniently making insurgencies merely a function of East-West contention, and thus overwhelmingly a military problem, obscures fundamental political problems facing the client regime as well as American decision-makers.

In retrospect, it can easily be argued that it was naive to attempt to reform Chiang Kai-shek and Ngo Dinh Diem—the policies failed. In light of the analysis presented in the case studies, however, is it any less naive to suggest that greater commitments alone would have "saved" their respective governments? The conservative critique tends to downplay, or even ignore, the political weaknesses, brutality, and sometimes irresponsible behavior of beleaguered client governments. It is not enough to say that the Communists or other radicals are ultimately worse, no matter how true that may be. Client governments that alienate their societies to a high degree are strategic liabilities, not assets.

Could the United States have "saved" a government in China which was squandering—and in some cases outright stealing—aid funds, whose armies were usually too sick to march because corrupt officials sold necessary medical supplies, which rewarded incompetence and punished initiative in its military leadership to ensure loyalty, and which, in effect, frantically searched for repressive mechanisms to avoid feeding its own people? Could the United States have "saved" a Vietnamese government which had alienated virtually the entire political spectrum, had brought down worldwide condemnation on itself, also rewarded incompetence and punished initiative in its military leadership to ensure loyalty, planned to assassinate Americans to demonstrate its own *raison d'être*, and was increasingly dominated by the mercurial Ngo Dinh Nhu? It is extremely doubtful that the answer would be a positive one in the absence of major changes in the very nature of the regimes, the goal of the reformist interventions. Nor is it likely that the Huk insurgency, given the endemic corruption, repressive nature, and irresponsibility of the Quirino regime, would have been defeated without the widespread reform program promoted by the United States.

By ignoring such difficult questions, the conservative descriptive analysis leads to the fatuous, if not dangerous, prescriptive conclusion that more commitment alone, without remedial action by the client government, would have somehow alleviated, or easily overcome, these problems. Had the successful reform program in the Philippines failed to defeat the Huk insurgency, conservatives would most likely have criticized that reformist intervention as naive. As President Kennedy noted after the Bay of Pigs debacle, success has many fathers, but failure is an orphan. What appears to be hubris in failure is visionary if successful.

This book should also put to rest the conservative claim that reformist interventions are simply the result of a moralistic, unilateral American policy. In all three cases, it was the intra-governmental as well as extra-governmental opposition to the policies of the client nation's leadership that provided the key in determining the reformist intervention. Interested allies also pressured the United States to "do something," often along reformist lines. Thus it was not only the Americans, but segments of the leadership in the client government itself and others, who saw the necessity for changes. Even the Ministry of National Defense of the Kuomintang, for example, implicitly agreed with American advice, *after* the retreat to Taiwan, that a most important element of an insurgency is the political support of the populace and that a military solution alone will not suffice. Though the Americans, and especially General Marshall and Ambassador Stuart, attempted to make this clear to the regime during the civil war, this advice was ignored by the dominant right wing of the party and by Chiang Kai-shek. Much of the left wing of the Kuomintang, however, agreed with the position and asked the United States to intervene to change governmental policy. Unfortunately, despite herculean efforts at persuasion and ineffective efforts at coercion, this proved impossible. Similar efforts were made by intra-governmental elites in the Philippines and Vietnam. Thus, reformist intervention is largely brought about by a *combination* of a particular American response to instability together with indigenous and international entreaties for reform.

The failures in China and Vietnam were not based on a "misunderstanding" of, let alone a lack of desire to defeat, the Communist insurgents, as charged by some conservatives. They were based on an inability to help create a coalition of forces capable of withstanding the military and political challenge of a highly motivated and organized enemy. It is extremely doubtful that this could have been accomplished through bolstering alone, given the depth of the delegitimization of the ruling groups, even among some of their closest political associates.

The attempts to reform the client states studied here were based more on a pragmatic policy response to the failings of the client government, and those failings as a causal factor in an increase in instability in the client's polity, than on a "naive, moralistic" American impulse to remake the world in its own image. It does no good to wish that the United States could "stay out of" the internal politics of the client and "get on with the war" against the insurgents. The insurgency is largely a function of those politics; that is, as expert after expert in methods of counterinsurgency and example after empirical example have made plain, an insurgency is political, economic, social, and military warfare. Ramon Magsaysay understood this; Chiang, Quirino, and Diem, despite their idealistic rhetoric and honorable intentions, never really did. Concentrating solely on the military effort has not been notably successful in achieving victory over insurgents. Both liberals and conservatives may have to face the fact that the United States may very well be inexorably dragged into the difficult task of reformist intervention if it does not want to withdraw from certain clients for security reasons.

The Ideological Critique: The United States Should Be Consistent

Those who emphasize ideological goals offer valuable contextual variables in understanding the oscillation that characterizes American interaction with the world. Though there is much to their descriptive analysis of the "missionary" approach to the external realm, juxtaposed with periods of relative passivity, these analysts consistently overemphasize the role of ideology in that oscillation. Ideological goals play an important role in American foreign policy, especially during reformist administrations. Yet so does reformist intervention as a pragmatic response to the instability in clients. If alleged American moralism were to disappear, the dilemma of how to deal with such instability would remain, and the promotion of reform is arguably a sensible, not necessarily moralistic, policy response.[7]

Americans can rise above ideological parochialism. Reformist interventions are more a policy response to the growing popularity of the insurgents, and their specific political program, than a knee-jerk liberal democratic reaction to the authoritarian nature of the client government. Thus, the ideological critique is partially correct in pointing to the internal reasons for the particular choices that are sometimes made in selecting which reforms to pursue, but it consistently underestimates the external necessity for such reforms (that is, the potential collapse of the client government, which threatens external security goals) and the relatively sophisticated political analysis of the client society by the United States that often determines reforms. This perspective is useful as a partially correct descriptive analytical tool, but it offers little in the way of prescriptive analysis other than a need for more consistency. It does not, moreover, answer the basic question of whether to aim for a consistently bolstering or reformist policy.

In sum, the liberal, conservative, and ideological critiques of the American role in the developing world are only partially useful in understanding the phenomenon they attempt to analyze. Examined collectively, they offer a valuable descriptive analysis of the incoherence and oscillation in, and the vibrant policy debate over, the role of the United States in the developing world. Examined discretely, they are much less useful because they only partially explain the complexities of the foreign policy process, the political dilemmas facing the client, and the conflicting values at stake. Thus, the descriptive conclusions drawn from viewing only one type of critique are inadequate for understanding the total reality of the policy process. If any one of them were followed faithfully as a prescription, the resulting policy would obscure important constraints on the capabilities of the United States.

For this reason, the prescriptive analyses stemming from the discrete use of the critiques are fundamentally flawed. Liberals are correct in telling us that the United States must actively promote change; conservatives are correct in telling us to have patience; those who adopt the ideological perspective are correct in telling us of the need for consistency. Collectively, they suggest a consistent, selective promotion of reform, with proper understanding of (by American standards) the sometimes glacial pace of change in the developing nations and the vagaries of idiosyncratic local conditions, as a general prescription for American policy toward the developing world. They all ignore or condemn, however, the level of intervention in the internal politics of client nations that may at times be necessary for the shaping of political development in these nations. There are no clean and neat ways to accomplish these reformist interventions, even in periods of relative calm.

In crisis situations, such as those in the case studies, the pace of reform must be quickened, and the level of reformist intervention greatly expanded, to meet the political, economic, social, military, and diplomatic exigencies of the emerging chaos. This will lead to much hard bargaining in difficult situations that will severely test the diplomatic acumen of the United States. It is to this problem that I now turn.

The Commitment Trap and the Management of Strategic Interdependence

There is a paradox in power relations between patrons and clients that I have termed the Commitment Trap: an inverse relationship between commitments and leverage in the bargaining relationship. When in the Commitment Trap, the patron nation finds itself in a greatly diminished bargaining position in a situation that intuitively it should dominate. Yet despite the fact that the case of the Philippines shares many of the characteristics of the bargaining relationships with China and Vietnam— that is, the overall public commitment of American prestige and the need to demonstrate resolve in supporting the client government in order to satisfy the four primary audiences (adversaries, allies, other clients, and domestic opinion)—the United States effectively used its leverage to promote reform in that society. The former colonial relationship between the United States and the Philippines is a necessary, but not sufficient, explanation for this success. The adept manipulation of the political, economic, and military factors of strategic interdependence was the key to a successful policy.

In the China and Vietnam cases, the use of commitments to gain leverage was sloppy and its role in the bargaining relationship poorly understood. This was due to a lack of recognition of the differences between, yet the essential indivisibility of, the psychological and behavioral aspects of commitments. Before proceeding with an analysis of how the bargaining was actually carried out, it will be useful to examine the variance in these aspects of commitments.

The Varying Types and Roles of Commitments

There are two ways in which the concept of commitment and its role in bargaining behavior should be viewed: psychological and behavioral. *Psychological commitments* are the sum total of declaratory policy and promises for aid which translate into a perception of support for the regime—to the client, the patron, and the other audiences. Though overwhelmingly psychological, in that they deal with perceptions and intentions and therefore directly reflect the expectations of clients and patrons alike, these commitments are also partly behavioral in the sense that to make a declaration or promise is an objective act. But their primary importance rests in their subjective, psychological consequences for the bargaining relationship. The patron will do better in bargaining if it can retain ambiguities in the relationship. Psychological commitments relate directly to that ambiguity, or lack thereof, in bargaining with the client government. In short, psychological commitments are subjectively important *promises* of support.

Behavioral commitments are specific programmatic segments of a support effort (political, military, and economic aid) that are primarily material and objective. In short, they deal with the *implementation* of promises to the client. The problem in bargaining arises when the patron overlooks the important subjective, perceptual consequences of making these objective commitments. In this regard, psychological and behavioral commitments are directly interrelated and indivisible within the bargaining relationship, because they both impinge upon the mutual perceptions of strategic interdependence and the future direction of policy. In addition, they are directly interrelated and indivisible within themselves, that is, if promises or implementation of support are given in one area, they will almost inexorably lead to further promises or implementation of support. It is not surprising that American decision-makers have not always recognized these complex interrelationships. Though they are often not recognized by the patron, however, they will be by the client.

There are generally two ways to view the relationship between leverage and commitments. The first, accepted by bolsterers, is that greater commitment brings greater leverage. This might be true in the long term, but not in the short term, especially in the crisis bargaining over internal reform. Policies based on this view show why prior bolstering undermines belated reform attempts: it is extremely difficult to question a commitment once it has been made. This is even more true for behavioral commitments than for psychological ones. Once aid programs are in the pipeline, and materials are perhaps stockpiled by the client, they are much more difficult to retrieve, and the client can resist bargaining threats to a relatively high degree. It is for this reason that clients constantly desire more concrete demonstrations of commitment, that is, material aid, even when they cannot absorb it easily, because this proves to internal and external audiences that the client government has the backing of the patron. In addition, it is more difficult for the patron to question psychological commitments, and the need for domestic justification increases, if material and human resources have already been expended in the policy. Thus, objective behavioral commitments produce important subjective results in the bargaining relationship over time.

The second view, recognized by reformers—though at times too late—is that a threat to commitments brings greater leverage, that is, a quid pro quo use of psychological and behavioral commitments to bargain for reform in a reciprocal *exchange process*. This differs from the idea of social exchange where both sides benefit in mutual trading of values, because the client does not see itself as benefiting from the exchange, though it actually may benefit in terms of legitimacy and mobilization of support. In patron-client quid pro quo bargaining over reform, then, there are winners and losers, though the difference between these terms is one of degree, not kind.

Within the context of the three case studies, the quid pro quo approach to leverage appears to be the more valid generalization, especially when compared to the consistent short-term loss of leverage that resulted when commitments were made on a relatively unconditional basis. This is true in short-term bargaining results as well as in general bargaining outcomes. Indeed, in virtually every instance, an increase in unconditional commitments ultimately meant a loss of bargaining leverage with the client. In contrast, whenever the United States received what it wanted in the promotion of elite and redistributive reforms, the bargaining was on a conditional, quid pro quo basis. That is *not* to say, however, that when the United States used a quid pro quo it always obtained what it wanted. But when it did, it was because of making commitments contingent upon specific actions of the client government and the acceptance of the assumption that reciprocal commitments were indivisible.

Thus leverage accrues, or is created, at two key points in the bargaining relationship: at the time when new commitments are promised (psychological), and at the time when commitments are actually implemented (behavioral). It is at these crucial moments that a quid pro quo has the best chance of ensuring leverage. If it is not used to induce the client to agree to *and* implement reciprocal commitments for reform at these points, however, there is a precipitous loss of leverage. That is, if American commitments are made without reciprocation from the client at *both* stages, it is unlikely that the reformist intervention will succeed. Leverage for reform was only created by a quid pro quo for commitments at these stages in an exchange process.

In the cases studied here, this was learned behavior. The lessons of China in bargaining with Chiang Kai-shek are important in this regard. Officials in the Truman administration learned the valuable lesson of the inverse relationship between commitments (especially behavioral ones—for example, Marshall's comment in October 1946 that the more you aided the Kuomintang the less you could get them to agree to) and leverage, and applied it directly to the Filipino context. The purge of the Far Eastern political analysts during the bolstering Eisenhower administration destroyed that institutional memory, and substituted the bolstering lesson drawn from China. The reformist lesson then had to be rediscovered during the early 1960s in Vietnam, only to be ignored in relations with that nation after 1963 in the rush to satisfy other audiences and achieve other goals.

Bargaining for Promises: Psychological Commitments

As noted earlier, bargaining for reform follows a two-stage process, promissory and implementation. At the promissory stage, there is bargaining over a package deal, that is, the acceptance of an overall program that deals with promises for reform by the client. In this stage, the quid pro quo in the three case studies was very successful. Chiang's promises to Marshall in January-February 1946, the Quirino-Foster Agreement of November 1950, and Diem's agreement in December 1961, for example, all represent the successful use of a quid pro quo approach for elite and redistributive reformist purposes.

It should be noted that the client governments were relatively insecure in their internal power position during this promissory stage. In fact, it was these crises that precipitated greater American concern in the first place. Chiang's alarm over the startling growth of the CCP in the final stages of World War II, Quirino's panic over the Huk offensives of the spring and fall of 1950, and Diem's fears aroused by the Viet Cong's September 1961 offensive all underscored to the clients their dependence on support from the United States.

In relations with clients, however, international systemic factors were even more crucial because they raised questions concerning ultimate American intentions and psychological commitments. The Soviet presence in Manchuria in 1945–1946 (Chiang), the Chinese Communist victory and the rise of radicalism in Southeast Asia in 1948–1950 and the outbreak of the Korean War (Quirino), and the proposed "neutralization" of Laos in 1961 (Diem) led to ambiguities in the minds of the clients concerning American intentions toward them. In general, the worse the Cold War became, and the more the United States felt a necessity to satisfy the four primary audiences by making commitments to the client, the more internal reform was successfully resisted. Within the context of ambiguity, however, at this stage of the bargaining the quid pro quo often succeeded.

Though bolsterers usually argue that such crises are precisely the time to give unconditional support to boost morale in the client government, and reformers and bolsterers alike feel an impulse to demonstrate resolve to the four primary audiences, in bargaining terms it is the worst time to do so. It may run against basic concepts of fair play, and certainly sounds inelegant, but the best approach for a patron in a reformist intervention at the promissory stage (though not necessarily at the implementation stage) may be to "hit them when they are down."

Bargaining for Implementation: Behavioral Commitments

It is during the second stage, the implementation of reforms, when the greatest problems arose in the three case studies in dealing with the clients, partly because psychological commitments per se reduced ambiguities in the bargaining relationship. Yet it was the divided and unconditional use of behavioral commitments that reduced ambiguity even more. In this regard, *only* in the Philippines, the successful reformist intervention, were behavioral commitments consistently kept on a quid pro quo basis and recognized as indivisible to ensure the implementation of the promises obtained in the first stage. In contrast, in China and Vietnam aid went forward without implementation of reform, reducing ambiguity over psychological commitments, and American policymakers were later reduced to searching frantically for ways to regain previous leverage. This process can be demonstrated in a more detailed examination of the way behavioral commitments were used in bargaining for implementation.

In China, Marshall divided the behavioral commitments by going forward with economic aid while withholding military aid. This fogged the ultimate extent of psychological commitments, sending mixed signals concerning how serious the patron was in demanding a quid pro quo at both stages; moreover, this was done while Chiang was reneging on promises for reform. It was not unreasonable for Chiang to assume that if the United States was going to grant him economic aid to prevent the collapse of the regime, it would eventually grant him military aid. Thus, a behavioral commitment through economic aid programs, in tandem with an incorrect assumption of an implicit commitment on the part of the Chinese due to a precipitous worsening of the Cold War in the spring of 1946, raised unreasonable expectations about the extent to which the United States was committed to the regime. This served neither American nor Kuomintang policy well.

Behavioral commitments, as used in bargaining for reforms, are correctly perceived by the client as indivisible, that is, if given in one area they are expected in other areas. Indeed, they are almost always given in other areas (that is, one type of behavioral commitment—for example, political support—is usually followed by others, for example, economic and/or military support) if the nation is considered strategically important. This undermined American bargaining leverage and the use of a quid pro quo with Chiang during the implementation stage by creating the mixed signals concerning the extent of psychological commitments. No matter how hard Marshall tried when the economic aid programs went forward without reform, he could not convince Chiang that further aid would be withheld unless promised reforms were implemented.

Though it might be argued that Chiang was lying all along, or reacting solely to internal political pressures, his actions prior to March 1946 belie this interpretation. Indeed, it is difficult to imagine why he went along with the reformist package deal in the promissory stage in the first place if not in response to the ambiguities in the psychological commitments raised by the death of Roosevelt, the end of World War II, the Hurley resignation, Truman's statement of December 15, 1945, the appointment of the distrusted (by Chiang) Marshall, and the quid pro quo presented him upon Marshall's arrival in China. Chiang had outwaited the Americans during more serious crises before, most notably the Stilwell controversy in 1944. In the previous crises, however, psychological commitments had been relatively unambiguous and indivisible because of the wartime alliance. Thus, the quid pro quo in the postwar relationship was successful in pressuring the client for promises of reform, but it was not credibly used for the implementation of the program because of a lack of understanding of the indivisibility of psychological and behavioral commitments.

Similar developments occurred in Vietnam in the aftermath of the Taylor Mission in 1961. The quid pro quo approach to reform, insisted upon by President Kennedy and Secretary Rusk, was successful in garnering promises of a package deal of elite and redistributive reforms in exchange for psychological commitments to Diem. During the implementation process in 1962, however, Diem balked at most reforms, and his stalling tactics were successful until 1963. Yet the behavioral commitments went forward because of the need to demonstrate resolve in the Cold War, the exigencies of the battlefield, and because the policy seemed to be working without the reforms in the short term. This seriously undermined American leverage when the regime began to unravel in early 1963, and there was a showdown on reform. Thus, mixed signals were also communicated during the implementation stage in Vietnam, and replaced ambiguities in the relationship with certitude on the part of the client. By the time of the Buddhist crisis of the summer of 1963, Diem and Nhu were again convinced that the United States was too involved in Vietnam to threaten credibly a quid pro quo. When the Americans initiated selective aid cuts in an attempt to regain the leverage of December 1961 by dividing the behavioral commitments, the policy failed because it could not cut support where this might have produced the most leverage—in military programs—since the patron was already heavily committed in that area. The United States instead moved toward supporting a coup, because by that time many State Department analysts saw it as the only way out of the leverage dilemma.

As in the China case, it could be argued that Diem, and especially Nhu, never intended to implement the reforms, and in fact this seems more likely than in the bargaining relationship with Chiang. Yet it is also difficult to imagine why Diem did not simply refuse the package deal offered in December 1961 and outwait the United States, tactics that had also worked quite well during crises in the past, if ambiguities in the psychological commitment in the face of the "neutralization" of Laos and the quid pro quo approach had not convinced him that he must exchange promises of reform for commitments. Thus, as in China, the quid pro quo was successful in gaining leverage with the client in the promissory stage but not in the implementation stage, because behavioral commitments without reform went forward, reducing ambiguities in the psychological commitment to the regime.

In contrast, the quid pro quo approach was used in both the promissory and implementation stages in the Philippines. The close association of fulfillment of patron promises for aid with fulfillment of client promises for reform created the dynamic of a reciprocal exchange process in United States–Filipino relations that led to a successful reformist intervention, even within a harsh Cold War international bargaining context. The implementation of reforms on an incremental, priority basis, though in close succession to maintain the indivisibility of psychological and behavioral commitments, was effective when used in tandem with the quid pro quo. The client was not confused about American resolve, nor in what it expected in exchange for its commitments. Success in one area spilled over into other areas. Thus, bargaining was successful because proper attention was paid to both types of commitments at both stages of the bargaining.

Although it might be argued that Quirino, even though he admittedly was under internal political constraints that neither Chiang nor Diem faced, was simply more likely to reform than the other leaders, his consistently bitter resistance to implementation of the reforms and his sometimes violent behavior toward opponents would discount this one-dimensional analysis. Quirino also tried to renege on his promises for reform, but was met with firm insistence of a quid pro quo for behavioral commitments at every point. Even within this context, however, it took a massive political intervention to prevent a retreat into repression in 1953 when the bolstering Eisenhower administration lessened the top-level pressure for reform. A quid pro quo approach is not a substitute for political intervention, but a complementary bargaining tool. In fact, though both are crucial, there appears to be an inverse relationship between the two: the higher the degree of successful bargaining for reform, the lower the necessity for political, economic, and military intervention to prevent the client government from collapsing.

A particularly acute internal crisis in the client nation is an important variable in the promissory stage, but not necessarily in the implementation stage. Though it is true that Chiang, Quirino, and Diem were greatly influenced by the relative strength of their internal power positions in their acquiescence to reformist pressures during the former stage, they were less so during the latter. Chiang and Diem were weaker politically in 1947 and late 1963 respectively than in early 1946 and late 1961 respectively (the promissory stage), and this weaker position presumably underscored their dependence on American support. Yet it was at that precise time that they put up the greatest resistance to reform. A more important factor was that the former periods were times when they believed the United States was inalterably committed to their regimes.

A client can argue that its internal power position is too secure to require reform (Chiang, 1946; Quirino, 1953; Diem, early 1963) or too insecure to implement it (Chiang, 1947; Quirino, 1950; Diem, late 1963.) The most salient bargaining issue appears to be not so much the client's relative internal security position, but its perception of American commitments and the alternatives to those commitments. The clients studied here only responded to reformist pressure, regardless of their perception of their internal power position, when those commitments were ambiguous. They were only kept consistently ambiguous during implementation, however, in the Philippines. Even when psychological commitments were made less ambiguous with the United States–Filipino Defense Treaty of 1951, the ambiguity over behavioral commitments was maintained by strict indivisibility and a quid pro quo at the implementation stage.[8]

Though it is clearly no panacea for the tough bargaining necessary to promote reform successfully in clients undergoing intense political instability, a quid pro quo approach to commitments—in both the promissory and the implementation stages—will make failure less likely. The indivisibility of psychological and behavioral commitments must be recognized. A skillful manipulation of those commitments is not impossible if the United States uses a strict quid pro quo approach in its bargaining behavior. This is not to say that this approach is an ideal way to bargain with clients, but one must consider the absolutely dreadful record of the unconditional use of commitments and the resulting paradoxical effects on leverage. It is only in relative terms that the quid pro quo approach is superior. Yet if the cases in this study are any indication, it is the best way to attempt a reformist intervention.

Given the potential for disaster in precipitous increases in commitments, and their paradoxical effect of often weakening rather than strengthening a client, the most serious thought must be given to making them in the first place. Before such commitments are made, the fundamental question in policy debates should be whether the client is actually strategically important. If it is decided that it is, however, decision-makers must accept the probability that commitments at one level, especially the military, will most likely lead to commitments at others. The more commitments are made, the stronger will be the pressures to make more still. The client will come to understand this and will attempt to use it to pass responsibility for its fate to the patron. Within this context, the United States might do better to concentrate on the potential effects of commitments on the bargaining relationship with the client rather than overemphasizing the importance of the primary audiences (adversaries, allies, other clients, and domestic groups.) This, of course, is easier said than done, and will require a high degree of political skill and courage at the top levels of government. The end of the Cold War should simplify this task, though it is unlikely to disappear as a policy dilemma.

Before proceeding to further analysis of the preferable strategy and tactics to be used in a quid pro quo approach, there is one more area, the bureaucratic and organizational constraints on signaling commitments in the bargaining relationship, that must first be examined. The sharp disagreements within the U.S. government over policy direction in China and Vietnam were important factors in the failure of the reformist interventions.

The Bureaucratic Effects on Bargaining

There was great contention within the U.S. government in the three cases studied concerning which bargaining approach to adopt, the pace of implementation of reforms, and the salience of various issue areas. In general terms, military officers, especially of the higher ranks, promoted a bolstering approach, while political officers, economic officers, and the CIA generally promoted a reformist one. This is because military officers tend to view the problem in military terms; political, economic, and intelligence officers tend to see it from a broader, more political perspective. The latter three bureaus are also more likely to recognize the indivisibility of behavioral commitments because of their programmatic functions within the government. Several caveats must be offered, however, in regard to drawing easy conclusions from these generalizations.

First, these are only broad tendencies, not hardened categorizations.

Generals Marshall and Lansdale and Admiral Spruance were among the strongest promoters of reform in the three cases—and all were professional soldiers. Yet they were reformist when they were acting in the capacity of political or intelligence, not military, officers. This suggests that the bureaucratic-functional role they were playing was a more important variable in the policies they espoused than a simplistic notion of the "liberal" civilians versus the "conservative" military. In contrast, the State Department during the Dulles years, especially following the purges of the early 1950s, was the center of bolstering sentiment within the U.S. government. Even so, as the bureaucratic infighting over policy in the cases demonstrates, there is a strong broad tendency for military officers to promote bolstering, and for political, economic, and intelligence officers to promote reform.

Second, bolsterers are generally in favor of economic and military reforms; it is in the areas of political and social reforms that they have reservations. Reformers, on the other hand, generally promote reform in all of the issue areas as a key to client stability.

Third, these tendencies should also be seen within the context of a difference in relative degree. No one was completely reformist, nor completely bolstering, in his preferred policy choices.

Finally, the perspectives on reform can diverge according to whether the policymaker is in Washington or in the field; that is, there are often splits within, as well as among, bureaucratic agencies. In China during World War II, political officers in the field were more reformist; their superiors in Washington were more bolstering. A split along similar lines appeared in the Philippines after 1952. In Vietnam from 1961 to 1963, decision-makers in Washington were more reformist; the ambassador and military chief in the field were more bolstering. At other times, there was a congruence between perceptions in Washington and the embassies.

Splits between Washington and the field are often a function of a dynamic perceptual process based on various developments: (1) on the battlefield; (2) within the client's political system; (3) within the embassy team; (4) in domestic and international opinion; (5) in the possible systemic consequences of actions taken; and (6) within the body politic. In general, field representatives are relatively more concerned with the first three considerations; Washington is relatively more concerned with the last three. All, however, are concerned with the overall developments as they pertain to the client in question.

With these caveats in mind, it is clear that there were relatively consistent bureaucratic splits along military bolstering and politically reformist lines in the three cases. The persistence of these splits suggests that they are based on varying perceptions within the bureaus of how to approach an insurgency; another cause is the functional specialization within the various bureaus of the government. At this point a brief analysis of the causes of insurgencies will be useful, since the differing perceptions of how to deal with instability are intimately linked to perceptions of its fundamental causes.

The Causes of Insurgency

Insurgencies have both immediate and underlying causes. The immediate cause is a highly organized, motivated, and disaffected group of elites, often receiving external aid and succor, who want to overthrow the government. Without such a group, revolution is impossible; the masses possess neither the expertise nor the organizational skills to effectuate such a vast and complicated undertaking. Though Marxists and other romantics portray revolutions as mass uprisings based in the objective, material conditions of a society, they have always been led by a relatively educated elite group from the middle or upper classes. Those who implicitly or explicitly accept the Marxist view confuse lower "class origins" with lower "class consciousness": the former is rarely, if ever, based in reality among the revolutionary leadership; the latter is always highly developed among that group and is the unifying dynamic in its opposition to the status quo.[9] Revolutionist doctors; lawyers, intellectuals, and other economic elites in the Third World are often blithely accepted, especially in the West, as the "real" representatives of the common people. These groups, however, have little actual chance of gaining widespread support unless there are fundamental underlying problems that create a potential for delegitimizing the political, economic, and social status quo. Without an immediate cause, revolution is impossible; without underlying causes, it is highly improbable. It is the combination of these two dynamics that creates a revolutionary environment.

The underlying causes of insurgencies are often a deep political and social inequality, a brutal economic reality for the vast majority, and a set of status-quo elites in power who are more concerned with protecting their privileged position than with mobilizing support through political, social, and economic power-sharing, even in moderate doses. When a political challenge is mounted by revolutionary elites, the status-quo elites typically respond with a repressive crackdown on all dissent. This may work in the short term, but often fails to work in the long term because it entails a growing discontent among the masses and the eventual further disaffection of oppositionist (as opposed to revolutionary), apolitical, or apathetic elites, including intra-governmental ones, through the growing centralization of power. If this development occurs, the government is faced with a dynamic revolutionary situation. Its actions, unfortunately, often exacerbate that situation as the instability spreads. In all three cases studied here, grievance-producing actions of the client government added to the precipitous growth of dissent and violence in its society.

Insurgencies in rural societies are thus characterized by their "triangularity": competition between opposing sets of elites for the loyalty of the masses. John Shy describes this process, and the typical responses from revolutionary and status-quo elites:

> Two armed forces contend less with each other than for the support and the control of the civilian population. Invariably, the government and its forces are reluctant to perceive this essential triangularity, while the rebels use whatever strength they can muster to break the links between governor and governed. Revolutionary violence is less an instrument of physical destruction than one kind of persuasion; the aim is to destroy responsiveness to the state, at first with the general population, ultimately among those who man the military and administrative arms of the state. Ideally, government ceases to function because no one any longer obeys; old authority is displaced by revolutionary organization without the massive confrontations of conventional warfare or the *force majeure* of the *coup d'état*. To organize revolution means going beneath the normal level of governmental operation, reaching the smallest social groups and even individuals, indoctrinating everyone so recruited, and of course using those forms of violence, particularly threats, terrorism, and irregular or guerrilla warfare, that are at once most difficult to stop and most likely to change docile, obedient subjects into unhappy, suggestible people.[10]

The struggle for the loyalty of the masses takes three typical strategic forms: *repression*, *reform*, or *revolution*. The status-quo elites typically adopt the first strategy in an attempt to destroy the immediate cause of rebellion, while avoiding dealing with the underlying causes because this would adversely affect their short-term and long-term power position. American reformist administrations, and their fellow reformers in the client society and government, adopt the first and second strategies to defeat the insurgency through simultaneous attention to the immediate and underlying causes of the rebellion. The revolutionary elites adopt the third strategy to turn latent dissent into blatant rebellion through exploitation of the underlying causes in order to gain support for the immediate cause. It is in this chaotic environment that the United States government must develop a policy.

The Bureaucratic-Functional Dilemma

The bureaucratic dilemma for the United States largely rests in the specialized functions of individual bureaus and the resultant divergence in perception over the salience of tasks. The U.S. government sends its military officers to the field to attend to the immediate cause and "stay out of" political, economic, and social questions; it sends its political, intelligence, and economic officers to attend to the underlying causes and "stay out of" military questions. Then surprise is often expressed that these two sets of officers tend to take highly divergent views concerning the relative importance of governmental programs. These disagreements should be expected. There is so much convergence in the respective issue areas—that is, the military, economic, social, and political dilemmas are so interrelated—that there will be inevitable clashes over their relative salience as a result of organizational specialization and a functional overlap in responsibilities.

Yet it is in the perception of the salience of issue areas where policy analysis can also transcend bureaucratic loyalties. Those military officers who recognized this interrelationship (Generals Marshall and Lansdale and Admiral Spruance) were reformist; those officers who viewed the immediate cause as most salient were bolsterers (Generals MacArthur and Harkins, Admiral Cooke). Those political officers who viewed the causes discretely and downplayed the salience of underlying causes (Walter Robertson, Frederick Nolting) were bolsterers; those who emphasized both underlying and immediate causes (John Carter Vincent, Myron Cowen, Averell Harriman) were reformist. Yet, in general, military officers tended to concentrate on the immediate causes, obscure the salience of underlying causes, and view the two discretely; the other agencies tended to view immediate and underlying causes symbiotically.

The bureaucratic wrangling over the salience of immediate and underlying causes is not narrowly based on infighting for influence, trying to catch the ear of the President, programmatic resources, or careerist opportunism, reasons often given in bureaucratic paradigms of U.S. policy. There are clear functional reasons for the contention based on the duties assigned to the respective bureaus. This largely reflects a wide asymmetry in the urgency of the programmatic responses to the instability. Political and economic change is generally painfully slow and the full effects, at best, are felt in the medium term, though the psychological benefits in support from the populace can be felt immediately (a primarily political, not military, question). Military programs, however, have an immediate and urgent salience to a deteriorating security situation (a primarily military, not political, question). Because of the urgency of the battlefield, the military resists threats to military behavioral commitments that are to be used as leverage in quid pro quo bargaining for reform programs in the other issue areas. Political and economic officers tend to see the various components of the reform program as indivisible. The bureaus therefore tend to split over perceptions of the probable effects of particular forms of bargaining—bolstering versus quid pro quo—on their respective specialized programmatic functions. The urgency of the battlefield turns military officers into bolsterers; the indivisibility of behavioral commitments, and of issue areas, turns civilian officers into advocates of a quid pro quo.

When an attempt is made to threaten a behavioral commitment in one issue area, in order to bargain for reform in other issue areas, the variance in programmatic urgency and bureaucratic response manifests itself in acute form. If the United States goes forward with a military commitment, which everyone recognizes is of primary but not singular importance, it lessens leverage for using economic and political commitments as bargaining tools because the client can assume that the United States will go forward in the economic and political areas to avoid damage to its reputation and prestige, which have already been invested in the military commitment. Given the varying perceptions and functions of the bureaus, the splits over policy are manifested in intragovernmental bargaining over behavioral commitments, and their effects on bargaining with the client, because it is the bureaus that are responsible for implementation.

This dilemma developed in China. In that case, the United States withheld its military aid on the advice of State Department reformers, and went forward with its economic aid on the advice of bolsterers, to convince Chiang that its psychological commitment was limited unless reforms were put through. As the military situation deteriorated in mid-1947, however, military officers argued forcefully that the urgency of the battlefield dictated that military aid must go forward lest the political and economic reforms become irrelevant through the collapse of the client. Reformist State Department personnel reluctantly agreed, and the bureaucratic dispute shifted in favor of the bolsterers. Even though the political, military, and economic reforms had not been implemented, Marshall half-heartedly agreed and resumed military aid in May 1947. The lack of a quid pro quo after that time, however, lessened leverage even further, and Marshall was reduced to sending General Wedemeyer to attempt to jolt the Kuomintang into action. Though it was not recognized at the time, economic commitments (1946–1947) and military commitments (after mid-1947) undermined whatever leverage the United States might have gained by altering the perception of psychological commitments, and led to the total abandonment of the quid pro quo advocated by the State Department. By 1949 the lesson had been learned, and a quid pro quo policy was initiated in the Philippines.

A similar situation developed in Vietnam. As the United States proceeded with its military programs in 1962, in spite of growing reservations in the State Department and outright opposition among civilian officers in the field, in order to attend to the immediate cause of the insurgency, it unwittingly squandered its leverage for reform to attend to underlying causes. When this was realized by civilian officers in Washington in late 1962 and early 1963, the bureaucratic debate over how to regain that leverage reached startling proportions. Neither bolstering military officers nor reformist civilian officers, however, ever solved this basic dilemma of how to regain leverage when extensive behavioral commitments had already been made to the client government without a quid pro quo.

In the Philippines, however, these bureaucratic splits were largely avoided and therefore were much less of a problem in bargaining with the client government. Many of the top-ranking military officers were as convinced of the need to attend simultaneously to immediate and underlying causes, with a slight precedence given to the former, as were the political officers. In fact, the military officers were at times even more reformist than State Department or embassy personnel. Military officers who were less convinced were quickly removed from positions of influence, maintaining programmatic unity. The Economic Cooperation Administration and CIA officers were also generally reformist, which added to policy coherence. This unity of purpose maintained a consistent bargaining position with the client government and allowed the quid pro quo use of commitments to proceed with relative cohesion during the crucial implementation stage. Though this is hardly sufficient to lead to successful bargaining, it was necessary to avoid the internal bureaucratic splits that undermined American policy in the China and Vietnam cases.

Bargaining and the Minimization of Noise

Internal incoherence is not the only reason bureaucratic splits should be avoided. They may, in fact, have adverse consequences for signaling commitments and bargaining. Indeed, these splits can clearly undermine policy with the client government.

The problem with signaling commitments amid intense internal policy debates can best be explained through the concept of the "signal-to-noise-ratio" (SNR). As any audiophile will recognize, the SNR is "the strength of the [desired] signal relative to the [undesired] strength of the confusing or distracting background stimuli."[11] In order to communicate a quid pro quo approach to the client government, the bureaucratic bolstering noise must be kept low relative to the reformist signal of resolve emanating from the top levels of government on the nature of American commitments. This is a separate problem from that of granting commitments in one area and withholding them in another, thereby sending mixed signals for reform. Though the latter is often a serious problem, the SNR dilemma manifests itself primarily in the field, in Congress, and among extra-governmental groups during policy implementation.

In China and Vietnam, the noise level emanating from bolsterers within the government (Admiral Badger in China, General Harkins and Ambassador Nolting in Vietnam) was quite high. Since bolsterers tend to see leverage as gained through the granting of commitments, they overemphasize the psychological commitment to particular officials in the client government, especially those to individual leaders. Bolstering noise, of course, may be amplified by other groups such as journalists (Henry Luce, Joseph Alsop, Marguerite Higgins) congressional bolsterers (Congressman Walter Judd), or other important personages (General MacArthur). A strong reformist signal, even from the President, is not sufficient to carry out effective bargaining. It may be negated by the expectations of the client, or simply by the perceived costs of the client's accession to reformist demands.[12] These developments, however, may be directly influenced by the level of bolstering noise. If the client government believes the United States is not united in its policy (thereby affecting its expectations), and that it can therefore outwait its patron (and minimize the threatened costs of not reforming), the American bargaining position will be greatly worsened. Indeed, if negative sanctions are not employed to demonstrate resolve, this may further undermine leverage attempts by leading the client to believe that the patron is bluffing. This is an eventuality that should be avoided by the patron, because all subsequent threats to commitments may then be viewed as bluffs.

This situation is more likely to occur if various bolstering officials increase noise relative to reformist signals. Even the appearance of disagreement can have this effect on the perceptions of the client government and society. The deep divisions within the bureaus in the field, let alone in Washington, were no secret to the Chinese and Vietnamese. Ambassador Hurley, for example, once threatened to punch another American official at a Chinese diplomatic reception for suggesting that the United States and the Kuomintang seek a rapprochement with the Chinese Communists during World War II, which happened to be American policy at the time. When incidents like this were added to the mixed signals in the confused use of commitments in bargaining, it is small wonder that Chiang was convinced that the United States was not entirely serious in its quid pro quo approach under Marshall. It should also be noted, however, that in the Philippines case, American congressional and public opinion tended to *strengthen* the reformist signal, thereby reinforcing, rather than undermining, American bargaining positions.

In general, bureaucratic and extra-governmental bolstering noise has three negative effects on U.S. bargaining for reform: (1) it calls into question the degree of resolve in making commitments contingent upon actions by the client; (2) it encourages stalling and cosmetic reform tactics on the part of the client; and (3) it allows the client to play one bureau or faction off against another, and exacerbates the internal dissension even further. The client will attempt to appeal to a bolstering bureau and make an end run around reformist ones to manipulate policymakers and garner commitments; it will also attempt to mobilize its "friends" in the United States to push for a bolstering policy. Such actions seriously and detrimentally affect the American bargaining position in an already difficult bargaining relationship.

Deep policy disputes can even have an effect on the political strategies of the enemy. The Chinese Communists spoke of the Hurley faction (bolsterers) and the "progressive" faction (reformers) within the U.S. government following the death of Roosevelt in 1945. It is no secret that the North Vietnamese in part aimed their policies and propaganda at congressional and other advocates of withdrawal from Vietnam. The policy debate itself, then, becomes a crucial element in whether that policy will succeed or fail.

Little can be done about extra-governmental or congressional noise in a democratic political system, except perhaps an appeal to reason— a notoriously ineffective device. Within the bureaucracy, however, steps can be taken to prevent noise that can undermine policy. Civil servants, unlike civilians or congressmen, are under orders. The SNR problem is greatly intensified if the debate is carried out through leaks to the press. If a reformist policy is decided upon, it is crucial that all members of the U.S. government in the field be equally dedicated to that end. Debate over policy cannot—and should not—be done away with; decision-makers need varying options to make effective policy, and democratic standards demand some form of accountability. But that debate must be carried out behind closed doors, and in the strictest secrecy possible in a democracy.

The bureaucratic noise problem, of course, is largely obviated if there is agreement over policy within the government, and that would be the optimal solution. In the Philippines, in contrast to China and Vietnam, the U.S. government presented a united front to the client for a total reform package that communicated the conditional nature of American commitments. This led to a much more united, coherent, and, it should be emphasized, successful policy. In all three of the cases, all of the agencies recognized the primacy of attending to the immediate cause of the insurgency. Only in the Philippines, however, was the indivisibility of commitments and the ultimate indivisibility of the immediate and underlying causes of the insurgency clearly understood by most officials. A program to educate military and civilian officers in each other's problems, the importance of each other's areas of responsibility, and the effects of commitments on the bargaining relationship might lead to an attenuation of the functional dilemma. The skillful manipulation of the bargaining relationship in the Philippines was a key to its successful outcome and should be used as a model for policy in other nations.

A programmatically coherent policy is a necessary, but hardly sufficient, prerequisite to successful bargaining. All bureaucratic elements must be made aware of the need to present a united front to the client. This is true if the general policy is either one of bolstering or reform, but especially in the latter case because of the potentially disastrous consequences of contradictory noise on the bargaining relationship. Though a coherent policy will hardly guarantee successful bargaining, it is necessary to avoid the programmatic and bureaucratic chaos of the China and Vietnam cases.

Bargaining Strategies and Tactics for the Internal and External Reformer

There are acute dilemmas involved in inducing reforms in a client government that is reluctant to implement them. The tasks for an external reformer are severely compounded when the degree of resistance from the client reaches the proportions that it did in the case studies. Attempting to promote reform while avoiding the collapse or total estrangement of a client government may be the most daunting diplomatic task that faces the United States.

In viewing the past and potential frequency with which this problem occurs, the question arises of which bargaining strategy and tactics are more likely to lead to a successful result. It is important to emphasize, however, that what follows represents broad generalizations based on the case studies and secondary literature, not algebraic equations for dealing with widely varying local conditions, cultures, and personalities.

With that caveat in mind, three conditions are explicitly assumed in the following analysis: (1) that a comprehensive reform policy has been decided upon by the U.S. government; (2) that a quid pro quo approach to psychological and behavioral commitments has been adopted at both the promissory and implementation stages; and (3) that the bureaucracy is relatively united in its approach to the client government. Given past performances by the U.S. government, these are weighty assumptions to make. They are necessary, however, to flesh out the strategic and tactical issues involved in bargaining for a reformist policy.

The Internal Reformer

In his analysis of Mustafa Kemal, the founder of modern Turkey, Samuel Huntington has examined the strategies and tactics open to a Third World reformer.[13] The probable choices for a strategy fall into two general categories: *blitzkrieg* and *fabian*. The blitzkrieg approach is comprehensive, and aims to introduce a host of reforms simultaneously to overcome the opposition to them. The idea is to make known the entire scope of the reform program and hope to obtain as much as possible. This is a questionable strategy in developing countries, however, because it will most likely coalesce opposition to particular segments of the program into a unified bloc against all reform. Status-quo economic elites, for example, would join with status-quo political, social, and military elites to prevent a program that threatened the position of all. A blitzkrieg strategy is therefore likely to mobilize "the wrong groups at the wrong time on the wrong issues."[14]

On the other hand, a fabian strategy, that used by Kemal, is an incremental, prioritized approach which suggests facing down one segment of opposition at a time to prevent this coalescence and to give the society and government time to adjust to the change inherent in reform. This strategy allows the reformer to choose which opposition group he will face when he deems it propitious, thereby maintaining strategic flexibility, and does not expend precious political capital waging a multi-front political struggle.

The task of a reformer is a difficult one; he must wage a simultaneous struggle against revolutionaries and reactionaries. The fabian strategy may be especially desirable in an insurgency, because the reformist government can concentrate more political capital on the revolutionaries and minimize expenditure on the reactionaries, while still going forward with moderate change in order to mobilize support. In this way, the reformer can wage his simultaneous two-front war against the revolutionaries (immediate cause) and reactionaries (underlying causes) while placing, properly so, more emphasis on the former.

The existence of an armed insurgent group could even be helpful here, because the reformer can then argue that the threat of revolution is greater than the threat of reform. Unfortunately, the reactionaries—being reactionaries—often do not see a clear distinction between the two. By adopting a fabian strategy, the reformer, if he is skillful, may be able to maintain the support of at least some of the reactionaries through an incremental approach and wage a more comprehensive struggle against the revolutionaries.

The tactics of reform also offer the blitzkrieg and fabian approaches as the two general patterns of choice. Here, however, the reformer might do better to adopt blitzkrieg tactics on individual issues. Since the minimization of opposition is crucial to success in deeply divided societies, where the government may be none too powerful, the reformer should move to defeat his opponents on specific issues before they have a chance to mobilize against the entire reform program. It is here that the centralization of power as the first stage in mobilizing support for the government is most important. If the reformer does not have the political wherewithal to overcome opposition, he will fail in the trying and might even fall from power.

For the internal reformer, then, a fabian strategy and blitzkrieg tactics appear to be the best approach to take, and possibly even more so during an insurgency. But this is for a reformer dealing with his own society and political system—a sovereign ruler. An external reformer attempting to promote reform in another society through diplomatic means has a very different set of dilemmas.

The External Reformer

For the external reformer, the question of strategy and tactics is as complicated as that for the internal reformer. The situation is even more difficult, however, because the constraints on the external reformer mean that he cannot wield power in anything approaching a similar manner. An internal reformer can exercise whatever power is available and mobilize it to serve a relatively narrow set of ends. The internal reformer believes that what he is doing is necessary, whereas the external reformer must filter the reform program through a reluctant client government that may not believe the program is necessary, or desirable, in the first place. This makes the leadership problem, that is, elite reform, and the implementation processes, actual rather than cosmetic changes, the most important elements in the external reformer's agenda. At the promissory and implementation stages, however, there are certain strategies and tactics that are more likely to succeed. These also tend to follow the blitzkrieg and fabian patterns of choice.

The external reformer must first gain acceptance of the reform program through a commitment from the client government for internal reform—the promissory stage of bargaining. The best strategy for doing so is the blitzkrieg, that is, attention to all areas of reform simultaneously. This is true for several reasons. First, as noted earlier, both psychological and behavioral commitments are indivisible in bargaining. It is therefore better in bargaining terms to make a package deal, letting the client know that major changes are expected and that, at least theoretically, refusal to reform in one area will threaten the entire aid program.

Second, the package deal is a necessary reference point for future bargaining. If only one form of commitment (political, economic, or military) is exchanged for one kind of reform, the client can later claim, with justification, that it never expected such a comprehensive reform program, and refuse to make further concessions. Since the patron's reputation would already be on the line, it is likely that it would have to acquiesce and increase the other commitments anyway. A package deal allows the external reformer to cry foul if the client government does not live up to its end of the bargain. This is a necessary component of normal diplomacy if the client later tries to renege, which in all probability it will.

Third, it is only fair to let the client know what is expected of it. The acceptance of commitments is almost as difficult as the granting of them, if they are made contingent upon reform. It must be recognized that there are nationalistic sensibilities involved. The trick is not simply to get tough; it is to get tough without appearing to do so. Within this context, issues of fairness should not be overlooked.

In short, the blitzkrieg strategy is preferable for the external reforming patron at the promissory stage because it is most likely that eventually the patron will be committed across the board in any event. This should be recognized and across-the-board commitments for reform obtained from the client government. Without the latter, bargaining for implementation will be much more difficult.

The blitzkrieg strategy has worked well in the promissory stage in bargaining for a reform package deal. In China, the Philippines, and Vietnam, the United States was promised comprehensive reforms by the client government through the effective use of a quid pro quo approach to bargaining. The problems remained in the implementation, or tactical, stage.

For tactics, the best approach for the external reformer is the fabian. The incremental implementation of reforms in the one successful case, the Philippines, followed a prioritized sequence in which the overall promises were broken down into segments (military, economic/social, political) that were carried out in close succession. This is the most difficult, and therefore the most important, area in bargaining for implementation: the reforms must be dealt with sequentially, but a close succession is required to maintain the indivisibility of behavioral commitments and the issue areas. Though the reforms in the Philippines were implemented in incremental sequence, the overall result was a comprehensive program. Thus a blitzkrieg strategy and fabian tactics, and a strict quid pro quo at the promissory and implementation stages, succeeded in this case in reforming the client government.

In contrast, in China and Vietnam, simultaneous reforms were promoted without the quid pro quo at the implementation stage, and the reforms never materialized. Blitzkrieg tactics were attempted, and the resistance to the implementation of the package deal was far greater. When Chiang attempted to push the total reform program simultaneously (military demobilization, political and economic power-sharing) at the Kuomintang Congress in March 1946, his intra-party opposition coalesced and blocked reform in any area. Though the left wing of the Kuomintang was in favor of the package deal, it was neither large nor powerful enough to overcome right-wing and centrist opposition. Since American commitments were going ahead in any event, Chiang could then renege on the promises for reform with minimal costs, that is, the costs of facing down a relatively unified internal opposition appeared greater than the potential costs of not acceding to American threats. In Vietnam, blitzkrieg tactics were also attempted in a simultaneous reform program (military delegation of authority, political and economic power-sharing). Diem successfully stalled on implementing much of the program, however, by invoking sovereignty at every turn, refusing to allow American oversight of the implementation of particular programs, avoiding State Department reformers in favor of military bolsterers, and obfuscating the issue areas with the manipulation of statistics in the Strategic Hamlet Program. By the time the United States fully discovered that the program was in fact not being implemented, it was already committed on the battlefield. By attempting too much too quickly, and abandoning the quid pro quo during implementation, the United States achieved very little.

There are several reasons for the efficacy of fabian tactics in the implementation stage. First, the external reformer cannot expect, nor force, the client government to transform itself virtually overnight. This may also cause the client government political problems at a time when it is already weak, as in the case of Chiang Kai-shek. These are proud and intelligent people with their own agenda; it is unrealistic to expect them to turn over the reins of government to a patron they see as uncomprehending, overbearing, and naive. This should not stop the patron from pursuing the reform program, but it should make the patron aware that there are sensibilities involved, especially in non-Western nations that perceive themselves as the past victims of imperialism and resent external pressure.

Second, it is not necessary to pursue reform in every issue area with equal vigor, and necessity should be the guiding principle for the external reformer. An analysis must be done of the most urgent issue areas based on the grievance-producing conditions that pertain in the strongest pockets of dissidence. A school program, for example, should not be pursued because it sounds nice back home, but because the masses actually desire education. In the case studies, the most salient grievance-producing issue areas where reform was needed were (1) military (especially the elimination of indiscriminate repression and corruption); (2) economic/social (especially land reform and social relations with rural elites); and (3) political (especially some form of participation for non-Communist opposition elites). In the Philippines, the reforms were implemented in the above sequence. In China and Vietnam they were never implemented.

Third, the client government typically does not possess the material or trained human resources to attend to all of the issue areas simultaneously. Unless the patron is willing to take over major areas of responsibility for the client government because of its superior resource base, the client government should not be expected to create miracles with its limited means. This is why a prioritized list should be devised at the implementation stage. The patron should not take direct responsibility for the reform programs for the following reasons: (1) it may hand the issue of nationalism over to the insurgents; (2) it makes the client even more dependent, in the worst sense of the word, on external aid; (3) it leads to a "let the Americans do it" attitude in the client that may lead to further involvement; and (4) it allows the client to avoid the remedial action needed to become self-sufficient. In short, it makes the client weaker, not stronger. Though selective direct responsibility may become necessary in a crisis, the patron should always avoid this to the greatest extent possible. The basic idea of reformist intervention is to get the client to take action itself, not to pass responsibility to the patron. A prioritized, incremental approach to reform is therefore the best that can be expected.

At first glance, it would seem that there is a paradox in the strategies and tactics of the internal and external reformer: the former, fabian strategy/blitzkrieg tactics; the latter, blitzkrieg strategy/fabian tactics. Fortunately—and this is perhaps the only fortunate aspect of this form of diplomacy—this is not the case.

The Symmetry of External Tactics and Internal Strategies

Though there are many asymmetries of interests in the patron-client relationship, there is a major symmetry in the bargaining for reform. The blitzkrieg strategy of the external reformer is not meant to obtain immediate, simultaneous reforms, but the formal promise of a comprehensive program and acquiescence in the patron's oversight of imple-

Table 2 Strategies and tactics of reform

EXTERNAL REFORMER		INTERNAL REFORMER
STRATEGY: BLITZKRIEG Psychological commitment Promissory stage		
TACTICS: FABIAN Behavioral commitment Implementation stage	=	STRATEGY: FABIAN Psychological commitment Promissory stage
		TACTICS: BLITZKRIEG Behavioral commitment Implementation stage

mentation. During implementation, the optimal tactics for the external reformer are fabian for a variety of reasons. Despite the many asymmetries in the overall relationship, there is a symmetry of interest in the pace of implementation in which *the optimal tactics for the external reformer translate into the optimal strategy for the internal reformer.* Table 2 provides a graphic representation of this phenomenon. It is in the crucial implementation stage, the most important in bargaining for reform, and in which there is the most failure, that the interests of the external reformer and the internal reformer are theoretically in congruence.

This has an added benefit for the external reformer. Since the client is a reluctant internal reformer, to say the least, the patron can guide it toward the optimal plan for implementation, whether the client desires a fabian strategy or not, by pursuing its own optimal tactics, *if* the patron can implement its policy preferences through a quid pro quo. In the Philippines, Quirino had no strategy for implementation; in fact, he resisted reform in any of the issue areas. Through following fabian tactics in bargaining, however, the United States forced him to adopt a fabian strategy that did not cause a coalescence of the opposition or an excessive strain on Filipino or American resources. When Magsaysay became president, however, he followed a blitzkrieg strategy; the United States offered little help after the return of stability, and the opposition from status-quo elites severely constrained his reform program.

Thus, a comprehensive, sequential reform program aiming at the most likely areas to produce opposition to the status quo and grievances against the client government, and within the context of a strictly quid pro quo bargaining approach at the promissory *and* implementation stages of reform, would seem to be the best possible bargaining posture.

A Final Word

This book has demonstrated that the record of the United States in the developing world during the Cold War era has been more complicated than the way it is generally portrayed in much of the historical and social science literature. Yet the positive achievements of that record have generally been overlooked in favor of relatively few, albeit spectacular, failures. It is disconcerting that a nation possessing the dynamism and resources of the United States has done so little to examine dispassionately its past successes as well as failures.

Americans do not have all the answers in terms of economic and political development, but they have often asked the right questions. Reformist interventions, whether for ideological or security purposes, or both, will always be difficult, but not necessarily impossible. The end of the Cold War will reduce but not eliminate the need to intervene. With a greater unity of purpose, a hard-headed realism concerning the limits of our capabilities, a less impatient attitude toward transitional political cultures, and a greater understanding of the processes of strategic interdependence with clients, the United States can accomplish a great deal in the future.

Notes · Index

Abbreviations

China White Paper	Special State Department Publication on China Policy of August 1949
CO	Country Files
COHP	Columbia University Oral History Program
DA	Dean Acheson Papers (HST)
DEPTEL	State Department Telegram
DF	Decimal Files
EMBTEL	Embassy Telegram
FRUS	Foreign Relations of the United States Series (State Department Publications)
GME	George M. Elsey Papers (HST)
GOLD	Special Telegram Designation for Marshall Mission Communications
HST	The Harry S. Truman Library, Independence, Missouri
JFK	The John F. Kennedy Library, Boston, Massachusetts
JFM	John F. Melby Papers (HST)
MJC	Michael J. Connelly Papers (HST)
MMC	Myron M. Cowen Papers (HST)
MMR	Marshall Mission Records (NA)
NA	The National Archives, Washington, D.C.
NSF	National Security Files
OF	The President's Office Files
ORE	Office of Regional Estimates
PA	Public Affairs Files
PP/GE	The Senator Gravel Edition of the Pentagon Papers
PP/GPO	US Government Edition of the Pentagon Papers
PPNF	Post-Presidential Name Files (HST)
PP/NYT	The New York Times Edition of the Pentagon Papers
PSEAD	Philippines and Southeast Asia Department
PSF	Presidential Secretary's Files
RG	Record Group
WAR	War Department Telegram
WMR	Wedemeyer Mission Records (NA)

Notes

Introduction

1. Not everyone would agree, and there is a vigorous policy debate over the question. On the importance of the "periphery," see Robert Pastor, *Condemned to Repetition: The United States and Nicaragua* (Princeton, N.J.: Princeton University Press, 1987), pp. 299–300; Steven R. David, "Why the Third World Matters," *International Security,* 14 (Summer 1989), 50–85; John Maxwell Hamilton, *Entangling Alliances: How the Third World Shapes Our Lives* (Washington, D.C.: Seven Locks Press, 1990); and Douglas J. Macdonald, "Post-Revisionism and Hyper-Realism as Paradigms of American Foreign Policy in the Non-European World," paper presented at the 1990 Annual Meeting of the American Political Science Association, San Francisco, August 31, 1990. For an account of how extended deterrence was applied to the periphery in the late 1940s, see Douglas J. Macdonald, "The Truman Administration and Global Responsibilities: The Birth of the Falling Domino Principle," in Robert Jervis and Jack Snyder, eds., *Dominoes and Bandwagons: Strategic Beliefs and Superpower Competition in the Eurasian Rimland* (New York: Oxford University Press, 1991), pp. 112–144. For the argument that the periphery is unimportant, see Stephen M. Walt, *The Origins of Alliances* (Ithaca, N.Y.: Cornell University Press, 1987); Stephen M. Walt, "The Case for Finite Containment: Analyzing U.S. Grand Strategy," *International Security,* 14 (Summer 1989), 5–49; Robert H. Johnson, "Exaggerating America's Stakes in Third World Conflicts," *International Security,* 10 (Winter 1984–1985), 32–68; Jerome Slater, "Dominos in Central America: Will They Fall? Does It Matter?" *International Security,* 12 (Fall 1987), 105–134; Stephen Van Evera, "Why Europe Matters, Why the Third World Doesn't: American Grand Strategy after the Cold War," *Journal of Strategic Studies,* 13 (June 1990), 1–51. For a mixed view, see Michael C. Desch, "The Keys That Lock Up the World: Identifying American Interests in the Periphery," *International Security,* 14 (Summer 1989), 86–121.

2. On the illegitimacy of nondemocratic governments and the resulting will-ingness among liberals of the left and right to intervene, see Michael W. Doyle, "Kant, Liberal Legacies, and Foreign Affairs, Part 2," *Philosophy and Public Affairs*, 12 (Fall 1983), 323–353. Criticism tends to come more from the left because so many of the regimes that are American clients have had rightist governments.

3. For a theory of alliances that includes domestic politics, see George Liska, *Nations in Alliance: The Limits of Interdependence* (Baltimore: The Johns Hop-kins Press, 1962); for a neorealist theory that largely ignores domestic politics, see Walt, *The Origins of Alliances*.

4. On how the domestic political weakness of a member government can threaten alliance stability, see Liska, *Nations in Alliance*, p. 44.

5. For this problem in his otherwise excellent critique of American policy in Vietnam, see Harry G. Summers, Jr., *On Strategy: A Critical Analysis of the Vietnam War* (Novanto, Calif.: Presidio Press, Dell Edition, 1982), pp. 221–239.

6. *The Counterinsurgency Era: U.S. Doctrine and Performance, 1950 to the Present* (New York: The Free Press, 1977).

7. This theme is covered in Macdonald, "Post-Revisionism and Hyper-Real-ism," especially pp. 19–24.

8. For example, see Lawrence S. Wittner, *American Intervention in Greece, 1943–1949* (New York: Columbia University Press, 1982); Stephen R. Shalom, *The United States and the Philippines: A Study of Neocolonialism* (Philadelphia: Institute for the Study of Human Issues, 1981); Michael Schaller, *The U.S. Crusade in China, 1938–1945* (New York: Columbia University Press, 1979). For an attempt to generalize many of these criticisms, see Michael H. Hunt, *Ideology and U.S. Foreign Policy* (New Haven: Yale University Press, 1987).

9. For some recent attempts to generalize from single cases by policy partici-pants, see Pastor, *Condemned to Repetition;* Gary Sick, *All Fall Down: America's Tragic Encounter with Iran* (New York: Random House, 1985); and Anthony Lake, *Somoza Falling: The Nicaraguan Dilemma: A Portrait of Washington at Work* (Boston: Houghton Mifflin, 1989).

10. For an excellent exception to this generalization about the literature, see John David Orme, *Political Instability and American Foreign Policy: The Middle Options* (New York: St. Martin's Press, 1989). See also Robert Pastor, "Preempting Revolutions: The Boundaries of U.S. Influence," *International Security*, 15 (Spring 1991), 54–86.

11. I have found the following works useful: Alexander George, "Case Studies and Theory Development: The Method of Structured, Focused Compari-son," in Paul G. Lauren, ed., *Diplomacy: New Approaches in History, Theory, and Policy* (New York: The Free Press, 1979), especially pp. 54–56; Harry Eckstein, "Case Study and Theory in Political Science," in F. I. Greenstein and Nelson W. Polsby, eds., *Handbook of Political Science*, Volume VII (Read-ing, Mass.: Addison-Wesley, 1975), pp. 79–138; Richard Cottam, *Competitive Interference and Twentieth Century Diplomacy* (Pittsburgh: University of Pitts-burgh Press, 1967); Arend Lijphart, "The Comparable-Cases Strategy in Comparative Research," *Comparative Political Studies*, 8 (July 1975), 158–

177; and Chalmers Johnson, "Political Science and East Asian Area Studies," *World Politics*, 26 (July 1974), especially pp. 562–574. My research design does not follow any of these works faithfully, but rather adopts elements from each.

12. Glenn H. Snyder and Paul Diesing, *Conflict among Nations: Bargaining, Decision Making and System Structure in International Crises* (Princeton, N.J.: Princeton University Press, 1977), pp. 6–9.

13. Johnson, "Political Science and East Asian Area Studies," p. 573.

14. Snyder and Diesing, *Conflict among Nations*, p. 23. David Baldwin points out that there has been excessive emphasis on negative sanctions and insufficient emphasis on positive sanctions in the power analysis literature. David A. Baldwin, "Power Analysis and World Politics: New Trends versus Old Tendencies," *World Politics*, 31 (January 1979), 192. The case studies demonstrate that a *combination* of positive and negative sanctions most often characterizes American reformist bargaining positions. In fact, negative sanctions were used most reluctantly because of a fear of collapse of the client government. Bolsterers, of course, advocate only positive sanctions to bargain with the client government.

15. George, "Case Studies and Theory Development," p. 48.

16. The literature on power is voluminous, but I have found the following works especially useful: Baldwin, "Power Analysis and World Politics"; David A. Baldwin, *Economic Statecraft* (Princeton, N.J.: Princeton University Press, 1985); Peter Bachrach and Morton S. Baratz, "Decisions and Non-decisions: An Analytic Framework," *American Political Science Review*, 57 (September 1963), 632–642; Andrew M. Scott, *The Revolution in Statecraft* (New York: Random House, 1965); and Jeffrey Hart, "Three Approaches to the Measurement of Power in International Relations," *International Organization*, 30 (Spring 1976), 289–305.

17. For the "power of the weak" in dealing with patrons, see Robert O. Keohane, "The Big Influence of Small Allies," *Foreign Policy*, No. 2 (Spring 1971), 161–182; Peter M. Blau, *Exchange and Power in Social Life* (New York: Wiley, 1964), pp. 118–119. As Coral Bell has pointed out, many of these threats are not credible in stable clients or allies. Coral Bell, *The Conventions of Crisis: A Study in Diplomatic Management* (London: Oxford University Press, 1971), p. 96. Thus, instability becomes a bargaining lever for vulnerable clients. On the need for small powers to "advertise" their weakness to get commitments from great powers, see also Liska, *Nations in Alliance*, p. 31. Robert Rothstein argues that this relative weakness is what defines a small power, in *Alliances and Small Powers* (New York: Columbia University Press, 1968), p. 29.

18. On the value of regional comparisons, see Johnson, "Political Science and East Asian Area Studies," p. 562.

1. American Policy toward the Third World

1. Selig Adler, *Isolationist Impulse: Its Twentieth Century Reaction* (New York: The Free Press, 1957), pp. 29–32, 90–111, 250–326; see also Robert Divine,

Second Chance: The Triumph of Internationalism in America during World War II (New York: Atheneum, 1967).

2. For the debates between Democrats and Republicans over the means of containment, see John Lewis Gaddis, *Strategies of Containment: A Critical Appraisal of Postwar American National Security Policy* (New York: Oxford University Press, 1982).

3. Barry Rubin, *Paved with Good Intentions: The American Experience in Iran* (New York: Penguin Press, 1981), pp. 56–57; for the Eurocentric strategy in the early years, see the testimony of Secretary of State George C. Marshall on February 20, 1948, in U.S. House of Representatives, *U.S. Policy in the Far East, Part One, Historical Series, Volume VII* (Washington, D.C.: Government Printing Office, 1976), p. 167.

4. Rubin, *Paved with Good Intentions*, p. 57.

5. Cole Blasier, *The Hovering Giant: U.S. Responses to Revolutionary Change in Latin America* (Pittsburgh: University of Pittsburgh Press, 1976), pp. 231–232; Bruce R. Kuniholm, *The Origins of the Cold War in the Near East: Great Power Conflict in Iran, Turkey, and Greece* (Princeton, N.J.: Princeton University Press, 1980), pp. xvii–xxi. For an analysis of this evolution in U.S. policy, see Douglas J. Macdonald, "The Truman Administration and Global Responsibilities: The Birth of the 'Falling Domino Principle,'" in Robert Jervis and Jack Snyder, eds., *Dominos and Bandwagons: Strategic Beliefs and Superpower Competition in the Asian Rimland* (New York: Oxford University Press, 1991), pp. 112–144.

6. Russell Buhite, *Soviet-American Relations in Asia, 1945–1954* (Norman: University of Oklahoma Press, 1981), pp. 2–5.

7. A patron-client relationship in international relations is characterized by three basic elements: (1) a sizable asymmetry in capabilities; (2) ties of mutual dependence; and (3) a general recognition of the relationship within the international system. See Christopher C. Shoemaker and John Spanier, *Patron-Client Relationships: Multilateral Crises in the Nuclear Age* (New York: Praeger, 1984), p. 13.

8. Rubin, *Paved with Good Intentions*, p. 57.

9. The quote is from a memorandum written by John Melby that Acheson used to brief President Truman on the Philippines on April 20, 1950. FRUS (1950), Volume VI, p. 1442.

10. The cable was sent on July 18, 1949. See Philip Jessup, *The Birth of Nations* (New York: Columbia University Press, 1974), p. 29. For the American reaction to the militant Cominform line taken after 1947 and the Communist uprisings in 1948 and 1949, see Macdonald, "The Truman Administration and Global Responsibilities."

11. Philip E. Tetlock, "Cognitive Style and Belief Systems in the British House of Commons," *Journal of Personality and Social Psychology*, 46 (1984), 373; Philip Tetlock, "Cognitive Style and Political Ideology," *Journal of Personality and Social Psychology*, 45 (1983), 124.

12. FRUS (1952–1954), Volume VIII, Part 2, p. 1798.

13. Arthur M. Schlesinger, Jr., *A Thousand Days: John F. Kennedy in the White House* (Boston: Houghton Mifflin, 1965), p. 224.

14. Lyndon B. Johnson, *The Vantage Point: Perspectives of the Presidency, 1963–1969* (New York: Holt, Rinehart and Winston, 1971), pp. 151–152; quoted in Barbara Tuchman, *The March of Folly: From Troy to Vietnam* (New York: Alfred A. Knopf, 1984), p. 252.

15. Quoted in Seymour Hersh, *The Price of Power: Kissinger in the Nixon White House* (New York: Summit Books, 1983), p. 188.

16. Iran, of course, was lost not to Communism, but to a right-wing reaction. For Carter and morality, see Lars Schoultz, *Human Rights and United States Policy toward Latin America* (Princeton, N.J.: Princeton University Press, 1981), p. 113 and n. 11; see Kirkpatrick's attacks on the Carter policy in Jeane Kirkpatrick, *Dictatorships and Double Standards: Rationalism and Reason in Politics* (New York: Simon and Schuster, 1982), pp. 23–52.

17. Truman: Robert M. Blum, *Drawing the Line: The Origins of the American Containment Policy in East Asia* (New York: W. W. Norton, 1982), pp. 38–49, 65–79; Eisenhower: Gary W. Reichard, "Divisions and Dissent: Democrats and Foreign Policy, 1952–1956," *Political Science Quarterly*, 93 (Spring 1978), 51–72, and Burton I. Kaufman, *Trade and Aid: Eisenhower's Foreign Economic Policy, 1953–1961* (Baltimore: The Johns Hopkins Press, 1982), pp. 162–165; Kennedy: for example, see Kissinger's criticisms of the Kennedy and Johnson administrations in Gaddis, *Strategies of Containment*, p. 278; Nixon: for Carter's criticism of Nixon and Ford, see Walter LaFeber, *America, Russia, and the Cold War, 1945–1980*, 4th ed. (New York: Wiley, 1980), pp. 288–292; Carter: see Kirkpatrick, *Dictatorships and Double Standards*, pp. 23–52; Reagan: see Walter Mondale's remarks on Reagan's Latin American policy in the *New York Times*, September 26, 1983, p. A7.

18. K. J. Holsti, *International Politics: A Framework for Analysis* (Englewood Cliffs, N.J.: Prentice-Hall, 1983), pp. 326–327. For primary evidence see also Draft Report, "Why Has the U.S. Embarked upon a Program of Aid to the Countries of Southeast Asia?" Harlan Cleveland to Dean Rusk (8/21/50), NA: DF: PSEAD: RG 59: 796.00: Box 1; Memo and attachment, "U.S. Objectives in Asia and the Pacific," Parelman to Gay (5/7/51), NA: DF: PSEAD: RG 59: 796.00: Box 5. Testifying before Congress in February 1977, Secretary of State Cyrus Vance stated that human rights would receive greater attention in the Carter administration, yet cautioned: "In each case we must balance a political concern for human rights against economic or security goals." Quoted in Schoultz, *Human Rights and Latin America*, p. 114.

19. Hans J. Morgenthau, *Politics among Nations*, 5th ed., rev. (New York: Alfred A. Knopf, 1978), pp. 7, 259–263, 551–553; George F. Kennan, *Realities of American Foreign Policy* (Princeton, N.J.: Princeton University Press, 1954), pp. 31–62; George F. Kennan, *The Cloud of Danger* (Boston: Little, Brown, 1977), pp. 41–46. Henry Kissinger's views are summarized in LaFeber, *America, Russia and the Cold War*, pp. 284–286, and David Landau, *Kissinger: The Uses of Power* (New York: Thomas Y. Crowell, 1974), pp. 38–40; Kirkpatrick's views can be seen in *Dictatorships and Double Standards*, pp. 23–52, and "U.S. Security and Latin America: Jeane Kirkpatrick and Critics," *Commentary*, April 1981, pp. 4, 6, 10–11, 14, 16, 18, 20. Kirkpatrick finds

the "parallels" in American policy in the "losses" of China, Cuba, Iran, and Nicaragua "suggestive." See ibid., p. 20.

20. George H. Quester, *American Foreign Policy: The Lost Consensus* (New York: Praeger, 1982), pp. 5–24.

21. Again, Morgenthau and Kennan would be exceptions here, and they argue for a far more selective use of power. Kennan argues, however, that the United States should only grant support to ruling groups that can utilize such support effectively. Thus, he was against aid to the Nationalists in China. Though this is a useful caveat, the United States cannot pick and choose its clients by this criterion alone. The exigencies of its security goals are largely determined by the geostrategic and political significance of the client nations, and their relationship with other allies and/or clients, not their indigenous potential for good government.

22. The political opposition also played this role before there was a widespread Communist threat in Latin America. See Theodore P. Wright, Jr., "Free Elections in the Latin American Policy of the United States," *Political Science Quarterly,* 74 (March 1959), 92.

23. U.S. House of Representatives, *U.S. Policy in the Far East,* p. 167. See also Marshall's remarks shortly after his return from China in U.S. Senate, *Executive Sessions of the Senate Foreign Relations Committee, Historical Series, Volume One* (Washington, D.C.: Government Printing Office, 1976), pp. 6–7.

24. EMBTEL 1070, Chapin (Manila) to Acheson (4/13/50), NA: DF: RG 59: 796.00: Box 4314.

25. Quoted in Letter, Takashi Oka to Joseph Harrison, overseas editor for the *Christian Science Monitor* (11/2/61), JFK: OF: CO: Vietnam, General, 1960–1961: Box 128. According to internal evidence in the letter, Harrison forwarded the letter to President Kennedy, who read it.

26. Amos Jordan, *Foreign Aid and the Defense of Southeast Asia* (New York: Praeger, 1962), p. 96; Robert Pastor, *Condemned to Repetition,* p. 300. China: Memo, John K. Fairbank to Dr. Knight Biggerstaff, HST: JFM: China File, General, 1945–1946: Box 1; Marshall testimony, U.S. House of Representatives, *U.S. Policy in the Far East,* p. 168; Dorothy Borg, "America Loses Chinese Good Will," *Far Eastern Survey,* February 23, 1949, pp. 37–45. Philippines: EMBTEL 983, Chapin (Manila) to Acheson (4/4/50), NA: DF: RG 59: 796.00: Box 4314; EMBTEL 988, Chapin (Manila) to Acheson (4/5/50), ibid.; EMBTEL 2322, Ambassador Spruance to Dulles (2/2/53), NA: DF: RG 59: 796.00: Box 4316. Vietnam: PP/GPO, Volume 2, Part IV, A, p. 14; EMBTEL 277, Trueheart to Rusk (8/21/63), JFK: NSF: CO: Vietnam, 8/21/63–8/23/63: Box 198.

27. Barbara Tuchman, *Stilwell and the American Experience in China, 1911–1945* (New York: Macmillan, 1971), chaps. 17–20; Michael Schaller, *The U.S. Crusade in China, 1938–1945* (New York: Columbia University Press, 1979), pp. 147–200.

28. PP/GE, Volume 1, p. 302; Edward G. Lansdale, *In the Midst of Wars: An American's Mission to Southeast Asia* (New York: Harper and Row, 1972), pp. 341–345; PP/GPO, Volume 2, Part IV, A4, pp. 16, 18, 33.

29. As quoted in Arthur Schlesinger, Jr., "Human Rights and the American Tradition," *Foreign Affairs,* 57 (1979), 224.

30. For this argument, see Samuel P. Huntington, *American Politics: The Promise of Disharmony* (Cambridge, Mass.: Harvard University Press, 1981), p. 238. For the developments of the mid-1970s, see Sandy Vogelgesang, *American Dream, Global Nightmare* (New York: Norton, 1980), pp. 129–133.

31. Huntington, *American Politics,* p. 246; see also Robert A. Packenham, *Liberal America and the Third World: Political Development Ideas in Foreign Aid and Social Science* (Princeton, N.J.: Princeton University Press, 1973), pp. 98–110.

32. See, for example, Richard J. Barnet, *Intervention and Revolution* (New York: Signet, 1972); Tuchman, *Stilwell and the American Experience,* pp. 672–673, 678; Melvin Gurtov, *The United States against the Third World: Antinationalism and Intervention* (New York: Praeger, 1974); Eric F. Goldman, *Rendezvous with Destiny: A History of Modern American Reform* (New York: Vintage, 1977), p. 344; Robert H. Johnson, "Exaggerating America's Stakes in Third World Conflicts," *International Security,* 10 (Winter 1985–1986), 32–68; Jerome Slater, "Dominos in Central America: Will They Fall? Does It Matter?" *International Security,* 12 (Fall 1987), 105–134.

33. Huntington, *American Politics,* pp. 246–259.

34. Quoted in ibid., p. 247.

35. Ibid., pp. 221–262; Quester, *American Foreign Policy,* pp. 59–62.

36. FRUS (1950), Volume VII, pp. 44, 89.

37. U.S. House of Representatives, *Investigation of Korean-American Relations,* Committee on International Relations, 95th Congress (October 31, 1978) (Washington, D.C.: Government Printing Office, 1978), pp. 21–25; Joungwon A. Kim, *Divided Korea: The Politics of Development* (Cambridge, Mass.: Harvard University Press, 1975), pp. 231–234, 248. See also "Presidential Task Force on Korea: Report to the National Security Council" (6/5/61), JFK: OF: CO: Korea, Security, 1961–1963: Box 120, pp. 1–38, and appendices; Memo, Rusk to President Kennedy (9/1/61), JFK: OF: CO: Korea, General, 1961: Box 120.

38. Donald Fraser, "Human Rights and U.S. Foreign Policy: Some Basic Questions Regarding Principles and Practice," *International Studies Quarterly,* 23 (June 1979), 181; for the improvement of conditions of political liberty in Latin America during Carter's term in office, see Schoultz, *Human Rights and Latin America,* pp. 356–358; Alfred Stepan, "The United States and Latin America: Vital Interests and the Instruments of Power," *Foreign Affairs,* 58 (1980), 691.

39. For a similar conclusion, see John David Orme, *Political Instability and American Foreign Policy: The Middle Options* (New York: St. Martin's, 1989), chaps. 1–2.

40. Memo, Truman to Acheson (8/2/51), HST: DA: Memoranda of Conversations, 1951: Box 66. Emphasis added.

41. Quoted in David McLellan, *Dean Acheson: The State Department Years* (New York: Dodd, Mead, 1976), pp. 195–196.

42. Ibid., pp. 196, 215; for Truman's objections to Franco on ideological grounds, see also LaFeber, *America, Russia, and the Cold War,* p. 130.

43. Franz Schurmann, *The Logic of World Power* (New York: Pantheon, 1974), pp. 55–56.

44. Herbert Feis, *The China Tangle: The American Effort in China from Pearl Harbor to the Marshall Mission* (New York: Atheneum, 1965), p. 272.

45. This is a common mistake made by those who simply see power as control over resources; see Jeffrey Hart, "Three Approaches to the Measurement of Power in International Relations," *International Organization,* 30 (Spring 1976), 290.

46. For the rural reform program in China, see the remarks of Harlan Cleveland, October 6–8, 1949, HST: Roundtable Discussion, "American Policy toward China": Volume II; for the revision of the Chinese Communist program in 1948, see Suzanne Pepper, *Civil War in China: The Political Struggle, 1945–1949* (Berkeley: University of California Press, 1978), pp. 316–330. The Communists experienced similar problems with their radical land reform in Manchuria during World War II. See Chong-sik Lee, *Revolutionary Struggle in Manchuria: Chinese Communism and Soviet Interest, 1922–1945* (Berkeley: University of California Press, 1983), pp. 310–311.

47. James C. Thomson, Jr., Peter W. Stanley, and John Curtis Perry, *Sentimental Imperialists: The American Experience in East Asia* (New York: Harper and Row, 1981), p. 118. Stanley points out that American promotion of education in the Philippines has been criticized as "irrelevant and denaturalizing." Most Filipinos, however, welcomed these programs at the time.

48. For example, Carl Oglesby and Richard Schaull, *Containment and Change* (New York: Macmillan, 1967); Teresa Hayter, *Aid as Imperialism* (Harmondsworth, England: Penguin, 1971); Edward Friedman and Mark Selden, eds., *America's Asia* (New York: Pantheon, 1971); N. D. Houghton, ed., *Struggle against History: United States Foreign Policy in an Age of Revolution* (New York: Simon and Schuster, 1968); William A. Williams, *The Tragedy of American Diplomacy,* 2nd ed. (New York: Delta, 1972); Gabriel Kolko, *Confronting the Third World: United States Foreign Policy, 1945–1980* (New York: Pantheon, 1988); Emily Rosenberg, *Spreading the American Dream: American Economic and Cultural Expansion, 1890–1945* (New York: Hill and Wang, 1982); Neil Sheehan, *A Bright Shining Lie: John Paul Vann and America in Vietnam* (New York: Random House, 1988), pp. 43, 130–131.

49. On the "ideological gloss" of U.S. policy, see Nina S. Adams, "The Last Line of Defense," in Noam Chomsky and Howard Zinn, eds., *The Pentagon Papers: Critical Essays* (Boston: Beacon Press, 1972), pp. 147–148.

50. Gabriel Kolko, *The Roots of American Foreign Policy* (Boston: Beacon Press, 1969), pp. 77, 79.

51. See, for example, Steven J. Rosen and James R. Kurth, eds., *Testing Theories of Economic Imperialism* (Lexington, Mass.: D. C. Heath, 1974); Robert W. Tucker, *The Radical Left and American Foreign Policy* (Baltimore: The Johns Hopkins Press, 1971); Robert Dallek, *The American Style of Foreign Policy*

(New York: Alfred A. Knopf, 1983), pp. 154–186; Quester, *American Foreign Policy*, pp. 25–54; Huntington, *American Politics*, pp. 221–262.

52. James R. Kurth, "Testing Theories of Economic Imperialism," in Rosen and Kurth, eds., *Testing Theories of Economic Imperialism*, p. 3.

53. PP/GPO, Volume 1, Part II, A3, pp. A47–A48. If India and Japan became Communist nations, it was argued, this would have had disruptive political effects in the Middle East and Western Europe. Yet some unsuccessfully continue to attempt the economic argument for Vietnam. See Patrick J. Hearden, *The Tragedy of Vietnam* (New York: HarperCollins, 1991).

54. Tucker, *The Radical Left and American Foreign Policy*, pp. 113–118.

55. Stephen Kane, "American Businessmen and Foreign Policy: The Recognition of Mexico, 1920–1923," *Political Science Quarterly*, 90 (Summer 1975), 311–312.

56. Cabinet Meeting (5/13/49), HST: MJC: Cabinet Meetings, January 3–December 30, 1949: Box 2.

57. Blum, *Drawing the Line*, pp. 65–103; Nancy B. Tucker, *Patterns in the Dust: Chinese-American Relations and the Recognition Controversy, 1949–1950* (New York: Columbia University Press, 1983); Warren I. Cohen, "The United States and China since 1945," in Warren I. Cohen, ed., *New Frontiers in American–East Asian Relations* (New York: Columbia University Press, 1983), pp. 137–138. See also HST: Robert Lovett Oral History: pp. 11–17.

58. See Letter, Lansdale to Cowen (6/11/53), HST: MMC: Personal Correspondence: Box 6. Edward G. Lansdale was one of the CIA's major operatives in the Philippines; Myron Cowen was the former ambassador to the Philippines, subsequently reassigned in Washington.

59. On the question of the government attempting to get business to serve the interests of the state (that is, security goals) rather than the other way around, see Benjamin Cohen, *The Question of Imperialism* (New York: Basic Books, 1973), p. 130.

60. Kenneth Waltz, *Foreign Policy and Democratic Politics: The American and British Experience* (Boston: Little, Brown, 1967), pp. 192, 194–195.

61. Blum, *Drawing the Line*, pp. 19–20; Nancy B. Tucker, "Nationalist China's Decline and Its Impact on Sino-American Relations, 1949–1951," in Dorothy Borg and Waldo Heinrichs, eds., *Uncertain Years: Chinese-American Relations, 1947–1950* (New York: Columbia University Press, 1980), pp. 165–166, n. 80.

62. Memo, Truman to Collector of Internal Revenue (6/11/51), HST: PSF: Subject File, China—I: Box 173; Memo, Truman to Secretary of the Treasury (6/11/51), ibid.; Memo, Truman to the Attorney General (6/11/51), ibid.

63. Kurth, "Testing Theories of Economic Imperialism," p. 6.

64. For example, Richard Ullman, "The 'Foreign World' and Ourselves: Washington, Wilson and the Democrat's Dilemma," *Foreign Policy*, No. 21 (Winter 1975–1976), 99–124; Arthur Schlesinger, Sr., "Tides in American Politics," *Yale Review*, 29 (December 1939), 217–230; Frank L. Klingberg, "Historical Alternations and U.S. Foreign Policy," *World Politics*, 4 (October 1951), 239–

273; Stephen Garret, "Foreign Policy and the American Constitution: The Bricker Amendment in Contemporary Perspective," *International Studies Quarterly*, 16 (June 1972), 187–220; Irving Kristol, "Consensus and Dissent in U.S. Foreign Policy," in Anthony Lake, ed., *The Legacy of Vietnam* (New York: New York University Press, 1976), pp. 80–101; Lucian Pye, "Foreign Aid and America's Involvement in the Developing World," in ibid., pp. 374–387; George Quester, "The Malaise of American Foreign Policy: Relating Past to Future," *World Politics*, 33 (October 1980), 82–95; Stanley Hoffman, *Primacy or World Order* (New York: McGraw-Hill, 1978); Dexter Perkins, *The American Approach to Foreign Policy* (New York: Atheneum, 1973), pp. 136–155.

65. For a perceptive analysis of this ideological dualism, see Pye, "Foreign Aid and America's Involvement," pp. 374–387.

66. Frederick Merk, *Manifest Destiny and Mission in American History* (New York: Vintage, 1966), p. 265. For a general treatment of the reform impulse during the Progressive Era, see Robert M. Crunden, *Ministers of Reform: The Progressives' Achievement in American Civilization, 1889–1920* (New York: Basic Books, 1982).

67. Pye, "Foreign Aid and America's Involvement," pp. 374–378.

68. See I. M. Destler, Leslie H. Gelb, and Anthony Lake, *Our Own Worst Enemy: The Unmaking of American Foreign Policy* (New York: Simon and Schuster, 1984).

2. The Politics of Oscillation

1. For a more extensive treatment of the history of U.S. policy in the Third World and the oscillation between the two approaches along party lines, see Douglas J. Macdonald, "'Adventures in Chaos': Reformism in U.S. Foreign Policy," (Ph.D. dissertation, Columbia University, 1986), chap. 2.

2. Cecil V. Crabb, Jr., *American Diplomacy and the Pragmatic Tradition* (Baton Rouge, La.: Louisiana State University Press, 1989), p. 5.

3. Barton J. Bernstein, "The New Deal: The Conservative Achievements of Liberal Reform," in Barton J. Bernstein, ed., *Towards a New Past* (New York: Vintage Press, 1969), pp. 263–282; James MacGregor Burns, *Roosevelt: The Lion and the Fox* (New York: Harcourt, Brace and World, 1956), pp. 234–246. Roosevelt used to defend his New Deal by saying, "Reform if you would preserve." Ibid., p. 238.

4. Franz Schurmann, *The Logic of World Power* (New York: Pantheon, 1974), pp. 47–48. Roosevelt suppressed his own reformist tendencies in U.S. foreign policy during World War II because he was well aware that opposition, presumably chiefly Republican, would form to any attempt to promote a "global New Deal." Eric F. Goldman, *Rendezvous with Destiny: A History of Modern American Reform* (New York: Vintage, 1977), p. 342. Schurmann argues that the United States enthusiastically, and somewhat arrogantly, embraced the "global New Deal" concept in the postwar era. I find that this was done reluctantly, and overwhelmingly as a reaction to internal political instability in clients and allies.

5. For example, Richard Nixon often felt closer ideologically to conservative Southern Democrats such as Senators Stennis (D–Miss.) and Long (D–La.) than with Republican liberals such as Senators Percy (R–Ill.) and Javits (R–N.Y.) John Ehrlichman, *Witness to Power* (New York: Pocket Books, 1982), p. 177. In the 1970s, Democrats tended to vote for human rights legislation to a higher degree than Republicans, with the exception of Southerners. Those who placed more emphasis on security goals were also generally less likely to vote for the legislation. See William P. Avery and David Forsythe, "Human Rights, National Security, and the U.S. Senate: Who Votes for What and Why," *International Studies Quarterly*, 23 (June 1979), 303–320.

6. For the Democrats as the party of change and the Republicans as the party of the status quo, see V. O. Key, Jr., *Politics, Parties and Pressure Groups* (New York: Thomas Y. Crowell, 1952), pp. 209–214, 239–240; Clinton Rossiter, *Parties and Politics in America*, 6th ed. (Ithaca, N.Y.: Cornell University Press, 1969), pp. 107–150; Nelson W. Polsby and Aaron Wildavsky, *Presidential Elections*, 6th ed. (New York: Charles Scribner's Sons, 1980), pp. 171–175. On the importance of ideology to the parties' membership and to the public, see Robert Axelrod, "Where the Votes Come From: An Analysis of Electoral Coalitions, 1952–1968," *American Political Science Review*, 66 (March 1972), 11–20. Pomper demonstrates that the "end of ideology" school of the 1950s may have been confined to that decade; Gerald M. Pomper, "From Confusion to Clarity: Issues and American Voters, 1956–1968," *American Political Science Review*, 66 (June 1972), 415–428. For the argument that Republican conservatism after Eisenhower represents a distinctive ideological entity, see A. James Reichley, "The Conservative Roots of the Nixon, Ford and Reagan Administrations," *Political Science Quarterly*, 96 (Winter 1981–82), 537–550.

7. Even the relatively moderate Eisenhower, however, ran for President in 1952 to "save" the nation from New Deal–Fair Deal "socialism." See John L. Gaddis, *Strategies of Containment: A Critical Appraisal of Postwar American National Security Policy* (New York: Oxford University Press, 1982), p. 127. When Eisenhower did attempt to protect and develop social and foreign aid programs, many in his own party fought these efforts in a coalition with Southern Democrats. See Stephen E. Ambrose, *Eisenhower: The President* (New York: Simon and Schuster, 1984), pp. 376–381.

8. As James Q. Wilson has pointed out, Ronald Reagan may have been the first Republican President since Theodore Roosevelt elected to induce change. James Q. Wilson, "Reagan and the Republican Revival," *Commentary*, October 1980, p. 25. (The article, of course, was written during the 1980 campaign.) That change, however, was to reduce, not enhance, the role of government in inducing further change in the future. It is the *combination* of the desire for relatively rapid change and a vigorous governmental role that distinguishes the ideological positions of the political parties.

9. Seyom Brown, *The Faces of Power: Constancy and Change in American Foreign Policy from Truman to Reagan*, 2nd ed. (New York: Columbia University Press, 1983).

10. Rossiter, *Parties and Politics*, p. 148. Coalitions for a shift in public approval for one party or the other also tend to follow national trends or "moods," not shifts in particular principles. Axelrod, "Where the Votes Come From," p. 17.

11. The concepts of cultural relativism and the missionary approach are perceptively examined in Lucian W. Pye, "Foreign Aid and America's Involvement in the Developing World," in Anthony Lake, ed., *The Legacy of Vietnam* (New York: New York University Press, 1976), pp. 373–377. Pye does not apply them to the respective political parties, however, but discusses the appeal to many Americans of both concepts.

12. Richard Minear, "Cross-Cultural Perception and World War II: American Japanists of the 1940s and Their Images of Japan," *International Studies Quarterly*, 24 (December 1980), 555–580. On domestic politics and views toward other nations, see Robert Jervis, *Perception and Misperception in International Politics* (Princeton, N.J.: Princeton University Press, 1976), pp. 283–286.

13. Key, *Parties, Politics and Pressure Groups*, pp. 209–214.

14. Ibid., p. 209.

15. Alexander George, *Presidential Decisionmaking in Foreign Policy: The Effective Use of Information and Advice* (Boulder, Colo.: Westview Press, 1980), pp. 26–34.

16. Ibid., p. 36.

17. See Acheson's remarks after leaving office during a series of meetings at Princeton University with other decision-makers and scholars. HST: DA: Princeton Seminars (July 2, 1953): Box 74. Marshall thought that Truman had the ability to make decisions to a rare degree.

18. See his remarks on this strategy at the cabinet meeting of November 26, 1948, HST: MJC: Notes on Cabinet Meetings, 1948: Box 2.

19. Thomas G. Patterson, "If Europe, Why Not China? The Containment Doctrine, 1947–1949," *Prologue*, 13 (Spring 1981), 19–38.

20. It is when issues are salient that the need for value conflict resolution is most common; Robert P. Abelson, "Modes of Resolution of Belief Dilemmas," *Journal of Conflict Resolution*, 3 (December 1959), 344.

21. Samuel P. Huntington, *Political Order in Changing Societies* (New Haven: Yale University Press, 1968), p. 41.

22. Ibid., pp. 1–92.

23. As Huntington and Barrington Moore have noted, it is necessary to centralize power in order to reform. Ibid., pp. 344–396; Barrington Moore, "Notes on the Process of Acquiring Power," *World Politics*, 8 (October 1955), 2. I am discussing here the attitudes of American decision-makers toward political stability, not whether one policy or the other is the most intelligent. Some of the paradoxes inherent in American biases against centralized power will be examined in the next chapter.

24. George, *Presidential Decisionmaking*, pp. 31–32; Philip E. Tetlock, "Cognitive Style and Belief Systems in the British House of Commons," *Journal of Personality and Social Psychology*, 46 (1984), 367; Philip E. Tetlock, "Cognitive Style and Political Ideology," *Journal of Personality and Social Psychology*, 45

(1983), 124; Abelson, "Modes of Resolution of Belief Dilemmas," pp. 344–345, 348.

25. See his testimony on April 29, 1953, in U.S. Senate, Committee on Foreign Relations, *Executive Sessions, Historical Series, Volume V* (Washington, D.C.: Government Printing Office, 1977), pp. 387–388. Note also the equation of American domestic politics with politics in other nations.

26. Ibid., pp. 387–388.

27. Gaddis, *Strategies of Containment,* p. 77 and note; see also Barry Rubin, *Paved with Good Intentions: The American Experience in Iran* (New York: Penguin Press, 1981), p. 57.

28. Robert A. Packenham, *Liberal America and the Third World: Political Development Ideas in Foreign Aid and Social Science* (Princeton, N.J.: Princeton University Press, 1973), pp. 69, 49–58; on Eisenhower's distaste for radical reformers see also Ambrose, *Eisenhower,* pp. 181–188.

29. Edward W. Chester, "Beyond the Rhetoric: A New Look at Presidential Inaugural Addresses," *Presidential Studies Quarterly,* 10 (Fall 1980), 580.

30. Yale H. Ferguson, "The United States and Political Development in Latin America: A Retrospect and a Prescription," in Yale H. Ferguson, ed., *Contemporary Inter-American Relations* (Englewood Cliffs, N.J.: Prentice-Hall, 1972), p. 373; Thomas L. Karnes, ed., *Readings in the Latin American Policy of the United States* (Tucson: University of Arizona Press, 1972), p. 273; on the alliance systems built by the administration, see Townsend Hoopes, *The Devil and John Foster Dulles* (Boston: Little, Brown, 1973), pp. 487–488. For a critique of Eisenhower's policies in the developing world, see Robert J. McMahon, "Eisenhower and Third World Nationalism," *Political Science Quarterly,* 101 (Fall 1986), 453–473.

31. Mary S. McAuliffe, "Dwight D. Eisenhower and Wolf Ladejinsky: The Politics of the Declining Red Scare, 1954–1955," *Prologue,* 14 (Fall 1982), 109–127; Edward G. Lansdale interview (May 29, 1982).

32. Gaddis, *Strategies of Containment,* p. 177; Schlesinger, *A Thousand Days: John F. Kennedy in the White House* (Boston: Houghton Mifflin, 1965), pp. 189–191; Rupert Emerson, "The Erosion of Democracy," *Journal of Asian Studies,* 20 (November 1960), 1–8.

33. Edwin Lieuwen, *Generals vs. Presidents: Neo-militarism in Latin America* (New York: Praeger, 1964), p. 4. On the Third World in general, see Hoopes, *The Devil and John Foster Dulles,* pp. 492–499; Charles C. Alexander, *Holding the Line: The Eisenhower Era, 1952–1961* (Bloomington: University of Indiana Press, 1975), p. 280; McMahon, "Eisenhower and Third World Nationalism," pp. 453–473. On aid policy in general, see Burton I. Kaufman, *Trade and Aid: Eisenhower's Foreign Economic Policy, 1953–1961* (Baltimore: Johns Hopkins Press, 1982).

34. On the shift in policy, see the remarks by Samuel Huntington in Richard M. Pfeffer, ed., *No More Vietnams? The War and the Future of American Foreign Policy* (New York: Harper and Row, 1968), p. 221; Amos Jordan, *Foreign Aid and the Defense of Southeast Asia* (New York: Praeger, 1962), pp. 23, 219; Charles Stevenson, *The End of Nowhere: American Policy toward Laos since 1954* (Boston: Beacon Press, 1972), pp. 80–81; Hoopes, *The Devil and John*

Foster Dulles, pp. 492–500. For Eisenhower's retrospective view of his limited conversion to reform, see Dwight D. Eisenhower, *The White House Years: Waging Peace, 1956–1961* (Garden City, N.Y.: Doubleday, 1965), pp. 514–539.

35. Ambrose, *Eisenhower,* pp. 376–381.
36. On Greece, see Seymour Hersh, *The Price of Power: Kissinger in the Nixon White House* (New York: Summit, 1983), pp. 136–140; and C. M. Woodhouse, *The Rise and Fall of the Greek Colonels* (New York: Franklin Watts, 1985), chap. 7. Nixon is quoted in U.S. House of Representatives, *Investigation of Korean-American Relations, Committee on International Relations, 95th Congress, October 31, 1978* (Washington, D.C.: Government Printing Office, 1978), p. 39.
37. Richard D. Mahoney, *JFK: Ordeal in Africa* (New York: Oxford University Press, 1983), p. 243.
38. Lars Schoultz, *Human Rights and United States Policy toward Latin America* (Princeton, N.J.: Princeton University Press, 1981), pp. 110–111.
39. Walter LaFeber, *America, Russia, and the Cold War, 1945–1980,* 4th ed. (New York: Wiley, 1980), pp. 284–285.
40. Sandy Vogelgesang, *American Dream, Global Nightmare* (New York: Norton, 1980), pp. 122–133.
41. Schoultz, *Human Rights and Latin America,* p. 122.
42. I disagree with Huntington's view that Reagan went "far beyond" Carter's more limited concern with human rights. There was a huge gap between the administration's rhetoric and its actions, at least during its first term. Samuel P. Huntington, "Will More Countries Become Democratic?" *Political Science Quarterly,* 99 (Summer 1984), 193. During its second term, it was clear that the Reagan administration had shifted toward promoting democratic change in the Philippines, Chile, South Korea, and, though less consistently, Haiti, among other nations.
43. Ronald Reagan and Charles Hobbs, *Ronald Reagan's Call to Action* (New York: Warner Books, 1976), pp. 23–24. The statement is historically and sociologically incorrect: (1) the United States never granted Social Security benefits to the vast majority of Filipinos; and (2) the extended family is alive and well in the Philippines.
44. William M. LeoGrande, "A Splendid Little War: Drawing the Line in El Salvador," *International Security,* 6 (Summer 1981), 43–44 and n. 32.
45. Nayan Chanda, "A Gloomy View of Reform and Rebellion from the U.S.," *Far Eastern Economic Review,* August 30, 1984, pp. 28–30.
46. See Seth Mydans, "Marcos and Aquino Stage Rival Manila Inaugurals; U.S. Backs Change in Regime," *New York Times,* February 25, 1986, pp. A1, A13.
47. Walter LaFeber, "The Reagan Administration and Revolutions in Central America," *Political Science Quarterly,* 99 (Spring 1984), 1–26.
48. Leslie H. Gelb, "U.S. Vows to Resist Despots of Right as well as of Left," *New York Times,* March 14, 1986, pp. A1, A7.
49. Abelson, "Modes of Resolution of Belief Dilemmas," pp. 346, 351; Jervis, *Perception and Misperception,* pp. 296–297; Tetlock, "Cognitive Style and Political Ideology," p. 124. See also W. Russell Neuman, "Differentiation

and Integration: Two Dimensions of Political Thinking," *American Journal of Sociology,* 86 (May 1981), 1236–66.

50. Tetlock, "Cognitive Style and Political Ideology," p. 124.
51. Rubin, *Paved with Good Intentions,* p. 62.
52. *Department of State Bulletin,* 22 (January 23, 1950), 116.
53. Ibid.
54. George E. Taylor, *The Philippines and the United States: Problems of Partnership* (New York: Praeger, 1964), pp. 5–6, 149, 198–199.
55. Rubin, *Paved with Good Intentions,* p. 57. On the concern that backing Kuomintang-style regimes in Asia would mark the United States as "reactionary" among the new nations of Asia, see Truman and Acheson's remarks, NSC Meeting (12/30/49), HST: PSF: NSC Meetings, 1949: Box 220.
56. Gaddis, *Strategies of Containment,* p. 85. See also Nancy B. Tucker, *Patterns in the Dust: Chinese-American Relations and the Recognition Controversy, 1949–1950* (New York: Columbia University Press, 1983), p. 23. In early 1949, the British requested a coordination of policy with the United States in Southeast Asia; the State Department made the objections noted in this paragraph. Memo, Sprouse to Graves (3/16/49), NA: Regional Affairs: PSEAD: Box 5. The quote is from Memo, Reed to Butterworth (3/25/49), ibid. For a theoretical treatment of the fear of "bandwagoning" in unstable regions, see Stephen M. Walt, *The Origins of Alliances* (Ithaca, N.Y.: Cornell University Press, 1987).
57. Tucker, *Patterns in the Dust,* pp. 2–3; David S. McLellan, *Dean Acheson: The State Department Years* (New York: Dodd, Mead, 1976), pp. 393, 395–396; Memorandum of Conversation, Dean Acheson and French Ambassador Bonnett (7/8/49), HST: DA: Memoranda of Conversations, 1949: Box 64. The Dutch and French were pressured to devolve power to indigenous governments. For Acheson's problems with the French, see McLellan, *Dean Acheson,* pp. 383, 393; PP/GPO, Volume I, Part II, A.2., pp. A35–A42.
58. McLellan, *Dean Acheson,* pp. 395–396.
59. For treatments of the American promotion of land reform during this period, see Roy L. Prosterman et al., "Land Reform and El Salvador," *International Security,* 6 (Summer 1981), 56–58; Rubin, *Paved with Good Intentions,* pp. 45–75; Andrew J. Grad, "Land Reform in Japan," *Pacific Affairs,* 21 (June 1948), 115–135; C. Clyde Mitchell, "Land Reform in South Korea," *Pacific Affairs,* 22 (June 1949), 144–154; Gary L. Olson, *U.S. Foreign Policy and the Third World Peasant: Land Reform in Asia and Latin America* (New York: Praeger, 1974), pp. 38–94; Russell King, *Land Reform: A World Survey* (Boulder, Colo.: Westview, 1977), pp. 207–217, 221–226, 379–383. Truman wanted to intervene against the reformist Arbenz regime in Guatemala, and actually initiated a policy of doing so. Acheson talked him out of it and the plan was aborted. See Richard H. Immerman, *The CIA in Guatemala: The Foreign Policy of Intervention* (Austin, Tex.: University of Texas Press, 1982), pp. 118–122.
60. As Blaufarb has pointed out, the basic premises of counterinsurgency strategy did not, as many believe, originate in the Kennedy administration, but rather during the Truman administration in Greece, Malaya, Burma, and

the Philippines. They were again accepted as the basis of policy late in the second Eisenhower administration. Douglas Blaufarb, *The Counterinsurgency Era: U.S. Doctrine and Performance, 1950 to the Present* (New York: The Free Press, 1977), p. 21.

61. Draft Report, "Why Has the U.S. Embarked upon a Program of Aid to the Countries of Southeast Asia?" Harlan Cleveland to Dean Rusk (8/21/50), NA: Political Affairs: PSEAD: RG 59: Box 1; Memo and Attachment, "U.S. Objectives in Asia and the Pacific," Parelman to Gay (5/7/51), NA: Regional Affairs: PSEAD: RG 59: Box 5.

62. Abelson, "Modes of Resolution of Belief Dilemmas," p. 351.   ‡

63. George Ball, *The Past Has Another Pattern: Memoirs* (New York: Norton, 1982), pp. 180–182; Blaufarb, *The Counterinsurgency Era*, pp. 57–62; Packenham, *Liberal America and the Third World*, pp. 59–85; Arthur Schlesinger, Jr., *A Thousand Days*, pp. 594–600. Ball sees the shift primarily as a difference in style rather than substance, but the record belies such a notion.

64. Theodore Sorenson, *Kennedy* (New York: Bantam, 1965), p. 616.

65. Schlesinger, *A Thousand Days*, p. 610. For a case study of Kennedy's reformist program in Iran, see James Goode, "Reforming Iran during the Kennedy Years," *Diplomatic History*, 15 (Winter 1991), 13–30.

66. Roger Hilsman, quoted in Blaufarb, *The Counterinsurgency Era*, p. 62.

67. Arthur Schlesinger describing approvingly the Truman-Acheson program promoted under Ramon Magsaysay in the Philippines, in Schlesinger, *A Thousand Days*, p. 541.

68. For a compelling argument that this approach was in fact never implemented by the army in Vietnam, see Andrew F. Krepinevich, Jr., *The Army and Vietnam* (Baltimore: The Johns Hopkins Press, 1986).

69. Packenham, *Liberal America and the Third World*, pp. 85–90, 93–97; Walter LaFeber, "Latin America Policy," in Robert Divine, ed., *Exploring the Johnson Years* (Austin, Tex.: University of Texas Press, 1981), pp. 63–85; Ferguson, "The United States and Political Development in Latin America," pp. 374–375; James D. Cochrane, "U.S. Policy towards the Recognition of Governments and Promotion of Democracy since 1963," *Journal of Latin American Studies*, 4 (November 1972), 272, 283.

70. Eric F. Goldman, *The Tragedy of Lyndon Johnson* (New York: Dell, 1969), p. 89.

71. LaFeber, "Latin American Policy," p. 67. For the shift from Kennedy's policy, see ibid., pp. 63–85; Cochrane, "U.S. Policy towards the Recognition of Governments," pp. 278–281; Ferguson, "The United States and Political Development in Latin America," pp. 372–375; Packenham, *Liberal America and the Third World*, pp. 85–98; Donald M. Dozer, "Recognition in Contemporary Inter-American Relations," *Journal of Inter-American Studies*, 8 (April 1966), 318–335.

72. LeoGrande, "A Splendid Little War," pp. 28–29.

3. The Perils and Paradoxes of Reformist Intervention

1. James N. Rosenau, "Intervention as a Scientific Concept," *Journal of Conflict Resolution*, 13 (June 1969), 149–171; Richard W. Cottam, *Competitive Inter-*

ference and Twentieth Century Diplomacy (Pittsburgh, Pa.: University of Pittsburgh Press, 1967), pp. 36–39. On positive and negative sanctions as the basis of diplomacy, see K. J. Holsti, *International Politics: A Framework for Analysis* (Englewood Cliffs, N.J.: Prentice-Hall, 1983), pp. 161–190. See also Richard Rosecrance, "Reward, Punishment and Interdependence," *Journal of Conflict Resolution,* 25 (March 1981), 31–46.

2. Arthur Schlesinger, Jr., *A Thousand Days: John F. Kennedy in the White House* (Boston: Houghton Mifflin, 1965), p. 769.

3. Quoted in Theodore P. Wright, Jr., "Free Elections in the Latin American Policy of the United States," *Political Science Quarterly,* 74 (March 1959), 91.

4. Irwin F. Gellman, *Roosevelt and Batista: Good Neighbor Diplomacy in Cuba, 1933–1945* (Albuquerque: University of New Mexico Press, 1973), pp. 34–83. On the question of difficulty in avoiding interventions, see also Robert Pastor, *Condemned to Repetition: The United States and Nicaragua* (Princeton, N.J.: Princeton University Press, 1987), p. 300. Interventions were once again regularly carried out in Latin America in the post–World War II period, especially after 1954. See Bryce Wood, *The Dismantling of the Good Neighbor Policy* (Austin, Tex.: University of Texas Press, 1985).

5. Samuel P. Huntington, *American Politics: The Promise of Disharmony* (Cambridge, Mass.: Harvard University Press, 1981), p. 251.

6. The basis of land reform, for example, "normally attempts a diffusion of wealth, income or productive capacity." Russell King, *Land Reform: A World Survey* (Boulder, Colo.: Westview Press, 1977), pp. 5–6. On the devolution of power see also Samuel P. Huntington, *Political Order in Changing Societies* (New Haven: Yale University Press, 1968), p. 7. Albert Hirschman states that reform is a change in which "the power of hitherto privileged groups is curbed and the economic position and social status of underprivileged groups [are] correspondingly improved." Quoted in ibid., p. 344. See also Wurfel's definition of social reform as "any governmental or governmentally encouraged action which is directed toward making more equal the economic and political—and even educational, medical or cultural—opportunities for all individuals and groups in society." David Wurfel, "Foreign Aid and Social Reform in Political Development: A Philippine Case Study," *American Political Science Review,* 53 (June 1959), 459.

7. This list is not exhaustive. Anti-corruption reforms can also fall into the category of a devolution of power if they are meant to ensure that aid reaches programs aimed at the client society. More strictly fiscal reforms (for example, balancing the budget, reduction of tariffs, and achieving a balance of payments) will also be included in the analyses in the case studies because they are directly related to the reformist intervention in terms of financing for the redistributive reforms. They are therefore viewed as directly interrelated by American diplomats.

8. It is often pointed out that reform, which encompasses relatively swift change, can be destabilizing. It can also have, as in the Philippines in the midst of a Communist insurgency, the opposite, stabilizing effect.

9. My thinking on this matter, and on the question of reform in general, has been greatly influenced by Huntington, *American Politics;* Huntington, *Political Order;* Eric Goldman, *Rendezvous with Destiny: A History of Modern*

American Reform (New York: Vintage, 1977); Robert Packenham, *Liberal America and the Third World: Political Development Ideas in Foreign Aid and Social Science* (Princeton, N.J.: Princeton University Press, 1973); Michael W. Doyle, "Kant, Liberal Legacies, and Foreign Affairs, Part 1," *Philosophy and Public Affairs*, 12 (Summer 1983), 205–235; Michael W. Doyle, "Kant, Liberal Legacies, and Foreign Affairs, Part 2," *Philosophy and Public Affairs*, 12 (Fall 1983), 323–353; and Louis Hartz, *The Liberal Tradition in America* (New York: Harcourt, Brace and World, 1955). The specific reforms the United States aimed for in China, the Philippines, and Vietnam will be discussed in detail in the case studies. For primary evidence that the United States aimed at a devolution of power and a curb on its arbitrary use by client governments, see the following: China: Cable "Gold" No. 1850, George C. Marshall to John McCloy (12/46), NA: DF: RG 59: MMR: Colonel Carter's File: Box 2; Philippines: Memo, "Actions That Should Be Taken by the Philippine Government," John Melby to Dean Rusk (5/5/50), NA: DF: RG 59: 796.00: Box 4314; Vietnam: Letter, President Kennedy to President Diem (8/4/61), JFK: NSF: CO: Vietnam, 8/61: Box 194. For similar programs planned for Laos and Korea in 1961, see the following: Laos: Memo, "A New Look at Laos," Kenneth T. Young (undated, but early 1961), JFK: OF: CO: Laos, General, 1/13/61: Box 121; Korea: Korean Task Force Report (June 12, 1961), in U.S. House of Representatives, *Investigation of Korean-American Relations*, Committee on International Relations, 95th Congress (12/31/78), pp. 165–166.

10. On this point in the Philippines, see George E. Taylor, *The Philippines and the United States: Problems of Partnership* (New York: Praeger, 1964), p. 157.
11. For example, see Richard Pipes, *Russia under the Old Regime* (New York: Scribner's, 1974), pp. 158–162. See also Joel Migdal, *Peasants, Politics, and Revolution: Pressures toward Political and Social Change in the Third World* (Princeton, N.J.: Princeton University Press, 1974), pp. 33–59.
12. Ibid., pp. 103–106, 226–256.
13. Stephen R. Shalom, *The United States and the Philippines: A Study of Neocolonialism* (Philadelphia: Institute for the Study of Human Issues, 1981), p. 80.
14. Ibid., pp. 79–80. For the effects of the reform program and U.S. aid on the insurgency based on the accounts of the rebels and the local peasants, see Benedict Kerkvliet, *The Huk Rebellion: A Study of Peasant Revolt in the Philippines* (Berkeley, Calif.: University of California Press, 1977), pp. 238–248.
15. Memo, Merchant to Rusk (4/19/50), NA: DF: RG 59: 796.00: Box 4314.
16. Pastor also argues that in a nation where the United States has a relationship of historical influence, it "cannot choose to be uninvolved." Pastor, *Condemned to Repetition*, p. 300.
17. For a discussion of the uneasiness which Americans felt toward the commitments made in the 1940s and 1950s, see Doris A. Graber, "The Truman and Eisenhower Doctrines in the Light of the Doctrine of Non-Intervention," *Political Science Quarterly*, 73 (September 1958), 321–334.
18. Quoted in William C. Olson, *The Theory and Practice of International Relations*, 8th ed. (Englewood Cliffs, N.J.: Prentice-Hall, 1991), p. 99.

19. China White Paper, p. 92.

20. For the foreign aid as security policy argument, see R. D. McKinlay and R. Little, "A Foreign Policy Model of U.S. Bilateral Aid Allocation," *World Politics*, 30 (October 1977), 58–86.

21. Huntington, *American Politics*, pp. 247–248.

22. One analyst argues that even a radical, virulently anti-American Mexico would not threaten the security interests of the United States. Jerome Slater, "Dominos in Central America: Will They Fall? Does It Matter?" *International Security*, 12 (Fall 1987), 105–134. It is extremely doubtful that most Americans would be, or should be, as sanguine about such a development.

23. See Kissinger's remarks in the printed transcript of *Firing Line*, "Is Bipartisanship Dead?" (Columbia, S.C.: Southern Educational Communications Association, 1984), p. 8. As noted earlier, Kissinger is a bolsterer who believes that "it is the task of the Department of State to conduct foreign policy and not domestic policy [in clients and allies]"; ibid. Samuel Huntington made the same point in 1968 about the liberal dilemma over intervention, in Richard M. Pfeffer, ed., *No More Vietnams? The War and the Future of American Foreign Policy* (New York: Harper and Row, 1968), p. 224.

24. David Baldwin demonstrates this in practical terms, that is, in the relative costs of various alternatives. David A. Baldwin, *Economic Statecraft* (Princeton, N.J.: Princeton University Press, 1985), pp. 118–130. It is just as salient in moral and ethical terms. See Arnold Wolfers, *Discord and Collaboration: Essays on International Politics* (Baltimore: The Johns Hopkins Press, 1962), pp. 47–65.

25. Cottam, *Competitive Interference*, pp. 32–33.

26. Holsti, *International Politics*, p. 65.

27. Quoted in Steven Goldstein, "Chinese Communist Policy toward the United States: Opportunities and Constraints, 1944–1950," in Dorothy Borg and Waldo Heinrichs, eds., *Uncertain Years: Chinese-American Relations, 1947–1950* (New York: Columbia University Press, 1980), pp. 241–242.

28. Rene Albrecht-Carrie, "How Far Should the U.S. Interfere?" *Political Science Quarterly*, 65 (December 1950), 493.

29. Quoted in John L. Gaddis, *Strategies of Containment: A Critical Appraisal of Postwar American National Security Policy* (New York: Oxford University Press, 1982), pp. 46–47 and note. See also Memo (unsigned) to Truman, "Chinese Instructions to Ambassador Koo" (5/10/49), HST: PSF: Subject File, China—I: Box 173. For Latin American influences on United States policy, see Lars Schoultz, *Human Rights and United States Policy toward Latin America* (Princeton, N.J.: Princeton University Press, 1981), pp. 48–65.

30. Cottam, *Competitive Interference*, pp. 69–75.

31. For a cogent argument that objective conditions tend to produce similar political behavior across widely divergent cultural contexts, see Barrington Moore, Jr., *Social Origins of Dictatorship and Democracy* (Boston: Beacon Press, 1967), pp. 159–161. For an unconvincing critique of this approach, see D. Michael Shafer, *Deadly Paradigms: The Failure of U.S. Counterinsurgency Policy* (Princeton, N.J.: Princeton University Press, 1988).

32. This model was extrapolated from my own study of the cases: China in the

1940s, the Philippines in the 1950s, and Vietnam in the 1960s, though many of these dilemmas are endemic to rural Third World societies. The variance in the situations in particular clients will be discussed in the case studies. Also helpful were the following: Huntington, *Political Order;* Moore, *Social Origins;* John Dunn, *Modern Revolutions: An Introduction to the Analysis of a Political Phenomenon* (New York: Cambridge University Press, 1972); Suzanne Pepper, *Civil War in China: The Political Struggle, 1945–1949* (Berkeley, Calif.: University of California Press, 1978); Kerkvliet, *The Huk Rebellion;* John H. Kautsky, ed., *Political Change in Underdeveloped Countries: Nationalism and Communism* (New York: John Wiley and Sons, 1962); Lucian W. Pye, "Transitional Asia and the Dynamics of Nation Building," in Marian D. Irish, ed., *World Pressures on American Foreign Policy* (Englewood Cliffs, N.J.: Prentice-Hall, 1964), pp. 154–171; James C. Scott, *The Moral Economy of the Peasant: Rebellion and Subsistence in Southeast Asia* (New Haven, Conn.: Yale University Press, 1976), pp. 65–68, 91–113.

33. For example, during the periods under examination in the case studies, these groups were in the forefront of anti-government opposition. For a similar problem under the Rhee regime in South Korea, see William A. Douglas, "Korean Students and Politics," *Asian Survey,* 2 (December 1963), 584–595. For a similar development among journalists under the Marcos regime in the Philippines in the early 1980s, see Guy Sacerdoti, "The Born-again Media," *Far Eastern Economic Review,* May 23, 1985, pp. 30–34, 36. On intellectuals in the Third World in general, and some of the definitional problems in making generalizations, see Edward Shils, "The Intellectuals in the Political Development of the New States," *World Politics,* 12 (April 1960), 329–368.

34. William B. Quandt, *Revolution and Political Leadership* (Cambridge, Mass.: MIT Press, 1969), pp. 14–15. For a personal account of this process in Vietnam from the perspective of a disillusioned participant, see Truong Nhu Tang, with David Chanoff and Doan Van Toai, *A Viet Cong Memoir: An Inside Account of the Vietnam War and Its Aftermath* (New York: Vintage, 1985).

35. On the ad hoc nature of American responses to crises in clients, see Cottam, *Competitive Interference,* pp. 1–2, 16–17.

36. Moore, *Social Origins,* p. 459. See also Scott, *Moral Economy,* pp. 91–113.

37. Quandt, *Revolution and Political Leadership,* p. 17.

38. Resistance to the mobilization of new groups is created because it involves an inherent shift in the balance of power within the society. Samuel P. Huntington and Joan M. Nelson, *No Easy Choice: Political Participation in Developing Countries* (Cambridge, Mass.: Harvard University Press, 1976), p. 29.

39. Huntington, *Political Order,* p. 157; Barrington Moore, "Notes on the Process of Acquiring Power," *World Politics,* 8 (October 1955), 2.

40. Sungjoo Han, *The Failure of Democracy in South Korea* (Berkeley, Calif.: University of California Press, 1974), pp. 103–177. See also Se-jin Kim, *The Politics of Military Revolution in Korea* (Chapel Hill, N.C.: University of North Carolina Press, 1971), pp. 27–35.

41. Huntington, *Political Order,* pp. 374–396.
42. Howard Boorman, ed., *Biographical Dictionary of Republican China,* Vol. 1 (New York: Columbia University Press, 1967), pp. 210–211. See also Taylor, *The Philippines and the United States,* p. 205.
43. Quoted in Huntington, *Political Order,* p. 19.
44. For the effects of personal loyalty on the military, see Alfred Stepan, *The Military in Politics: Changing Patterns in Brazil* (Princeton, N.J.: Princeton University Press, 1971), pp. 165–168; for the effects on government in the Third World in general, see Lucian Pye, *Politics, Personality, and Nation Building: Burma's Search for Identity* (New Haven, Conn.: Yale University Press, 1962), p. 69. For this problem as a cause of the attempted coups against Diem in 1960 and 1962, see PP/GPO, Volume 2, Part IV, A, pp. 17, 20. For the problem in the Philippines in the 1970s and 1980s under the Marcos regime, see Guy Sacerdoti, "Military in the Wings," *Far Eastern Economic Review,* December 6, 1984, pp. 15–17.
45. Quoted in Lloyd Eastman, *Seeds of Destruction: Nationalist China in War and Revolution, 1937–1949* (Stanford, Calif.: Stanford University Press, 1984), p. 146. It should be noted that there were competent Kuomintang generals, but they were not considered sufficiently loyal to Chiang. Ibid., pp. 142–143. See also Tang Tsou, *America's Failure in China, 1941–1950* (Chicago: University of Chicago Press, 1963), pp. 384–385.
46. Nancy B. Tucker, *Patterns in the Dust: Chinese-American Relations and the Recognition Controversy, 1949–1950* (New York: Columbia University Press, 1983), pp. 65–66.
47. Edward G. Lansdale interview (May 29, 1982).
48. COHP: V. K. Wellington Koo Oral History, Volume V, Part F, reel 2, p. 1014.
49. Huntington and Nelson, *No Easy Choice,* pp. 18, 20–25, 78.
50. For an early exposition of this view, see Zbigniew Brzezinski, "The Politics of Underdevelopment," *World Politics,* 9 (October 1956), 55–75. See also Sylvia Ann Hewlett, "Human Rights and Economic Realities: Tradeoffs in Historical Perspective," *Political Science Quarterly,* 94 (Fall 1979), 453–473; Robert M. Marsh, "Does Democracy Hinder Economic Development in the Latecomer Developing Nations?" *Comparative Social Research,* 2 (1979), 215–248.
51. For example, the International Monetary Fund and lender nations forced an economic austerity program on the democratic government of Ghana that led to a military coup in the early 1970s. Ronald Libby, "External Cooptation of a Less Developed Country's Policy Making: The Case of Ghana, 1969–1972," *World Politics,* 29 (October 1976), 67–89. See also Richard S. Olson, "Economic Coercion in World Politics: With a Focus on North-South Relations," *World Politics,* 31 (July 1979), 485–492. For this problem in the Philippines in the early 1950s, see Wurfel, "Foreign Aid and Social Reform in Political Development"; Robert S. Stephens, "The Prospect for Social Progress in the Philippines," *Pacific Affairs,* 23 (June 1950), 140–141.
52. HST: Roundtable Discussion, American Policy toward China (October 6–

8, 1949): Volume II. The American approach to the Third World has been criticized for just that, that is, assuming that economic development will axiomatically lead to a democratic political development. See Packenham, *Liberal America and the Third World,* pp. 174–182; Huntington and Nelson, *No Easy Choice,* p. 20.

53. For example, see Glen C. Dealy, "The Pluralistic Latins," *Foreign Policy,* No. 57 (Winter 1984–85), 111–115, 122–123. The sequence here is wrong since Locke lived before Rousseau. See also Wright, "Free Elections in the Latin American Policy of the United States," pp. 89–112.

54. Pipes, *Russia under the Old Regime,* pp. 112–138.

55. Lloyd Eastman, *The Abortive Revolution: China under Nationalist Rule, 1927–1937* (Cambridge, Mass.: Harvard University Press, 1974), pp. 140–180.

56. See map entitled "Democracy in Various Degrees," *New York Times,* January 19, 1986, p. E2.

57. Germany and Japan were reformed during their respective occupations. Italy was largely reformed and stabilized from without through the effective use of American aid and covert action in a successful reformist intervention that was very influential on later policies. See James E. Miller, *The United States and Italy, 1940–1950: The Politics and Diplomacy of Stabilization* (Chapel Hill, N.C.: University of North Carolina Press, 1986).

58. Huntington and Nelson, *No Easy Choice,* p. 29.

59. Cited in Robert Jervis, "Realism, Game Theory, and Cooperation," *World Politics,* 40 (April 1988), 318–319.

60. For this development in Vietnam, see Geoffrey Warner, "The United States and the Fall of Diem, Part One," *Australian Outlook,* 28 (December 1974), 245.

61. Robbins Burling, *The Passage of Power: Studies in Political Succession* (New York: Academic Press, 1974), p. 264.

62. See Marshall's remarks, HST: Roundtable Discussion, American Policy toward China (October 6–8, 1949): Volume II.

63. Marshall quoted (February 14, 1947) in U.S. Senate, *Executive Sessions of the Senate Foreign Relations Committee (Historical Series), Eightieth Congress, 1947–1948, Volume I* (Washington, D.C.: Government Printing Office, 1976), p. 6.

64. John Melby, *The Mandate of Heaven: A Record of Civil War, China 1945–1949* (Garden City, N.Y.: Anchor, 1971), pp. 227–228.

65. On Quirino, see Memo, Acheson to Truman (February 2, 1950), HST: PSF: Subject File: Philippines, Folder II: Box 185; on Diem, see Edward G. Lansdale interview (May 29, 1982).

66. Burling, *The Passage of Power,* p. 263. Factional politics was a major problem for the Kuomintang; see Eastman, *Seeds of Destruction,* p. 122.

67. Eastman, *Seeds of Destruction,* p. 129.

68. Ibid., pp. 170–171. The term in brackets was translated by Eastman.

69. For the argument that like-minded decision-making groups are more apt to miscalculate policy decisions, see Irving Janis, *GroupThink,* 2nd. ed. rev. (Boston: Houghton Mifflin, 1983), pp. 2–13, 242–259.

70. Thomas C. Schelling, *Arms and Influence* (New Haven, Conn.: Yale University Press, 1966), pp. 49, 65–66.

71. Howard S. Becker, "Notes on the Concept of Commitment," *American Journal of Sociology*, 66 (July 1960), 33. Schelling notes that if commitments were easy to get out of, they would be worthless. Schelling, *Arms and Influence*, pp. 65–66.

72. On the distinction between behavioral and psychological commitments, see Richard Little, *Intervention: External Involvement in Civil Wars* (Totowa, N.J.: Rowman and Littlefield, 1975), pp. 138–139.

73. Roland A. Paul, *American Military Commitments Abroad* (New Brunswick, N.J.: Rutgers University Press, 1974), pp. 8–13. On the manipulation of aid to clarify commitments, see Baldwin, *Economic Statecraft*, p. 102.

74. E. Abramson et al., "Social Power and Commitment," *American Journal of Sociology*, 23 (February 1958), 16.

75. For a discussion of this dynamic, see Baldwin, *Economic Statecraft*, p. 24.

76. For a discussion of this point, see Glenn H. Snyder and Paul Diesing, *Conflict among Nations: Bargaining, Decision Making and System Structure in International Crises* (Princeton, N.J.: Princeton University Press, 1977), pp. 431–435.

77. For Soviet problems in influencing clients, see Christopher C. Shoemaker and John Spanier, *Patron-Client State Relationships: Multilateral Crises in the Nuclear Age* (New York: Praeger, 1984).

78. Quoted in Pfeffer, ed., *No More Vietnams?*, p. 230.

79. Kenneth N. Waltz, *Foreign Policy and Democratic Politics: The American and British Experience* (Boston: Little, Brown, 1967), p. 194; PP/GE, Volume 1, p. 253; Thomas Schelling, *The Strategy of Conflict* (New York: Oxford University Press, 1963), pp. 22–28; Stanley Karnow, *Vietnam: A History* (New York: Viking, 1983), p. 383; Leslie Gelb and Richard Betts, *The Irony of Vietnam: The System Worked* (Washington, D.C.: The Brookings Institution, 1979), pp. 83–84; Michael Handel, *Weak States in the International System* (London: Frank Cass, 1981); Robert O. Keohane, "The Big Influence of Small Allies," *Foreign Policy*, No. 2 (Spring 1971), 161–182. See also the remarks of Alexander Haig and Dean Rusk on Vietnam, "Secretaries of State in Conference," as broadcast on WNEW, New York, April 2, 1984.

80. Quoted in the *New York Times,* April 18, 1991; cited in Fred Barnes, "Winners and Losers: A Postwar Balance Sheet," *The National Interest*, 24 (Summer 1991), 45.

81. DEPTEL 279, Rusk to Lodge (8/29/63), JFK: NSF: CO: Vietnam, 8/24/63–8/31/63: Box 198. See also the following: China: HST: Philip Sprouse Oral History: p. 62; Philippines: Letter, John Allison to Harlan Cleveland (no date, but 11/50), NA: PA: PSEAD: RG 59: Box 1.

82. Quoted in Larry Berman, *Planning a Tragedy: The Americanization of the War in Vietnam* (New York: Norton, 1983), p. 108.

83. Paul, *American Military Commitments Abroad*, p. 4; on multiple audiences during crises, see Snyder and Diesing, *Conflict among Nations*, pp. 223–225; on signaling, see Robert Jervis, *The Logic of Images in International Relations* (Princeton, N.J.: Princeton University Press, 1970), pp. 18–40.

84. Memo of telephone conversation, James Reston and Averell Harriman (2/15/62), JFK: NSF: CO: Vietnam, 2/62: Box 195.

85. Milovan Djilas, *The Progress of a Revolutionary* (New York: Universe Books, 1983), p. 188.
86. William J. Duiker, *The Communist Road to Power in Vietnam* (Boulder, Colo.: Westview Press, 1981), p. 226.
87. Kerkvliet, *The Huk Rebellion,* p. 243.
88. See the remarks of Dean Acheson and Averell Harriman, NSC Meeting (6/29/50), HST: PSF: NSC Meetings, 1950: Box 220.
89. Quoted in Ross Terrill, "John Carter Vincent and the American 'Loss' of China," in Ross Terrill and Bruce Douglas, eds., *China and Ourselves* (Boston: Beacon Press, 1969), p. 130.
90. Memorandum of conversation (4/29/61), JFK: NSF: CO: Laos, Volume II, 6/61 *(sic)*: Box 130.
91. Theodore J. Lowi, "Making Democracy Safe for the World: National Politics and Foreign Policy," in James Rosenau, ed., *Domestic Sources of Foreign Policy* (New York: The Free Press, 1967), pp. 315–323.
92. On this point, see Schelling, *Arms and Influence,* p. 55. Weinstein argues that this view is peculiarly American, but this seems unlikely. Franklin Weinstein, "The Concept of Commitment in International Relations," *Journal of Conflict Resolution,* 13 (March 1969), 39–56.
93. This latter concept can be seen in a variety of situations in the concept of public goods; see Mancur Olson, Jr., *The Logic of Collective Action* (Cambridge, Mass.: Harvard University Press, 1965), pp. 5–52. The basic idea is that if a good or service is provided regardless of one's actions, it is logical to be inactive. On the need to "boost morale," see EMBTEL 545, Nolting to Rusk (10/25/61), JFK: NSF: CO: Vietnam, 10/20/61–10/26/61: Box 194; EMBTEL 575, Nolting to Rusk (10/31/61), JFK: NSF: CO: Vietnam, 10/27/61–10/31/61: Box 194; EMBTEL 661, Nolting to Rusk (11/16/61), JFK: NSF: CO: Vietnam, 11/16/61–11/17/61: Box 195.
94. Gary Sick, *All Fall Down: America's Tragic Encounter with Iran* (New York: Random House, 1985), pp. 31, 34.
95. John W. Thibault and Harold H. Kelley, *The Social Psychology of Groups* (New York: John Wiley and Sons, 1959). See also Lawrence E. Grinter, "Bargaining between Saigon and Washington: Dilemmas of Linkage Politics during War," *Orbis,* 18 (Fall 1974), 837–867.
96. Snyder and Diesing, *Conflict among Nations,* pp. 145–147.
97. Gary May, *China Scapegoat: The Diplomatic Ordeal of John Carter Vincent* (Washington, D.C.: New Republic Books, 1979), pp. 128–129.
98. Quoted in Barbara Tuchman, *Stilwell and the American Experience in China, 1911–1945* (New York: Bantam, 1972), p. 518.
99. This was said openly in front of Americans in China during the Marshall Mission. Melby, *Mandate of Heaven,* p. 120.
100. See Marshall's testimony on the views of Chen Li-fu, a leader of the "CC Clique" in the Kuomintang (February 20, 1948), in U.S. House of Representatives, *United States Policy in the Far East, Part I, Volume VII, Historical Series, Executive Sessions* (Washington, D.C.: Government Printing Office, 1976), p. 164.
101. Personal communication from Dr. Dorothy Borg. Dr. Borg visited Am-

bassador John Leighton Stuart at that time following a session of the latter with Hu Shih, a leading Chinese intellectual and former ambassador to the United States. Stuart was quite frustrated at his inability to convince Hu that this was not the case.

102. Schelling, *Arms and Influence,* p. 52.

103. PP/GE, Volume 1, p. 253.

104. Vietnamese officers told the Americans that this had the effect of discrediting U.S. personnel in Vietnam, who were seen as an extension of the Diem regime. ACTION MEMO 37, Lodge to Rusk (9/20/63), JFK: NSF: CO: Vietnam, 9/18/63–9/21/63, State Cables: Box 200.

105. Quoted in Karnow, *Vietnam: A History,* p. 383.

106. On the increase in leverage, see Grinter, "Bargaining between Saigon and Washington," p. 848; on the improvement in land reform, see Roy L. Prosterman, "Land-to-the-Tiller in South Vietnam: The Tables Turn," *Asian Survey,* 10 (August 1970), 751–764.

107. Quoted in Golda Meir, *My Life* (London: Futura, 1976), p. 322.

108. Quoted in Joel Brinkley, "Negotiating with Shamir Can Be All Give and No Take," *New York Times,* June 16, 1991, p. E2.

109. Quoted in Thomas L. Friedman, "America's Failure in Lebanon," *New York Times Magazine,* April 8, 1984, p. 37.

110. Ibid., p. 37.

111. Unnamed European official, quoted in ibid., pp. 42, 44.

112. For this development in El Salvador, see William LeoGrande, "A Splendid Little War: Drawing the Line in El Salvador," *International Security,* 6 (Summer 1981), 46.

4. The Marshall Mission, 1946

1. See, for example, Secretary of State Marshall's testimony in Executive Session on February 20, 1948, in U.S. House of Representatives, *United States Policy in the Far East, Part One, Volume VII, Historical Series* (Washington, D.C.: Government Printing Office, 1976), p. 168.

2. William W. Stueck, Jr., *The Road to Confrontation: American Policy toward China and Korea, 1947–1950* (Chapel Hill, N.C.: University of North Carolina Press, 1981), pp. 33–74.

3. Quoted in Tang Tsou, *America's Failure in China, 1941–1950* (Chicago: University of Chicago Press, 1963), p. 362.

4. For background, see Paul Varg, *The Closing of the Door: Sino-American Relations, 1936–1946* (Lansing, Mich.: Michigan State University Press, 1973); Gary May, *China Scapegoat: The Diplomatic Ordeal of John Carter Vincent* (Washington, D.C.: New Republic Books, 1979); Herbert Feis, *The China Tangle: The American Effort in China from Pearl Harbor to the Marshall Mission* (New York: Atheneum, 1965). Chinese names of persons and places in this book are rendered as they appeared in the American documents at the time, that is, according to the Wade-Giles system (without the diacritical marks). Thus, the Nationalist Party is rendered Kuomintang rather than Guomindang.

5. Albert C. Wedemeyer, *Wedemeyer Reports!* (New York: Henry Holt and Sons, 1958), p. 279; Lloyd Eastman, *Seeds of Destruction: Nationalist China in War and Revolution, 1937–1949* (Stanford, Calif.: Stanford University Press, 1984), pp. 132, 136–137, 140–141, 144–147, 157; Hsi-cheng Chi, *Nationalist China at War: Military Defeats and Political Collapse, 1937–1945* (Ann Arbor, Mich.: University of Michigan Press, 1982), pp. 37, 161–164; John Boyle, *China and Japan at War, 1937–1945* (Stanford, Calif.: Stanford University Press, 1972), pp. 318–319; Lionel Chassin, *The Communist Conquest of China* (Cambridge, Mass.: Harvard University Press, 1965), p. 85; Varg, *The Closing of the Door,* pp. 75–78; May, *China Scapegoat,* pp. 88, 94.

6. John Dunn, *Modern Revolutions: An Introduction to the Analysis of a Political Phenomenon* (New York: Cambridge University Press, 1972), p. 92; Suzanne Pepper, *Civil War in China: The Political Struggle, 1945–1949* (Berkeley, Calif.: University of California Press, 1978), p. 95; Chi, *Nationalist China at War,* pp. 149–150, 169–175; "OSS Report on Chinese Inflation" (5/15/45), General William Donovan to Truman, HST: PSF: Subject File: China—I: Box 173. For U.S.-Kuomintang relations during the war, see Russell Buhite, *Patrick J. Hurley and American Foreign Policy* (Ithaca, N.Y.: Cornell University Press, 1973); Feis, *The China Tangle.*

7. May, *China Scapegoat,* pp. 96–104; China White Paper, pp. 55–56; Varg, *The Closing of the Door,* pp. 72–73, 100; James Reardon-Anderson, *Yenan and the Great Powers: The Origins of Chinese Communist Foreign Policy, 1944–1946* (New York: Columbia University Press, 1979), pp. 21–30.

8. Varg, *The Closing of the Door,* pp. 72–73, 100, 164–165, 169; May, *China Scapegoat,* pp. 96–104, 112–113; Buhite, *Patrick J. Hurley and American Foreign Policy,* p. 177. Buhite cites some changes made, but they were cosmetic ones only. See also COHP: Wellington Koo Oral History, Volume V, Part E, reel 2: pp. 706–707; Reardon-Anderson, *Yenan and the Great Powers,* p. 31; Feis, *The China Tangle,* pp. 145–162, 174–175; China White Paper, pp. 59–100; Wedemeyer, *Wedemeyer Reports!,* p. 295.

9. Varg, *The Closing of the Door,* pp. 84, 224; Feis, *The China Tangle,* pp. 174–175.

10. Feis, *The China Tangle,* pp. 181–182; May, *China Scapegoat,* pp. 132–134; Wedemeyer, *Wedemeyer Reports!,* pp. 344–348; Memo, Patterson and Forrestal to Byrnes (no date, but following SWNCC meeting of 11/20/45), NA: DF: RG 59: MMR, 1944–1948: Marshall/Byroade File, Volume I: Box 1.

11. For the background of U.S.-Soviet relations in the immediate postwar period, see Russell Buhite, *Soviet-American Relations in Asia, 1945–1954* (Norman, Okla.: University of Oklahoma Press, 1981).

12. "China Regional Directive" (11/14/45), NA: DF: RG 59: 796.00: Box 7006.

13. EMBTEL 224, Sprouse (Kunming) to Byrnes (10/5/45), NA: DF: RG 59: 796.00: Box 7006; Memo (unsigned) to Byrnes (11/17/45), ibid.; EMBTEL 261, Sprouse (Kunming) to Byrnes (11/27/45), ibid.; Memo, John K. Fairbank to Dr. Knight Biggerstaff (12/6/45), HST: JFM: China File, General, 1945–1946: Box 1; Pepper, *Civil War in China,* pp. 44–52; Eastman, *Seeds of Destruction,* p. 39.

14. Memo, Marshall to Truman (5/18/54), HST: PPNF: General Marshall—I: Box 57.
15. Memo, James Shepley to Truman (2/28/46), HST: PSF: China, 1946: Box 173.
16. Ibid.
17. For a Nationalist Chinese view, see William L. Tung, *Revolutionary China* (New York: St. Martin's Press, 1973), pp. 299, 301. In discussions with Chiang at the time, Tung, a former Kuomintang diplomat, relates that Chiang was very worried over continued American and British support during this period. Ibid., pp. 304–305.
18. Tsou, *America's Failure in China,* p. 373; Buhite, *Soviet-American Relations in Asia,* p. 40.
19. For the claims of the CCP and Kuomintang on violations in early 1946, see FRUS, (1946), Volume IX, pp. 342–349, 352–353, 366–368; EMBTEL 108, Smyth to Byrnes (1/15/46), NA: DF: RG 59: 796.00: Box 7007; EMBTEL 171, Smyth to Byrnes (1/26/46), ibid.
20. EMBTEL (no number—unsigned) to Byrnes, (1/25/46), NA: DF: RG 59: 796.00: Box 7007; Memo, Marshall to Truman (5/18/54), HST: PPNF: General Marshall—I: Box 57.
21. EMBTEL 251, Smyth to Byrnes (2/9/46), NA: DF: RG 59: 796.00: Box 7007.
22. On the various political factions, see Chien Tuan-sheng, *The Government and Politics of China* (Cambridge, Mass.: Harvard University Press, 1950), pp. 350–362; Tung, *Revolutionary China,* pp. 295–297; John F. Melby, *The Mandate of Heaven: A Record of Civil War, China 1945–1949* (New York: Anchor, 1971), pp. 42–43; Lloyd Eastman, *The Abortive Revolution: China under Nationalist Rule, 1927–1937* (Cambridge, Mass.: Harvard University Press, 1974), pp. 31–84, 93–96; Eastman, *Seeds of Destruction,* pp. 30, 32, 35, 101–102; Chester Ronning, *A Memoir of China in Revolution* (New York: Pantheon, 1974), p. 80; Tsou, *America's Failure in China,* pp. 374–378; Reardon-Anderson, *Yenan and the Great Powers,* pp. 30–32; May, *China Scapegoat,* pp. 208–209; COHP: Wellington Koo Oral History, Volume V, Part F, reel 2: pp. 756, 758–759, 993–995, 1012–14; Memo, Richard M. Service to Hurley (1/23/45), NA: DF: RG 59: 796.00: Box 7005; Memo, "Some Features of China's Intra-party Struggle," Bureau of Foreign and Domestic Commerce (11/28/45), HST: PSF: China, 1945: Box 173; FRUS (1946), Volume IX, pp. 178–188.
23. FRUS (1946), Volume IX, pp. 137–143, 380; GOLD 98, Marshall to Byrnes, Acheson (1/24/46), NA: DF: RG 59: MMR: Box 15.
24. Ibid.; Memo, Koji Ariyoshi (Yenan) to Fairbank, Connors (2/3/46), HST: JFM: China File, General, 1945–46: Box 1.
25. FRUS (1946), Volume IX, pp. 148–153, 206–207; Letter, Truman to Marshall (2/2/46), HST: PSF: Subject File, Foreign Affairs: Box 183.
26. EMBTEL 1164 (unsigned) to Byrnes (2/10/46), NA: DF: RG 59: 796.00: Box 7007; EMBTEL 304, Smyth to Byrnes (2/10/46), ibid.; FRUS (1946), Volume IX, pp. 154–155.

27. FRUS (1946), Volume IX, pp. 430–434, 441, 516–528. General Chang Fa-kwei has the added dubious distinction, at least in Asian anti-Communist circles, of having released Ho Chi Minh from Nationalist Chinese prison in 1944, and aiding the latter in setting up the Viet Minh in northern Vietnam.

28. Ibid., pp. 11, 17–18, 75–76, 427–428, 438–441, 448–453, 513–516, 538, 612, 757, 937, 940; COHP: Wellington Koo Oral History, Volume V, Part F, reel 2: pp. 1008, 1012; Buhite, *Soviet-American Relations in Asia,* p. 41; Chien, *The Government and Politics of China,* p. 379; Memo, Melby (2/23/46), HST: JFM: China File, General, 1945–1946: Box 1; EMBTEL 188, Smyth to Byrnes (1/30/46), NA: DF: RG 59: 796.00: Box 7007; Reardon-Anderson, *Yenan and the Great Powers,* pp. 139–140.

29. Eastman, *Seeds of Destruction,* p. 116.

30. Chiang quoted by unnamed source in Taiwan who was present at the meeting, in ibid., p. 117.

31. In late February, Chiang had asked Marshall to be present in Chungking in early March, as the latter told Truman, "in case the meeting developed precariously." FRUS (1946), Volume IX, pp. 444–446. On March 18, Chiang informed Byrnes and Marshall that the "worries I expressed [to Marshall over his ability to control the right wing] in Chungking" were over. He now had complete control of the situation, said Chiang, and Marshall "need not worry." This was *after,* according to the Eastman account, he had told the party that he would never reach agreement with the CCP. Memo, Pace to Truman (for Chiang to Marshall, Byrnes), (3/18/46), HST: PSF: Subject File, China—I: Box 173.

32. Reardon-Anderson, *Yenan and the Great Powers,* pp. 145, 151, 153, 155.

33. China White Paper, pp. 144–154; FRUS (1946), Volume IX, pp. 156–158, 167–169, 173–175, 177 (note), 538–540; Reardon-Anderson, *Yenan and the Great Powers,* pp. 145, 151, 153, 155; Varg, *The Closing of the Door,* pp. 101, 205–206; Memo (undated and unsigned), "China Theater" (4/46), HST: PSF: Subject File, China—I: Box 173; George C. Marshall, *Marshall's Mission to China* (Arlington, Va.: University Publications of America, 1976), p. 104.

34. China White Paper, pp. 149–156; EMBTEL 4 (unsigned—Mukden) to Byrnes (3/27/46), NA: DF: RG 59: MMR: Miscellaneous File—I: Box 7; FRUS (1947), Volume VII, p. 1065; Memo, Marshall to Truman (5/18/54), HST: PPNF: General Marshall—I: Box 57; Pepper, *Civil War in China,* p. xvi; Buhite, *Soviet-American Relations in Asia,* p. 42; Ronning, *A Memoir of China in Revolution,* p. 95; Reardon-Anderson, *Yenan and the Great Powers,* pp. 155–157; May, *China Scapegoat,* p. 144.

35. FRUS (1946), Volume IX, pp. 513, 528–529, 535–538, 603–605, 737–738; Memo, "Statements of Chiang Kai-shek and Chou En-lai" (3/10/46), NA: DF: RG 59: MMR: General Marshall's Return to China File: Box 1; Letter, Chiang to Truman (3/11/46), HST: OF: 150 (1945–1946): Box 632; Letter, Chiang to Truman (3/30/46), ibid.; WAR 83515, Marshall to Chiang (4/5/46), NA: DF: RG 59: MMR: Miscellaneous File, Marshall, George C.: Box 8; Melby, *The Mandate of Heaven,* p. 120; Varg, *The Closing of the Door,* p. 218; COHP: Wellington Koo Oral History, Volume V, Part F, reel 2: pp. 1037–38, 1040; HST: Philip Sprouse Oral History: p. 62. Sprouse's

view was shared by Canadian diplomats. Ronning, *A Memoir of China in Revolution,* pp. 106–107.

36. For the narrowing of options for a superpower patron in a tense bipolar system, see Glenn H. Snyder and Paul Diesing, *Conflict among Nations: Bargaining, Decision Making and System Structure in International Crises* (Princeton, N.J.: Princeton University Press, 1977), pp. 30–31, 441–445.

37. FRUS (1946), Volume IX, pp. 166–167, 528–529, 603–605; Letter, Chiang to Truman (3/11/46), HST: OF: 150 (1945–1946): Box 632; Letter, Chiang to Truman (3/30/46), ibid.; COHP: Wellington Koo Oral History, Volume V, Part F, reel 2: pp. 1037–38, 1040; Buhite, *Soviet-American Relations in Asia,* pp. 47–50; Walter LaFeber, *America, Russia and the Cold War, 1945–1980,* 4th ed. (New York: Wiley, 1980), pp. 34–40.

38. Marshall, *Marshall's Mission to China,* p. 380.

39. On Marshall's altered view of Soviet intervention, see Steven I. Levine, "A New Look at American Mediation in the Chinese Civil War: The Marshall Mission and Manchuria," *Diplomatic History,* 3 (Fall 1979), 349–376.

40. GOLD 681, Marshall to Truman (5/12/46), NA: DF: RG 59: MMR: Vincent File: Box 54; Letter, Marshall to Truman (6/30/46), ibid.; DEPTEL 414, Acheson to Marshall (7/4/46), ibid.; Memo of conversation, Melby and Chen Li-fu (6/13/46), HST: JFM: China File, General, 1945–1946: Box 1; COHP: Wellington Koo Oral History: Volume V, Part F, reel 2, pp. 1037–38, 1040; HST: Philip Sprouse Oral History: p. 62; Ronning, A *Memoir of China in Revolution,* pp. 106–107.

41. U.S. House of Representatives, *United States Policy in the Far East,* p. 164.

42. Ibid.; Marshall Testimony (2/14/47), U.S. Senate, *Executive Sessions, Historical Series, Volume I* (Washington, D.C.: Government Printing Office, 1976), p. 5.

43. FRUS (1946), Volume IX, pp. 339–340, 1361–1362; DEPTEL (unnumbered), Truman to Marshall (5/10/46), NA: DF: RG 59: MMR: Vincent File: Box 54; Letter, Marshall to Truman (6/17/46), ibid.; Harry B. Price, *UNRAA in China, 1945–1947, Operational Analysis Papers, No. 53* (Washington, D.C.: United Nations Relief and Rehabilitation Administration, 1948), pp. 10–11, 22–23, 69–71, 75–116, 122; Marshall Testimony (2/14/47), *Executive Sessions, Historical Series, Volume I,* p. 5; Marshall Testimony (2/20/48), U.S. House of Representatives, *United States Policy in the Far East,* p. 164; COHP: Wellington Koo Oral History, Volume V, Part F, reel 2: p. 1020.

44. Letter, Marshall to Truman (6/26/46), NA: DF: RG 59: MMR: Vincent File: Box 54; WAR 92916, Carter to Marshall (6/28/46), ibid.; GOLD 1526, Marshall to Acheson (9/18/46), ibid.; FRUS (1946), Volume IX, p. 1394; FRUS (1946), Volume X, pp. 753–755; Marshall, *Marshall's Mission to China,* pp. 453–454.

45. GOLD 1032, Marshall to Acheson, Vincent (7/2/46), NA: DF: RG 59: MMR: Vincent Files: Box 54; DEPTEL 414, Acheson, Vincent to Marshall (7/4/46), ibid.

46. FRUS (1946), Volume IX, p. 1390. On the perceived need by the Americans for agrarian reforms and rural elections to settle disputes and gather support for the Kuomintang, see ibid., pp. 1350–52.

47. Quoted in John R. Beal, *Marshall in China* (Garden City, N.Y.: Doubleday, 1970), p. 177.
48. Marshall Testimony, U.S. House of Representatives, *United States Policy in the Far East, Part 1*, pp. 167–168; GOLD 1165, Marshall to Truman (7/22/46), NA: DF: RG 59: MMR: Box 2; EMBTEL 1400, Stuart to Byrnes (8/29/46), NA: DF: RG 59: MMR: Incoming Cables File—September, 1946: Box 13; FRUS (1946), Volume IX, pp. 1374–86, 1399–1426; Varg, *The Closing of the Door*, pp. 82–83, 205–206; Pepper, *Civil War in China*, pp. 42–93.
49. GOLD 1210, Marshall to Truman (7/30/46), NA: DF: RG 59: MMR: Vincent Files: Box 54; DEPTEL 539, Acheson to Marshall (8/1/46), ibid.; Memo, "Proposed Presidential Press Statement," Carter to Acheson (8/6/46), ibid.; Memo of conversation, Vincent and Koo (8/13/46), ibid.; GOLD 1283, Marshall to Acheson (8/10/46), NA: DF: RG 59: MMR: Box 2; FRUS (1946), Volume IX, pp. 1380–84, 1389; "Crop" quote of Marshall's in U.S. House of Representatives, *United States Policy in the Far East, Part 1*, p. 180; Chien, *The Government and Politics of China*, p. 382; Ronning, *A Memoir of China in Revolution*, p. 108; Tsou, *America's Failure in China*, p. 354; Marshall, *Marshall's Mission to China*, pp. 195–197.
50. Navy Message (unnumbered), Forrestal to Marshall (8/1/46), NA: DF: RG 59: MMR: Box 59; Letter, Marshall to Truman (8/2/46), NA: DF: RG 59: MMR: Vincent Files: Box 54; GOLD, Marshall to Truman (8/16/46), ibid.; Intelligence Report, "Implementation of Soviet Objectives in China" (9/15/47), HST: PSF: Central Intelligence Reports, ORE, 1947: Box 254; FRUS (1946), Volume IX, p. 1452; Reardon-Anderson, *Yenan and the Great Powers*, pp. 158–159; Marshall, *Marshall's Mission to China*, p. 444; Beal, *Marshall in China*, pp. 163, 171–172.
51. GOLD 1334, Marshall to Truman, Acheson (8/17/46), NA: DF: RG 59: MMR: Vincent Files: Box 54.
52. Memo, Vincent to Acheson (8/21/46), NA: DF: RG 59: MMR: Vincent Files: Box 54.
53. GOLD 1367, Marshall to Truman, Acheson (8/23/46), NA: DF: RG 59: MMR: Vincent Files: Box 54; GOLD 1422, Marshall to Truman, Acheson (8/30/46), ibid.; Memo, Connolly to Thorpe (2/13/47), HST: Office of the Assistant Secretary of State for Economic Affairs: China Files: Box 16; May, *China Scapegoat*, p. 148; Marshall, *Marshall's Mission to China*, pp. 394–403; Eastman, *Seeds of Destruction*, pp. 158–163; Marshall quoted on American interests in Beal, *Marshall in China*, p. 23.
54. Beal, *Marshall in China*, p. 178.
55. GOLD 1587, Marshall to Acheson (10/2/46), NA: DF: RG 59: MMR: Vincent File: Box 54.
56. GOLD 1600, Marshall to Truman (10/5/46), NA: DF: RG 59: MMR: Vincent File: Box 54; Marshall to Truman (10/5/46), ibid.; GOLD 1627, Marshall to Truman (10/10/46), ibid.; GOLD 1628, Marshall to Truman (10/10/46), ibid.
57. Quoted in Beal, *Marshall in China*, p. 246.
58. For the final negotiations, see GOLD 1491, Marshall to Truman (9/13/46),

NA: DF: RG 59: MMR: Vincent File: Box 54; Memo, Vincent to Clayton (9/26/46), ibid.; GOLD 1587, Marshall to Acheson (10/2/46), ibid.; Memo of Conversation, Vincent and Acheson (10/3/46), ibid.; WAR 82325, Acheson to Marshall (10/4/46), ibid.; DEPTEL 5318, Acheson to Byrnes (Paris) (10/5/46), ibid.; GOLD 1600, Marshall to Truman (10/5/46), ibid.; GOLD 1605, Marshall to Truman (10/5/46) ibid.; GOLD 1627, Marshall to Truman (10/10/46), ibid.; GOLD 1628, Marshall to Truman (10/10/46), ibid.; GOLD 1663, Marshall to Truman (10/17/46), ibid.; GOLD 1695, Marshall to Truman (10/26/46), ibid.; GOLD 1589, Marshall to Acheson (10/1/46), NA: DF: RG 59: MMR: Box 2; GOLD 1603, Marshall to Carter (10/5/46), ibid.; GOLD 1662, Marshall to Carter (10/17/46), ibid.; Chien, *The Government and Politics of China*, pp. 320–329, 380; Ronning, *A Memoir of China in Revolution*, p. 115.
59. GOLD 1804, Marshall to Truman, Acheson (11/23/46), NA: DF: RG 59: MMR: Vincent File: Box 54.
60. WAR 86851, Carter (for Truman) to Marshall (12/3/46), NA: DF: RG 59: MMR: Box 2.
61. Memo of conversation, Messrs. Thorpe, Wood, Dort and Chinese Minister Plenipotentiary Tan Shao-hwa (12/27/46), HST: Office of Assistant Secretary of State for Economic Affairs: China File: Box 16. Tan requested $2 billion in unrestricted aid.
62. WAR 83538, Carter to Marshall (10/19/46), NA: DF: RG 59: MMR: Carter File: Box 2; GOLD 1676, Caughey to Carter (10/21/46), ibid.; WAR 86819, Carter (from McCloy) to Marshall (12/3/46), ibid.; GOLD 1850, Marshall to Carter (to McCloy) (12/4/46), ibid.
63. Editorial quoted in Nancy B. Tucker, *Patterns in the Dust: Chinese-American Relations and the Recognition Controversy, 1949–1950* (New York: Columbia University Press, 1983), p. 146.
64. Quoted in Barbara Tuchman, *Stilwell and the American Experience in China, 1911–1945* (New York: Bantam, 1972), p. 673.

5. Reform's Last Hurrah, 1947–1948

1. Letter, Truman to Williams (2/25/47), HST: PSF: Subject File, China—I: Box 173; Memo, Byrnes to Marshall (1/3/47), HST: PSF: Subject File, Foreign Affairs: Box 183; William Stueck, *The Road to Confrontation: American Policy toward China and Korea, 1947–1950* (Chapel Hill, N.C.: University of North Carolina Press, 1981), pp. 36–37, 39, 48–49; John Melby, *The Mandate of Heaven: A Record of Civil War, China 1945–1949* (Garden City, N.Y.: Anchor, 1971), pp. 80–89; Russell Buhite, *Soviet-American Relations in Asia, 1945–1954* (Norman, Okla.: University of Oklahoma Press, 1981), p. 55.
2. FRUS (1947), Volume VII, pp. 944–946, 951–953; Stueck, *The Road to Confrontation*, p. 39.
3. WAR 92363, War Department to General Lucas (2/18/47), NA: DF: RG 59: MMR: Outgoing Cables, 1947 File: Box 13; Stueck, *The Road to Confrontation*, p. 39.

4. FRUS (1947), Volume VII, pp. 6–12, quote on p. 12.

5. Ibid., pp. 6, 786–789, 791, 795–797, 946–950; Stueck, *The Road to Confrontation*, pp. 36–37, 41, 48–49; John R. Skretting, "Republican Attitudes toward the Administration's China Policy, 1945–1949" (Ph.D. dissertation, University of Iowa, 1952), p. 36.

6. Memo, Marshall to Forrestal (2/11/47), HST: PSF: Subject File, China—I: Box 173; Memo, Patterson to Marshall (2/26/47), ibid.; WAR 90664, Marshall to Stuart, Underwood (1/27/47), NA: DF: RG 59: MMR: Vincent File: Box 54.

7. FRUS (1947), Volume VII, pp. 16–17, 19–29, 42–43, 46–47; GOLD 1915, Underwood to Marshall (1/9/47), NA: DF: RG 59: MMR: Box 2; GOLD 1917, Underwood to Marshall (1/9/47), NA: DF: RG 59: MMR: Vincent File: Box 54; Norstad to MacArthur, Underwood (2/11/47), NA: DF: RG 59: MMR: Outgoing Cables, February, 1947: Box 13.

8. FRUS (1947), Volume VII, pp. 48–49, 53–54; Suzanne Pepper, *Civil War in China: The Political Struggle, 1945–1949* (Berkeley, Calif.: University of California Press, 1978), pp. 109–110; Chester Ronning, *A Memoir of China in Revolution* (New York: Pantheon, 1974), p. 118.

9. Cabinet Meeting (3/7/47), HST: MJC: White House File, Set II: Box 2. The remarks are obviously paraphrased by the president's secretary, Matthew Connelly.

10. Ibid.

11. FRUS (1947), Volume VII, p. 1108; EMBTEL 625, Stuart to Marshall (3/21/47), HST: PSF: Subject File, China—I: Box 173; EMBTEL 923, Smith (Moscow) to Acheson (3/21/47), HST: PSF: Subject File, Foreign Affairs: Box 183; Nancy B. Tucker, *Patterns in the Dust: Chinese-American Relations and the Recognition Controversy, 1949–1950* (New York: Columbia University Press, 1983), pp. 10–11.

12. FRUS (1947), Volume VII, pp. 34–35, 45–46, 48–49, 54–58; Tang Tsou, *America's Failure in China, 1941–1950* (Chicago: University of Chicago Press, 1963), pp. 379–382; EMBTEL 625, Stuart to Marshall (3/21/47), HST: PSF: Subject File, China—I: Box 173.

13. FRUS (1947), Volume VII, pp. 18, 27–28, 30–32, 40–41, 43–44, 51–52; EMBTEL 213, Stuart to Marshall (2/6/47), NA: DF: RG 59: MMR: State Department Folder: Box 12.

14. EMBTEL 531, Stuart to Marshall (3/12/47), HST: PSF: Subject File, China—I: Box 173; EMBTEL 844, Marshall (Moscow) to Stuart (3/16/47), ibid.; EMBTEL 625, Stuart to Marshall (3/21/47), ibid.; Pepper, *Civil War in China*, pp. 110–111.

15. Eastman argues compellingly that low levels of ammunition were not, in fact, a problem for the Kuomintang, in Lloyd Eastman, *Seeds of Destruction: Nationalist China in War and Revolution, 1937–1949* (Stanford, Calif.: Stanford University Press, 1984), pp. 159–161 (and note), 203–204.

16. FRUS (1947), Volume VII, pp. 831–833, 954–957, 959–960, 966–968; Executive Order 9843, in *Department of State Bulletin* (5/4/47), p. 821; China White Paper, pp. 944–945, 968; Stueck, *The Road to Confrontation*, pp. 37–38.

17. Marshall quoted in Gary May, *China Scapegoat: The Diplomatic Ordeal of John Carter Vincent* (New York: New Republic Books, 1979), p. 159. The source of the quote was John Carter Vincent, who was present at the meeting. By the fall of 1948, 75 percent of Kuomintang equipment was lost to the CCP. China White Paper, p. 357.

18. China White Paper, p. 356; Stueck, *The Road to Confrontation*, p. 38; Tsou, *America's Failure in China, 1941–1950*, p. 357; Buhite, *Soviet-American Relations in Asia*, pp. 62–63. For the critique of the lack of ammunition argument, based on Kuomintang sources, see Eastman, *Seeds of Destruction*, pp. 159–161 and note, 203–204.

19. FRUS (1947), Volume VII, pp. 185–187, 1065–1141, 1184–89; Pichon P. Y. Loh, *The Early Chiang Kai-shek* (New York: Columbia University Press, 1971), pp. 132–133; Albert C. Wedemeyer, *Wedemeyer Reports!* (New York: Henry Holt and Sons, 1958), p. 295. Memo of Conversation, Koo, Tan, Clayton, Ness (6/17/47), HST: Office of Assistant Secretary of State for Economic Affairs: China File: Box 16; Tsou, *America's Failure in China*, p. 384.

20. Quoted in David Lilienthal, *Journals: Volume VII* (New York: Harper and Row, 1964), pp. 200–201.

21. FRUS (1947), Volume VII, pp. 795–797; Walter Millis, ed., *The Forrestal Diaries* (New York: Viking, 1951), pp. 245, 285–289; Letter, Marshall to Patterson (3/4/47), HST: PSF: China 1947: Box 173; EMBTEL 809, Stuart to Marshall (6/18/47), NA: DF: RG 59: 796.00: Box 7013; EMBTEL 1335, Stuart to Marshall (6/19/47), ibid.; Memo, "The Joint Chiefs of Staff Study of Military Aspects of U.S. China Policy," Vincent to Marshall (6/20/47) ibid.; EMBTEL 1355, Stuart to Marshall (6/20/47), ibid.; EMBTEL 1364, Stuart to Marshall (6/21/47), ibid.; Memo, Willard Thorpe to Marshall (6/24/47), HST: Office of Assistant Secretary of State for Economic Affairs: China File: Box 16; Cabinet Meeting (6/27/47), HST: MJC: White House Files, Set II: Box 2; Memo, "Memo for Use in Presenting to the President the Problem of Military Assistance to the Chinese National Armies," Vincent to Marshall (6/27/47), NA: DF: RG 59: MMR: Vincent File: Box 54; HST: Philip Sprouse Oral History: p. 80; Stueck, *The Road to Confrontation*, pp. 44–46; Buhite, *Soviet-American Relations in Asia*, p. 63 and note 38; Skretting, "Republican Attitudes toward the Administration's China Policy," p. 79; William Stueck, *The Wedemeyer Mission: American Politics and Foreign Policy during the Cold War* (Athens, Ga.: University of Georgia Press, 1984), pp. 7–10, 12, 30.

22. For example, Domestic: Wedemeyer, *Wedemeyer Reports!*, pp. 382, 388; Tsou, *America's Failure in China, 1941–1950*, pp. 452–454; Stueck, *The Road to Confrontation*, pp. 46–47; Bureaucratic: Ernest R. May, *The Truman Administration and China, 1945–1949* (New York: Lippincott, 1975), p. 21; Information: Gary May, *China Scapegoat*, p. 160; Buhite, *Soviet-American Relations in Asia*, pp. 63–64. The various approaches are covered in John H. Feaver, "The Truman Administration and China" (Ph.D. dissertation, University of Oklahoma, 1980), pp. 310–312 and note 12a, and synthesized in Stueck, *The Wedemeyer Mission*, pp. 7–28.

23. Stueck, *The Wedemeyer Mission,* p. 16.
24. For the little background information available on Marshall's thinking on the matter, see FRUS (1947), Volume VII, pp. 635–638; Stueck, *The Wedemeyer Mission,* pp. 16–17, 58; HST: Philip Sprouse Oral History: p. 80.
25. FRUS (1947), Volume VII, pp. 646–650, 741–759.
26. Ibid., p. 767.
27. Ibid., pp. 645–646, 650, 676, 696; Stueck, *The Wedemeyer Mission,* pp. 11, 18, 28–29; Ronning, *A Memoir of China in Revolution,* p. 120.
28. See the series of reports, most unsigned, given to Wedemeyer dated July 5 and 11 in "Briefing Folder" and "China Current Situation, July 11, 1946," NA: DF: RG 59: WMR: Box 1. See also Letter, Wedemeyer to Marshall (8/8/47), HST: PSF: China, 1947: Box 173; EMBTEL 21, Wedemeyer to Marshall (8/18/47), HST: PSF: Subject File, China—I: Box 173; Stueck, *The Wedemeyer Mission,* pp. 23, 30, 36–42.
29. FRUS (1947), Volume VII, pp. 970–977; Memo, Cooke to Wedemeyer (undated), NA: DF: RG 59: WMR: Briefing Folder: Box 1; Memo, Lucas to Director, Plans and Operations Division, War Department (8/19/47), NA: DF: RG 59: WMR: AAG Proposed Directive: Box 1; Stueck, *The Road to Confrontation,* p. 49; Stueck, *The Wedemeyer Mission,* pp. 31–34, 39.
30. Unsigned Memo (7/5/47), NA: DF: RG 59: WMR: Briefing Folder: Box 1; Unsigned Memo (7/11/47), NA: DF: RG 59: WMR: China—Current Situation: Box 1.
31. FRUS (1947), Volume VII, pp. 656–672, 675–677, 684–688, 691–692, 718–719, 721–730, 735–738, 741–759, 906–908; Letters (8/47), NA: DF: RG 59: WMR: China—Letters and Memos: Box 1; Letters (8/47), NA: DF: RG 59: WMR: American Chamber of Commerce, Shanghai: Box 1; HST: Philip Sprouse Oral History: pp. 22–25, 82.
32. Letter, Melby to Butterworth (8/27/47), HST: JFM: Personal Correspondence File, 1947: Box 6; Letter, Melby to "Maggie" (11/5/47), ibid.; Letter, Wedemeyer to Marshall (8/8/47), HST: PSF: China, 1947: Box 173; HST: Philip Sprouse Oral History: p. 87.
33. Quoted by Stuart in FRUS (1947), Volume VII, p. 764.
34. FRUS (1947), Volume VII, pp. 760–761.
35. For the reaction to the statements, see ibid., pp. 761–778; Wedemeyer Report (9/19/47), HST: PSF: Subject File, China—I: Box 173; Stueck, *The Wedemeyer Mission,* pp. 45–46, 49–51; Tsou, *America's Failure in China, 1941–1950,* pp. 385–386.
36. Stuart quotes from China White Paper, pp. 829–831; see also Eastman, *Seeds of Destruction,* pp. 106–107; Stueck, *The Wedemeyer Mission,* pp. 47–50, 88, 90–91.
37. FRUS (1947), Volume VII, pp. 306–308, 777–784, 892–895; China White Paper, pp. 262–264, 269–270; Memo, Marshall to Truman (undated), HST: PSF: Subject File, China—I: Box 173; Memo, Humelsine to Connelly (9/25/47), ibid.; Memo, Miss Dennison to Thorpe (9/18/47), HST: Office of the Assistant Secretary of State for Economic Affairs: China File: Box 16; Letter, Reverend Fred McGuire to Jessup (1/18/50), ibid.; John Melby, Diary Entry (12/22/47), HST: JFM: China File: Box 1; Stueck, *The Road to Con-*

frontation, pp. 51–52; Stueck, *The Wedemeyer Mission,* pp. 88, 90–92; Buhite, *Soviet-American Relations in Asia,* pp. 64–66.

38. Memo, Butterworth to Clifford, Truman (11/12/47), HST: PSF: China, 1947: Box 173; FRUS (1947), Volume VII, pp. 892, 895–897, 902, 908–912, 917–918, 978–979, 981; Memo, Wedemeyer to Truman (10/21/47), HST: PSF: China, 1947: Box 173; Memo, Butterworth to Thorpe (11/4/47), HST: Office of Assistant Secretary of State for Economic Affairs: China File: Box 16; China White Paper, p. 264; see Judd's remarks to Marshall (2/20/48), U.S. House of Representatives, *U.S. Policy in the Far East, Part I, Volume VII* (Washington, D.C.: Government Printing Office, 1976), pp. 179, 185, 333.

39. Stueck, *The Wedemeyer Mission,* pp. 90–92, 95, 103–104.

40. FRUS (1947), Volume VII, pp. 908–912; China White Paper, pp. 268–269, 371, 374, 833–834 and note 14, 840; Ronning, *A Memoir of China in Revolution,* p. 121.

41. Memo, State Department Special Poll (12/19/47), HST: Office of Assistant Secretary of State for Economic Affairs: China File: Box 16; Butterworth quote in HST: Walton Butterworth Oral History: p. 41.

42. See his testimony in U.S. House of Representatives, *U.S. Policy in the Far East, Part 1,* pp. 166–167, 173, 333, 355–356; Memo, Butterworth to Thorpe (12/30/47), HST: Office of Assistant Secretary of State for Economic Affairs: China File: Box 16; Memo of Conversation with Tan Shao-hwa (11/13/47), ibid.; Memo of Press and Radio News Conference of Secretary Marshall (11/12/47), ibid.; Memo, Tan Shao-hwa to Penfield (11/24/47), ibid.; China White Paper, pp. 371, 374; FRUS (1947), Volume VII, pp. 898, 982; Marshall's remarks at Cabinet Meeting (11/14/47), HST: MJC: White House File, Set II: Box 2.

43. Eastman, *Seeds of Destruction,* pp. 172–201; Memo, Butterworth to Clifford, Truman (11/12/48), HST: PSF: Subject File, China—I: Box 173; Letter, Melby to Davies (4/29/48), HST: JFM: China File, G-P, 1948: Box 3; Memo, John F. Melby (6/20/48), HST: JFM: Philippine File, Southeast Asia Folder: Box 8; Memo, Merchant to Melby (6/10/48), HST: JFM: Personal Correspondence, 1945–1952: Box 6; Letter, Butterworth to Merchant (4/15/48), HST: Office of the Assistant Secretary of State for Economic Affairs: China File: Box 16; FRUS (1948), Volume VIII, pp. 237–239; Buhite, *Soviet-American Relations in Asia,* p. 74; Ronning, *A Memoir of China in Revolution,* p. 128.

44. Quoted in Gary May, *China Scapegoat,* p. 196.

6. Saving the Philippine Republic, 1950–1951

1. Memo, "Possible Postponement Philippine Independence," Moffat to Acheson (12/27/45), NA: Regional Affairs: PSEAD: RG 59: Box 6.

2. Quoted in James C. Thomson, Jr., Peter W. Stanley, and John Curtis Perry, *Sentimental Imperialists: The American Experience in East Asia* (New York: Harper and Row, 1981), p. 120.

3. David Wurfel, "The Philippines," in George McT. Kahin, ed., *Governments*

and Politics in Southeast Asia (Ithaca, N.Y.: Cornell University Press, 1964), pp. 679–693; Glenn May, *Social Engineering in the Philippines: The Aims, Execution and Impact of American Colonial Policy, 1900–1913* (Westport, Conn.: Greenwood Press, 1980); Thomson, Stanley, and Perry, *Sentimental Imperialists*, pp. 112–119; Jose V. Abueva, *Ramon Magsaysay: A Political Biography* (Manila: Solidaridad, 1971), pp. 24–25; Willard Elsbree, "The Philippines," in Rupert Emerson, ed., *Representative Government in Southeast Asia* (Cambridge, Mass.: Harvard University Press, 1955), p. 93; Robert B. Asprey, *War in the Shadows*, Vol. 1 (Garden City, N.Y.: Doubleday, 1975), pp. 197–215; Stuart C. Miller, "The American Soldier and the Conquest of the Philippines," in Peter W. Stanley, ed., *Reappraising an Empire: New Perspectives on Philippine-American History* (Cambridge, Mass.: Harvard University Press, 1984), pp. 13–34; John M. Gates, *Schoolbooks and Krags: The United States Army in the Philippines, 1898–1902* (Westport, Conn.: Greenwood Press, 1973). A journalistic history is provided in Stanley Karnow, *In Our Image: America's Empire in the Philippines* (New York: Random House, 1989).

4. Abueva, *Ramon Magsaysay*, pp. 58–59 (and note 16); Wurfel, "The Philippines," pp. 694–695; Benedict J. Kerkvliet, *The Huk Rebellion: A Study of Peasant Revolt in the Philippines* (Berkeley, Calif.: University of California Press, 1977), pp. 5–8, 11–25, 54–59; Robert S. Stephens, "The Prospect for Social Progress in the Philippines," *Pacific Affairs*, 23 (June 1950), 145–147.

5. Wurfel, "The Philippines," pp. 696, 698–699; Stephen R. Shalom, *The United States and the Philippines: A Study of Neocolonialism* (Philadelphia: Institute for the Study of Human Issues, 1981), pp. 1–4, 7–10; for the devastation in rural areas, see L. King Quan, "UNRRA in the Philippines, 1946–1947," *Operational Analysis Papers*, No. 50 (Washington, D.C.: United Nations Relief and Rehabilitation Administration, 1948). The Huks later changed their name to Hukbong Mapagpalaya ng Bayan, or the "People's Liberation Army," presumably to emulate the Communist Chinese movement. Shalom and Kerkvliet find that the Huks were "reluctant rebels" who simply acted in self-defense in reaction to attacks from the government and landlords: Shalom, *The United States and the Philippines*, pp. 68–69; Kerkvliet, *The Huk Rebellion*, pp. 110–118, 143–155. In fact, there is virtually no discussion of Huk violence at all except within this context. I find this a very one-dimensional argument. Though both use sources that list Huk atrocities, these incidents are virtually ignored in their analyses.

6. Abueva, *Ramon Magsaysay*, p. 93 (and note 19); Shalom, *The United States and the Philippines*, pp. 33–37, 43–50; Wurfel, "The Philippines," p. 698; HST: Richmond Keech Oral History: pp. 14–16; Cabinet Meeting (2/1/46), HST: MJC: White House File, Set II: Box 2. Negotiations over War Damage payments continued into the 1970s. For a Filipino view, see Bonifacio S. Salamanca, "The Negotiation and Disposition of the Philippine War Damage Claims: A Study in Philippine-American Diplomacy, 1951–1972," in Stanley, *Reappraising an Empire*, pp. 261–284.

7. Shalom, *The United States and the Philippines,* pp. 16, 27–28; Wurfel, "The Philippines," pp. 696–698; Kerkvliet, *The Huk Rebellion,* pp. 125–126, 133–143, 261–262; Frederick Whyte, "Note on the Philippine Election," *Pacific Affairs,* 19 (June 1946), 193–198; Memo, Patterson to Marshall (4/7/47), NA: DF: RG 59: 796.00: Box 952.

8. EMBTEL 1750, Lockett to Marshall (9/13/48), NA: DF: RG 59: 896.00: Box 7144; EMBTEL 1200, Lockett to Marshall (11/29/48), ibid.; EMBTEL 1695, Lockett to Marshall (8/29/48), ibid.; EMBTEL 1681, Lockett to Marshall (9/4/48), ibid.; EMBTEL 1729, Lockett to Marshall (9/10/48) ibid.; EMBTEL 1749, Lockett to Marshall (9/13/48), ibid.; EMBTEL 1750, Lockett to Marshall (9/13/48), ibid.; EMBTEL 1752, Lockett to Marshall (9/13/48), ibid.; Philippine Armed Forces (hereafter, AFP) Intelligence Summary, No. 142 (9/13/48), ibid.; Letter, McDaniel to Ely (7/1/49), NA: DF: RG 59: 896.00: Box 7145; Letter, Davies to Melby, HST: JFM: Personal Correspondence, 1945–1952: Box 6; Abueva, *Ramon Magsaysay,* pp. 122, 129.

9. AIRGRAM A-3, Lockett to Marshall (1/10/49), NA: DF: RG 59: 896.00: Box 7144; EMBTEL 138, Lockett to Marshall (1/14/49), ibid.; AFP Intelligence Summary, No. 166 (2/28/49), ibid.; AFP Intelligence Summary No. 169 (3/21/49), ibid.; AFP Intelligence Summary No. 170 (3/27/49), ibid.; EMBTEL 311, Lockett to Acheson (3/21/49), NA: DF: RG 59: 896.00: Box 7145; EMBTEL 1126, Lockett to Acheson (4/28/49), ibid.; EMBTEL 561, Lockett to Acheson (6/16/49), ibid.; AIRGRAM A-481, Hester to Acheson (10/17/49), ibid.; Memo and Attachment, Ely to Butterworth (10/15/49), NA: Regional Affairs: RG 59: PSEAD: Box 17.

10. Memo, Ely to Butterworth (2/21/49), NA: DF: RG 59: 896.00: Box 7144; AIRGRAM A-81, Lockett to Acheson (2/21/49), ibid.; EMBTEL 454, Lockett to Acheson (2/21/49), ibid.; EMBTEL 196, Lockett to Acheson (2/23/49), ibid.; Memo, Ely to Butterworth (3/4/49), NA: DF: RG 59: 896.00: Box 7145; EMBTEL 599, Lockett to Acheson (3/9/49), ibid.; Memo, Ely to Butterworth (3/9/49), ibid.; EMBTEL 270, Lockett to Acheson (3/10/49), ibid.; Memo, Ely to Butterworth (3/15/49), ibid.; EMBTEL 681, Lockett to Acheson (3/15/49), ibid.

11. Memo, Reed to Butterworth (3/25/49), NA: Regional Affairs: RG 59: PSEAD: Box 5. See also Memo, Sprouse to Graves (3/16/49), ibid.

12. Memo of conversation, Acheson, Butterworth, Pace, Freese, Steelman, Murphy, Spingarn (3/16/49), HST: GME: Spingarn File: Foreign Relations— Philippine Affairs: No Box; Memo of conversation, Acheson, Butterworth, Pace, Freese, Steelman, Murphy, Spingarn (8/16/49), ibid.; Memo of conversation, Rusk, Cowen, Ely, Steelman, Johnson, Eisenhower, and others (5/19/49), NA: DF: RG 59: 896.00: Box 952; Memo, Ely to Butterworth (6/10/49), ibid.

13. EMBTEL 282, Lockett to Acheson (3/14/49), NA: DF: RG 59: 896.00: Box 7145; Memo, Ely to Allison (2/2/49), NA: DF: RG 59: 896.00: Box 952; Memo, Lockett to Ely (2/16/49), ibid.; Memo, Ely to Allison (3/16/49), ibid.; Memo, Berkner to Butterworth (6/17/49), ibid.; Memo, Butterworth to

Berkner (6/20/49), ibid.; Memo, Bell to Berkner (6/24/49), ibid.; Cabinet Meeting (7/1/49), HST: MJC: Cabinet Meetings, 1/3/49–12/30/49—Set II: Box 2.

14. Memo, Ely to Metzger (10/21/49), NA: Country Files: RG 59: PSEAD: Philippines—Miscellaneous Correspondence, 1938–1949: Box 16.

15. EMBTEL 1717, Lockett to Acheson (7/12/49), NA: DF: RG 59: 896.00: Box 7145; EMBTEL 2269, Cowen to Acheson (9/28/49), ibid.; EMBTEL 833, Cowen to Acheson (10/6/49), ibid.; EMBTEL 2398, Cowen to Acheson (10/14/49), ibid.; EMBTEL 2485, Hester to Acheson (10/28/49), ibid.; Memo and attachment, Ely to Butterworth (10/18/49), NA: Regional Affairs: RG 59: PSEAD: Box 17; Air Pouch 307, Cowen to Acheson (3/15/50), NA: DF: RG 59: 796.00: Box 4314; Abueva, *Ramon Magsaysay*, pp. 140–142.

16. EMBTEL 2503, Hester to Acheson (10/31/49), NA: DF: RG 59: 896.00: Box 7145; Memo, Henderson (Cebu) to Hester (Manila) (11/14/49), ibid.; EMBTEL 2561, Hester to Acheson (11/9/49), ibid.; Memo, Ely to Butterworth (11/22/49), ibid.; EMBTEL 2471, Hester to Acheson (10/26/49), NA: DF: RG 59: 896.00: Box 952; Air Pouch 307, Cowen to Acheson (3/15/49), NA: DF: RG 59: 796.00: Box 4314; Embassy Briefing, Melby Survey Mission (9/18/50), HST: JFM: Melby Chronological File, 1950 (September 16–30): Box 10; Elsbree, "The Philippines," p. 105; Abueva, *Ramon Magsaysay*, pp. 140–142 (and notes 2 and 3).

17. Abueva, *Ramon Magsaysay*, pp. 140–142 (and notes 2 and 3); Air Pouch 307, Cowen to Acheson (3/15/50), NA: DF: RG 59: 796.00: Box 4314; Memo, Henderson (Cebu) to Hester (Manila) (11/14/49), NA: DF: RG 59: 896.00: Box 7145; Elsbree, "The Philippines," p. 105.

18. EMBTEL 2629, Hester to Acheson (11/19/49), NA: DF: RG 59: 896.00: Box 7145; EMBTEL 2629, Hester to Acheson (11/19/49), ibid.; EMBTEL 2659, Cowen to Acheson (11/23/49), ibid.; EMBTEL 2668, Cowen to Acheson (11/26/49), ibid.; EMBTEL 2694, Cowen to Acheson (11/29/49), ibid.; EMBTEL 2730, Cowen to Acheson (12/2/49), ibid.; EMBTEL 3, Cowen to Acheson (1/3/50), NA: DF: RG 59: 796.00: Box 4314; EMBTEL 32, Cowen to Acheson (1/4/50), ibid.; Memo, Cansler (Iloilio) to Cowen (Manila) (1/19/50), ibid.; Memo, McKinnon (Pao) to Cowen (Manila) (1/24/50), ibid.; Air Pouch 307, Cowen to Acheson (3/15/50), ibid.

19. JUSMAG was a joint organization of the various American military services, not a joint Filipino-American organization.

20. EMBTEL 2731, Melby to Acheson (12/2/49), NA: DF: RG 59: 896.00: Box 952; EMBTEL 2769, Cowen to Acheson (12/8/49), ibid.; EMBTEL 2613, Cowen to Acheson (11/17/49), ibid.; Air Pouch 307, Cowen to Acheson (3/15/50), NA: DF: RG 59: 796.00: Box 4314.

21. EMBTEL 56, Cowen to Acheson (1/6/50), NA: DF: RG 59: 796.00: Box 4314; Memo, Martin to Secretary of the Treasury (2/1/50), HST: Alphabetical File: Philippine Islands, General, 1946–1951: Snyder File: No Box.

22. Letter, Melby to Cowen (2/3/50), HST: JFM: Philippine Islands, Cowen-Melby Correspondence, 1949–1950: Box 7; Letter, Cowen to Thomas Dewey (2/18/52), HST: MMC: Personal Correspondence: Box 6; Memo of

conversation, Truman, Quirino, Acheson, Elizalde (2/4/50), HST: DA: Memoranda of conversations, 1950: Box 65.

23. Letter, Rice to Melby (11/15/49), HST: JFM: Personal Correspondence, 1945–1952: Box 6; EMBTEL 194, Cowen to Acheson (1/17/50), NA: DF: RG 59: 796.00: Box 4314; Memo, Wanamaker to Cowen (2/2/50), ibid.; EMBTEL 452, Cowen to Acheson (2/13/50), ibid.; Air Pouch 177, Chapin to Acheson (2/14/50), ibid.; EMBTEL 578, Cowen to Acheson (2/23/50) ibid.; Air Pouch 328, Cowen to Acheson (3/17/50), ibid.; Air Pouch 1057, Cowen (Rice) to Acheson (1/24/51), HST: JFM: Philippine File, General, 1950–1952: Box 7.

24. DEPTEL 551, Acheson to Chapin (3/31/50), NA: DF: RG 59: 796.00: Box 4314.

25. EMBTEL 931, Chapin to Acheson (3/30/50), NA: DF: RG 59: 796.00: Box 4314; EMBTEL 942, Chapin to Acheson (3/31/50), ibid.; EMBTEL 946, Chapin to Acheson (3/31/50), ibid.; DEPTEL 551, Acheson to Chapin (3/31/50), ibid.; EMBTEL 941, Chapin to Acheson (3/31/50), ibid.; DEPTEL 1472, Rusk to Acheson (London) (3/31/50), ibid.; EMBTEL 954, Chapin to Acheson (4/1/50), ibid.; EMBTEL 984, Chapin to Acheson (4/4/50), ibid.; EMBTEL 1004, Chapin to Wright (4/5/50), ibid.; Acheson's "chaos" quote in Memo, Rusk to Webb, Acheson (5/17/50), ibid.

26. Memo, Cowen to Melby (1/18/50), HST: JFM: Philippine File, Cowen-Melby Correspondence, 1949–50: Box 7; EMBTEL 354, Cowen to Acheson (2/1/50), NA: DF: RG 59: 796.00: Box 4314; EMBTEL 383, Cowen to Acheson (2/3/50), ibid.; EMBTEL 711, Cowen to Acheson (3/9/50), ibid.; DEPTEL 405, Acheson to Cowen (3/10/50), ibid.; DEPTEL 471, Acheson to Cowen (3/20/50), ibid.; Memo of Conversation, Romulo and Jessup (3/31/50), ibid.; EMBTEL 1011, Chapin to Acheson (4/8/50), ibid.; EMB-TEL 1195, Cowen to Acheson (4/26/50), ibid.; DEPTEL 714, Acheson to Cowen (4/22/50), ibid.; Memo, Ely to Rusk (3/31/50), NA: Political Affairs: Country Files: PSEAD: RG 59: Box 16; Abueva, *Ramon Magsaysay,* pp. 146–147 (and note 7).

27. EMBTEL 1070, Chapin to Acheson (4/13/50), NA: DF: RG 59: 796.00: Box 4314.

28. EMBTEL 693, Cowen to Acheson (3/8/50), NA: DF: RG 59: 796.00: Box 4314; Air Pouch 474, Chapin to Acheson (4/17/50), ibid.; EMBTEL 1197, Cowen to Acheson (4/26/50), ibid.; EMBTEL 1293, Cowen to Acheson (5/4/50), ibid.; EMBTEL 1308, Cowen to Acheson (5/5/50), ibid.; EMBTEL 1319, Cowen to Acheson (5/8/50), ibid.; EMBTEL 1350, Cowen to Acheson (5/10/50), ibid.; EMBTEL 1399, Cowen to Acheson (5/12/50), ibid.; EMB-TEL 1386, Cowen to Acheson (5/12/50), ibid.; EMBTEL 1425, Cowen to Acheson (5/16/50), ibid.; EMBTEL 1540, Cowen to Rusk (5/26/50), ibid.; EMBTEL 1594, Cowen to Acheson (6/1/50), ibid.; EMBTEL 1611, Cowen to Rusk (6/3/50), ibid.; EMBTEL 1731, Cowen to Acheson (6/15/50), ibid.; Letter, Cowen to Melby (4/24/51), HST: JFM: Philippine File, Cowen-Melby Correspondence, 1951: Box 8; Richard E. Welch, Jr., "America's Philippine Policy in the Quirino Years (1948–1953): A Study in Patron-Client Diplomacy," in Stanley, *Reappraising an Empire,* pp. 291–292.

29. Minutes, Interdepartmental Meeting on the Far East, with representatives from Defense, Treasury, Agriculture, Army, Economic Cooperation Administration, Commerce, Budget, and Labor (including Rusk, Sprouse, Lacy, Ely, Cowen, Ladejinsky, and others) (4/13/50), NA: DF: RG 59: 796.00: Box 4314.

30. Ibid.

31. EMBTEL 1063, Chapin to Cowen (4/13/50), NA: DF: RG 59: 796.00: Box 4314; Memo, Merchant to Acheson (4/10/50), ibid.; Acheson's briefing of Truman is summarized in Memo, Rusk to Webb, Acheson (5/17/50), ibid. See also FRUS (1950), Volume VI, pp. 1440–44.

32. Letter, Cowen to Dewey (2/18/52), HST: MMC: Personal Correspondence: Box 6; DEPTEL 841, Rusk to Cowen (5/13/50), NA: DF: RG 59: 796.00: Box 4314; Memo, Ely to Rusk (5/24/50), ibid.; EMBTEL 1530, Cowen to Acheson (5/25/50), ibid.; Letter, Melby to Cowen (6/1/50), HST: JFM: Philippine File, Cowen-Melby Correspondence, 1949–1950: Box 7.

33. Memo, Merchant to Acheson (4/10/50), NA: DF: RG 59: 796.00: Box 4314; Memo of Meeting, James Webb and Senator Connally (5/10/50), ibid.

34. Air Pouch 421, Turner (Bangkok) to Acheson (6/3/50), NA: DF: RG 59: 796.00: Box 4314. The journal was the *USSR Bulletin.*

35. EMBTEL 111, Cowen to Acheson (7/10/50), NA: DF: RG 59: 796.00: Box 4315; EMBTEL 103, Cowen to Acheson (7/13/50), ibid.

36. Air Pouch 814, Cowen to Acheson (6/28/50), NA: DF: RG 59: 796.00: Box 4314; DEPTEL 1460, Acheson to Cowen (7/18/50), ibid.; Air Pouch 213, Cowen to Acheson (8/21/50), ibid.

37. EMBTEL 53, Cowen to Acheson (7/7/50), NA: DF: RG 59: 796.00: Box 4315; EMBTEL 97, Cowen to Acheson (7/13/50), ibid.; EMBTEL 200, Cowen to Acheson (7/25/50), ibid.; EMBTEL 211, Cowen to Acheson (7/26/50), ibid.; EMBTEL 220, Cowen to Acheson (7/27/50), ibid.

38. CIA, ORE 33–50, "Prospects for Stability in the Philippines" (8/10/50), HST: PSF: Central Intelligence Reports-ORE, 1950: Box 257

39. EMBTEL 53, Cowen to Acheson (7/7/50), NA: DF: RG 59: 796.00: Box 4315; EMBTEL 385, Cowen to Acheson (8/16/50), ibid.; EMBTEL 412, Cowen to Rusk (8/18/50), ibid.; EMBTEL 414, Cowen to Acheson (8/19/50), ibid.; EMBTEL 415, Cowen to Acheson (8/19/50), ibid.; Letter, Rice to Wanamaker (8/21/50), ibid.; DEPTEL 299, Acheson to Cowen (8/22/50), ibid.; EMBTEL 431, Cowen to Acheson (8/22/50), ibid.; EMBTEL 442, Cowen to Acheson (8/23/50), ibid.; Air Pouch 437, Cowen to Acheson (10/2/50), ibid.; Air Pouch 511, Cowen to Acheson (11/11/50), ibid.; Abueva, *Ramon Magsaysay,* pp. 155–156 (and note 17).

40. This is a key point in terms of leverage, and deserves further discussion here. For the Filipino pressure, see Abueva, *Ramon Magsaysay,* pp. 141, 154–156 (and note 17); on the embassy's pressure, see the retrospective admission in Letter, Cowen to Thomas Dewey (2/18/52), HST: MMC: Personal Correspondence: Box 6; on State's pressure, Edward G. Lansdale interview (October 11, 1983). A former Filipino official told Dr. William Overholt that President Truman sent a telegram directly to Quirino telling him to appoint Magsaysay as Secretary of Defense or risk losing U.S.

military aid. Personal Communication from Dr. William Overholt (September 27, 1984). I have been unable to find further evidence on this point, but it should be noted that some documents remain classified. General Lansdale would only state that this was handled "at the Undersecretary [of State] level," which would have been Dean Rusk. Edward G. Lansdale interview (October 11, 1983). Contacted by letter, Rusk declined to comment on this point, though he generally agreed that my account is accurate. Lansdale's biographer, Cecil Currey, argues that Assistant Secretary of State Livingston Merchant and other Americans "urged" Quirino to appoint Magsaysay without too much resistance, but Currey characteristically ignores Filipino pressures. Cecil B. Currey, *Edward Lansdale: The Unquiet American* (Boston: Houghton Mifflin, 1988), p. 84. Stanley Karnow argues that Merchant gave Quirino an ultimatum, but his only source listed is Currey, who is much more careful in his choice of words. Karnow's journalistic practice of eschewing footnotes makes it impossible to assess his research. Moreover, he also ignores internal political pressures on Quirino as a major factor. Karnow, *In Our Image*, p. 346. As in the Currey and Karnow accounts, it is quite common for American analysts to ignore the Filipinos and make it an "American show."

41. Lansdale quoted in Currey, *Edward Lansdale*, p. 91. On events in the Philippines, see Edward G. Lansdale, *In the Midst of Wars: An American's Mission to Southeast Asia* (New York: Harper and Row, 1972), pp. 24–84; Douglas Blaufarb, *The Counterinsurgency Era: U.S. Doctrine and Performance, 1950s to the Present* (New York: Free Press, 1977), pp. 23, 27–33, 35, 37–40; Abueva, *Ramon Magsaysay*, pp. 28–33, 158, 160–163; Joseph B. Smith, *Portrait of a Cold Warrior: Second Thoughts of a Top CIA Agent* (New York: G. P. Putnam's, 1976), pp. 91, 94–95, 105–106, 109–112. On Lansdale's "invention" of Magsaysay, see ibid., pp. 94–95; L. Fletcher Prouty, *The Secret Team: The CIA and Its Allies in Control of the World* (New York: Ballantine, 1973), pp. 38–39, 67, 93, 99.

42. *Deadly Paradigms: The Failure of U.S. Counterinsurgency Policy* (Princeton, N.J.: Princeton University Press, 1988), chap. 8.

43. Kerkvliet, *The Huk Rebellion*, pp. 208–209, 235, 238–242, 268.

44. Blaufarb, *The Counterinsurgency Era*, pp. 27–33; Lansdale, *In the Midst of Wars*, pp. 43, 47–48; Abueva, *Ramon Magsaysay*, pp. 160–163; Robert B. Asprey, *War in the Shadows*, Vol. 2 (Garden City, N.Y.: Doubleday, 1975), pp. 824–832.

45. EMBTEL 111, Cowen to Acheson (7/14/50), NA: DF: RG 59: 796.00: Box 4315; Memo, Acheson to Truman (8/31/50), HST: PSF: Subject File, Philippines (File II): Box 185; Memo, Truman to Acheson (9/2/50), ibid. (also in NA: DF: RG 59: 796.00: Box 4315).

46. Memo of conversation, Truman, Bell, General Richard Marshall (9/11/50), HST: DA: Memos of conversations, 1950: Box 65; Wurfel, "The Philippines," pp. 70–71; George E. Taylor, *The Philippines and the United States: Problems of Partnership* (New York: Praeger, 1964), pp. 144–146.

47. Report, Melby to FMACC "Joint State-Defense MDAP Survey Mission for Southeast Asia" (9/29/50), HST: JFM: Chronological File, 1950: Box 10.

48. Embassy Briefing (Melby Mission) (9/18/50), HST: JFM: Chronological File, 1950: Box 10; JUSMAG Briefing (Melby Mission) (9/18/50), ibid.; Philippines Armed Forces Briefing (Melby Mission) (9/19/50), ibid.; EMBTEL 752, Melby to Lacy (9/27/50), ibid.; Melby, General Erskine to Acheson (9/28/50), ibid.; Memo, Ely to Lacy (9/20/50), NA: DF: RG 59: 796.00: Box 4315; Taylor, *The Philippines and the United States*, pp. 143–144.

49. CIA, ORE 58–50, "Critical Situations in the Far East," HST: PSF: Central Intelligence: ORE, 1950: Box 257.

50. NSC 84/2, "The Position of the United States with Respect to the Philippines" (11/9/50), HST: PSF: NSC Meeting No. 71 Folder: Box 210.

51. Mangahas quoted in Taylor, *The Philippines and the United States*, p. 140.

52. Letter, Melby to Lacy (9/30/50), HST: JFM: Chronological File, 1950: Box 10; EMBTEL 819, Cowen to Acheson (10/4/50), NA: DF: RG 59: 796.00: Box 4315; Memo, Ely to Rusk (10/27/50), ibid.; EMBTEL 1263, Chapin to Acheson (11/14/50), ibid.; Memo of Conversation, Merchant, Ely, Quasha, Soriano (11/16/50), ibid.; Letter, Cowen to Melby (4/2/51), HST: JFM: Philippine File, Cowen-Melby Correspondence, 1950: Box 8.

53. EMBTEL (unnumbered), Foster to Acheson (11/14/50), HST: PSF: Subject File, Telegrams, Manila: No Box; Letter, Chapin to Melby (12/19/50), HST: JFM: Philippine File, General, 1950–1952: Box 7; FRUS (1951), Volume VI, p. 1514 (and note 5); Taylor, *The Philippines and the United States*, pp. 142–144; Shalom, *The United States and the Philippines*, pp. 82–83.

54. EMBTEL 1003, unsigned to Acheson (10/23/50), NA: DF: RG 59: 796.00: Box 4315; EMBTEL 1460, Chapin to Acheson (11/30/50), ibid.; Clippings, *New York Times* and *Washington Post* (10/24/50), HST: GME: Foreign Relations, Philippine Affairs: No Box; Lansdale, *In the Midst of Wars*, pp. 60–67. Speaker Perez was not named in the captured documents, but the embassy suspected him of being an unnamed "government official" referred to in them because his wife's checkbook was found in the Huks' possession and had not been reported lost or stolen. For a summary of the raids and captured documents, see Air Pouch 1057, Cowen, Rice to Acheson (1/24/51), HST: JFM: Philippine File, General, 1950–52: Box 7.

55. Letter, Cowen to Melby (1/30/51), HST: JFM: Philippines, Cowen-Melby Correspondence, January–March, 1951: Box 8; Air Pouch 948, Chapin to Acheson (1/3/51), NA: DF: RG 59: 796.00: Box 4315; FRUS (1951), Volume VI, p. 1504.

56. Letter, Melby to Cowen (2/13/51), HST: JFM: Philippines, Cowen-Melby Correspondence, January–March, 1951: Box 8; Letter, Melby to Cowen (2/20/51), ibid.; Letter, Cowen to Melby (3/29/51), ibid.; Letter, Melby to Cowen (4/10/51), ibid.; Letter, Cowen to Hobbs (2/27/51), ibid.; Letter, Melby to Cowen (4/9/51), ibid.

57. FRUS (1951), Volume VI, pp. 1513–14 (and notes 2 and 3); Letter, Melby to Cowen (2/20/51), HST: JFM: Philippines, Cowen-Melby Correspondence, 1951: Box 8; Letter, Cowen to Melby (4/6/51), ibid.; Letter, Cowen to Melby (4/12/51), ibid.; Letter, Cowen to Melby (4/13/51), ibid.; Letter, Cowen to Melby (4/23/51), ibid.; EMBTEL 1972, Chapin to Acheson (1/11/51), NA: DF: RG 59: 796.00: Box 4315; EMBTEL 2725, Cowen to Lacy (3/10/51),

ibid.; EMBTEL 2893, Cowen to Acheson (3/26/51), ibid.; Memo of Conversation, Melby, Cowen (4/5/51), ibid.

58. Air Pouch 1638, Harrington to Acheson (5/14/51), NA: DF: RG 59: 796.00: Box 4315; EMBTEL 3812, Harrington to Acheson (5/31/51), ibid.; EMBTEL 21, Cowen to Acheson (7/2/51), ibid.; EMBTEL 381, Cowen to Acheson (7/26/51), ibid.; EMBTEL 646, Cowen to Acheson (8/11/51), ibid.; EMBTEL 703, Cowen to Acheson (8/17/51), ibid.; EMBTEL 737, Cowen to Acheson (8/21/51), ibid.; Letter, Cowen to Melby (7/25/51), HST: JFM: Philippines, Cowen-Melby Correspondence, 1951: Box 8; Letter, Harrington to Melby (9/6/51), HST: JFM: Philippines, General, 1951–1952: Box 7; Letter, Melby to Harrington (10/10/51), ibid.

59. FRUS (1951), Volume VI, pp. 1517, 1522–23, 1530–31; Letter, Melby to Cowen (3/20/51), HST: JFM: Philippines, Cowen-Melby Correspondence, January-March, 1951: Box 8; Letter, Cowen to Melby (4/16/51), ibid.; Clipping, *Manila Times* (8/4/51), HST: JFM: Philippines, Cowen-Melby Correspondence, 1951: Box 8; Cowen, "Notes for the Undersecretary's Staff Meeting" (6/8/51), HST: MMC: Personal Correspondence: Box 7; Air Pouch 1289, Cowen to Acheson (3/5/51), NA: DF: RG 59: 796.00: Box 4315.

60. EMBTEL 2893, Cowen to Acheson (3/26/51), NA: DF: RG 59: 796.00: Box 4315; EMBTEL 3445, Harrington to Acheson (5/3/51), ibid.; EMBTEL 108, Cowen to Acheson (7/9/51), ibid.; Letter, Cowen to Melby (4/20/51), HST: JFM: Philippines, Cowen-Melby Correspondence, 1951: Box 8. See also Taylor, *The Philippines and the United States,* pp. 173, 205–206; Shalom, *The United States and the Philippines,* pp. 134–135.

61. EMBTEL 729, Cowen to Rusk (8/21/51), NA: DF: RG 59: 796.00: Box 4315.

62. Ibid.; see also Letter, Cowen to Melby (8/11/51), HST: JFM: Philippines, Cowen-Melby Correspondence, 1951: Box 8.

63. Air Pouch 1640, Harrington to Acheson (5/14/51), NA: DF: RG 59: 796.00: Box 4315; EMBTEL 3249, Cowen to Acheson (4/17/51), ibid.; Air Pouch 275, Harrington to Acheson (8/22/51), ibid.

64. Air Pouch 1240, Cowen to Acheson (2/26/51), NA: DF: RG 59: 796.00: Box 4315; EMBTEL 3936, Harrington to Acheson (6/8/51), ibid.; EMBTEL 70, Cowen to Acheson (7/5/51), ibid.; Letter, James Bell (Manila) to Wanamaker (10/16/51), ibid.

65. Wurfel, "The Philippines," pp. 701–702 (especially note 36); Edward G. Lansdale interview (May 29, 1982).

66. Letter, Bell to Wanamaker (10/16/51), NA: DF: RG 59: 796.00: Box 4315; EMBTEL 808, Harrington to Acheson (8/27/51), ibid.; EMBTEL 1060, McKelvey to Sullivan (9/18/51), ibid.; DEPTEL 67, unsigned to Cowen (9/28/51), ibid.; Letter, Cowen to Melby (8/13/51) and attachment, HST: JFM: Philippines, Cowen-Melby Correspondence, 1951: Box 8; Smith, *Portrait of a Cold Warrior,* pp. 107–108; Lansdale, *In the Midst of Wars,* pp. 90–91; Blaufarb, *The Counterinsurgency Era,* pp. 33–35; Elsbree, "The Philippines," p. 106; Edward G. Lansdale interview (May 29, 1982).

67. Memo of conversation, Truman, Cowen, Quirino, Elizalde (9/14/51), HST:

JFM: Philippines, General, 1950–1952: Box 7; Memo, Melby to Lacy, Merchant, Rusk (9/17/51), ibid.

68. EMBTEL 1229, Harrington to Acheson (10/1/51), NA: DF: RG 59: 796.00: Box 4315; EMBTEL 1301, Harrington to Acheson (10/8/51), ibid.; EMBTEL 1307, Harrington to Acheson (10/8/51), ibid.; EMBTEL 1649, Cowen to Acheson (11/5/51), ibid.; EMBTEL 1700, Cowen to Acheson (11/8/51), ibid.; Memo, Wanamaker to Lacy (11/16/51), ibid.; EMBTEL 1808, Harrington to Acheson (11/17/51), ibid.

69. EMBTEL 1784, Harrington to Acheson (11/15/51), NA: DF: RG 59: 796.00: Box 4315; Memo, Wanamaker to Lacy (11/16/51), ibid.; EMBTEL 1808, Harrington to Acheson (11/17/51), ibid.; EMBTEL 1828, Harrington to Acheson (11/19/51), ibid.; EMBTEL 1840, Harrington to Acheson (11/20/51), ibid.; EMBTEL 1858, Harrington to Acheson (11/21/51), ibid.; EMBTEL 1844, Harrington to Acheson (11/21/51), ibid.; EMBTEL 1867, Harrington to Acheson (11/23/51), ibid.; EMBTEL 2023, Sternberg to Acheson (12/6/51), ibid.; EMBTEL 1199, Heath (Saigon) to Acheson (12/13/51), ibid. The British also expressed interest in the American operations in the Philippines, in order to adopt some measures to combat their own Communist insurgency in Malaya. Edward G. Lansdale interview (May 29, 1982).

70. Memo, Webb to Truman (12/6/51), HST: OF: 1055 (1950–1953) Folder: Box 1573.

71. EMBTEL 1739, Cowen to Acheson (11/13/51), NA: DF: RG 59: 796.00: Box 4315; Memo, Allison to Webb (11/28/51), ibid.; EMBTEL 2000, Harrington to Acheson (12/4/51), ibid.; EMBTEL 2012, Harrington to Acheson (12/5/51), ibid.; DEPTEL 1763, Webb to Embassy (12/11/51), ibid.; Memo, Cowen (U.S.) to Melby (12/3/51), HST: JFM: Philippines, Cowen-Melby Correspondence, 1951: Box 8; Memo, Webb to Truman (12/6/51), HST: OF: 1055 (1950–1953) Folder: Box 1573; Abueva, *Ramon Magsaysay,* pp. 197–198.

72. Memo of conversation, Truman and Acheson (10/8/51), HST: DA: Memoranda of conversation, 1951: Box 66; Memo of conversation, Truman and Acheson (12/17/51), ibid.; Memo of conversation, Truman and Acheson (12/20/51), ibid.; Letter, Cowen to Truman (10/10/51), HST: JFM: Philippines, Cowen-Melby Correspondence, 1951: Box 8; Letter, Cowen to Melby (10/19/51), ibid.; Memo of conversation, Webb and Truman (10/29/51), NA: DF: RG 59: 796.00: Box 4315; Thomas B. Buell, *The Quiet Warrior: A Biography of Admiral Raymond A. Spruance* (Boston: Little, Brown, 1974), pp. 401–405.

7. A New Government, Despite Washington, 1952–1953

1. Air Pouch 971, Harrington to Acheson (1/21/52), NA: DF: RG 59: 796.00: Box 4316; EMBTEL 2651, Harrington to Acheson (1/28/52), ibid.; EMBTEL 2353, Harrington to Acheson (1/7/52), ibid.; Air Pouch 1004, Harrington to Acheson (1/29/52), ibid.; EMBTEL 2502, Harrington to Acheson (1/17/52), ibid.; EMBTEL 2743, Harrington to Acheson (2/4/52), ibid.;

EMBTEL 2951, Spruance to Acheson (2/20/52), ibid.; Air Pouch 1168, Spruance to Acheson (3/7/52), ibid.; Letter, Bell to Melby (2/26/52), HST: JFM: Philippines, General, 1950–1952: Box 7.

2. Air Pouch 1168, Spruance to Acheson (3/7/52), NA: DF: RG 59: 796.00: Box 4316; EMBTEL 3433, Spruance to Acheson (3/31/52), ibid.; Letter, Bell to Melby (2/15/52), HST: JFM: Philippines, General, 1950–1952: Box 7; George E. Taylor, *The Philippines and the United States: Problems of Partnership* (New York: Praeger, 1964), pp. 206–207.

3. EMBTEL 3514, Spruance to Acheson (4/4/52), NA: DF: RG 59: 796.00: Box 4316; Air Pouch 1339, Spruance to Acheson (4/15/52), ibid.; EMBTEL 3598, Spruance to Acheson (4/16/52), ibid.

4. Memo, Tyson to Lacy (1/24/52), NA: Regional Affairs: RG 59: PSEAD File: Box 5; Memo, Simmons to Connelly (6/4/52), HST: OF: 1055 File (1950–1953): Box 1573; EMBTEL 4191, Spruance to Acheson (6/4/52), NA: DF: RG 59: 796.00: Box 4316.

5. Stephen R. Shalom, *The United States and the Philippines: A Study of Neocolonialism* (Philadelphia: Institute for the Study of Human Issues, 1981), p. 124.

6. Letter, Cowen to Spruance (4/29/52), HST: MMC: General Correspondence, 1948–1953: Box 13.

7. Thomas B. Buell, *The Quiet Warrior: A Biography of Admiral Raymond A. Spruance* (Boston: Little, Brown, 1974), pp. 404–406.

8. Air Pouch 189, Spruance to Acheson (8/12/53), NA: DF: RG 59: 796.00: Box 4316; Jose Abueva, *Ramon Magsaysay: A Political Biography* (Manila: Solidaridad, 1971), pp. 220–223.

9. One of this younger generation of leaders who gathered around Magsaysay was Benigno Aquino, later assassinated in 1983 during the Marcos regime.

10. EMBTEL 871, Spruance to Acheson (9/22/52), NA: DF: RG 59: 796.00: Box 4316; EMBTEL 907, Spruance to Acheson (9/24/52), ibid.

11. Air Pouch 439, Braddock to Acheson (10/13/52), NA: DF: RG 59: 796.00: Box 4316; Air Pouch 869, Spruance to Dulles (2/6/53), ibid.; DEPTEL 263, Bruce to Spruance (11/5/52), ibid.

12. Quoted in Abueva, *Ramon Magsaysay,* p. 224 (note 10).

13. EMBTEL 1351, Spruance to Acheson (11/7/52), NA: DF: RG 59: 796.00: Box 4316; EMBTEL 1601, Spruance to Allison (12/3/52), ibid.; EMBTEL 2144, Spruance to Acheson (1/19/53), ibid.; EMBTEL 2192, Spruance to Allison (1/22/53), ibid.; EMBTEL 2208, Spruance to Allison (1/23/53), ibid.; Buell, *The Quiet Warrior,* pp. 407–408; Edward G. Lansdale, *In the Midst of Wars: An American's Mission to Southeast Asia* (New York: Harper and Row, 1972), pp. 102–104; Abueva, *Ramon Magsaysay,* pp. 224–227; Shalom, *The United States and the Philippines,* pp. 88–89.

14. EMBTEL 1386, Spruance to Acheson (11/10/52), NA: DF: RG 59: 796.00: Box 4316; EMBTEL 1592, Spruance to Acheson (12/3/52), ibid.; EMBTEL 1679, Spruance to Acheson (12/10/52), ibid.; EMBTEL 1680, Spruance to Acheson (12/10/52), ibid.; EMBTEL 1689, Spruance to Acheson (12/11/52), ibid.; Letter, Lacy to Bonsal (12/15/52), ibid.; EMBTEL 1716, Spruance to Allison (12/15/52), ibid.; EMBTEL 1727, Spruance to Acheson (12/15/52), ibid.; DEPTEL 1846, Acheson to Spruance (12/24/52), ibid.; EMBTEL

1875, Spruance to Acheson (12/26/52), ibid.; EMBTEL 1905, Spruance to Acheson (12/29/52), ibid.; Shalom, *The United States and the Philippines,* pp. 84–85.

15. DEPTEL 1932, Allison to Spruance (1/3/53), NA: DF: RG 59: 796.00: Box 4316; EMBTEL 1953, Spruance to Allison (1/5/53), ibid.; Air Pouch 78, Peterson (Cebu) to Dulles (1/29/53), ibid.; Air Pouch 87, Peterson (Cebu) to Dulles (2/7/53), ibid.; EMBTEL 2644, Spruance to Dulles (2/28/53), ibid.; EMBTEL 2657, Spruance to Dulles (3/2/53), ibid.; EMBTEL 2658, Spruance to Dulles (3/2/53), ibid.; Despatch 982, Spruance to Dulles (3/5/53), ibid.; EMBTEL 2753, Spruance to Dulles (3/10/53), ibid.

16. EMBTEL 2837, Spruance to Dulles (3/17/53), NA: DF: RG 59: 796.00: Box 4316; Air Pouch 102, Peterson (Cebu) to Dulles (3/23/53), ibid.; EMBTEL 2881, Spruance to Dulles (3/23/53), ibid.; EMBTEL 3085, Spruance to Dulles (4/12/53), ibid.; Air Pouch 1277, Spruance to Dulles (5/12/53), ibid.; Willard Elsbree, "The 1953 Philippine Elections," *Pacific Affairs,* 27 (March 1954), 7–8; Edward G. Lansdale interview (May 29, 1982).

17. EMBTEL 2050, Spruance to Dulles (1/12/53), NA: DF: RG 59: 796.00: Box 4316; Willard Elsbree, "The Philippines," in Rupert Emerson, ed., *Representative Government in Southeast Asia* (Cambridge, Mass.: Harvard University Press, 1955), pp. 110–111.

18. EMBTEL 2149, Spruance to Acheson (1/14/53), NA: DF: RG 59: 796.00: Box 4316; Air Pouch 869, Spruance to Dulles (2/6/53), ibid.; EMBTEL 2410, Spruance to Dulles (2/9/53), ibid.; EMBTEL 2818, Spruance to Dulles (3/16/53), ibid.; EMBTEL 2735, Spruance to Dulles (3/8/53), ibid.

19. Quirino's daughter, however, had been gunned down by the Japanese in the final days of the war. This personal loss had apparently insulated him somewhat from "collaboration" charges.

20. EMBTEL 2783, Spruance to Dulles (3/12/53), NA: DF: RG 59: 796.00: Box 4316; EMBTEL 3336, Spruance to Dulles (5/7/53), NA: DF: RG 59: 796.00: Box 4317; EMBTEL (unnumbered), Spruance to Dulles (5/8/53), ibid.; EMBTEL 3359, Spruance to Dulles (5/11/53), ibid.; EMBTEL 3747, Spruance to Dulles (6/17/53), ibid.; Air Pouch 174, Spruance to Dulles (8/7/53), ibid.; EMBTEL 252, Spruance to Dulles (7/30/53), ibid.

21. Air Pouch 869, Spruance to Dulles (2/6/53), NA: DF: RG 59: 796.00: Box 4316; EMBTEL 2441, Spruance to Dulles (2/11/53), ibid.; EMBTEL 2773, Spruance to Dulles (3/12/53), ibid.; Air Pouch 1167, Spruance to Dulles (4/14/53), NA: DF: RG 59: 796.00: Box 4317; Air Pouch 1458, Spruance to Dulles (6/19/53), ibid.

22. EMBTEL 2123, Spruance to Acheson (1/16/53), NA: DF: RG 59: 796.00: Box 4316; DEPTEL 2934, Dulles to Spruance (3/24/53), ibid.; EMBTEL 2948, Spruance to Dulles (3/29/53), ibid.; EMBTEL 2962, Spruance to Dulles (3/30/53), ibid.; EMBTEL 2966, Spruance to Dulles (3/31/53), ibid.; EMBTEL 2967, Spruance to Dulles (3/31/53), ibid.; EMBTEL 2986, Spruance to Dulles (4/1/53), NA: DF: RG 59: 796.00: Box 4317; EMBTEL 2996, Spruance to Dulles (4/2/53), ibid.; Shalom, *The United States and the Philippines,* pp. 88–89.

23. EMBTEL 2959, Spruance to Dulles (3/30/53), NA: DF: RG 59: 796.00: Box

4316; EMBTEL 2966, Spruance to Dulles (3/31/53), ibid.; Air Pouch 1112, Lacy to Dulles (4/1/53), NA: DF: RG 59: 796.00: Box 4317; EMBTEL 2967, Spruance to Dulles (3/31/53), ibid.; EMBTEL 2981, Spruance to Allison (4/1/53), ibid.; EMBTEL 2986, Spruance to Dulles (4/1/53), ibid.; Buell, *The Quiet Warrior,* pp. 414–415.

24. COHP: Walter Robertson Oral History: pp. 19–21.

25. DEPTEL 2840, Dulles to Spruance (3/13/53), NA: DF: RG 59: 796.00: Box 4316.

26. Ibid.; DEPTEL 2854, Dulles to Spruance (3/14/53), NA: DF: RG 59: 796.00: Box 4316; DEPTEL 2189, Dulles to Spruance (3/17/53), ibid.; Buell, *The Quiet Warrior,* pp. 413–414.

27. EMBTEL 2857, Spruance to Dulles (3/19/53), NA: DF: RG 59: 796.00: Box 4316; EMBTEL 2866, Spruance to Dulles (3/20/53), ibid.; EMBTEL 2928, Spruance to Dulles (3/26/53), ibid.

28. EMBTEL 2036, Spruance to Allison (1/11/53), NA: DF: RG 59: 796.00: Box 4316; DEPTEL 2719, Dulles to Spruance (3/5/53), ibid.; Letter, Lansdale to Cowen (6/11/53), HST: MMC: Personal Correspondence, 1951–1961: Lansdale File: Box 6; Lansdale, *In the Midst of Wars,* pp. 106–109, 116, 120–121; Edward G. Lansdale interview (May 29, 1982); Shalom, *The United States and the Philippines,* pp. 118–121.

29. For example, DEPTEL 3645, Smith, Bonsal to Spruance (5/29/53), NA: DF: RG 59: 796.00: Box 4317; Letter, Robertson to Spruance (6/13/53), ibid.

30. Letter, Senator J. William Fulbright to Thruston Morton (4/20/53), NA: DF: RG 59: 796.00: Box 4317; EMBTEL 3466, Spruance to Dulles (5/22/53), ibid.; DEPTEL 3645, Smith, Bonsal to Spruance (5/29/53), ibid.; EMBTEL 3594, Spruance to Dulles (6/3/53), ibid.; EMBTEL 3692, Spruance to Dulles (6/12/53), ibid.; Letter, Robertson to Spruance (6/16/53), ibid.; Letter, Spruance to Robertson (6/24/53), ibid.

31. EMBTEL 35, Spruance to Dulles (7/3/53), NA: DF: RG 59: 796.00: Box 4317; EMBTEL 49, Spruance to Dulles (7/7/53), ibid.; Letter, Dr. Macario Bautista to Dulles (7/7/53), ibid.; Letter, James Bell to Bautista (7/7/53), ibid.; Lansdale, *In the Midst of Wars,* pp. 109–113; Shalom, *The United States and the Philippines,* pp. 90–91; Letter, Lansdale to Cowen (6/11/53), HST: MMC: Personal Correspondence, 1951–1961: Lansdale File: Box 6; Edward G. Lansdale interview (May 29, 1982).

32. EMBTEL 3890, Spruance to Dulles (6/29/53), NA: DF: RG 59: 796.00: Box 4317; DEPTEL 13, Dulles to Spruance (7/24/53), ibid.; Air Pouch 115, Spruance to Dulles (7/27/53), ibid.; Memo, Armstrong to Bonsal (8/13/53), ibid.; EMBTEL 498, Spruance to Dulles (9/2/53), ibid.; EMBTEL 712, Spruance to Dulles (9/28/53), ibid.; EMBTEL 808, Lacy to Dulles (10/7/53), ibid.; Air Pouch 415, Lacy to Dulles (10/14/53), ibid.; EMBTEL 1021, Spruance to Dulles (11/3/53), ibid.; Lansdale, *In the Midst of Wars,* pp. 116–120; Edward G. Lansdale interview (May 29, 1982); Edward G. Lansdale interview (October 11, 1983); Buell, *The Quiet Warrior,* p. 417; Willard Elsbree, "The 1953 Philippine Presidential Election," pp. 9–11.

33. Air Pouch 80, Spruance to Dulles (7/20/53), NA: DF: RG 59: 796.00: Box

4317; Air Pouch 115, Spruance to Dulles (7/27/53), ibid.; EMBTEL 271, Spruance to Dulles (8/3/53), ibid.; Air Pouch 324, Spruance to Dulles (9/18/53), ibid.; Air Pouch 481, Spruance to Dulles (10/28/53), ibid.; Air Pouch 500, Eileen Donovan (Negros Occidental) to Dulles (11/6/53), ibid.; Air Pouch 591, Spruance to Dulles (12/3/53), ibid.

34. EMBTEL 377, Spruance to Dulles (8/17/53), NA: DF: RG 59: 796.00: Box 4317; EMBTEL 1059, Spruance to Dulles (11/7/53), ibid.; EMBTEL 1078, Spruance to Dulles (11/11/53), ibid.; Joseph B. Smith, *Portrait of a Cold Warrior: Second Thoughts of a Top CIA Agent* (New York: G. P. Putnam's Sons, 1976), p. 112.

35. Cannon's quote is from Shalom, *The United States and the Philippines,* pp. 87–92; see also Buell, *The Quiet Warrior,* pp. 416–417, 471; Edward G. Lansdale interview (May 29, 1982).

36. Shalom, *The United States and the Philippines,* pp. 87–92; Buell, *The Quiet Warrior,* pp. 416–417, 471; Letter, Lansdale to Cowen (6/4/53), HST: MMC: Personal Correspondence, 1951–1961: Lansdale Folder: Box 6; Edward G. Lansdale interview (May 29, 1982). For the Filipino government's specific complaints about Lansdale's actions, see Memo, Day to Drumwright (11/6/53), NA: DF: RG 59: 796.00: Box 4317.

37. EMBTEL 292, Spruance to Dulles (8/5/53), NA: DF: RG 59: 796.00: Box 4317; Memo of conversation, Day, Bell, A. H. Tange (Minister of Australian Embassy, Washington) (8/7/53), ibid.; EMBTEL 503, Spruance to Dulles (9/2/53), ibid.; DEPTEL 617, Dulles to Spruance (9/3/53), ibid.; EMBTEL 550, Spruance to Dulles (9/8/53), ibid.; DEPTEL 653, Dulles to Spruance (9/9/53), ibid.; EMBTEL 742, Spruance to Dulles (10/2/53), ibid.; EMBTEL 768, Lacy to Dulles (10/5/53), ibid.; EMBTEL 877, Lacy to Dulles (10/16/53), ibid.; EMBTEL 833, Lacy to Dulles (10/10/53), ibid.

38. Air Pouch 261, Spruance to Dulles (8/31/53), NA: DF: RG 59: 796.00: Box 4317; EMBTEL 599, Spruance to Dulles (9/16/53), ibid.; EMBTEL 876, Lacy to Dulles (10/16/53), ibid.; EMBTEL 877, Lacy to Dulles (10/16/53), ibid.; DEPTEL 1043, Smith to Lacy (10/16/53), ibid.; DEPTEL 1102, Dulles to Embassy (10/21/53), ibid.; EMBTEL 996, Lacy to Dulles (10/29/53), ibid.; EMBTEL 1058, Spruance to Dulles (11/6/53), ibid.; EMBTEL 1079, Spruance to Dulles (11/11/53), ibid.; Lansdale, *In the Midst of Wars,* p. 121; Edward G. Lansdale interview (May 29, 1982). It is clear from the marginal comments on embassy telegrams, made by State analysts in Washington, that the State Department was very hostile to any attempt to favor sides in the election.

39. DEPTEL 740, Smith to Spruance (10/18/53), NA: DF: RG 59: 796.00: Box 4317; DEPTEL 1885, Smith to Spruance (10/21/53), ibid.; EMBTEL 792, Lacy to Dulles (10/6/53), ibid.; EMBTEL 812, Lacy to Dulles (10/8/53), ibid.; Memo, Day to Drumwright (11/6/53), ibid.

40. EMBTEL 1078, Spruance to Dulles (11/11/53), NA: DF: RG 59: 796.00: Box 4317; EMBTEL 1087, Spruance to Dulles (11/12/53), ibid.; EMBTEL 1129, Spruance to Dulles (11/17/53), ibid.; EMBTEL 1151, Spruance to Dulles (11/19/53), ibid.; EMBTEL 1181, Spruance to Dulles (11/24/53), ibid.; Letter, Bell to Lacy (11/20/53), ibid.; Letter, Lacy to Bell (12/2/53),

ibid.; Elsbree, "The Philippines," pp. 112–113; Eisenhower quoted in Smith, *Portrait of a Cold Warrior,* pp. 113–115.

41. Shalom, *The Philippines and the United States,* pp. 118–121, 125–126; Russell King, *Land Reform: A World Survey* (Boulder, Colo.: Westview, 1977), pp. 320–321; Abueva, *Ramon Magsaysay,* pp. 371–374; Jose Abueva, "Bureaucratic Politics in the Philippines," in Lucian Pye, ed., *Cases in Comparative Politics: Asia* (Boston: Little, Brown, 1970), pp. 223–239; Taylor, *The Philippines and the United States,* p. 206; Gary L. Olson, *United States Foreign Policy and the Third World Peasant* (New York: Praeger, 1974), pp. 82–84; David Wurfel, "Foreign Aid and Social Reform in Political Development: A Philippine Case Study," *American Political Science Review,* 53 (June 1959), 456–482; David Wurfel, "Philippine Agrarian Reform under Magsaysay, Part One," *Far Eastern Survey,* 27 (January 1958), 7–15; David Wurfel, "Philippine Agrarian Reform under Magsaysay, Part Two," *Far Eastern Survey,* 27 (February 1958), 23–30; Edward G. Lansdale interview (May 29, 1982); Edward G. Lansdale interview (October 11, 1983). For the return of reformist intervention in the Kennedy years, see Shalom, *The United States and the Philippines,* pp. 119–121; Olson, *United States Foreign Policy and the Third World Peasant,* p. 87; Taylor, *The Philippines and the United States,* pp. 226–228.

42. Air Pouch 591, Spruance to Dulles (12/3/53), NA: DF: RG 59: 796.00: Box 4317.

8. The New Commitment to Diem, 1961

1. HST: Lucius D. Battle Oral History: pp. 22–23.
2. The Vietnamese, like the Koreans, Japanese, and Chinese, place the surname first. Unlike the others, however, the Vietnamese commonly refer to persons by their given name. I will follow the common usage of American and Vietnamese officials by referring to the Vietnamese by their given names. For example, President Ngo Dinh Diem will be referred to as President Diem.
3. For a highly critical account of the domestic forces behind such backing, see Robert Scheer, *How the United States Got Involved in Vietnam* (Santa Barbara, Calif.: Center for the Study of Democratic Institutions, 1965). For a more balanced and comprehensive account, see Russell H. Fifield, *Americans in Southeast Asia* (New York: Thomas Y. Crowell, 1973).
4. Ellen Hammer, "Progress Report on Southern Viet Nam," *Pacific Affairs,* 30 (September 1957), 221–235; William J. Duiker, *The Communist Road to Power in Vietnam* (Boulder, Colo.: Westview Press, 1981), pp. 174, 181–182; PP/GPO, Volume 2, Part IV, A, p. 17; Roy Jumper and M. Normand, "Vietnam," in George McT. Kahin, ed., *Governments and Politics of Southeast Asia* (Ithaca, N.Y.: Cornell University Press, 1964), pp. 409–410; Edward G. Lansdale, *In the Midst of Wars: An American's Mission to Southeast Asia* (New York: Harper and Row, 1971), p. 355. On the training of the South Vietnamese army in the early years, see Brigadier General James Lawton Collins, *The Development and Training of the South Vietnamese Army, 1950–1972*

(Washington, D.C.: Government Printing Office, 1975), pp. 1–18; Ronald Spector, *Advice and Support: The Early Years, 1941–1960* (Washington, D.C.: Center of Military History, 1983).

5. Naval Message, CINCPAC to RUEPDA/DIA (3/14/63), JFK: NSF: CO: Vietnam, 3/1/63–3/19/63: Box 197.

6. Duiker, *The Communist Road to Power*, pp. 174, 181, 183–186; PP/GPO, Volume 2, Part IV, A, 4, pp. "pp," "qq"; PP/GE, Volume 1, pp. 260–265.

7. Joseph Buttinger, *Vietnam: A Dragon Embattled*, Vol. 2 (New York: Praeger, 1967), pp. 935–946; Douglas Pike, *Viet Cong: The Organization and Techniques of the National Liberation Front of South Vietnam* (Cambridge, Mass.: MIT Press, 1966), pp. 71–73; PP/GPO, Volume 2, Part IV, A, pp. 17–18; Duiker, *The Communist Road to Power*, p. 175; Memo, Robert Johnson to Rostow (10/6/61), JFK: NSF: CO: Vietnam, 10/4/61–10/9/61: Box 194.

8. Buttinger, *A Dragon Embattled*, pp. 946–981; Jumper and Normand, "Vietnam," pp. 427, 431–432; PP/GPO, Volume 2, Part IV, A, 4, p. 20; Roy Jumper, "Mandarin Bureaucracy and Politics in South Viet Nam," *Pacific Affairs*, 30 (March 1957), 47–58; Robert Scigliano and Wayne Snyder, "The Budget Process in South Vietnam," *Pacific Affairs*, 33 (March 1960), 48–60; Lloyd D. Musolf, "Public Enterprise and Development Perspectives in South Vietnam," *Asian Survey*, 3 (August 1963), 357–371; Nguyen Tuyet Mai, "Electioneering: Vietnamese Style," *Asian Survey*, 2 (November 1962), 11–18; Milton C. Taylor, "South Viet-Nam: Lavish Aid, Limited Progress," *Pacific Affairs*, 34 (Fall 1961), 242–256; John C. Donnell, "National Renovation Campaigns in Vietnam," *Pacific Affairs*, 32 (March 1959), 73–88; Bernard Fall, *The Two Vietnams: A Military and Political Analysis* (New York: Praeger, 1963), pp. 254–315.

9. PP/GPO, Volume 2, Part IV, A, 4, pp. 33–35, "pp," "qq"; Jumper and Normand, "Vietnam," p. 440; Buttinger, *A Dragon Embattled*, pp. 942–946; Pike, *Viet Cong*, p. 72; Stephen Pelz, "John F. Kennedy's 1961 War Decisions," *Journal of Strategic Studies*, 4 (December 1981), 357. For journalistic accounts, see Stanley Karnow, *Vietnam: A History* (New York: Viking, 1983), pp. 233–235, 677; Robert Shaplen, *The Lost Revolution: The United States in Vietnam, 1946–1966* (New York: Harper and Row, 1966), pp. 128–129, 132–139, 140–142.

10. This synopsis of Lansdale's views is based on two lengthy interviews he granted in May 1982 and October 1983. For a glowing, uncritical account of Lansdale's exploits and viewpoint, see Cecil B. Currey, *Edward Lansdale: The Unquiet American* (Boston: Houghton Mifflin, 1988). Though I have strong disagreements with him in some policy areas, such as the quid pro quo bargaining approach, I much admired Lansdale, his views, and his activities in Asia in the 1950s and 1960s.

11. Quoted in PP/GPO, Volume 10, p. 74; Edward G. Lansdale interview (May 29, 1982); Edward G. Lansdale interview (October 11, 1983).

12. Rostow later placed this meeting in early February. His memo at the time, however, shows that Lansdale first met with Kennedy on January 28. Walt W. Rostow, *The Diffusion of Power: An Essay in Recent History* (New York:

MacMillan, 1972), pp. 264–265; Memo, Rostow to Bundy (1/30/61), JFK: NSF: CO: Vietnam, Volume I, 1/61–3/61: Box 193. On Kennedy's "keen interest" in the Lansdale report, see Memo, Bundy to McNamara, Rusk, Dulles (1/27/61), ibid. On the influence of Lansdale's report on decision-making in 1961, see also Maxwell D. Taylor, *Swords and Ploughshares* (New York: W. W. Norton, 1972), pp. 220–221.

13. Memo, Rostow to Bundy (1/30/61), JFK: NSF: CO: Vietnam, Volume I, 1/61–3/61: Box 193. See also Pelz, "1961 War Decisions," pp. 357–359.
14. Memo, Kennedy to Rusk, McNamara (1/30/61), JFK: NSF: CO: Vietnam, Volume I, 1/61–3/61: Box 193; Memo, Komer to Rostow (2/1/61), ibid.; Herbert Parmet, *JFK: The Presidency of John F. Kennedy* (New York: Dial Press, 1983), pp. 136–138, 140; Arthur Schlesinger, Jr., *Robert Kennedy and His Times* (New York: Ballantine, 1978), pp. 495–496. The best work on military resistance to the "new" counterinsurgency doctrine is Andrew Krepinevich, Jr., *The Army and Vietnam* (Baltimore: Johns Hopkins University Press, 1986).
15. DEPTEL 1054, Rusk to Durbrow (2/3/61), JFK: NSF: CO: Vietnam, Volume I, 1/61–3/61: Box 193.
16. Letter, Young to Rostow (2/17/61), JFK: NSF: CO: Vietnam, Volume I, 1/61–3/61: Box 193.; Pelz, "1961 War Decisions," p. 359.
17. EMBTEL 1453, Durbrow to Rusk (3/11/61), JFK: CO: Vietnam, Volume I, 1/61–3/61: Box 193; Memo, Bundy to Battle (3/14/61), ibid.; Memo, Rostow to Kennedy (3/29/61), ibid.; Airgram A-28, Saigon to Bangkok (8/31/61) JFK: NSF: CO: Vietnam, 8/61: Box 194.
18. Hagerty quote from Memo, Baughman [?] (12/31/60), JFK: OF: CO: Laos, General, 1/61–3/61: Box 121; Memo, "The Outlook for Southeast Asia in Mid-November, 1960," ibid.; Memo, Rusk to Kennedy (2/2/61), ibid.; Memo, "A New Look at Laos," Kenneth Young (undated), ibid.; see Phouma's request for a neutralist Laos in a message sent through Senator Mike Mansfield, Memo, Mansfield to Kennedy (1/21/61), ibid.; Dr. Bernard Fall, "Communist Subversion in SEATO Areas," (6/1/60), JFK: Pre-Presidential Transition Files: Task Force Reports: Box 1073; Parmet, *JFK*, pp. 134–135; Charles A. Stevenson, *The End of Nowhere: American Policy toward Laos since 1954* (Boston: Beacon Press, 1973), pp. 92–142; Pelz, "1961 War Decisions," p. 364.
19. DEPTEL 1567, Rusk to Moscow (3/23/61), JFK: NSF: CO: Vietnam, Volume I, 1/61–3/61: Box 193; DEPTEL 1455, Rusk to all embassies (3/23/61), ibid.
20. EMBTEL 1684, Bangkok to Rusk (3/20/61), JFK: NSF: CO: Vietnam, Volume I, 1/61–3/61: Box 193; EMBTEL 1686, Bangkok to Rusk (3/20/61), ibid.; EMBTEL 1689, Bangkok to Rusk (3/20/61), ibid.; EMBTEL 1723, Bangkok to Rusk (3/23/61), ibid.; Parmet, *JFK*, pp. 96, 135, 139–146; Stevenson, *The End of Nowhere*, pp. 143–154.
21. Stevenson, *The End of Nowhere*, pp. 155–179.
22. Letter, J. William Fulbright to Kennedy (3/24/61), JFK: OF: CO: UN-Vietnam, General, 1962 (*sic*): Box 128.

23. Parmet, *JFK,* pp. 96, 141–146; Schlesinger, *Robert Kennedy,* p. 757; Ronald Steel, *Walter Lippman and the American Century* (New York: Vintage, 1981), p. 530.

24. Parmet, *JFK,* pp. 96, 99, 155, 176–177, 193–196; Pelz, "1961 War Decisions," pp. 364–366, 378–379; Schlesinger, *Robert Kennedy,* pp. 757–758; Steel, *Walter Lippman,* pp. 530–533.

25. Memo of Interdepartmental Meeting (4/29/61), JFK: NSF: CO: Laos, Volume II, 6/61 (*sic*): Box 130; Memo, Rostow to Kennedy (3/29/61), JFK: NSF: CO: Vietnam, Volume I, 1/61–3/61: Box 193; DEPTEL 1456, Rusk to Bangkok (3/23/61), ibid.; Memo, "Operations against North Vietnam," Gilpatric to Kennedy (3/29/61), JFK: NSF: CO: Vietnam, Volume I, 4/1/61–4/24/61: Box 193; Memo, Rostow to Kennedy (4/3/61), ibid.; Memo, McNamara to Kennedy (4/20/61), ibid.; Memo, McNamara to Gilpatric (4/20/61), ibid.; Memo, Gilpatric to Kennedy (4/27/61), JFK: NSF: CO: Vietnam, 4/25/61–4/31/61: Box 193; Memo, Rostow to Bundy, Robert Johnson, Owen (5/3/61), JFK: NSF: CO: Vietnam, 5/3/61–5/7/61: Box 193; Parmet, *JFK,* pp. 135, 178–179; Schlesinger, *Robert Kennedy,* pp. 757–758.

26. EMBTEL 1599, Durbrow to Rusk (4/12/61), JFK: NSF: CO: Vietnam, 4/1/61–4/24/61: Box 193; EMBTEL 1606, Durbrow to Rusk (4/15/61), ibid.

27. Memo of Phone Message, Lansdale to Rostow (4/14/61), JFK: NSF: CO: Vietnam, 4/1/61–4/24/61: Box 193.

28. Memo, Battle to Dungan (4/4/61), JFK: NSF: CO: Vietnam, 4/1/61–4/24/61: Box 193; Memo (unsigned), "Status of the Counter Insurgency Plan for Vietnam, Annex A," JFK: NSF: CO: Vietnam, 4/25/61–4/31/61: Box 193; Memo (unsigned), "A Program of Action: To Prevent Communist Domination of South Vietnam," (5/1/61), JFK: NSF: CO: Vietnam, 5/1/61–5/2/61: Box 193; EMBTEL 1656 (Part 2), Durbrow to Rusk (5/2/61), JFK: NSF: CO: Vietnam, 5/3/61–5/7/61: Box 193; Memo, Harriman to Rusk, Kennedy (5/4/61), ibid.

29. Memo, "Putting U.S. Troops into Vietnam," Komer to Bundy, Rostow (5/4/61), JFK: NSF: CO: Vietnam, 5/3/61–5/7/61: Box 193; Memo (unsigned), "U.S. Military Forces in South Vietnam," (5/5/61), ibid.; EMBTEL 1656, Durbrow to Rusk (5/3/61), ibid.; Memo (unsigned), "Viet-Nam NSC Paper," (5/10/61), JFK: NSF: CO: Vietnam, 5/8/61–5/19/61: Box 193; EMBTEL 1752, Nolting to Rusk (5/16/61), ibid.; Memo, Rostow to Kennedy (5/12/61), JFK: OF: CO: Communist China, 1961: Box 114; CIA Memo, "The Chances of a PRC Thrust into Southeast Asia," (5/11/61), ibid.

30. Memo, "The Possibility of a Coup in South Viet Nam," Robert Johnson to Rostow (5/24/61), JFK: NSF: CO: Vietnam, 5/20/61–5/24/61: Box 193; EMBTEL 2782, Galbraith (New Delhi) to Rusk (5/22/61), ibid.; DEPTEL (unnumbered), Rusk to Saigon, London, Ottawa, Paris, New Delhi (5/26/61), JFK: NSF: CO: Vietnam, 5/25/61–5/31/61: Box 193; Memo, Young to Bundy, Rostow (4/29/61), JFK: NSF: CO: Vietnam, 4/25/61–4/31/61: Box 193; Memo, Sorensen to Kennedy (4/28/61), ibid.; DEPTEL 2084, Rusk to New Delhi, London, Paris, Saigon, Ottawa, Geneva (7/1/61), JFK: NSF: CO: Vietnam, 7/1/61–7/4/61: Box 193; Pelz, "1961 War Decisions," pp. 367–

369; Parmet, *JFK,* pp. 151–153; Shaplen, *The Lost Revolution,* p. 197; Karnow, *Vietnam,* p. 237.

31. Letter, Diem to Kennedy (5/15/61), JFK: OF: CO: Vietnam Security 1961: Box 128a; EMBTEL 1767, Nolting to Rusk (5/18/61), JFK: NSF: CO: Vietnam, 5/8/61–5/19/61: Box 193; Memo, Robert Johnson to Rostow (5/19/61), ibid.; DEPTEL 1390, Bowles to Nolting (5/19/61), ibid.; DEPTEL 1422, Bowles to Nolting (5/20/61), JFK: NSF: CO: Vietnam, 5/20/61–5/24/61: Box 193; DEPTEL 1432, Rusk to Nolting (5/23/61), ibid.; Pelz, "1961 War Decisions," pp. 369–370; Leslie Gelb and Richard Betts, *The Irony of Vietnam: The System Worked* (Washington, D.C.: The Brookings Institution, 1978), p. 72.

32. Robert Scigliano, *South Vietnam: Nation under Stress* (Boston: Houghton Mifflin, 1963), p. 209.

33. DEPTEL 1433, Rusk to Nolting (5/23/61), JFK: NSF: CO: Vietnam, 5/20/61–5/24/61: Box 193; EMBTEL 1794, Nolting to Rusk (5/24/61), ibid.; EMBTEL 1786, Nolting to Rusk (5/24/61), ibid.; EMBTEL 1800, Nolting to Rusk (5/26/61), JFK: NSF: CO: Vietnam, 5/25/61–5/31/61: Box 193; Memo, Rostow to Kennedy (5/26/61), ibid.; EMBTEL 1802, Nolting to Rusk (5/26/61), ibid.; EMBTEL 1803, Nolting to Rusk (5/27/61), ibid.; DEPTEL 1462, Rusk to Nolting (5/29/61), ibid.; Shaplen, *The Lost Revolution,* p. 153.

34. Memo, Rostow to Kennedy (6/21/61), JFK: NSF: CO: Vietnam, 6/19/61–6/30/61: Box 193; Memo, Rostow to Alexis Johnson (6/23/61), ibid.; Memo, Robert Johnson to Rostow (8/2/61), JFK: NSF: CO: Vietnam, 8/61: Box 194; Steel, *Walter Lippman,* pp. 530–533; Pelz, "1961 War Decisions," pp. 371–372. The CIA telegram outlining the leak is sanitized and does not identify the source of the information. In a memo from Robert Johnson to Rostow two days later, however, the source is identified as a North Vietnamese diplomat. CIA Telegram (7/12/61), JFK: NSF: CO: Vietnam, 7/14/61–7/21/61: Box 193; Memo, Robert Johnson to Rostow (7/14/61), ibid. Another rare reference to "informants" working for the United States in North Vietnam can be found in Frank Snepp, *Decent Interval: An Insider's Account of Saigon's Indecent End Told by the CIA's Chief Strategy Analyst* (New York: Vintage, 1978), p. 111.

35. Memo, Cottrell to McNaughty (7/8/61), JFK: NSF: CO: Vietnam, 7/5/61–7/13/61: Box 193; EMBTEL 225, Nolting to Rusk (8/12/61), JFK: NSF: CO: Vietnam, 8/61: Box 194; Parmet, *JFK,* pp. 197–201; Kennedy quoted in Gelb and Betts, *The Irony of Vietnam,* p. 70.

36. EMBTEL 1805, Nolting to Rusk (5/29/61), JFK: NSF: CO: Vietnam, 5/25/61–5/31/61: Box 193; EMBTEL 1817, Nolting to Rusk (5/30/61), ibid.; EMBTEL 1838, Nolting to Rusk (6/2/61), ibid.; Shaplen, *The Lost Revolution,* pp. 155–157; Jumper and Normand, "Vietnam," pp. 437, 449.

37. EMBTEL 1837, Nolting to Rusk (6/2/61), JFK: NSF: CO: Vietnam, 6/1/61–6/2/61: Box 193; Letter, Diem to Kennedy (6/9/61), JFK: OF: Vietnam, General, 1963 (*sic*): Box 128a; Memo, Robert Johnson to Rostow (6/14/61), JFK: NSF: CO: Vietnam, 6/3/61–6/18/61: Box 193; DEPTEL 1498, Rusk to Nolting (6/6/61), ibid.; DEPTEL 1840, Rusk to French Embassy (6/26/61),

JFK: NSF: CO: Vietnam, 6/19/61–6/30/61: Box 193; Airgram A-73, Nolting
to Rusk (9/1/61), JFK: NSF: CO: Vietnam, 9/61: Box 194; Pelz, "1961 War
Decisions," p. 372.

38. Memo, Robert Johnson to Rostow (6/15/61), JFK: NSF: CO: Vietnam,
6/13/61–6/18/61: Box 193; Memo of Conversation, Kennedy, Thuan,
McNaughty, Wood (6/14/61), ibid.; Memo, Robert Johnson to Rostow
(6/20/61), JFK: NSF: CO: Vietnam,6/19/61–6/30/61: Box 193; EMBTEL
1923, Nolting to Rusk (6/22/61), ibid.; Letter, Kennedy to Diem (7/3/61),
JFK: NSF: CO: Vietnam, 7/1/61–7/4/61: Box 193; Memo of Conversation,
Kennedy and General Clifton (7/3/61), ibid.; EMBTEL 1026, CHMAAG to
Rusk (7/10/61), JFK: NSF: CO: Vietnam, 7/5/61–7/13/61: Box 193; Office
Memo, CHMAAG to Nolting (7/13/61), ibid.; EMBTEL 70, Nolting to Rusk
(7/14/61), JFK: NSF: CO: Vietnam, 7/14/61–7/21/61: Box 193.

39. EMBTEL 70, Nolting to Rusk (7/14/61), JFK: NSF: CO: Vietnam, 7/14/61–
7/21/61: Box 193; Staley Mission, "Summary Joint Action Program"
(7/22/61), JFK: NSF: CO: Vietnam, 7/22/61–7/26/61: Box 193; Memo, Robert Johnson to Rostow (7/27/61), JFK: NSF: CO: Vietnam, 7/27/61–7/31/61:
Box 193; DEPTEL 106, Rusk to Nolting (7/27/61), ibid.; DEPTEL 113,
Rusk to Nolting (7/28/61), ibid.; Memo, "Staley Report on Vietnam," Rusk
to Kennedy (7/28/61), ibid.; Memo, Robert Johnson to Rostow (8/1/61),
JFK: NSF: CO: Vietnam, 8/61: Box 194; DEPTEL 140, Ball to Nolting
(8/4/61), ibid.

40. EMBTEL 192, Nolting to Rusk (8/8/61), JFK: NSF: CO: Vietnam, 8/61:
Box 194; EMBTEL 218, Nolting to Rusk (8/11/61), ibid.; DEPTEL 184,
Rusk to Nolting (8/12/61), ibid.; Memo, Robert Johnson to Rostow (8/16/61),
ibid.; DEPTEL 208, Rusk to Nolting (8/18/61), ibid.; DEPTEL 226, Rusk
to Nolting (8/24/61), ibid.; EMBTEL 277, Nolting to Rusk (8/25/61), ibid.;
EMBTEL 298, Nolting to Rusk (8/31/61), ibid.

41. Army Message 1473, CHMAAG to CINCPAC (9/10/61), JFK: NSF: CO:
Vietnam, 9/61: Box 194;; Memo, Robert Johnson to Rostow (9/15/61), ibid.;
EMBTEL 385, Nolting to Rusk (9/20/61), ibid.; Army Message 1534,
CHMAAG to CINCPAC (9/21/61), ibid.; Memo, Robert Johnson to Rostow
(9/22/61), ibid.; Army Message 1570, CHMAAG to CINCPAC (9/25/61),
ibid.; EMBTEL 405, Nolting to Rusk (9/26/61), ibid.; CIA Memo, "Security
Conditions in Kien Hoa Province; Changes in Communist Tactics; Presence
of High-Level Communists in Southwest Viet-Nam" (11/22/61), JFK: NSF:
CO: Vietnam, 11/21/61–11/23/61: Box 195; Pelz, "1961 War Decisions,"
pp. 74–75.

42. Memo, "The Vietnamese-Cambodian Border Control Problem," Robert
Johnson to Rostow (9/7/61), JFK: NSF: CO: Vietnam, 9/61: Box 194; EMB-
TEL 366, Nolting to Rusk (9/15/61), ibid.; EMBTEL 371, Nolting to Rusk
(9/17/61), ibid.; EMBTEL 414, Nolting to Rusk (9/28/61), ibid.; DEPTEL
344, Bowles to Nolting (9/25/61), ibid.; EMBTEL 401, Nolting to Rusk
(9/26/61), ibid.; Memo, "Internal Security in Viet-Nam," Cottrell to Rusk,
and others (9/1/61), ibid.; "Joint State-Defense Message" (9/20/61), ibid.;
DEPTEL 337, Bowles to Nolting (9/22/61), ibid.

43. EMBTEL 428, Nolting to Rusk (10/3/61), JFK: NSF: CO: Vietnam, 10/1/61–
10/3/61: Box 194; DEPTEL 392, Rusk to Nolting (10/6/61), JFK: NSF: CO:
Vietnam, 10/4/61–10/9/61: Box 194; EMBTEL 486, Nolting to Rusk
(10/13/61), JFK: NSF: CO: Vietnam, 10/12/61–10/15/61: Box 194; EMB-
TEL 502, Nolting to Rusk (10/17/61) JFK: NSF: CO: Vietnam, 10/16/61–
10/19/61: Box 194; EMBTEL 504, Nolting to Rusk (10/18/61), ibid.; EMB-
TEL 556, Nolting to Rusk (10/28/61), JFK: NSF: CO: Vietnam, 10/27/61–
10/31/61: Box 194; EMBTEL 421, Nolting to Rusk (10/1/61), JFK: NSF:
CO: Vietnam, 10/61: Box 194; Letter, Kennedy to the King of Laos
(4/19/61), JFK: OF: CO: Vietnam, General, 1963 (*sic*): Box 128a; Jumper
and Normand, "Vietnam," p. 424.
44. Quoted in Schlesinger, *Robert Kennedy,* p. 761.
45. EMBTEL 427, Nolting to Rusk (10/2/61), JFK: NSF: CO: Vietnam, 10/1/61–
10/3/61: Box 194; Department of Defense Memo, "Concept for Intervention in Viet-Nam" (10/5/61), ibid.; EMBTEL 448, Nolting to Rusk (10/8/61),
JFK: NSF: CO: Vietnam, 10/4/61–10/9/61: Box 194; EMBTEL 457, Nolting
to Rusk (10/9/61), ibid.; Memo, Joint Chiefs of Staff to General Maxwell
Taylor (10/9/61), ibid.; EMBTEL 462, Nolting to Rusk (10/10/61), JFK:
NSF: CO: Vietnam, 10/10/61–10/11/61: Box 194; EMBTEL 471, Nolting
to Rusk (10/11/61), ibid.; Memo, "Conversation with Major Taylor, USMC,
in Regard to his Views on the Military Situation" (10/12/61), JFK: NSF:
CO: Vietnam, 10/12/61–10/15/61: Box 194; Pelz, "1961 War Decisions,"
pp. 375–376.
46. DEPTEL 389, Rusk to Nolting (10/5/61), JFK: NSF: CO: Vietnam, 10/4/61–
10/9/61: Box 194.
47. DEPTEL 333, Bowles to Nolting (9/22/61), JFK: NSF: CO: Vietnam, 9/61:
Box 194; EMBTEL 414, Nolting to Rusk (9/28/61), ibid.; DEPTEL 371,
Rusk to Nolting (10/3/61), JFK: NSF: CO: Vietnam, 10/1/61–10/3/61: Box
194; DEPTEL 374, Rusk to Nolting (10/3/61), ibid.; Memo, Robert Johnson
to Rostow, "Civic Action in South Viet-Nam" (10/6/61), JFK: NSF: CO:
Vietnam, 10/4/61–10/9/61: Box 194; CIA Memo, "Bloc Support of the
Communist Effort against the Government of Vietnam" (10/5/61), ibid.;
Memo, Robert Johnson to Rostow, "Economic Assistance for Viet Nam"
(10/10/61), JFK: NSF: CO: Vietnam, 10/10/61–10/11/61: Box 194; Memo,
Robert Johnson to Rostow, "Various Military Items for Viet Nam"
(10/10/61), ibid.; Memo, Robert Johnson to Rostow, "Concept for Intervention in Viet Nam" (10/10/61), ibid.; EMBTEL 467, Nolting to Rusk
(10/10/61), ibid.; DEPTEL 484, Rusk to Bangkok (10/10/61), ibid.; DEPTEL
416, Ball to Nolting (10/11/61), ibid.; EMBTEL 469, Nolting to Rusk
(10/11/61), ibid.; Pelz, "1961 War Decisions," p. 377.
48. Quoted in CIA Report, "Belief of Senior Vietnamese Officials for Need of
State of National Emergency and Government Reforms" (10/17/61), JFK:
NSF: CO: Vietnam, 10/16/61–10/19/61: Box 194.
49. Ibid.; EMBTEL 479, Nolting to Rusk (10/12/61), JFK: NSF: CO: Vietnam,
10/12/61–10/15/61: Box 194; Unsigned Memo (10/18/61), ibid.; EMBTEL
545, Nolting to Rusk (10/25/61), JFK: NSF: CO: Vietnam, 10/20/61–

10/26/61: Box 194; EMBTEL 556, Nolting to Rusk (10/28/61), JFK: NSF: CO: Vietnam, 10/27/61–10/31/61: Box 194; EMBTEL 575, Nolting to Taylor (Baguio), ibid.

50. Letter, Harriman to Schlesinger (10/17/61), JFK: OF: Vietnam, 1963– (sic): Box 128a.

51. Taylor's initial report from Baguio on 11/1/61 is in PP/GPO, Volume 11, pp. 331–336; Memo, State Department to Kennedy, "Developments in Viet Nam between General Taylor's Visits: October, 1961–October, 1962" (10/8/62), JFK: NSF: CO: Vietnam, 10/7/62–10/17/62: Box 197; see also Gelb and Betts, *The Irony of Vietnam*, pp. 74–75; Rostow, *The Diffusion of Power*, pp. 277, 279.

52. PP/GPO, Volume 11, pp. 343–344; Gelb and Betts, *The Irony of Vietnam*, pp. 76–77.

53. SECTO 6, Rusk (Tokyo) to State Department (11/1/61), JFK: NSF: CO: Vietnam, 11/1/61–11/2/61: Box 194; Memo, Harriman to Kennedy (11/11/61), JFK: NSF: CO: Vietnam, 11/11/61–11/13/61: Box 195; DEPTEL 587, Rusk to Nolting (11/12/61), ibid.; Memo, Alexis Johnson to McGeorge Bundy, Rostow, Taylor (11/11/61), JFK: OF: Vietnam, General, 1963– (sic): Box 128a.

54. Memo, "List of Supporters of U.S. Troops in South Viet Nam" (11/61), JFK: OF: Vietnam, General, 1963 (sic): Box 128a; Memo, "Talks with Nehru" (11/8/61), ibid.; Memo, Alexis Johnson to McGeorge Bundy (11/28/61), ibid.; Memo, "State Department Position Paper on Viet Nam for Prime Minister Nehru's Visit" (11/6–9/61), ibid.; Letter, Galbraith to Kennedy (11/8/61), JFK: NSF: CO: Vietnam, 11/8/61–11/10/61: Box 194; DEPTEL 608, Rusk to Nolting (11/14/61), JFK: NSF: CO: Vietnam, 11/14/61–11/15/61: Box 195; EMBTEL 2587, Gavin (Paris) to Rusk (11/15/61), ibid.

55. DEPTEL 545, Bowles to Nolting (11/4/61), JFK: NSF: CO: Vietnam, 11/3/61–11/7/61: Box 194; EMBTEL 608, Nolting to Rusk (11/7/61), ibid.; Memo for the President, "Questions for the Meeting on South Vietnam, 12:00 p.m., 11/11/61" (11/11/61), JFK: OF: Vietnam, General, 1963– (sic): Box 128a; PP/GE, Volume 2, pp. 110–116; Gelb and Betts, *The Irony of Vietnam*, pp. 76–77.

56. Larry Berman, *Planning a Tragedy: The Americanization of the War in Vietnam* (New York: Norton, 1982), pp. 22–23; Pelz, "1961 War Decisions," p. 379; Rostow, *The Diffusion of Power*, pp. 278–279; Taylor, *Swords and Ploughshares*, pp. 248–249; the Hilsman quotes are from Memo, Hilsman to Rusk, "General Taylor's Recommendations on South Vietnam" (11/16/61), JFK: NSF: CO: Vietnam, Memos and Records, 11/1/61–11/16/61: Box 195.

57. DEPTEL 618, Rusk to Nolting (11/15/61), JFK: NSF: CO: Vietnam, 11/14/61–11/15/61: Box 195.

58. Ibid.; see also Draft Telegram, Rusk to Nolting (11/15/61), JFK: OF: CO: Vietnam, General, 1963 (sic): Box 128a; Memo, Hilsman to Rusk, "General Taylor's Recommendations on South Vietnam" (11/16/61), JFK: NSF: CO: Vietnam, Memos and Records, 11/1/61–11/16/61: Box 195.

59. EMBTEL 678, Nolting to Rusk (11/18/61), JFK: NSF: CO: Vietnam, 11/18/61–11/20/61: Box 195.
60. "Task Force Status Report on CIP" (11/28/61), JFK: NSF: CO: Vietnam, Memos and Reports, 11/1/61–11/16/61 (*sic*): Box 195; EMBTEL 647, Nolting to Rusk (11/14/61), JFK: NSF: CO: Vietnam, 11/14/61–11/15/61: Box 195; EMBTEL 650, Nolting to Rusk (11/14/61), ibid.; EMBTEL 702, Nolting to Rusk (11/24/61), JFK: NSF: CO: Vietnam, 11/24/61–11/25/61: Box 195; EMBTEL 707, Nolting to Rusk (11/25/61), ibid.; EMBTEL 707, Nolting to Rusk (11/25/61), ibid.; EMBTEL 708, Nolting to Rusk (11/25/61), ibid.; EMBTEL 715, Nolting to Rusk (11/27/61), JFK: NSF: CO: Vietnam, 11/26/61–11/28/61: Box 195; Telegram, CINCPAC to JCS (11/28/61), ibid.; Memo, Alexis Johnson to McGeorge Bundy (11/28/61), JFK: OF: CO: Vietnam, General, 1963– (*sic*): Box 128a.
61. DEPTEL 683, Rusk to Nolting (11/25/61), JFK: NSF: CO: Vietnam, 11/24/61–11/25/61: Box 195; EMBTEL 704, Nolting to Rusk (11/25/61), ibid.; Telegram, CHMAAG to Rusk (11/26/61), JFK: NSF: CO: Vietnam, 11/26/61–11/28/61: Box 195; Memo, "Status Report of the Military Actions Resulting from the NSC Meeting, 11 November 1961," ibid.; DEPTEL 694, Rusk to Nolting (11/27/61), ibid.; EMBTEL 722, Nolting to Rusk (11/28/61), ibid.; Memo, Alexis Johnson to Bundy (11/28/61), JFK: OF: CO: Vietnam, 1963– (*sic*): Box 128a; Memo, "Status Report on the Instructions to Ambassador Nolting Prepared by Task Force, Vietnam, DOS, November 28, 1961," ibid.
62. Memo, Alexis Johnson to Bundy (11/28/61), JFK: OF: CO: Vietnam, General, 1963– (*sic*): Box 128a; EMBTEL 729, Nolting to Rusk (11/29/61), JFK: NSF: CO: Vietnam, 11/29/61–11/30/61: Box 195.
63. For representative examples, see Shaplen, *The Lost Revolution,* pp. 154–155; Fall, *The Two Vietnams,* pp. 278–279.
64. EMBTEL 756, Nolting to Rusk (12/4/61), JFK: NSF: CO: Vietnam, 12/3/61–12/5/61: Box 195.
65. Ibid.
66. Ibid.
67. Memo, McNamara to Army Chief of Staff (12/21/61), JFK: NSF: CO: Vietnam, 1/6/62–1/12/62 (*sic*): Box 195; "Memo for the Record" (1/6/62), ibid.; EMBTEL 2499, Jones (London) to Rusk (1/5/62), JFK: NSF: CO: Vietnam, 1/1/62–1/5/62: Box 195; Schlesinger, *Robert Kennedy,* p. 762.

9. Successes and Failures, 1962–1963

1. On the split in general, see Leslie Gelb and Richard Betts, *The Irony of Vietnam: The System Worked* (Washington, D.C.: The Brookings Institution, 1979), pp. 81–82.
2. For military resistance to the civilian counterinsurgency strategy, see Andrew Krepinevich, *The Army and Vietnam* (Baltimore: Johns Hopkins University Press, 1986).
3. Richard Betts points out that most State Department and middle-level CIA

officials were reformist (political approach); high-level military officials and the top officials of the CIA favored bolstering (military approach). Gelb and Betts, *The Irony of Vietnam,* pp. 81–82. On the top officials of the CIA, see also Thomas Powers, *The Man Who Kept the Secrets: Richard Helms and the CIA* (New York: Washington Square, 1979), p. 206. I would add economic officials in the Treasury Department, the Agency for International Development, and the United States Operations Mission to the reformist column. See, for example, Memo, Robert Johnson to Rostow (10/13/61), JFK: NSF: CO: Vietnam, 10/12/61–10/15/61: Box 194.

4. Douglas Blaufarb, *The Counterinsurgency Era: U.S. Doctrine and Performance, 1950 to the Present* (New York: The Free Press, 1977), pp. 79–82. For the differences in the approaches, see Roger Hilsman, "Two American Counterstrategies to Guerrilla Warfare: The Case of Vietnam," in Tang Tsou, ed., *China in Crisis,* Vol. 2 (Chicago: University of Chicago Press, 1968), pp. 269–303. For Hilsman's contemporary view, see Roger Hilsman, "A Strategic Concept for South Vietnam" (2/2/62), JFK: NSF: CO: Vietnam, Reports and Memos, 1/62–2/62: Box 195. For a recent military critique of the political approach, see Colonel Harry G. Summers, Jr., *On Strategy: A Critical Analysis of the Vietnam War* (Novato, Calif.: Presidio Press, 1982), pp. 229–230. For a British critique of the U.S. military approach from a member of the Thompson Mission, see Dennis J. Duncanson, *Government and Revolution in Vietnam* (New York: Oxford University Press, 1968), pp. 303–311. Duncanson mistakenly argues that the political approach was rejected by all Americans. In fact, it was rejected by the U.S. military and the Ngos, and Duncanson has very little that is constructive to say about how the latter were to be convinced to go along. Not surprisingly, his main complaint is that British advice was allegedly not followed. For the influence of the Thompson Mission on the State Department, which had reached many similar conclusions independently, see Hilsman, *To Move a Nation: The Politics of Foreign Policy in the Administration of John F. Kennedy* (New York: Doubleday, 1967), pp. 429–435.

5. Quoted in Arthur Schlesinger, Jr., *Robert Kennedy and His Times* (New York: Ballantine, 1978), p. 762.

6. Quoted in Bernard Fall, *The Two Vietnams: A Military and Political Analysis* (New York: Praeger, 1963), pp. 265–266.

7. Maxwell Taylor, *Sword and Ploughshares* (New York: Norton, 1972), p. 249.

8. William Colby, with James McCargar, *Lost Victory: A Firsthand Account of America's Sixteen Year Involvement in Vietnam by the Former Director of the CIA* (New York: Contemporary Books, 1989), pp. 75–76.

9. JCS Memo, "Project Beef Up" (2/21/62), JFK: OF: CO: Vietnam, General, 1963 (*sic*): Box 128a; EMBTEL 963, Nolting to Rusk (1/24/63), JFK: NSF: CO: Vietnam, 1/13/62–1/31/62: Box 195; EMBTEL 1008, Nolting to Rusk (2/3/62) JFK: NSF: CO: Vietnam, 2/62: Box 195.

10. For American complaints over Diem's stalling on the rural programs, see EMBTEL 1289, Nolting to Rusk (4/10/62), JFK: NSF: CO: Vietnam, 4/1/62–4/10/62: Box 196; EMBTEL 1581, Nolting to Rusk (6/8/62), JFK: CO: Vietnam, 6/1/62–6/8/62: Box 196; EMBTEL 884, Trueheart to Rusk

(1/3/62), JFK: NSF: CO: Vietnam, 1/1/62–1/5/62: Box 195. See also Fall, *The Two Vietnams,* pp. 279–280; Roy Jumper and M. Normand, "Vietnam," in George McT. Kahin, ed., *Governments and Politics of Southeast Asia* (Ithaca, N.Y.: Cornell University Press, 1964), p. 448; JFK: Roger Hilsman Oral History: pp. 20–21.

11. "Flash" Telegram, Nolting to White House (2/27/62, Saigon time; 2/26/62, Washington time), JFK: OF: CO: Vietnam, General, 1962: Box 128; Telegram, General Harkins to White House (2/27/62, Saigon time; 2/26/62, Washington time), ibid.; Telegram, Nolting to DIRNSA, White House (2/27/62), JFK: NSF: CO: Vietnam, 2/62: Box 195; EMBTEL 1100, Nolting to Rusk (2/27/62), ibid.; Stanley Karnow, *Vietnam: A History* (New York: Viking, 1983), pp. 263–265.

12. Robert Shaplen, *The Lost Revolution: The United States in Vietnam, 1946–1966* (New York: Harper and Row, 1966), p. 160.

13. On the reports of progress throughout 1962, see Army Message, CINCPAC to JCS (4/16/62), JFK: NSF: CO: Vietnam, 4/11/62–4/16/62: Box 196; CIA Information Report, "Training Courses on the Strategic Hamlet Program" (5/16/62), JFK: NSF: CO: Vietnam, 5/11/62–5/16/62: Box 196; Army Message, COMUSMACV to AIG 924 (9/8/62), JFK: NSF: CO: Vietnam, 9/1/62–9/14/62: Box 196; Memo, "Developments in Viet-Nam between General Taylor's Visits October, 1961—October, 1962," State Department to President Kennedy (10/8/62), JFK: NSF: CO: Vietnam, 10/7/62–10/17/62: Box 197. Though the reports were hardly gushing in their praise of the program, they generally viewed it as concrete progress on the political and social front. McNamara quoted in Karnow, *Vietnam,* p. 254. Ho's revision in Navy Message, CINCPAC to RUEPDA/DIA (3/14/63), JFK: NSF: CO: Vietnam, 3/1/63–3/19/63: Box 197. On the *agroville* program of the 1950s, see Joseph J. Zasloff, "Rural Resettlement in South Vietnam: The Agroville Program," *Pacific Affairs,* 35 (Winter 1962–63), 327–340.

14. This analysis of the Strategic Hamlet Program is based on the following sources: Hilsman, *To Move a Nation,* pp. 429–435, 441; Duncanson, *Government and Revolution,* pp. 311–327; Karnow, *Vietnam,* pp. 254–259; Blaufarb, *The Counterinsurgency Era,* pp. 114–115; Robert L. Gallucci, *Neither Peace Nor Honor: The Politics of American Military Policy in Vietnam* (Baltimore: Johns Hopkins University Press, 1975), pp. 27–28; Milton E. Osborne, *Strategic Hamlets in South Vietnam: A Survey and a Comparison,* Data Paper No. 55 (Ithaca, N.Y.: Cornell University, 1965); Eric M. Bergerud, *The Dynamics of Defeat: The Vietnam War in Hau Nghia Province* (Boulder, Colo.: Westview, 1991), pp. 33–38. For settlement patterns in Vietnamese villages, see also Gerald Hickey, *Village in Vietnam* (New Haven: Yale University Press, 1964), pp. 12, 53–54. For rare, retrospective defenses of the program, see Walt W. Rostow, *The Diffusion of Power: An Essay in Recent History* (New York: MacMillan, 1972), p. 281; and Colby, *Lost Victory,* pp. 102–103.

15. Thompson quoted in Karnow, *Vietnam,* p. 259 (see also pp. 256–257); Fall, *The Two Vietnams,* pp. 197–198; Duncanson, *Government and Revolution,* p. 325.

16. On the negotiations over Laos and the problems with Diem, see EMBTEL

1652, Nolting to Rusk (6/25/62), JFK: NSF: CO: Vietnam, 6/24/62–6/30/62: Box 196; CONFERENCE 1190, Tubby, Harriman (Geneva) to Rusk (7/7/62), JFK: NSF: CO: Vietnam, 7/7/62–7/10/62: Box 196; Letter, Kennedy to Diem (7/9/62), JFK: OF: CO: Vietnam, General, 1963 (sic): Box 128a; Memo, Forrestal to Kennedy (9/24/62), ibid.; EMBTEL 326, Nolting to Rusk (9/20/62), JFK: NSF: CO: Vietnam, 9/15/62–9/21/62: Box 196; Charles Stevenson, *The End of Nowhere: American Policy toward Laos since 1954* (Boston: Beacon Press, 1972), pp. 155–192.

17. Jumper and Normand, "Vietnam," p. 448; Shaplen, *The Lost Revolution,* pp. 155–156; Duncanson, *Government and Revolution,* p. 318; Blaufarb, *The Counterinsurgency Era,* pp. 115–116.

18. Memo, Forrestal to Kaysen (8/6/62), JFK: NSF: CO: Vietnam, 8/1/62–8/14/62: Box 196; Memo, Forrestal to McGeorge Bundy (8/8/62), JFK: NSF: Meetings and Memoranda: Staff Memoranda, Forrestal, 6/62–10/62: Box 320.

19. Memo, Forrestal to Kaysen, Bundy (8/18/62), JFK: NSF: CO: Vietnam, 8/15/62–8/22/62: Box 196; Memo, Brubeck to O'Donnell, McGeorge Bundy (8/29/62), JFK: OF: CO: Vietnam, General, 1963 (sic): Box 128a; Memo, Brubeck to McGeorge Bundy (9/22/62), ibid.

20. Quoted in Karnow, *Vietnam,* p. 258.

21. For some of the particular problems of and with the press in Saigon during 1962, see DEPTEL 7, Rusk to Nolting (7/3/62), JFK: NSF: CO: Vietnam, 7/1/62–7/6/62: Box 196; Teletype, COMUSMACV to JCS (7/5/62), ibid.; Memo, General Dodge to General Clifton (7/8/62), JFK: NSF: CO: Vietnam, 7/7/62–7/10/62: Box 196; DEPTEL (unnumbered), Rusk to Nolting (9/14/62), JFK: NSF: CO: Vietnam, 9/1/62–9/14/62: Box 196; Jumper and Normand, "Vietnam," p. 443. For the administration's problems with the press in 1962–1963, see John Mecklin, *Mission in Torment: An Intimate Account of the U.S. Role in Vietnam* (Garden City, N.Y.: Doubleday, 1965); for Kennedy's attempts to manipulate the press in 1963, some successful and some not, see M. Kern, P. Levering, and R. Levering, *The Kennedy Crises: The Press, the Presidency, and Foreign Policy* (Chapel Hill, N.C.: University of North Carolina Press, 1983), pp. 141–191.

22. For Halberstam's views on Vietnam during this period, see David Halberstam, *The Best and the Brightest* (New York: Fawcett, 1972), pp. 224–368; for Higgins's views, see Marguerite Higgins, *Our Vietnam Nightmare* (New York: Harper and Row, 1965).

23. As quoted in Schlesinger, *Robert Kennedy,* p. 769.

24. Memo, Forrestal to President Kennedy (12/18/62), JFK: NSF: CO: Vietnam, 12/62: Box 197.

25. This account of the Mansfield report and of Kennedy's reaction is drawn from Karnow, *Vietnam,* p. 268, and Herbert Parmet, *JFK: The Presidency of John F. Kennedy* (New York: Dial Press, 1980), p. 327.

26. Memo, Hilsman and Forrestal, especially "Eyes Only Annex: Performance of U.S. Mission" (1/25/63), JFK: NSF: CO: Vietnam, 1/10/63–1/30/63: Box 197; JFK: Roger Hilsman Oral History: pp. 20–21.

27. JFK: Roger Hilsman Oral History: pp. 20–21; Memo, Forrestal to President

Kennedy (1/28/63), JFK: NSF: CO: Vietnam, 1/10/63–1/30/63: Box 197; JFK: Roger Hilsman Oral History: pp. 20–21; Hilsman, *To Move a Nation,* pp. 463–467.

28. CIA Memo, "Current Status of the War in South Vietnam" (1/11/63), JFK: NSF: CO: Vietnam, 1/10/63–1/30/63: Box 197.

29. DEPTEL 688, Rusk to Nolting (1/13/63), JFK: NSF: CO: Vietnam, 1/10/63–1/30/63: Box 197. On the renewed military capacity of the Viet Cong beginning in late 1962, see Army Message, COMUSMACV to AIG 924, JCS (12/6/62), JFK: NSF: CO: Vietnam, 12/62: Box 197.

30. Quoted in Navy Message, CINCPAC to RUEPDA/DIA (3/14/63), JFK: NSF: CO: Vietnam, 3/1/63–3/19/63: Box 197.

31. Navy Message, CINCPAC to JCS (3/9/63), JFK: NSF: CO: Vietnam, 3/1/63–3/19/63: Box 197.

32. Navy Message, CINCPAC to RUEAHQ/DIA (3/20/63), JFK: NSF: CO: Vietnam, 3/20/63–3/29/63: Box 197; EMBTEL 844, Nolting to Rusk (3/26/63), ibid.

33. Army Message, CINCPAC to JCS (3/26/63), JFK: NSF: CO: Vietnam, 3/20/63–3/29/63: Box 197; Memo, Brubeck to McGeorge Bundy (4/3/63), JFK: NSF: CO: Vietnam, 4/1/63–4/18/63: Box 197.

34. Quoted in Geoffrey Warner, "The United States and the Fall of Diem: Part I," *Australian Outlook,* 28 (December 1974), 248–249. For the opinion that Nhu's threats were not believed by "serious people" in Washington, see JFK: Roger Hilsman Oral History: p. 33.

35. Hilsman, *To Move a Nation,* pp. 468–470; Duncanson, *Government and Revolution,* pp. 326–334; Karnow, *Vietnam,* pp. 278–281. For a treatment highly critical of the Buddhists and their politicization in 1963, see Edwin F. Black, "The Role of Buddhism in the Overthrow of Diem," *Orbis,* 14 (Winter 1971), 992–1011.

36. This was the finding of the United Nations Commission sent to study the problem. Unfortunately, its report was issued after Diem's assassination. Black, "The Role of Buddhism," p. 1009. On the lack of systematic repression of the Buddhists under Diem, see also Guenter Lewy, *America in Vietnam* (New York: Oxford University Press, 1978), p. 26.

37. EMBTEL 107, Helble to Rusk (6/3/63), JFK: NSF: CO: Vietnam, 6/1/63–6/5/63: Box 197; DEPTEL 1170, Hilsman to Trueheart (6/3/63), ibid.; DEPTEL 1171, Rusk to Trueheart (6/3/63), ibid.; Army Message, COMUSMACV to CINCPAC (6/3/63), ibid.; EMBTEL 1100, Trueheart to Rusk (6/4/63), ibid.; EMBTEL 1104, Trueheart to Rusk (6/4/63), ibid.; Army Message, COMUSMACV to CINCPAC (6/4/63), ibid.; Navy Message, CINCPAC to CINCPAC (Wellington, New Zealand), JCS (6/5/63), ibid.; Memo, McNamara to President Kennedy (6/6/63), JFK: NSF: CO: Vietnam, 6/6/63–6/15/63: Box 197; Army Message, COMUSMACV to CINCPAC (6/6/63), ibid.

38. EMBTEL 1146, Trueheart to Rusk (6/11/63), JFK: NSF: CO: Vietnam, 6/6/63–6/15/63: Box 197; EMBTEL 1155, Trueheart to Rusk (6/11/63), ibid.; EMBTEL 1163, Trueheart to Rusk (6/12/63), ibid. On the reaction in the United States and the multiple pressures to "do something," see

Hilsman, *To Move a Nation,* pp. 473–474; Mecklin, *Mission in Torment,* pp. 153–187. On the self-immolations in June, see Malcolm W. Browne, *The New Face of War* (New York: Bobbs-Merrill, 1965), pp. 175–182.

39. Tran Van Don, *Our Endless War: Inside Vietnam* (San Rafael, Calif.: Presidio Press, 1978), p. 84.

40. EMBTEL 1136, Trueheart to Rusk (6/9/63), JFK: NSF: CO: Vietnam, 6/6/63–6/15/63: Box 197; EMBTEL 1137, Trueheart to Rusk (6/9/63), ibid.

41. EMBTEL 1137, Trueheart to Rusk (6/9/63), JFK: NSF: CO: Vietnam, 6/6/63–6/15/63: Box 197; DEPTEL 1199, Rusk to Trueheart (6/10/63), ibid. Trueheart's good friend and mentor, Ambassador Nolting, apparently never forgave him for these actions. After leaving Vietnam, they reportedly never again spoke to each other.

42. EMBTEL 10072, Trueheart, Brent to Rusk, Hilsman, Janow (5/28/63), JFK: NSF: CO: Vietnam, 5/18/63–5/31/63: Box 197; DEPTEL 1219, Rusk to Trueheart (6/14/63), JFK: NSF: CO: Vietnam, 6/6/63–6/15/63: Box 197; EMBTEL 1195, Trueheart to Rusk (6/16/63), JFK: NSF: CO: Vietnam, 6/16/63–6/24/63: Box 197.

43. EMBTEL 106, Nolting to Rusk (7/18/63), JFK: NSF: CO: Vietnam, 7/1/63–7/20/63: Box 198.

44. Ibid.; EMBTEL 107, Nolting to Rusk (7/19/63), ibid.; EMBTEL 111, Nolting to Rusk (7/19/63), ibid.; EMBTEL 159, Nolting to Rusk (8/1/63), JFK: NSF: CO: Vietnam, 8/1/63–8/20/63: Box 198; EMBTEL 160, Nolting to Rusk (8/1/63), ibid.

45. EMBTEL 173, Nolting to Rusk (8/3/63), JFK: NSF: CO: Vietnam, 8/1/63–8/20/63: Box 198; EMBTEL 178, Nolting to Rusk (8/4/63), ibid.; EMBTEL 190, Nolting to Rusk (8/8/63), ibid.; EMBTEL 191, Nolting to Rusk (8/8/63), ibid.

46. EMBTEL 212, Nolting to Rusk (8/13/63), JFK: NSF: CO: Vietnam, 8/1/63–8/20/63: Box 198; EMBTEL 226, Nolting to Rusk (8/14/63), ibid.; EMBTEL 230, Nolting to Rusk (8/14/63), ibid.; EMBTEL 249, Trueheart to Rusk (8/17/63), ibid.; TOAID, Saigon to AID (8/17/63), ibid.; Parmet, *JFK,* p. 326.

47. CIA Information Report, "Comments of Ngo Dinh Nhu on Possible Changes in U.S. Policy toward South Vietnam" (8/27/63), JFK: NSF: CO: Vietnam, 8/24/63–8/31/63: Box 198; EMBTEL (unnumbered), Helble (Hue) to Rusk (8/18/63), JFK: NSF: CO: Vietnam, 8/1/63–8/20/63: Box 198; State Research Memo, RFE-75 (8/21/63), JFK: OF: CO: Vietnam, General, 1963: Box 128a; Jumper and Normand, "Vietnam," p. 457.

48. EMBTEL (unnumbered), Trueheart to Rusk (8/20/63), JFK: NSF: CO: Vietnam, 8/1/63–8/20/63: Box 198; EMBTEL 267, Trueheart to Rusk (8/21/63), JFK: NSF: CO: Vietnam, 8/21/63–8/23/63: Box 198; EMBTEL 269, Trueheart to Rusk (8/21/63), ibid.; EMBTEL 271, Trueheart to Rusk (8/21/63), ibid.; EMBTEL 273, Trueheart to Rusk (8/21/63), ibid.; EMBTEL 3, Helble (Hue) to Rusk (8/21/63), ibid.; EMBTEL 292, Trueheart to Rusk (8/21/63), ibid.; State Research Memo RFE-75 (8/21/63), JFK: OF: Vietnam, General, 1963: Box 128a.

49. On the multiple pressures for policy changes, see DEPTEL 226, Ball to Trueheart (8/21/63), JFK: NSF: CO: Vietnam, 8/21/63–8/23/63: Box 198;

EMBTEL 288, Trueheart to Lodge (Tokyo) (8/21/63), ibid.; Navy Message, CINCPAC to JCS (8/21/63), ibid.; EMBTEL 357, Lodge to Rusk (8/27/63), JFK: NSF: CO: Vietnam, 8/24/63–8/31/63: Box 198.

50. Navy Message, CINCPAC to JCS (8/23/63), JFK: NSF: CO: Vietnam, 8/21/63–8/23/63: Box 198; EMBTEL 324, Lodge to Rusk (8/24/63), JFK: NSF: CO: Vietnam, 8/24/63–8/31/63: Box 198.

51. Memo, Forrestal to Kennedy (8/24/63), JFK: NSF: Vietnam, 8/24/63–8/31/63: Box 198; EMBTEL 329, Lodge to Rusk (8/24/63), ibid.; Powers, *The Man Who Kept the Secrets,* p. 208; Schlesinger, *Robert Kennedy,* p. 769; Parmet, *JFK,* p. 332; "Untold Story of the Road to War in Vietnam," *U.S. News and World Report* (hereafter cited as *USNWR*), 95 (October 10, 1983), 48–49. For a reformer's account, see Hilsman, *To Move a Nation,* pp. 483–494; for a bolsterer's account, see Taylor, *Swords and Ploughshares,* pp. 292–295. For a harsh assessment of Kennedy's policy, and the reformers in particular, see Ellen Hammer, *A Death in November: America in Vietnam, 1963* (New York: Oxford University Press, 1987).

52. Memo, Forrestal to Kennedy (8/26/63), JFK: OF: CO: Vietnam, General, 1963: Box 128a; DEPTEL 248, Rusk to Lodge (8/26/63), JFK: NSF: CO: Vietnam, 8/24/63–8/31/63: Box 198.

53. The split formed along the following lines: Pro-Coup: Averell Harriman (State), George Ball (State), Roger Hilsman (State), Michael Forrestal (White House), and Henry Cabot Lodge (Ambassador); Anti-Coup: Maxwell Taylor (JCS), Robert McNamara (Defense), John McCone (CIA), Vice-President Johnson, and Ambassador Fritz Nolting (then in Washington). Schlesinger, *Robert Kennedy,* p. 770. Secretary of State Dean Rusk avoided a strong association with either side, at least according to Schlesinger.

54. Kennedy quoted in *USNWR,* p. 50; Memo, Forrestal to Kennedy (8/26/63), JFK: OF: CO: Vietnam, General, 1963– : Box 128a; EMBTEL 335, Lodge to Rusk (8/26/63), JFK: NSF: CO: Vietnam, 8/24/63–8/31/63: Box 198.

55. Quoted in Karnow, *Vietnam,* p. 288.

56. Teletype, Taylor to Harkins (8/28/63), JFK: NSF: CO: Vietnam, 8/24/63–8/31/63: Box 198; Karnow, *Vietnam,* pp. 287–289.

57. PP/NYT, pp. 194–200, 202–204; *USNWR,* pp. 50–51; DEPTEL 284, Rusk to Lodge (8/30/63), JFK: NSF: CO: Vietnam, 8/24/63–8/31/63: Box 198; EMBTEL 391, Lodge to Rusk (8/31/63), ibid.; Halberstam, *Best and Brightest,* pp. 328–333; Karnow, *Vietnam,* p. 290.

58. PP/NYT, p. 203.

59. Memo of conversation, Hilsman, Lisagor, Sidey, Higgins (9/3/63), JFK: NSF: CO: Vietnam, 9/1/63–9/10/63: Box 199.

60. There is some controversy over Nhu's alleged addiction. State Department files show that Thuan, and others such as Vo Van Hai, in fact made the charge to United States officials. Memo, "The Problem of Nhu," Hughes to Rusk (10/15/63), JFK: NSF: CO: Vietnam, 9/16/63–9/21/63, Action Plans: Box 200. Thuan later denied ever having said it. General Don argues that Nhu was not an opium addict, but smoked "very strong cigarettes," whatever that means. Don, *Our Endless War,* p. 54. The important point for policymaking is that many Americans believed it was true.

61. DEPTEL 313, Rusk to U.S. Embassy (9/3/63), JFK: OF: CO: Vietnam, General, 1963– : Box 128a.

62. Ibid.; see also DEPTEL 335, Hilsman to Lodge (9/5/63), ibid.; EMBTEL 423, Lodge to Rusk (9/6/63), ibid.; TOAID 643, Lodge to AID/W (9/6/63), JFK: NSF: CO: Vietnam, 9/1/63–9/10/63, State Cables, Part II: Box 199.

63. Research Memo RFE-78, Thomas L. Hughes (INR) to Rusk (9/11/63), JFK: NSF: CO: Vietnam, 9/11/63–9/17/63, Memos and Miscellaneous, Part I: Box 199. For accounts that emphasize American fear of a separate peace, see Karnow, *Vietnam,* p. 292; Gabriel Kolko, *Anatomy of a War: Vietnam, the United States and the Modern Historical Experience* (New York: Pantheon, 1986), p. 117.

64. EMBTEL 937, Lyon (Paris) to Rusk (8/29/63), JFK: NSF: CO: Vietnam, 8/24/63–8/31/63: Box 198; "Memo of a Conference with the President" (9/3/63), JFK: NSF: Meetings and Memos: Meetings on Vietnam, 9/1/63– 9/10/63: Box 317; Research Memo RFE-78, Thomas L. Hughes (INR) to Rusk (9/11/63), JFK: NSF: CO: Vietnam, 9/11/63–9/17/63, Memos and Miscellaneous, Part I: Box 199; Jumper and Normand, "Vietnam," p. 457; Karnow, *Vietnam,* pp. 291–292.

65. Memo of a Conference with the President (10/3/63), JFK: NSF: Meetings and Memos: Meetings on Vietnam, 9/1/63–9/10/63: Box 317; DEPTEL 317, Rusk to Lodge (10/3/63), ibid.

66. See two CIA Information Reports: (1) "Ngo Dinh Nhu's Interpretation of Recent U.S. Government Actions"; and (2) "Imminent Arrest of Potential Civilian Oppositionists" (8/28/63), JFK: NSF: CO: Vietnam, 8/24/63– 8/31/63: Box 198; also EMBTEL 7, Helble (Hue) to Rusk [with pencil notation that President Kennedy had read the cable] (8/31/63), ibid.; Teletype, Rusk to the White House (9/7/63), JFK: NSF: CO: Vietnam, 9/1/63– 9/10/63, State Cables, Part II: Box 199; EMBTEL 454, Lodge to Rusk (9/9/63), ibid.

67. DEPTEL 279, Rusk to Lodge (8/29/63), JFK: NSF: CO: Vietnam, 8/24/63– 8/31/63: Box 198.

68. DEPTEL 349, Rusk to Lodge (9/6/63), JFK: NSF: Meetings and Memos: Meetings on Vietnam, 9/1/63–9/10/63: Box 317; Memo of Presidential Conference on Vietnam (9/10/63), ibid.; Report from General Krulak on His Trip to Vietnam (9/10/63), ibid.; EMBTEL 453, Mendenhall to Hilsman (9/9/63), JFK: OF: CO: Vietnam, General, 1963: Box 128a; Memo, Mecklin to Murrow (9/10/63), JFK: NSF: CO: Vietnam, 9/1/63–9/10/63, Memos and Miscellaneous: Box 199; Memo, Murrow to Bundy (9/10/63), ibid. Kennedy quoted in Karnow, *Vietnam,* p. 293. For Thompson's pessimistic report, see EMBTEL 633, Lodge to Rusk (10/5/63), JFK: NSF: CO: Vietnam, 9/22/63– 10/5/63: Box 200.

69. Memo, "Meeting at the State Department" (9/10/63), JFK: NSF: Meetings and Memoranda, Vietnam: Meetings on Vietnam, 9/1/63–9/10/63: Box 317; "Memorandum of Conference with the President" (9/11/63), JFK: NSF: Meetings and Memoranda: Meetings on Vietnam, 9/11/63–9/12/63: Box 317.

70. "Memorandum for the Record" (9/23/63), JFK: NSF: CO: VN: State Cables, 9/22/63–10/5/63: Box 200.

71. Draft Memo, "Background Guidance for Questions about the Country Team in South Vietnam" (10/2/63), JFK: NSF: CO: Vietnam, 9/22/63–10/5/63, Memos and Miscellaneous: Box 200; DEPTEL 907, Ball to Lodge (10/4/63), JFK: NSF: CO: Vietnam, 9/22/63–10/5/63: Box 200; Larry Berman, *Planning a Tragedy: The Americanization of the War in Vietnam* (New York: Norton, 1982), p. 27; Karnow, *Vietnam*, pp. 293–295.

72. Memo, "Meeting in the Situation Room (Without the President)" (10/3/63), JFK: NSF: Meetings and Memoranda: Meetings on Vietnam, 10/1/63–10/5/63: Box 317.

73. "Report to the Executive Committee" (10/3/63), JFK: NSF: CO: VN: Memos and Miscellaneous, 9/22/63–10/5/63: Box 200; "Report to the Executive Committee" (10/4/63), JFK: OF: CO: VN: Vietnam Security, 1963: Box 128a; "Draft Telegram to Saigon; Eyes Only for Ambassador Lodge" (10/5/63), JFK: NSF: Meetings and Memoranda: Meetings on Vietnam, 10/1/63–10/5/63: Box 317. On the instructions to AID to implement aid reductions, see AIDTO 915, Rusk to Bundy (10/5/63), JFK: NSF: CO: State Cables, 9/22/63–10/5/63: Box 200; DEPTEL 576, Kennedy to Lodge (10/14/63), JFK: NSF: CO: Vietnam, 10/6/63–10/14/63, State Cables: Box 200.

74. Memo, Bundy to Lodge (10/5/63), JFK: NSF: CO: Vietnam, 10/6/63–10/14/63: Box 200; for the psychological effects of the cuts on the business community in Saigon beginning in October, see EMBTEL 748, Lodge to Rusk (10/19/63), JFK: NSF: CO: Vietnam, State Cables, 10/15/63–10/28/63: Box 201; Memo, Forrestal to Bundy (10/21/63), ibid.

75. EMBTEL 632, Lodge to Rusk (10/4/63), JFK: NSF: CO: Vietnam, 9/22/63–10/5/63: Box 200; EMBTEL 640, Lodge to Rusk (10/5/63), ibid.; EMBTEL 647, Lodge to Rusk (10/7/63), JFK: NSF: CO: Vietnam, 10/6/63–10/14/63, State Cables: Box 200; EMBTEL 653, Lodge to Rusk (10/7/63), ibid.; EMBTEL 654, Lodge to Rusk (10/7/63), ibid.; EMBTEL 677, Lodge to Rusk (10/10/63), ibid.; Jumper and Normand, "Vietnam," p. 448. Hilsman's account of the regime notes that the "most pitiful" victims of Nhu's prisons were young women. Hilsman, *To Move a Nation*, p. 521.

76. PP/NYT, pp. 182–183; George Ball, *The Past Has Another Pattern: Memoirs* (New York: Norton, 1982), p. 373; Don, *Our Endless War*, pp. 95–99.

77. PP/NYT, pp. 181–187, 219–229; emphasis also in Karnow, *Vietnam*, p. 300.

78. On the fake coup plan, see Shaplen, *The Lost Revolution*, pp. 204–206; Karnow, *Vietnam*, pp. 303–304.

79. EMBTEL 816, Lodge to Rusk (10/30/63), JFK: NSF: CO: Vietnam, State and Defense Cables, 10/29/63–10/31/63: Box 201.

80. EMBTEL 841, Lodge to Rusk (11/1/63), JFK: NSF: CO: Vietnam, State Cables, 11/1/63–11/2/63: Box 201. Obviously garbled words in the quotes from this cable have been corrected for ease of reading.

81. EMBTEL 11, Helble (Hue) to Rusk (11/2/63), JFK: NSF: CO: Vietnam, 11/1/63–11/2/63, State Cables: Box 201.

82. On the coup and its aftermath, see CIA Memo, "The Coup in South Vietnam" (11/1/63), JFK: OF: CO: Vietnam, General, 1963– : Box 128a; CIA Memo, "The Situation in Vietnam" (11/2/63), ibid.; EMBTEL 11, Helble (Hue) to Rusk (11/2/63), JFK: NSF: CO: Vietnam, 11/1/63–11/2/63, State Cables: Box 201; DEPTEL 2333, Rusk to U.S. Embassy in Paris (11/4/63), ibid.; EMBTEL 923, Lodge to Rusk (11/5/63), ibid.; Jumper and Normand, "Vietnam," p. 435; Berman, *Planning a Tragedy*, pp. 28–29.

83. DEPTEL 704, Rusk to Lodge (11/3/63), JFK: NSF: CO: Vietnam, 11/3/63–11/5/63, State Cables: Box 201; EMBTEL 917, Lodge to Rusk (11/4/63), ibid.

84. Quoted in Berman, *Planning a Tragedy*, p. 108.

Conclusion: Bargaining in Chaos

1. Since reformist interventions take time to work, and reformist periods have lasted such a relatively short time, there may be a lag time between the approaches that gives bolstering too much credit for aiding in the return of stability in the short term. For example, the relative stability in clients in the first Eisenhower administration may have been the result of the longer-term effects of Truman's reformist policies. Similarly, the Reagan administration may have reaped the longer-term benefits of Carter's reformist policies. Then again, a bolsterer would suggest that the reformist periods were disruptive intervals based on flawed policies that bolstering had to correct. Much more research has to be done on the ultimate effects of the respective policies; I am pointing here to general tendencies.

2. It might be suggested that the citizens of a country that probably had a presidential election stolen through fraud as recently as 1960, followed by Watergate, Koreagate, Arabscam, Irangate, and the Savings and Loan scandals of the 1990s, as well as numerous lesser scandals, might exercise a greater degree of humility when judging democratic development and good government in "less politically developed" nations.

3. The best work on the paradoxes inherent in promoting democracy and reform in the Third World has been done by Samuel P. Huntington, and much of this chapter is based on his analysis. See especially Samuel P. Huntington, *Political Order in Changing Societies* (New Haven: Yale University Press, 1968), and *American Politics: The Promise of Disharmony* (Cambridge, Mass.: Harvard University Press, 1981), pp. 221–262. On the inherently unsatisfactory nature of reform, see Samuel P. Huntington, "Reform and Stability in South Africa," *International Security*, 6 (Spring 1982), 20. For a relatively pessimistic view of the potential spread of democracy, see Samuel P. Huntington, "Will More Countries Become Democratic?" *Political Science Quarterly*, 99 (Summer 1984), 197–199.

4. Huntington, "Will More Countries Become Democratic?" pp. 196–197. Huntington does not correlate these movements toward democracy with particular American administrations, but with American power. I agree that American power is an extremely important variable, and its correlation with the spread of democratic values and reform is strong, but the willingness

to promote reform programs is equally important. *Both* American power
and ideals are necessary to make a difference. Huntington agrees with this
formulation, but in his analysis often assumes that reformist interventions
are a constant. I find that they are variables, depending on which party is
in power (with the exception of Lyndon Johnson).

5. See Alan Riding, "Brazil Welcomes Jimmy Carter on Latin Tour," *New York Times,* October 9, 1984, p. A11.

6. For reasons enumerated in Chapter 1, I have chosen not to analyze the radical critique of American policy in this section. Since the evidence for the alleged economic causes of American interventions is relatively slight, I have concentrated on the clash between security and ideological goals. A further critique of the radical position can be found in Douglas J. Macdonald, "'Adventures in Chaos': Reformism in American Foreign Policy" (Ph.D. dissertation, Columbia University, 1987), pp. 751–754.

7. For an excellent treatment of the complex role of pragmatism in American foreign policy, see Cecil V. Crabb, Jr., *American Diplomacy and the Pragmatic Tradition* (Baton Rouge, La.: Louisiana State University Press, 1989).

8. For a theoretical treatment of the need for Third World leaders to balance internal and external political forces, see Steven R. David, "Explaining Third World Alignment," *World Politics,* 43 (January 1991), 233–256.

9. On the distinction between class origins and class consciousness among revolutionary leaders, see William B. Quandt, *Revolution and Political Leadership* (Cambridge, Mass.: MIT Press, 1969), p. 13.

10. John Shy, *A People Numerous and Armed: Reflections on the Military Struggle for American Independence* (New York: Oxford University Press, 1976), pp. 198–199. The quote is from page 199.

11. For "signal-to-noise-ratio" in general, see Alexander L. George, *Presidential Decisionmaking in Foreign Policy* (Boulder, Colo.: Westview Press, 1980), p. 73.

12. Ibid., p. 73.

13. Huntington, *Political Order,* pp. 344–362.

14. Ibid., p. 347.

Index